SO-FAI-244

Early Church Records of Delaware County Pennsylvania

Volume 1

John Pitts Launey
and *F. Edward Wright*

HERITAGE BOOKS
2007

HERITAGE BOOKS

AN IMPRINT OF HERITAGE BOOKS, INC.

Books, CDs, and more—Worldwide

For our listing of thousands of titles see our website
at
www.HeritageBooks.com

Published 2007 by
HERITAGE BOOKS, INC.
Publishing Division
65 East Main Street
Westminster, Maryland 21157-5026

Copyright © 1997 John Pitts Launey and F. Edward Wright

All rights reserved. No part of this book may be reproduced or
transmitted in any form or by any means, electronic or mechanical,
including photocopying, recording or by any information storage
and retrieval system without written permission from the author,
except for the inclusion of brief quotations in a review.

International Standard Book Number: 978-1-58549-424-8

CONTENTS

INTRODUCTION

CHESTER MONTHLY MEETING
CHESTER, PENNSYLVANIA

ST. PAUL'S PROTESTANT EPISCOPAL CHURCH
CHESTER, PENNSYLVANIA

INDEX

iii

DELAWARE COUNTY

PENNSYLVANIA

1789

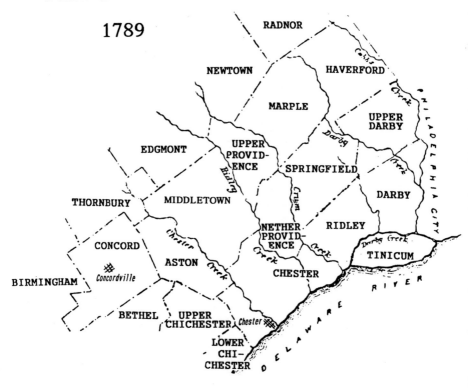

INTRODUCTION

The port town of Chester was established as an English colony on the Delaware River in 1660 under the name "Upland." Quakers began arriving in large numbers in 1677 from western England, many from the county of Chester, and quickly outnumbered the existing residents. By 1683 Upland Township had been partitioned to form Chester Township, and the town of Upland was renamed Chester.

Additional Friends from western England and northeastern Ireland rapidly expanded the population into the balance of southern Chester County and in 1789 a proposal was made before the Pennsylvania Assembly to move the county seat from Chester on the river to a more central location. Representatives from the borough of Chester blocked the proposal, which led to a compromise that allowed the county seat to be moved to Bradford Township and the creation of Delaware County with its county seat in Chester.

SOCIETY OF FRIENDS (QUAKERS)

The Religious Society of Friends, frequently known as the Quaker movement, began in England during the 1650s primarily due to the dedication, inspiration and leadership of a simple, Yorkshire tailor named George Fox. The movement took its members from the ranks of the Church of England that grew dissatisfied with its corrupt and often politically oriented leaders and doctrine. The motivation to abandon land and position in England, Ireland and Wales and begin again in America was supplied by persecution from a Puritan dominated government and an intolerant crown.

Seeing the use of repetitive ritual and ceremony as fundamentally evil, Friends created a society carefully avoiding these practices. Rather than wedding ceremonies, public marriages were held in private homes or meeting houses and consisted of a personal declaration of affection between the couple. Baptism in any form and the sacrament known as Communion or the Lord's Supper in other denominations was not practiced. It was considered an important breach of discipline for any member to attend a ceremony sponsored by another denomination, even if the wedding or funeral involved a close family member.

The child of two Quaker parents was accepted as a member by birthright and all the events of his life were automatically recorded; however, a child born to one parent in good standing and one disowned parent had no birthright. Even if the second parent was later reinstated, the child still had to be sponsored for membership. It was important, therefore, to keep meticulously accurate records of births, marriages, movements, disownments, and reinstatements.

In the early years, there was no formal requirement to record deaths. Some meetings saw the need to record this event and did so with great care. Other meetings only recorded burials and still others saw no need at all. Gradually, all meetings came to see the importance of these records and by the middle of the 18th century, both deaths and burials were noted in special books, often with additional information, such as the exact place and time of day when death occurred, length of illness, cause of death and individuals in attendance.

Every monthly meeting had two copies of the Book of Discipline, one each for the Men's and Women's Meetings. This volume, sometimes know as The Rules of Discipline, specified in detail how Friends should conduct their daily affairs. Violations of discipline ran the full spectrum of human behavior. Many forms of diversion and entertainment common in those days were forbidden to Friends, including music, singing, dancing, social gatherings of young members beyond the hours of early evening, associating socially with members of other societies, horse racing, betting, games of chance, hawking, and fox hunting. Alcohol was not forbidden, but drinking to excess, operating a tavern or frequenting "houses of diversion" were serious causes for discipline. Selling alcohol to the Indians was considered the most serious liquor related offense.

Near the heart of Quaker discipline was the avoidance of human conflict. Anger, arguing, harsh language directed at another individual, particularly another Friend, and fighting were causes for condemnation, as was the support or encouragement of these activities. Quakers were not permitted to engage in military or naval operations, fill requisitions or transport food or supplies for the military, produce or supply firearms for military use, pay money to military authorities for any reason or rendering any form of aid or comfort to either side of an armed conflict. Active members of a Monthly Meeting were exempt from military service by legislation until after the French and Indian

War; however, following this conflict new legislation mandated service in the militia for every young man of military age. Failure to enroll, refusal to take the Test and Oath of Allegiance, or absence on muster days was punishable by a stiff fine amounting to as much as £20 for each offense. Drill or muster days were held each month, and each day missed incurred an additional fine, which the Society forbade its members to pay. This resulted in the forced confiscation and auction of personal property. Household furniture, farm equipment, cash, personal items of gold or silver and livestock were seized and sold at the nearest town. Friends with means and property could afford the loss, but subsistence farmers were in danger of losing everything. The choice before these men was between insolvency and disownment.

In addition to rules of moral conduct, the Book of Discipline also specified the procedure to be followed in an orderly marriage. At a monthly meeting, the couple would announce their intentions to marry for the first time. If one of the two young people were not a Friend, he or she was told the procedure necessary to request membership. If both were already members, they were instructed to bring letters of consent from their parents, or bring the consenting parents, to the next meeting. If one were a member of a different Monthly Meeting, which was often the case, he or she was instructed to also bring a "certificate of clearness to marry" from that meeting. This letter would testify to his good standing within the meeting and specify his or her freedom from engagements or other marriages. Next, a committee of two or more was appointed to interview the couple, their parents and acquaintances to determine if any objection existed to the marriage.

At a subsequent Monthly Meeting, usually the next one, the couple again appeared and announced their continued intentions to marry. Appropriate letters of consent and clearness were delivered to the clerk who read them to the meeting and made the proper notations in the minutes. Following a report from the committee stating that no objection was found, the couple was granted liberty to proceed with the approval of the meeting. The marriage gathering was usually held in the verge of the bride's meeting and Friends were appointed to attend the event to ensure that orderly procedure was followed. They were also required to report the orderly completion of the marriage at the following Monthly Meeting, deliver the certificate to the clerk and see that the certificate was properly recorded. The Overseer of the

Monthly Meeting was responsible for all records and would then examine the entry to make certain all was correct.

A number of years passed before a reliable system for recording certificates was established. If for any reason the marriage certificate was not recorded, certain assumptions can be made from the minutes. According to an entry at the beginning of the minutes for Woodbridge Monthly Meeting held in Union County, New Jersey, "it can be assumed that the marriage took place one week after the date permission was granted or three weeks before the date it was reported accomplished." A comparison of the minutes and properly recorded certificates shows this statement to be highly accurate although unexpected exceptions can be found.

The procedure for an orderly marriage within the discipline usually took five weeks from the first announcement to the marriage day. This delay was deemed necessary to give the couple time to cool off and consider. With disturbing frequency, couples elected to bypass procedure and marry outside of Friends by ceremonies performed by a "hireling priest," a minister of another denomination, or by a Justice or magistrate. This occurred in nearly half the marriages and was always cause for disciplinary action. If the member wished to remain in unity with Friends, he or she was required to bring a letter condemning the act to a Monthly Meeting and read it before Friends. The individual was also required to bring a copy of the marriage certificate. If the person charged were truly contrite and no corrections were necessary in the condemnation letter, Friends could elect to accept the letter and continue in unity. If conditions did not appear to be in order, the meeting usually continued the case until the following Monthly Meeting. Failure to accept and follow the order of discipline usually lead to disownment. The most serious marriages out of unity were those involving close relatives such as first cousins. Marriages between second cousins were always discouraged but usually permitted, and marriages between third cousins were both permitted and common. Unlike assumptions that can be made from entries in the minutes granting permission to marry or reporting its accomplishment, no assumptions can be made from entries reporting marriages out of unity because the marriage may have occurred from days to years prior to the entry.

Friends believed that the use of the names of the days and months was a "vulgar practice" because the origin of many of these names could be traced back to pagan gods, such as the Viking god "Thor" for Thursday, or deified rulers, such as Julius Caesar, Caesar Augustus and Octavian. Consequently, Friends numbered their days and months. Two calendars, the Julian and Gregorian, were in use by Friends during the period of this book, each with a different number corresponding to the name of the month. Briefly the rule is this: For dates before November 1, 1751, the 1st month of the year was March, the 2nd was April and so on; from November 1, 1751 to the present, January was designated the 1st month.

SOCIETY OF FRIENDS: PLACES OF MEETING
FROM CHESTER AND CONCORD MEETING MINUTES

The Society of Friends was organized around the concept of meetings rather than church services, each having its own purpose, authority and responsibilities. The smallest and most numerous was the meeting for worship known formally as a Particular Meeting. These consisted of as few as two households to as many as ten, and were located in any suitable and convenient spot, usually the homes of members. Particular Meetings were established, or "settled" by, a Monthly Meeting. Every member of a Particular Meeting was also a member of a Preparative Meeting, which was also settled by a Monthly Meeting and jointly held with men and women during the week prior to the Monthly Meeting. Their purpose was to set the agenda for the next business meeting. Marriage intentions, requests for certificates of clearance to marry, requests for certificates of removal and matters of policy and discipline were first published and discussed here.

The bulk of responsibility for the Society fell to the Monthly Meeting. These meetings were responsible for the spiritual and physical well-being of all members of Particular and Preparative Meetings. The men held their meeting separate from the women and were authorized to issue and receive certificates, grant permissions to marry, oversee discipline and disown members. Monthly Meetings were settled by, and responsible to, the Quarterly Meeting.

Quarterly Meetings were made up of selected members of each Monthly Meeting within its service area, known as its verge or compass. Matters of policy discussed in a Monthly Meeting were written in the form of a "memorandum" and submitted to the Quarterly Meeting. If the issue only pertains to the verge of the Quarterly Meeting, it was treated on that level, and decisions were written in the form of "advice" and distributed to all Monthly Meetings within its verge. Matters affecting members outside the responsibility of the Quarterly Meetings was deferred to the Yearly Meeting.

Each nation, kingdom and principality had at least one separate and autonomous Yearly Meeting. The number of Yearly Meetings organized depended upon the number of Quarterly Meetings in an area. Its purpose was to deal with issues of importance to all Friends within the bounds of the Meeting, such as: Should the Society permit or stand against slavery? Should the requirements for marriage be relaxed? Does the Society have a responsibility to educate and train black Americans?

Two to three hundred years ago, every Friend was familiar with all of the meetings and most of the families within the verge of his or her Quarterly Meeting, and clerks usually did not see the need to detail locations in the minutes. Most of these meetings have long since disappeared along with any witnesses to their existence. The following meetings appear in the Chester and Concord minutes of the men's and women's Monthly Meetings:

Abington Monthly Meeting, Jenkintown, Abington Twp, formerly Philadelphia Co., now Montgomery Co., PA, near and N.W. of Philadelphia. Settled 1683. Know as Dublin Monthly Meeting from 1687 to 1710 and included Tacony (Frankford) and Poetquesink (Byberry) Meetings.
Arch Street Meeting, common expression of Philadelphia Monthly Meeting at Arch Street held at 4th and Arch Streets, Philadelphia, Philadelphia Co., PA. Settled 1682. Also the site of the Quarterly and Yearly Meetings.
Ashford Monthly Meeting, one of three locations for Matlock/Monyash/Ashford Monthly Meeting, N.W. county palatine of Derby, northwest England. Matlock, a parish 2 mi. E. by S.E. of Winser; Monyash, a chapelry in the parish of Bakewell 4 mi. W. by S.W. of Bakewell; Ashford, a chapelry in the parish of Bakewell 2 mi. N.W. by W. of Bakewell.

Ballenacre, Ballinacree, Ballenacris Monthly Meeting, Antrim County, northeast Ireland. [Exact location and correct spelling not found.]

Ballinderry Monthly Meeting, town of Ballinderry, 12 mi. S.W. of Belfast, Upper Massereene Province, south Antrim County, northeast Ireland. [Also appears as Ballendery, Balendery and Bellanderie.]

Ballycaine Monthly Meeting, Ballycaine, Wicklow Co., Ireland.

Ballynadee Select Meeting, Antrim Co., northeast Ireland.

Baltimore Meeting, Baltimore County, north Maryland. Settled 1792 as a Monthly Meeting.

Bethlehem Meeting, Quakertown, Hunterdon Co., East Jersey. Settled for worship by Chesterfield Monthly Meeting, Burlington Co., in 1731 and known after 1747 as Kingwood Preparative Meeting, later known as Quakertown Monthly Meeting.

Bradford Monthly Meeting, Marshallton, Bradford Twp, Chester Co., PA. Settled as a Monthly Meeting in 1737 by Chester Quarterly Meeting.

Bridgetown Monthly (and Quarterly) Meeting, Bridgetown, Carlisle Bay, Island of Barbadoes [later spelled Barbados], southeastern most island in the West Indies.

Bristol Monthly Meeting, major port town of Bristol on the Bristol Channel, urban county of Bristol between the counties of Glocester and Somerset on the west coast of England.

Buckingham Monthly Meeting, Lahaska, Buckingham Twp, Bucks Co., PA. Settled for worship in 1701 by Falls Monthly Meeting; Preparation ca. 1705; Monthly Meeting 1720.

Burlington Monthly Meeting, town and twp of Burlington, Burlington Co., West Jersey. Settled 1681.

Burmingham [Birmingham] Meeting, town and twp of Birmingham, Chester Co., PA. Settled for worship in 1704 by Concord Meeting; Preparative Meeting 1726; Monthly Meeting 1815.

Bush Creek Preparative Meeting, held at Bush Creek Meeting House, central Frederick (Frederic) Co., Maryland. Settled 1772; belonging to Pipe Creek Monthly Meeting.

Bush River Meeting, Newberry District, later Newberry Co., South Carolina.

Byberry Meeting, Poetquesink, near and N.E. of Philadelphia, formerly Philadelphia Co., now Montgomery Co., PA. Settled for worship 1683; Preparation 1701 attached to Abington Monthly Meeting; eventually merged with Abington Monthly Meeting.

Caln Meeting, Coatesville, Chester Co., PA. Settled for worship and Preparation prior to 1716 by Concord Monthly Meeting.

Cane Creek Monthly Meeting, Alamance Co., North Carolina, near and east of present day Greensboro. Settled 1751.

Carlow Monthly Meeting, town and county of Carlow, Ireland.

Carver's Creek Monthly Meeting, Bladen Co., North Carolina. Settled 1745.

Catawissa Meeting, Catawissa, 2 mi. S. of Bloomburg, Columbia Co., PA. Settled 1787 with Roaring Creek Meeting for worship; elevated to a meeting for worship and Preparation in 1794 under authority of Exeter Monthly Meeting by Philadelphia Quarterly Meeting. Catawissa and Roaring Creek Preparative Meetings were combined in 1795 to form Catawissa Monthly Meeting.

Ceacil [Cecil] Monthly Meeting, Lynch, formerly Cecil Co., now Kent Co., Maryland. Settled 1698 out of Third Haven Monthly Meeting.

Chester Monthly Meeting, known first as Chichester and Upland Monthly Meeting, town and twp of Chester on the Delaware River, formerly Chester Co., Delaware Co. since 1789, PA. By 1722 Chester Monthly Meeting was responsible for the following Preparative Meetings: Chester, Springfield, Providence, Middletown, Goshen, Newtown and Uwchlan.

Chester Monthly Meeting, Pomona, Kent Co., Maryland. Settled for worship at Chester Neck in 1679 by Third Haven Monthly Meeting and transferred to Cecil Monthly Meeting in 1698 when the Preparative Meeting was settled.

Chesterfield Monthly Meeting, market town and twp of Chesterfield, county palatine of Derby, northwest England.

Chesterfield Monthly Meeting, town and twp of Chesterfield, Burlington County, West Jersey.

Chichester Meeting, Boothwyn, Chichester Twp, formerly Chester Co., now Delaware Co., PA. Settled for worship in 1682 by Chester Monthly Meeting; Preparation 1684 and became part of Concord and Chichester Monthly Meeting.

Choptank Meeting, Choptank, Caroline Co., MD. Settled for worship before 1679 under Third Haven Monthly Meeting. In 1734 the meeting was moved to Third Haven and established as a preparative meeting. Later held at Easton, Talbot Co., MD.

Cohansey Meeting, town of Greenwich, Gloucester Co., West Jersey. Settled for worship in 1686 under Salem Monthly Meeting; Preparative Meeting 1760. Cohansey became part of Greenwich Monthly Meeting in 1783.

Coldbeck [Caldbeck] Monthly Meeting, town and parish of Caldbeck, 12 mi. S. by S.W. of Carlisle, county of Cumberland, north west coast of England on the Irish Sea. George Fox lived here for a number of years and established one of the first meetings.

Concord Monthly Meeting, Concordville, Concord Twp, formerly Chester Co., now Delaware Co., PA. Settled in 1684 as Chichester Monthly Meeting and was alternately held in Concord and Chichester until 1729 when it was settled in Concord and renamed Concord Monthly Meeting.

Cork 3 Week Meeting, town and parish of Cork at the headwaters of Cork Harbour, Cork County, southern coast of Ireland.

Cost Hill [Cootehill] Monthly Meeting, town of Cootehill, N.E. Cavan Co., north central Ireland. [Also appears as Colehill.]

Crooked Run Monthly Meeting, located near the village of Nineveh, formerly Frederick Co., now Warren Co., Virginia. Settled by Hopewell Friends in 1781.

Crosswicks Preparative Meeting, Crosswicks Creek, Nottingham Twp, formerly Burlington Co., later made part of Hunterdon Co., and now part of south Mercer Co., New Jersey. Meeting under the authority of Chesterfield Monthly Meeting, Chesterfield Twp, Burlington Co., West Jersey. [Also known as Chesterfield Monthly Meeting at Crosswicks Creek.]

Darby Monthly Meeting, Darby, near and southwest of Philadelphia, Darby Twp, formerly Chester Co., now in the Welsh Tract of Delaware Co., PA. Settled 1684 out of Chester Monthly Meeting. [Also appears as Darby Creek Monthly Meeting.]

Delobourn Monthly Meeting, Montgomeryshire, North Wales.

Dublin Monthly Meeting, market port town of Dublin, Dublin County, east central coast of Ireland.

Dublin Monthly Meeting, later known as Abington Monthly Meeting, Jenkintown, Abington Twp, formerly Philadelphia Co., now Montgomery Co., PA, near and north of Philadelphia. Settled 1683 and known as Dublin Meeting from 1687 to 1710 when it was changed to Abington Monthly Meeting. Dublin (Abington) Meeting included Tacony (Frankford) and Poetquesink (Byberry) Preparative Meetings.

Duck Creek Monthly Meeting, Smyrna, New Castle Co., Delaware. Settled as a monthly meeting out of Newark (Kennett) Monthly Meeting in 1705 by Chester Quarterly Meeting. In 1830, Duck Creek Monthly Meeting was merged with Motherkiln Monthly Meeting to form Camden Monthly Meeting.

Dudley Monthly Meeting, market town and parish of Dudley, extreme northern edge of the county of Worcester, England.

Duns Creek Monthly Meeting, Bladen County, south central North Carolina.

Evesham Monthly Meeting, market town of Evesham, 15 mi. S.E. of Worcester, county of Worcester, west central England.

Evesham Monthly Meeting, Mount Laurel, formerly Evesham Twp, now Mount Laurel Twp, 3 mi. from Moorestown, Burlington Co., West Jersey. Settled 1760 as a monthly meeting out of Haddonfield Monthly Meeting by authority of Salem Quarterly Meeting.

Exeter (Oley) Monthly Meeting, Stonersville, Exeter Twp, Berks Co., PA. Oley Meeting for worship est. 1724; Preparative Meeting est. 1725; reorganized and renamed Exeter Monthly Meeting in 1737.

Fairfax Monthly Meeting, Waterford, formerly Prince William Co., now Laudoun Co., VA. Settled 1744 by Chester Quarterly Meeting.

Falls Monthly Meeting, Fallsington, Falls Twp, Bucks Co., PA. Settled 1683 by Burlington Quarterly Meeting.

Falmouth Monthly Meeting, port town and parish of Falmouth in the hundred of Kerrier, county of Cornwall, extreme southwest England on the English Channel.

Flushing Monthly Meeting, Flushing, Long Island, New York.

Frandley (Frandly) Monthly Meeting, county palatine of Chester, England.

Frankford Preparative Meeting, Penn and Orthodox Streets, Philadelphia, PA. Settled for worship in 1682 under the name Tacony Meeting. Between 1683 and 1805, Frankford Meeting was know as Oxford Meeting.

Goose Creek Monthly Meeting, Lincoln, Loudoun Co., Virgina. Settled before 1757. A second Goose Creek Monthly Meeting was settled in Bedford County, Virginia, in 1794 and continued for 20 years.

Goshen Monthly Meeting, Goshenville, Goshen Twp, Chester Co., PA. Meeting for worship settled in 1702; Preparative Meeting ca. 1703; Monthly Meeting 1722 with authority over Goshen, Newtown and Willistown Preparative Meetings.

Grace Street 2 Week Meeting, common expression for London 2 Week Meeting at Grace Street, London, England.

Great Strictland Monthly Meeting, township of Great Strickland in the parish of Moreland West, 6 mi. S.E. by S. of Penrith, county of Westmoreland, England.

Great Valley Monthly Meeting, Strafford, Tredyffrin Twp in the Welsh
Tract of Chester Co., PA. Settled for worship ca. 1731. [Also appears
as Valley Meeting.]
Gunpowder Monthly Meeting, 16 mi. N.E. of the city of Baltimore and
18 mi. N.W. of Little Falls Meeting on the Gunpowder River,
Baltimore Co., MD. Settled 1716 and in the early years included
Patapsco and Elk Ridge Preparative Meetings. [Also known as Forks
of Gunpowder Monthly Meeting.]
Gwynedd Monthly Meeting, North Wales
Gwynedd Monthly Meeting, town and township of Gwynedd, formerly
Philadelphia County, now Montgomery Co., PA. Settled for worship
1700 by Radnor Monthly Meeting; Preparative Meeting 1702;
Monthly Meeting 1714.
Haddonfield Monthly Meeting, Haddonfield, Newton Twp, formerly
Gloucester Co., now Camden Co., West Jersey. Settled in 1686 in
Newton Twp under the name Newton Monthly Meeting. Removed to
the town of Haddonfield in the 12th mo, 1721/2, and renamed
Haddonfield Monthly Meeting.
Hardshaw-West Monthly Meeting, Liverpool, county of Lancaster,
northwest coast of England at the mouth of the River Mersey. [Also
appears as Hardshaw and Hartshaw.]
Harford Meeting, Harford Co., Maryland.
Haverford Meeting, town and twp of Haverford, formerly Chester Co.,
now in the Welsh Tract of Delaware Co., PA. Settled for worship in
1684 by Philadelphia Quarterly Meeting under Radnor Monthly
Meeting; Preparative Meeting 1701.
Henreco Monthly Meeting, Henreco Co., near and south of Richmond,
VA.
Hopewell Monthly Meeting, 7 mi. N.E. of Winchester, Frederick Co.,
VA. Settled 1734 by Chester Quarterly Meeting.
Horsham Monthly Meeting, town and twp of Horsham, formerly
Philadelphia Co., now Montgomery Co., PA. Monthly Meeting est.
1783 out of Abington Monthly Meeting. [Also appears as Horshan
and Harsham.]
Horslydowne Monthly Meeting, London, England.
Indian Springs Monthly Meeting, Sandy Spring, Montgomery Co.,
Maryland.
Kendall [Kendal] Monthly Meeting, town and parish of Kendal, 10 mi.
S.W. of Hutton, southwest county of Westmoreland, northwest
England.

Kennett Meeting, Kennett Square, Chester Co., PA. Settled for worship about 1707 as part of Newark Monthly Meeting, New Castle Co., Delaware; Preparative Meeting 1712. In 1760 Kennett was merged with Newark and renamed Kennett Monthly Meeting. The names Kennett and Newark were commonly used interchangeably.

Killcomon [Killcommon] Monthly Meeting, Killcommon, 6 Irish mi. S.W. of Wicklow, Wicklow Co., east Ireland.

Kingwood Meeting, Quakertown, Hunterdon Co., New Jersey. Settled 1731 for worship and known as Bethlehem Meeting until 1747 when the name was officially changed to Kingwood. Settled 1756 for Preparation. In 1859 the name was changed to Quakertown Monthly Meeting.

Lancaster Monthly Meeting, port borough and parish of Lancaster, northern coast of the county palatine of Lancaster, northwest coast of England.

Lavington Monthly Meeting, town and parish of East Lavington, 6 mi. S. of Devizes, county of Wilts, southwest England.

Leek Monthly Meeting, town and parish of Leek, 23 mi. N. by N.E. of Stafford, county of Stafford, west central England.

Lisbourn [Lisburn] Monthly Meeting, town of Lisburn, Upper Massereene Province, south Antrim Co., northeast Ireland.

London 2 Week Meeting at Grace Street, London, England. Same as Grace Street 2 Week Meeting, London.

Londongrove [London Grove] Meeting, town and twp of London Grove, Chester Co., PA. Settled 1792 as a Monthly Meeting from members of New Garden Monthly Meeting.

Long Island Yearly Meeting, first held in 1696 at Flushing, Long Island, NY; in 1746 moved to Westbury, Long Island; and in 1794 moved to New York City.

Lurgan Monthly Meeting, market town of Lurgan, 3 mi. S. of Lough Neagh, Down Co., northern Ireland.

Mansfield Meeting, Mansfield, Mansfield Twp, Burlington Co., West Jersey. Settled for worship in 1730 under both Burlington and Chesterfield Monthly Meetings; Preparative Meeting 1776.

Matlock Meeting, one of three locations for Matlock/Monyash/Ashford Monthly Meeting, northwest county palatine of Derby, northwest England. Matlock, a parish 2 mi. E. by S.E. of Winser; Monyash, a chapelry in the parish of Bakewell 4 mi. W. by S.W. of Bakewell; Ashford, a chapelry in the parish of Bakewell 2 mi. N.W. by W. of Bakewell.

Merion Meeting, town and twp of Merion, formerly Philadelphia Co., now Montgomery Co., near and northwest of Philadelphia, PA. Settled for worship in 1682; attached to Radnor/Haverford Monthly Meeting in 1684; and elevated to Merion Preparative Meeting in 1701. [Also appears as Merrian, Marian and Merrien.]

Middletown Meeting, Langhorne, Middletown Twp, Bucks County, PA. Settled for worship about 1680 by Falls Monthly Meeting, Bucks Co.; merged with Neshaminy Monthly Meeting in 1683 and known collectively as Neshaminy Monthly Meeting until about 1706 when it became known as Middletown Monthly Meeting.

Milverton Monthly Meeting, town and parish of Milverton, 3 mi. N. by N.W. of Wellington, southwest county of Somerset, southwestern England.

Minehead Monthly Meeting, port town and parish of Minehead on the Bristol Channel, west county of Somerset, southwestern England. [Ancient spelling: Manheved.]

Monallen [Menallen] Monthly Meeting, Menallen, 9 mi. N. of Gettysburg, formerly Menallen Twp, now Butler Twp, Adams Co., south central Pennsylvania.

Moneyash [Monyash] Monthly Meeting, one of three locations for Matlock/Monyash/Ashford Monthly Meeting, northwest quarter of the county palatine of Derby, northwest England: Matlock, a parish 2 mi. E. by S.E. of Winser; Monyash, a chapelry in the parish of Bakewell 4 mi. W. by S.W. of Bakewell; Ashford, a chapelry in the parish of Bakewell 2 mi. N.W. by W. of Bakewell.

Motherkill [Motherkiln] Monthly Meeting, Camden, Kent Co., Delaware. Settled for worship ca. 1712 by Duck Creek Monthly Meeting; Preparative Meeting 1728; Monthly Meeting 1788.

Mount Holly Monthly Meeting, town of Mount Holly, formerly Northampton Twp, now Mount Holly Twp, Burlington Co., West Jersey. Settled for worship in 1684 under the name Northampton Meeting; Preparative Meeting before 1762; Monthly Meeting 1776. Name changed to Mount Holly Meeting ca. 1772.

Mountrath Meeting, town of Mountrath, 12 mi. S.W. of Kildare, Queens County, central Ireland.

Nailsworth Monthly Meeting, chapelry of Nailsworth, partly in the parishes of Horsley and Minchin-Hampton, but chielfly in the parish of Avening, 2 mi. S.W. by W. of Minchin-Hampton, county of Gloucester, England

Namptwich [Nantwich] Monthly Meeting, town and parish of Nantwich, 20 mi. S.E. by E. of Chester, county palatine of Chester, northwest England.

Nantucket Monthly Meeting, Nantucket Island near Cape Cod, southeast Massachusetts.

Newgarden Monthly Meeting, Carlow Co., Ireland

Newgarden [New Garden] Monthly Meeting, Toughkenamon, New Garden Twp, Chester Co., PA. Settled for worship 1714; Preparation 1715; Monthly Meeting 1718.

New Garden Monthly Meeting, Guilford Co., North Carolina. Settled in 1754.

New Garden Monthly Meeting, Rowan Co., North Carolina.

Newport Monthly Meeting, Newport, R.I.

Newton (Haddonfield) Monthly Meeting, Newton Twp, formerly Gloucester Co., now Camden Co., West Jersey. Settled as Newton Monthly Meeting between 1682 and 1686 by Salem Quarterly Meeting. Removed to town of Haddonfield, also in Newton Twp, and renamed Haddonfield Monthly Meeting in the 12th mo. 1721/2. Woodbury Monthly Meeting was formed from the membership of Haddonfield Meeting in 1784.

Newtown Meeting, town of Newtown, parish of Tattenhall, county palatine of Chester, northwest England.

New York Yearly Meeting, held in Flushing, Long Island, in 1696, moved to Westbury, Long Island, in 1746, and finally moved to New York City in 1794.

Noble Street Meeting, common expression for Philadelphia Monthly Meeting for the Northern District, 6th and Noble Streets, Philadelphia, PA. Settled 1772 from Philadelphia Monthly Meeting at Arch Street.

Norton Meeting, parish of Norton, 2 mi. N. of Stockton, county palatine of Durham, extreme northeast coast of England.

Nottingham Monthly Meeting, town and county of Nottingham, north central England.

Nottingham Meeting, Nottingham Twp, south Chester Co., settled in 1730. Area became part of Cecil Co., Maryland, in 1769.

Oblong Monthly Meeting, Oblong, Northeast Twp, Dutchess Co., New York. Settled 1784

Oley (Exeter) Meeting, Stonersville, Exeter Twp, Berks Co., PA. Settled for worship before 1724 by Gwynedd Monthly Meeting; Preparative Meeting 1725; Monthly Meeting 1737 under the name of Exeter Monthly Meeting.

Opeckon Monthly Meeting, near Martinsburg and Hopewell on Opeckon Creek, Frederick Co., Virginia. First appeared in records in 1737.

Orange Street Meeting, common expression for Philadelphia Monthly Meeting for the Southern District, 8th and Orange Streets, Philadelphia, PA. Settled 1772 from Philadelphia Monthly Meeting at Arch Street.

Oxford (Frankford) Meeting, Philadelphia, PA. Settled 1683 as Tacony Meeting; known as Oxford Meeting from 1685 to 1805 under Abington Monthly Meeting.

Pardshaw Cragg [Pardsey Hall] Monthly Meeting, township of Pardsey, 4 mi. S.S.W. of Cockermouth, parish of Dean, county of Cumberland, England. [Also expressed Parshaw Hall, Pardsay Hall and Pardsey Hall Monthly Meeting.]

Philadelphia Monthly Meeting at Arch Street, commonly known as Arch Street Meeting, held at 4th and Arch Streets, Philadelphia, PA. Settled as a Monthly Meeting in 1682; also the site of Philadelphia Quarterly Meeting and later, Philadelphia Yearly Meeting. Arch Street Meeting was divided into Monthly Meetings for the Northern District (Noble St.) and Southern Districts (Orange St.) in 1772.

Philadelphia Monthly Meeting for the Northern District, 6th and Noble Streets, Philadelphia, PA, commonly known as Noble Street Meeting. Settled by Philadelphia Quarterly Meeting in 1772 from Arch Street Monthly Meeting.

Philadelphia Monthly Meeting for the Southern District, 8th and Orange Streets, Philadelphia, PA, commonly known as Orange Street Meeting, later moved to Pine Street. Settled by Philadelphia Quarterly Meeting in 1772 from Arch Street Monthly Meeting.

Pine Street Monthly Meeting. Philadelphia Monthly Meeting for the Southern District was first held on Orange Street, but soon moved to Hill Meetinghouse on the south side of Pine Street and became commonly known as Pine Street Meeting.

Pipe Creek Monthly Meeting, near Union Bridge, formerly Frederick Co., now Carroll County, Maryland. Met alternately at Pipe Creek and Bush Creek. [Also expressed Pipecreek Monthly Meeting.]

Plymouth Meeting, town of Plymouth Meeting, PA. Settled for worship in 1702 by Radnor Monthly Meeting; Preparative Meeting 1703. Transferred to Gwynedd Monthly Meeting in 1714.

Pownalfee [Pownal-Fee] Monthly Meeting, township of Pownal-Fee, 4 mi. S.W. of Stockport, parish of Wilmslow, county palatine of Chester, England. [Also expressed Pennalfee and Penalsee.]

Pont-y-Moile Monthly Meeting, village of Pont-y-Moile, 1.8 mi. E. by N.E. (bearing 079oT) from Pontypoole on the old stage road from Newport to Abergavenny, county of Monmouth, western England. [Also appears as Pant-y-moile, Pant moile, Ponty moile and Pentmoile.]

Providence Meeting, Providence, later Media, Providence Twp, formerly Chester Co., now Delaware Co., PA. Settled for worship in 1684; Preparation 12th mo, 1698/9. Held at the house of Thomas Marshall before 1700 and can be found referred to a "Thomas Marshall's Meeting.

Purchase Monthly Meeting, Purchase, 10 mi. W. by N.W. of Yonkers, south Westchester Co., New York

Radnor Monthly Meeting, market town of Radnor, Radnorshire, South Wales.

Radnor Monthly Meeting, Radnor, Radnor Twp, formerly Chester Co., now in the Welsh Tract of Delaware Co., PA. Settled 1684 as Haverford Monthly Meeting and after 1698 met alternately in Haverford, Merion, and Radnor. In 1796 the meeting was settled in Radnor and renamed Radnor Monthly Meeting.

Reading Monthly Meeting, market town of Reading, 39 mi. W. by S.W. of London on the road to Bath, county of Berks, England.

Redstone Monthly Meeting, Pembrokeshire, South Wales. [Also appears as Redstone General Meeting.]

Richland (Swamp, Great Swamp) Meeting, Quakertown, Richland Twp, Bucks Co, PA. Settled for worship 1721 under the name Swamp or Great Swamp Meeting; Preparation 1725; Monthly Meeting 1742 and renamed Richland Monthly Meeting.

Robeson Meeting, Birdsboro, Berks Co., PA. Settled for worship 1740; Preparation 1741; Monthly Meeting 1789.

Sadsbury Monthly Meeting, Christiana, Sadsbury Twp, Chester Co., PA. Settled 1737 out of New Garden Monthly Meeting.

Salem Monthly Meeting, town, twp and county of Salem, West Jersey. Settled 1677.

Saratoga Monthly Meeting, New York.

Sedberg [Sedbergh] Monthly Meeting, market town and parish of Sedbergh, West riding of the county of York between counties of York and Westmoreland, north England.

Settle Monthly Meeting, market town of Settle, parish of Giggleswick, West riding of the county of York, 59 mi. W. by N.W. of York, northern England.

Shrewsbury Monthly Meeting, Shrewsbury, Monmouth Co., East Jersey. Settled 1672.

Southern District Monthly Meeting, 8th and Orange Streets, later Pine Street, Philadelphia, PA. Official name: Philadelphia Monthly Meeting for the Southern District. [Also appears as Orange Street Meeting and Pine Street Meeting.]

South River Monthly Meeting, formerly Bedford Co., now Campbell Co., VA. Settled in 1757.

Springfield Preparative Meeting, Springfield, Springfield Twp, formerly Chester Co., now Delaware Co., PA. Settled for worship in 1696 under Chester Monthly Meeting (PA); Preparative Meeting 1698/9.

Stafford Monthly Meeting, market town, parish and county of Stafford, west central England.

Talcot Monthly Meeting, Radnorshire, South Wales.

Thornbury Preparative Meeting, Thornbury Twp, formerly Chester Co., now southwest Delaware Co., PA.

Third Haven Monthly Meeting, Easton, Talbot Co., Maryland. Settled for worship in 1676; Preparative Meeting 1693.

Upper Providence Preparative Meeting, Upper Providence Twp, formerly Chester Co., now Delaware Co., PA.

Upper Springfield Meeting, present day Columbus, Springfield Twp, Burlington Co., West Jersey. Settled for worship in 1727; Preparative Meeting 1776; Monthly Meeting 1781 by Burlington Quarterly Meeting from members of Burlington, Chesterfield and Mount Holly Monthly Meetings.

Uwchlan Monthly Meeting, Lionville, Uwchlan Twp, in the Welch Tract of Chester Co., PA. Settled for worship 1712 by Chester Monthly Meeting; Preparative Meeting 1714 or 1716; Monthly Meeting 1763 by Chester Quarterly Meeting out of Goshen Monthly Meeting.

Valley (Great Valley) Meeting, Strafford, Tredyffrin Twp in the Welsh Tract of Chester Co., PA. Settled for worship ca. 1731; Preparative Meeting 1810.

Waltham Abbey Monthly Meeting, town and parish of Waltham-Abbey, 12 mi. N.E. of London, county of Essex, England.

Warrington Meeting, held 14 mi. N.W. of York, Warrington Twp, York County, PA. Settled as a Monthly Meeting 1745.

Westbury Monthly Meeting, Nassau Co., Long Island, New York. First met for worship as early as 1657, formally settled as Woodledge Monthly Meeting in 1671. [Also met at Farms, Lusum and Jericho.]

Westland Monthly Meeting, Washington Co., PA.

West River Meeting, Anne Arundel Co., Maryland.

Whitney [Witney] Monthly Meeting, town and parish of Witney, 11 mi. N.W. of Oxford, county of Oxford (Oxon), England. Spelled Whitteney before the Norman conquest.

Wilmington Monthly Meeting, town of Wilmington, New Castle Co., Delaware.

Wolverhampton Monthly Meeting, town and parish of Wolverhampton, 16 mi. S. of Stafford, county of Stafford, England.

Woodbury Monthly Meeting, town of Woodbury, Gloucester Co., West Jersey. Settled 1710 for worship; Preparation 1717; Monthly Meeting 1784 out of Haddonfield Monthly Meeting by Salem Quarterly Meeting.

Woodhall Monthly Meeting, county of Cumberland, England.

Worchester Monthly Meeting, market town and county of Worchester, England.

Wrightsborough Monthly Meeting, Town Creek, 16 mi. from Appling, McDuffie Co., Georgia.

Wrightstown Monthly Meeting, town and twp of Wrightstown, Bucks Co., PA. Settled 1686.

York Monthly Meeting, town of York, East riding of the county of York, northern England.

CHESTER MONTHLY MEETING

Chester Monthly Meeting was settled in 1681 under the name "Chichester and Upland Monthly Meeting" by Burlington General Meeting in New Jersey. This meeting was intended to serve Friends living in the area of Marcus Hook and Upland (Chester). The meeting was first held at the homes of Robert Wade of Chichester and later at the home of William and Elizabeth Clayton, Jr. Three meetings for worship were settled within the first six months to be held at the courthouse in Chichester, at the house of William Woodmanson, and at the house of John Simcock in Ridley Twp.

The first meeting house was a simple, stone structure built in 1693 and measured fifteen feet square. It was located on a small lot at the end of Edgmont Avenue near 2nd Street. The basic structure was enlarged in 1701 by a brick addition. By the end of 1721, Chester Monthly Meeting consisted of seven meetings for preparation located in the borough of Chester and the townships of Springfield, Providence, Middletown, Goshen, Newtown and Uwchlan. A new and considerably larger meeting house was built of red and black brick in 1736 on Market Street in Chester.

SAINT PAUL'S PROTESTANT EPISCOPAL CHURCH

The first church building, known as Old Saint Paul's, was built on a small piece of land in the borough of Chester in 1702. This particular plot had been in used as a public burial ground for the previous 40 years at least, a fact that would eventually return to haunt the congregation. No burial records were maintained for this period and no stones marked the graves; nevertheless, it was believed that the new chapel was positioned apart from the grave sites on undisturbed land.

The church building was made of stone with a floor consisting of flat, stone slabs laid directly on the ground. The first sermon was preached in the new chapel on the 3rd day of May, 1703, by Rev. John Talbot. When members of the congregation died, the family had the option of burying their kinsman in the graveyard or in a grave dug under the floor of the chapel. If the family had the means, the stone over the grave was carved with the name of the deceased and his vital dates, but most of the flooring stones were left unmarked. Some incomplete records were kept of the burials under the church; however, church leaders and wealthy members tended to be recorded while members of lesser influence and means were not. Consequently, no one knew how many graves accumulated under the church over the next 150 years.

In 1850 the decision was made to pull down Old Saint Paul's and build a considerably larger church building. Digging for the new foundation hardly began when it was discovered the ground was laced with graves, one upon another. It was said in a newspaper article describing the event that "hardly a spade could be turned without exposing ancient bones." This so disturbed the congregation that a new site on Third Street was selected for the new building. Regrettably, by this time Old Saint Paul's was gone.

CHESTER MONTHLY MEETING
BIRTHS AND DEATHS

John Allen of Newtown, d. 12th da, 2nd mo, 1720.
George and Mary Ashbridge. Children: John Ashbridge, b. 1st da, 6th
mo, 1702, d. 1747; George Ashbridge, b. 19th da, 12th mo, 1703/4, d.
6th da, 3rd mo, 1773; Jonathan Ashbridge, b. 25th da, 9th mo, 1705;
Mary Ashbridge, b. 10th da, 11th mo, 1710/11, d. 20th da, 11th mo,
1745; Elizabeth Ashbridge, b. 6th da, 12th mo, 1708/9, d. 18th da,
12th mo, 1767; Aaron Ashbridge, b. 25th da, 12th mo, 1712/3, d. 5th
mo, 1776; Hannah Ashbridge, b. 26th da, 2nd mo, 1715, d. 13th da,
9th mo, 1793; Phebe Ashbridge, b. 26th da, 8th mo, 1717, d. 14th da,
6th mo, 1784; Lydia Ashbridge, b. 20th da, 11th mo, 1719/20; Joseph
Ashbridge, b. 9th da, 5th mo, 1723, d. 1796.
Joel and Ann Baily. Children: Mary Baily, b. 10th da, 9th mo, 1688;
Ann Baily, b. 10th da, 10th mo, 1691; Daniel Baily, b. 3rd da, 10th
mo, 1693; Isaac Baily, b. 24th da, 10th mo, 1695; Joel Baily, b. 17th
da, 12th mo, 1697.
Joseph and Mary Baker. Child: John Baker, b. 11th da, 10th mo, 1686.
Robert and Susanna Baker. Children: Mary Baker, b. 24th da, 12th
mo, 1711; Elizabeth Baker, b. 10th da, 5th mo, 1713; Ann baker, b.
1st da, 12th mo, 1715/6.
Robert and Hannah Barber. Children: Eleanor Barber, b. 1st da, 11th
mo, 1718; John Barber, b. 13th da, 8th mo, 1720; Robert Barber, b.
10th da, 10th mo, 1722; Thomas Barber, b. 20th da, 10th mo, 1724;
Nathaniel Barber, b. 9th da, 9th mo, 1727; Elizabeth Barber, b. 24th
da, 1st mo, 1729; Mary Barber, b. 8th da, 3rd mo, 1732.
James and Mary Barton. Children: Abner Barton, b. 5th da, 4th mo,
1757; Sarah Barton, b. 15th da, 8th mo, 1758; Adam Barton, b. 17th
da, 12th mo, 1760; Mary Barton, b. 12th da, 9th mo, 1762.
James and Elizabeth Bartram. Child: Mary Bartram, b. 12th da, 9th
mo, 1727, d. 16th da, 10th mo, 1756.
John and Mary Beals. Children: John Beals, b. 28th da, 7th mo, 1685;
William Beals, b. 1st da, 2nd mo, 1687; Jacob Beals, b. 28th da, 7th
mo, 1689; Mary Beals, b. 24th da, 1st mo, 1691/2; Patience Beals, b.
16th da, 4th mo, 1695.
Robert and Jane Benson. Children: John Benson, b. 19th da, 12th mo
1714; James Benson, b. 22nd da, 6th mo, 1717; Hannah Benson, b.
31st da, 1st mo, 1720.

William and Mary Bevan. Children: Elizabeth Bevan, b. 1st mo, 1706; Ann Bevan, b. 7th mo, 1708; Mordecai Bevan, b. 1st mo, 1710; Benjamin Bevan, b. 9th mo, 1711.

William Bevan, d. 17th da, 10th mo, 1715.

Joseph and Sarah Bishop of Upper Providence. Children: Thomas Pratt Bishop, 21st da, 12th mo, 1792; Randall Bishop, b. 18th da, 4th mo, 1795; Tamar Bishop, b. 3rd da, 12th mo, 1796; Emily Bishop, b. 23rd da, 6th mo, 1799; Joel Bishop, b. 26th da, 2nd mo, 1801; Orpha Bishop, b. 10th da, 12th mo, 1803; Jeremiah Bishop, b. 6th da, 10th mo, 1805.

Sarah Bishop, wife of Joseph, d. 17th da, 7th mo, 1809.

Charles Booth. Children: Mary Booth, b. 15th da, 1st mo, 1706; Lidia Booth, b. 24th da, 1st mo, 1707; Jonathan Booth, b. 28th da, 1st mo, 1709.

John and Frances Bowater. Children: Mary Bowater, b. 23rd da, 6th mo, 1685; William Bowater, b. 19th da, 11th mo, 1686; Elizabeth Bowater, b. 23rd da, 11th mo, 1688; Ann Bowater, b. 3rd da, 6th mo, 1690; Alice Bowater, b. 8th da, 12th mo, 1692; Phebe Bowater, b. 17th da, 2nd mo, 1697.

Thomas and Sarah Bowater. Children: Sarah Bowater, b. 17th da, 6th mo, 1688; Thomas Bowater, b. 28th da, 1st mo, 1690.

Sarah Bowater, wife of Thomas, d. 26th da, 2nd mo, 1692.

Asher Brassey, son of Thomas of Chester, d. 22nd da, 2nd mo, 1683.

Thomas Brassey, d. 16th da, 7th mo, 1690.

Peter and Mary Britton. Child: Elizabeth Britton, b. 25th da, 12th mo, 1692.

Daniel and Judith Broom. Children: James Broom, b. 8th da, 9th mo, 1726; Mary Broom, b. 25th da, 9th mo, 1728; Daniel Broom, b. 25th da, 12th mo, 1730/1; Thomas Broom (twin), b. 20th da, 3rd mo, 1734; Betty Broom (twin), b. 20th da, 3rd mo, 1734.

Susanna Broomall, wife of John, d. 19th da, 12th mo, 1798.

James and Hannah Broomall. Children: Thomas D., b. 5th da, 8th mo, 1799; John Broomall, b. 6th da, 7th mo, 1800; Abraham Broomall, b. 20th da, 7th mo, 1801, d. 20th da, 6th mo, 1875; Daniel Broomall, b. 23rd da, 6th mo, 1802; Susanna Broomall, b. 20th da, 8th mo, 1803; James Broomall, b. 29th da, 4th mo, 1805; James Broomall, b. 30th da, 10th mo, 1806, d. 19th da, 11th mo, 1825, age 19, at Thornbury, buried at Middletown; Hannah D. Broomall, b. 4th da, 6th mo, 1813.

James and Hannah Browne of Marcus Hook. Child: James Browne, b. 17th da, 1st mo, 1681.

William and Ann Browne. Children: Mercer Browne, b. 27th da, 12th 1685; Ann Browne, b. 1st da, 10th mo, 1687; William Browne, b. 21st da, 7th mo, 1689; John Browne, b. 3rd da, 5th mo, 1691; Richard Browne, b. 13th da, 1st mo, 1693; Thomas Browne, b. 17th da, 11th mo, 1694.

✶ David and Mary Cadwalader. Child: David Cadwalader, b. 26th da, 5th mo, 1719.

John and Judith Calvert of Providence Twp. Children: Daniel Calvert, b. 6th da, 5th mo, 1685; Mary Calvert, b. 19th da, 12th mo, 1687.

John and Hannah Calvert. Children: Nathaniel Calvert, b. 4th da, 12th mo, 1745/6; Lydia Calvert, b. 19th da, 12th mo, 1746/7.

Robert and Lydia Carter. Children: Prudence Carter, b. 6th da, 11th mo, 1689; John Carter, b. 8th da, 4th mo, 1691, d. 21st da, 2nd mo, 1693; Hannah Carter, b. 22nd da, 12th mo, 1692.

John and Hannah Churchman. Children: George Churchman, b. 13th da, 7th mo, 1697; Dinah Churchman, b. 7th da, 6th mo, 1699; Susanna Churchman, b. 13th da, 7th mo, 1701.

William and Susanna Cloud. Child: Sally Ann Cloud, b. 16th da, 1st mo, 1796.

Elizabeth Cobourn, wife of Thomas, d. 6th da, 3rd mo, 1688.

Joseph and Sarah Cobourn. Children: Sarah Cobourn, b. 20th da, 1st mo, 1718/9; Caleb Cobourn (twin), b. 6th da, 12th mo, 1720/1; Joshua Cobourn (twin), b. 6th da, 12th mo, 1720/1.

Rachel Cobourn, wife of Thomas, d. 7th da, 12th mo, 1720.

Bartholomew Coppock, Sr., d. 20th da, 12th mo, 1718/9 in Marple Twp, age near 73.

Bartholomew and Helen Coppock. Child: Hannah Coppock, b. 9th da, 10th mo, 1684.

Bartholomew Coppock, Jr., son of Bartholomew and Margaret (Yarwood) Coppock, Sr., and his 1st wife, Rebecca Minshall. Child: Margaret Coppock, b. 21st da, 4th mo, 1706; Moses Coppock, b. 2nd da, 5th mo, 1708.

Rebecca (Minshall) Coppock, 1st wife of Bartholomew Coppock, Jr., d. 29th da, 5th mo, 1708.

Bartholomew Coppock, Jr., and his 2nd wife, Phebe Massey, widow. Children: Rebecca Coppock, b. 14th da, 5th mo, 1711; Sarah Coppock, b. 22nd da, 7th mo, 1712; Esther Coppock, b. 12th da, 10th mo, 1714; Martha Coppock, b. 2nd da, 11th mo, 1716/7.

Bartholomew Coppock, Jr., d. 8th da, 2nd mo, 1720

Phebe (Massey) Coppock, 2nd wife of Bartholomew Coppock, Jr., d. 27th da, 12th mo, 1749/50.

Jonathan and Jane Coppock. Children: Sarah Coppock, b. 21st da, 8th mo, 1712; Hannah Coppock, b. 4th da, 1st mo, 1716; Rachel Coppock, b. 13th da, 1st mo, 1719.

Caleb Cowpland and his 1st wife, Mary. Child: William Cowpland, b. 26th da, 10th mo, 1717, d. 7th mo, 1728.

Mary Cowpland, 1st wife of Caleb, d. 5th da, 8th mo, 1719.

Caleb Cowpland and his 2nd wife, Sarah. Children: David Cowpland, b. 31st da, 10th mo, 1722; Jonathan Cowpland, b. 11th mo, 1724/5; Agnes Cowpland, b. 4th da, 6th mo, 1727; Caleb Cowpland, b. 15th da, 3rd mo, 1730; Grace Cowpland, b. 18th da, 12th mo, 1732/3, d. 17th da, 10th mo, 1756.

Caleb Cowpland, Sr., d. 12th da, 10th mo, 1757, age 67, buried at Chester.

Sarah Cowpland, 2nd wife of Caleb Cowpland, Sr., d. 28th da, 3rd mo, 1758 age 68.

John and Mary Coxe. Children: Jane Coxe, b. 3rd da, 3rd mo, 1752; Ellen Coxe, b. 14th da, 6th mo, 1753; Israel Coxe, b. 16th da, 10th mo, 1756; Sarah Coxe, b. 7th da, 10th mo, 1758; Mary Coxe, b. 1st da, 12th mo, 1760; Lawrence Coxe, b. 1st da, 9th mo, 1762; Amy Coxe, b. 2nd da, 5th mo, 1764.

John Coxe, Sr., d. 27th da, 6th mo, 1771, age 41.

Mary Coxe, widow of John Coxe, Sr., d. 4th da, 7th mo, 1784 in Chester.

Charles and Hannah Crossley. Children: Elizabeth Crossley, b. 30th da, 2nd mo, 1725; John Crossley, b. 22nd da, 8th mo, 1727; Samuel Crossley, b. 31st da, 8th mo, 1732.

Randall and Sarah Croxen. Children: Randall Croxen, b. 25th da, 1st mo, 1708; John Croxen, b. 13th da, 9th mo, 1706; Thomas Croxen, b. 5th da, 9th mo, 1707; Samuel Croxen, b. 6th da, 10th mo, 1709; Jonathan Croxen, b. 6th da, 10th mo, 1711.

Abraham and Elizabeth Darlington. Children: Mary Darlington, b. 14th da, 1st mo, 1717; Deborah Darlington, b. 13th da, 7th mo, 1719.

Jesse and Amy Darlington of Middletown. Children: Martha Darlington, b. 9th da, 7th mo, 1788; Rhoda Darlington, b. 9th da, 5th mo, 1790; Mark Darlington, b. 8th da, 1st mo, 1794, d. 4th da, 10th mo, 1794; Edward Darlington (twin), b. 14th da, 9th mo, 1795; Samuel Darlington (twin), b. 14th da, 9th mo, 1795; Benjamin Darlington (trip), b. 23rd da, 8th mo, 1797, d. 8th da, 10th mo, 1807; Joshua Darlington (trip), b. 23rd da, 8th mo, 1797, d. same day; Thomas Darlington (trip), b. 23rd da, 8th mo, 1797; Jared Darlington, b. 15th da, 8th mo, 1799; Amy Darlington, b. 11th da, 9th mo, 1805.

Ellis David, d. 17th da, 1st mo, 1720 in Goshen.

Rowland Davis, son of Ellis and Jane Davis, d. 12th da, 2nd mo, 1707.

David and Jane Davis. Children: Hannah Davis, b. 1st da, 5th mo, 1710; Richard Davis, b. 3rd da, 3rd mo, 1712; Ellis Davis, b. 24th da, 10th mo, 1714; Sarah Davis, b. 20th da, 7th mo, 1715; Jonathan Davis, b. 4th da, 6th mo, 1717; Amos Davis, b. 26th da, 3rd mo, 1717

Thomas and Rachel Dell. Child: Mary Dell, b. 16th da, 7th mo, 1734, d. 5th da, 10th mo, 1801.

Sarah Dell, dau. of Thomas and Mary, d. 27th da, 7th mo, 1714.

Mary Dell, d. 11th da, 9th mo, 1751, age 81.

Thomas Dell, d. 15th da, 6th mo, 1750, age 84.

Peter and Sarah Dicks. Children: Joseph Dicks, b. 26th da, 3rd mo, 1717; James Dicks, b. 18th da, 6th mo, 1718; Nathan Dicks, b. 2nd da, 11th mo, 1719; Sarah Dicks, b. 19th da, 1st mo, 1720; Peter Dicks, b. 23rd da, 10th mo, 1722.

Joseph and Ann Dicks. Children: James Dicks, b. 10th da, 4th mo, 1746; Frederick Dicks, b. 13th da, 12th mo, 1747; Esther Dicks, b. 21st da, 1st mo, 1748/9; Peter Dicks, b. 8th da, 5th mo, 1752 N.S.; Ann Dicks, b. 3rd da, 3rd mo, 1755; Sarah Dicks, b. 22nd da, 3rd mo, 1758; Lydia Dicks, b. 18th da, 4th mo, 1761.

Peter and Sarah Dicks. Children: Jane Dicks, b. 4th da, Nov 1751; Roger Dicks, b. 30th da, 7th mo, 1753, d. 29th da, 12th mo, 1808.

Peter Dicks, d. 25th da, 8th mo, 1760.

Sarah Dicks, widow of Peter, d. 25th da, 11th mo, 1793, age 82.

Morgan and Cassandra Druet. Children: Benjamin Druet, b. at sea, 20th da, 5th mo, 1677; Mary Druet, b. 22nd da, 2nd mo, 1680.

Elizabeth Dutton, dau. of John and Mary Dutton, d. 23rd da, 10th mo, 1682.

Thomas and Hannah Dutton. Child: Sarah Dutton, b. 7th da, 12th mo, 1760.

Virgil and Bethsheba Eaches. Children: Homer Eaches, b. 15th da, 7th mo, 1792; Joseph Eaches, b. 14th da, 11th mo, 1793; Obed Eaches, b. 18th da, 9th mo, 1795; Hiram Eaches, b. 11th da, 7th mo, 1797, d. 20th da, 9th mo, 1801; Edna Eaches, b. 9th da, 2nd mo, 1799, d. 27th da, 9th mo, 1801; Betsy Eaches, b. 24th da, 12th mo, 1800, d. 20th da, 9th mo, 1801; Mehala Eaches, b. 5th da, 11th mo, 1802; Abner Eaches, b. 21st da, 10th mo, 1804; Preston Eaches, b. 3rd da, 2nd mo, 1807.

John and Jane Edge. Children: John Edge, b. beginning of the 5th mo, 1685; Jacob Edge, b. 8th da, 3rd mo, 1690.

John Edge, d. 10th da, 5th mo, 1711 in Nether Providence Twp, age about 65.

Jacob and Sarah Edge. Children: Hannah Edge, b. 18th da, 6th mo, 1713; Jane Edge, b. 3rd da, 9th mo, 1715; Abigail Edge, b. 28th da, 8th mo, 1717; Sarah Edge, b. 19th da, 9th mo, 1719, d. 23rd da, 7th mo, 1728.

Sarah Edge, widow of Jacob Edge, dau. of Rees and Hannah Jones, b. 25th da,7th mo, 1690, m. 2nd Caleb Cowpland.

George and Ann Edge. Children: Mary Edge, b. 18th da, 11th mo, 1742/3; John Edge, b. 10th mo, 1744; Sarah Edge, b. 24th da, 8th mo, 1746; Ann Edge, b. 26th da, 12th mo, 1748.

John and Hannah Edwards. Children: Pennock Edwards, b. 26th da, 6th mo, 1782; Nathan Edwards, b. 6th da, 2nd mo, 1784; John Edwards, b. 15th da, 7th mo, 1786; Sarah Edwards, b. 27th da, 2nd mo, 1788.

John and Mary Eblen. Children: Hannah Eblen, b. 2nd da, 1st mo, 1746; Eliza Eblen, b. 15th da, 4th mo, 1748; Mary Eblen, b. 14th da, 4th mo, 1750; Rachel Eblen, b. 30th da, 7th mo, 1753; Samuel Eblen, b. 18th da, 7th mo, 1755; Elizabeth Eblen, b. 12th da, 7th mo, 1757; John Eblen, b. 16th da, 4th mo, 1759; Isaac Eblen, b. 6th da, 5th mo, 1761.

James and Phebe Emlen. Children: Ann Emlen, b. 9th da, 6th mo, 1784; Mary Emlen, b. 13th da, 8th mo, 1786; Samuel Emlen, b. 6th da, 3rd mo, 1789; Phebe Emlen, b. 30th da, 8th mo, 1790; James Emlen, b. 17th da, 6th mo, 1792.

Phebe Emlen, wife of James, d. 25th da, 10th mo, 1793, age 35.

Isaac and Abigail Engle. Children: John Roberts Engle, b. 15th da, 8th mo, 1793; Elizabeth Engle, b. 16th da, 10th mo, 1796; Abigail Engle, b. 29th da, 12th mo, 1798; Margaret Engle, b. 16th da, 8th mo, 1802; Isaac Engle, b. 10th da, 12th mo, 1804.

Abigail Engle, wife of Isaac, b. at Chester, d. 24th da, 4th mo, 1833 at S. Providence, age 67.

John and Mary Evans. Children: Thomas Evans, b. 24th da, 7th mo, 1713; Solomon Evans, b. 23rd da, 7th mo, 1714; David Evans, b. 12th da, 5th mo, 1716; Jonathan Evans, b. 2nd da, 10th mo, 1718.

Cadwalader and Ann Evans. Children: Pennell Evans, b. 1st da, 8th mo, 1731; Hannah Evans, b. 3rd da, 9th mo, 1733; Alice Evans, b. 4th da, 10th mo, 1735; Robert Evans, b. 17th da, 4th mo, 1738; Sarah Evans, b. 14th da, 9th mo, 1740, d. 27th da, 6th mo, 1743; Ann Evans, b. 6th da, 12th mo, 1742/3; Thomas Evans, b. 4th da, 3rd mo, 1745, d. 1786; Joseph Evans, b. 18th da, 4th mo, 1747, d.

27th da, 9th mo, 1756; Mary Evans. b. 28th da, 4th mo, 1750, d. 7th da, 10th mo, 1756; Jane Evans, b. 5th da, 12th mo, 1752; Catharine Evans, b. 10th da, 11th mo, 1754, d. 15th da, 9th mo, 1756.
Ann Evans, widow of Cadwalader Evans, b. 2nd da, 8th mo, 1711, d. 25th da, 1st mo, 1803, age 92.
Isaac and Ann Eyre. Children: Jonas Eyre, b. 28th da, 4th mo, 1767; Lewis Eyre, b. 23rd da, 3rd mo, 1769; William Eyre, b. 22nd da, 3rd mo, 1771; Preston Eyre, b. 17th da, 2nd mo, 1774; Mary Eyre, b. 9th da, 3rd mo, 1776; Isaac Eyre, b. 19th da, 4th mo, 1778.
Nicholas and Katharine Fairlamb. Children: Mary Fairlamb, b. 19th da, 7th mo, 1705; Samuel Fairlamb, b. 20th da, 10th mo, 1707, d. 20th da, 5th mo, 1708; Katharine Fairlamb, b. 8th da, 4th mo, 1709; Hannah Fairlamb, b. 19th da, 8th mo, 1711.
Robert and Mary Fairlamb of Middletown. Children: Alice Fairlamb, b. 24th da, 6th mo, 1792; Sarah Fairlamb, b. 12th da, 8th mo, 1794; Frederick Augustus Fairlamb, b. 14th da, 3rd mo, 1796; John Harry Fairlamb, b. 15th da, 5th mo, 1799; Susannah Fairlamb, b. 2nd da, 5th mo, 1801; Mary Fairlamb, b. 10th da, 4th mo, 1803; Robert Pennell Fairlamb, b. 1st da, 10th mo, 1804; Samuel Fairlamb, b. 13th da, 3rd mo, 1806.
Walter and Rebecca Faucit. Children: Rebecca Faucit, b. 24th da, 1st mo, 1695/6; Mary Faucit, b. 25th da, 9th mo, 1697; Sarah Faucit, b. 30th da, 7th mo, 1699, d. 4th da, 8th mo, 1701; Sarah Faucit, b. 10th da, 3rd mo, 1702; Elizabeth Faucit, b. 5th da, 3rd mo, 1704.
Grace Faucit, wife of Walter, d. 30th da, 9th mo, 1686.
Esther Faucit, dau. of Walter and Grace Faucit, d. 4th da, 5th mo, 1687
Joseph Faucit, son of Walter and Grace Faucit, d. 7th da, 4th mo, 1690.
Walter Faucit, d. 23rd da, 1st mo, 1704.
Edward and Mary Fell of Springfield Twp. Children: William Fell, b. 27th da, 5th mo, 1779, d. 7th da, 3rd mo, 1814; Thomas Fell, b. 3rd/4th da, 6th mo, 1781; Beulah Fell, b. 27th da, 2nd mo, 1783; Benjamin Fell, b. 14th da, 7th mo, 1785; Edward Fell, b. 28th da, 6th mo, 1787; Maria Fell, b. 22nd da, 7th mo, 1790; Gulielma Fell, b. 27th da, 2nd mo, 1792; Joseph Fell, b. 24th da, 2nd mo, 1794; Deborah Fell, b. 12th da, 5th mo, 1798.
Mary Fell, wife of Edward, d. 17th da, 8th mo, 1818 in Springfield Twp, age 65.
Edward Fell, widower of Mary, d. 28th da, 12th mo, 1825 in Lower Providence Twp, buried in Springfield Twp.
Mary Few, widow of Richard Few, Jr., d. 13th da, 1st mo, 1686.

Richard Few, d. 25th da, 9th mo, 1688.

Thomas and Rebecca Garrett. Children: William Garrett, b. 5th da, 12th mo, 1705; Samuel Garrett, b. 1st da, 5th mo, 1708; Susanna Garrett, b. 6th da, 9th mo, 1711.

George Gleave, d. 25th da, 9th mo, 1688.

John and Elizabeth Gleave. Children: George Gleave, b. 21st da, 9th mo, 1707; John Gleave, b. 22nd da, 2nd mo, 1709, d. 25th da, 2nd mo, 1720; Esther Gleave, b. 10th da, 10th mo, 1712; Rachel Gleave, b. 8th da, 8th mo, 1715; Isaac Gleave, b. 8th da, 8th mo, 1719; John Gleave, b. 2nd da, 2nd mo, 1721; Elizabeth Gleave, b. 6th da, 10th mo, 1721, d. 6th da, 7th mo, 1727.

Elizabeth Gleave, wife of John Gleave, d. 11th da, 8th mo, 1727 at age 46.

Elizabeth Goodwin, d. 10th da, 9th mo, 1739, age 87.

William and Rebecca Gorsuch. Children: Hannah Gorsuch, b. 16th da, 2nd mo, 1731; John Gorsuch, b. 7th da, 9th mo, 1732, d. 24th da, 11th mo, 1732; Lydia Gorsuch, b. 13th da Nov 1733; John Gorsuch, b. 23rd da Nov 1735; Thomas Gorsuch, b. 26th da, 12th mo, 1737/8, d. 12th da, 6th mo, 1744; Mary Gorsuch, b. 2nd da, 6th mo, 1739; Elizabeth Gorsuch, b. 17th da, 3rd mo, 1741, d. 28th da, 6th mo, 1742; Ebenezer Gorsuch, b. 24th da, 11th mo, 1742/3.

Henry Hale and Abigail Graham of Chester. Children: Eleanor Graham, b. 17th da, 7th mo, 1761; Mary Graham, b. 4th da, 1st mo, 1764; William Graham, b. 13th da, 2nd mo, 1766; Henrietta Graham, b. 27th da, 4th mo, 1768; Dorothea Graham, b. 22nd da, 6th mo, 1770; Catharine Graham, b. 2nd da, 1st mo, 1773; Henry Hale Graham, b. 24th da, 5th mo, 1777, d. 21st da, 7th mo, 1777; Abigail Graham, b. 19th da, 4th mo, 1780; Maria Graham, b. 29th da, 11th mo, 1782.

William and Rachel Gray. Children: Martha Gray, b. 7th da, 5th mo, 1793; William Gray, b. 9th da, 10th mo, 1795.

Robert and Hannah Green of Edgmont Twp. Children: Abel Green, b. 12th da, 2nd mo, 1784; Joseph Green, b. 2nd da, 9th mo, 1785; Jane Green, b. 14th da, 3rd mo, 1787; Lewis Green, b. 3rd da, 1st mo, 1789; Lydia Green, b. 12th da, 12th mo, 1790; Robert Green, b. 1st da, 10th mo, 1793; David Green, b. 3rd da, 4th mo, 1795; Hannah Green, b. 2nd mo, 1797; Samuel Green, b. 2nd da, 6th mo, 1798; James Green, b. 11th da, 3rd mo, 1800; Mary Green, b. 15th da, 11th mo, 1804; Edward Green, b. 15th da, 8th mo, 1807.

William and Rebecca Gregory of Edgmont Twp. Children: John Gregory, b. 16th da, 12th mo, 1685; William Gregory, b. 2nd da, 10th mo, 1687; Elizabeth Gregory, b. 14th da, 9th mo, 1690; Mary

Gregory, b. 10th da, 9th mo, 1691; Simon Gregory, b. 30th da, 9th mo, 1694; Shouah Gregory, b. 6th da, 9th mo, 1696; Edmund Gregory, b. 25th da, 2nd mo, 1699.

William Gregory, yeoman, d. not recorded; Will: dated 20th da, 6th mo, 1703, proven 17 Jun 1704.

Joseph and Sarah Griffith. Children: Isaac Griffith, b. 9th da, 1st mo, 1799; Eli Griffith, b. 21st da, 11th mo, 1800; Everard Griffith, b. 15th da, 6th mo, 1803; Hannah Griffith, b. 19th da, 1st mo, 1805.

Joseph and Priscilla Grissel. Child: Agnes Grissel, b. 19th da, 4th mo, 1784, d. 16th da, 9th mo, 1821.

Agnes Guest, wife of Simon Guest, dau. of John and Elizabeth Salkeld, d. 17th da, 12th mo, 1769.

John and Elizabeth Haines of Middletown. Child: David Haines, b. 13th da, 1st mo, 1719.

Samuel and Mary Hall. Children: John Hall, b. 27th da, 2nd mo, 1691; Elizabeth Hall, b. 29th da, 11th mo, 1693; George Hall, b. 1st da, 3rd mo, 1695; Ann Hall, b. 11th da, 3rd mo, 1698; Samuel Hall, b. 25th da, 6th mo, 1701.; Thomas Hall, b. 24th da, 4th mo, 1704.

David and Hannah Hall of Marple Twp. Children: Beulah Hall, b. 10th da, 1st mo, 1796; William Hall, b. 19th da, 5th mo, 1797; Samuel Hall, b. 30th da, 9th mo, 1798; Deborah Hall, b. 17th da, 7th mo, 1800; Susanna Hall, b. 19th da, 1st mo, 1802; Julian Hall, b. 20th da, 3rd mo, 1804; Hannah Hall, b. 23rd da, 11th mo, 1805; David Hall, b. 5th da, 7th mo, 1812.

Hannah Hall, wife of David, d. 29th da, 12th mo, 1817, age 40, buried in Springfield Twp.

David Hall, widower of Hannah, d. 1st da, 1st mo, 1842, age 76, buried in Springfield Twp.

William and Margaret Hammans. Children: Mary Hammans, b. 28th da, 1st mo, 1710; Martha Hammans, b. 6th da, 7th mo, 1713; Sarah Hammans, b. 28th da, 3rd mo, 1720; William Hammans, b. 31st da, 6th mo, 1723; Hannah Hammans, b. 26th da, 2nd mo, 1727/8.

Margaret Hammans, wife of William Hammans, d. 4th da, 9th mo, 1731, age 46.

Samuel and Sarah Hampton. Children: Mary Hampton, b. 15th da, 1st mo, 1754; Sarah Hampton, b. 2nd da, 11th mo, 1755; Elizabeth Hampton, b. 8th da, 2nd mo, 1758.

Caleb and Hannah Harrison. Children: Caleb Harrison, b. 13th da, 11th mo, 1714; John Harrison, b. 29th da, 1st mo, 1716; Hannah Harrison, b. 29th da, 1st mo, 1718.

Joshua and Eliza Harrison of Springfield Twp. Children: Caleb Harrison, b. 12th da, 1st mo, 1792; Catharine Harrison, b. 21st da, 9th mo, 1795; Joshua Harrison, b. 16th da, 9th mo, 1797; Samuel Pancoast Harrison, b. 19th da, 11th mo, 1799; Seth Harrison, b. 30th da, 12th mo, 1801; John Fairlamb Harrison, b. 2nd da, 2nd mo, 1804.

Joseph and Mary Harvey. Children: Joseph Harvey, b. 18th da, 7th mo, 1710; Alice Harvey, b. 10th da, 10th mo, 1713; Mary Harvey, b. 1st da, 1st mo, 1718.

Joshua and Elizabeth Hastings. Child: Mary Hastings, b. 16th da, 6th mo, 1685.

Elizabeth Hastings, wife of John Hastings of Providence Twp, d. and buried 2nd da, 2nd mo, 1684.

John and Sarah Heacock of Middletown. Child: Ann Heacock, b. 24th da, 6th mo, 1742.

John Heacock, d. 13th da, 11th mo, 1794, age 80.

Joseph and Jane Helsby. Child: Mary Helsby, b. 6th da, 3rd mo, 1713.

John and Mary Hibberd. Child: Jacob Hibberd, b. 3rd da, 10th mo. 1752, d. 13th da, 9th mo, 1827.

Jacob and Sarah Hibberd of Middletown. Children: Mary Hibberd, b. 17th da, 7th mo, 1779; Hannah Hibberd, b. 9th da, 1st mo, 1781; John Hibberd, b. 4th da, 1st mo, 1783; Thomas Hibberd, b. 14th da, 10th mo, 1785; Jacob Hibberd, b. 11th da, 1st mo, 1787; Phineas Hibberd, b. 11th da, 12th mo, 1792, d. 24th da, 8th mo, 1808; Phebe Hibberd, b. 12th da, 9th mo, 1794, d. 20th da, 5th mo, 1808; Samuel Hibberd, b. 8th da, 1st mo, 1797; Jesse Hibberd, b. 10th da, 10th mo, 1801, d. 28th da, 8th mo, 1808; Susanna Hibberd (twin), b. 27th da, 9th mo, 1803; Sarah Hibberd (twin), b. 27th da, 9th mo, 1803; Abraham Hibberd, b. 21st da, 6th mo, 1806, d. 25th da, 1st mo, 1807.

Sarah (Dutton) Hibberd, wife of Jacob, dau. of Thomas and Hannah Dutton, b. 7th da, 12th mo, 1760.

John and Mary Hill of Middletown. Children: William Hill (twin), b. 31st da, 10th mo, 1761; Joseph Hill (twin), b. 31st da, 10th mo, 1761; Humphrey Hill, b. 5th da, 10th mo, 1763; Hannah Hill, b. 5th da, 8th mo, 1765; Ann Hill, b. 15th da, 12th mo, 1767; Rachel Hill, b. 25th da, 2nd mo, 1770; Mary Hill, b. 1st da, 2nd mo, 1772; Lydia Hill, b. 5th da, 11th mo, 1774; Lacy Hill, b. 31st da, 10th mo, 1776; John Hill, b. 27th da, 4th mo, 1779; Deborah Hill, b. 12th da, 10th mo, 1781; Sidney Hill, b. 22nd da, 6th mo, 1785; Norris Hill, b. 23rd da, --, 1788.

John Hill of Middletown, d. 10th da, 2nd mo, 1814, buried at
Middletown.

Mary Hill, widow of John, d. 4th da, 4th mo, 1827, age 84.

James and Elizabeth Hind. Child: James Hind b. 15th da, 1st mo,
1723/4.

Hannah Hind, wife of James, d. 24th da, 5th mo, 1716.

Abigail Hinkson of Middletown, b. 24th da, 11th mo, 1765.

Daniel and Jane Hoopes. Children: Grace Hoopes, b. 17th da, 7th mo,
1697; Ann Hoopes, b. 23rd da, 10th mo, 1698, d. 13th da, 3rd mo,
1704; Mary Hoopes, b. 22nd da, 9th mo, 1700; Hannah Hoopes, b.
25th da, 5th mo, 1702; Joshua Hoopes, b. 29th da, 4th mo, 1704;
Jane Hoopes, b. 14th da, 5th mo, 1706; Ann Hoopes, b. 3rd da, 12th
mo, 1707, d. 14th da, 7th mo, 1728; Daniel Hoopes, b. 27th da, 10th
mo, 1710; John Hoopes, b. 17th da, 8th mo, 1711; Abraham Hoopes,
b. 12th da, 4th mo, 1713; Thomas Hoopes, b. 22nd da, 10th mo 1714;
Elizabeth Hoopes (twin), b. 13th da, 1st mo, 1716; Stephen Hoopes
(twin), b. 13th da, 1st mo, 1716; Nathan Hoopes, b. 16th da, 1st mo,
1718; Walter Hoopes, b. 11th da, 1st mo, 1719; Sarah Hoopes, b.
25th da, 5th mo, 1720; Christian Hoopes, b. 30th da, 8th mo, 1723.

John and Ruth Hoskins. Children: John Hoskins, b. 24th da, 12th mo,
1699; Stephen Hoskins, b. 18th da, 12th mo, 1701/2; George
Hoskins, b. 8th da, 8th mo, 1703; Joseph Hoskins, b. 30th da, 4th
mo, 1705; Mary Hoskins, b. 1st da, 8th mo, 1707.

John Hoskins, husband of Ruth, d. 26th da, 8th mo, 1716.

John and Ann Houlston. Child: John Houlston, b. 19th da, 9th mo,
1686.

John Houlston, Jr., husband of Ann Houlston, son of John and
Elizabeth Houlston, Sr., d. 17th da, 4th mo, 1688.

John Houlston, Sr., d. 12th da, 3rd mo, 1699.

Elizabeth Houlston, widow of John Houlston, Sr., d. 8th da, 3rd mo,
1702.

Henry Howard, son of Richard, was christened 22 Dec 1689 in England.

Henry and Hannah Howard. Children: Grace Howard, b. 11th da, 3rd
mo, 1721; Mary Howard, b. 11th da, 8th mo, 1722; John Howard, b.
4th da, 2nd mo, 1725; Peter Howard, b. 15th da, 1st mo, 1726/7;
Hannah Howard, b. 15th da, 2nd mo, 1729; Rebecca Howard, b. 4th
da, 9th mo, 1731; Henry Howard, b. 26th da, 10th mo, 1733, d. 2nd
da, 11th mo, 1757; Richard Howard, b. 9th da, 3rd mo, 1736; James
Howard, b. 9th da, 11th mo, 1738.

Rees and Elizabeth Howell. Children: David Howell, b. 29th da, 5th mo, 1702; Susanna Howell, b. 7th da, 3rd mo, 1706, d. 22nd da, 8th mo, 1720; Rees Howell, b. 16th da, 3rd mo, 1710.

Jacob and Sarah Howell. Children: Benjamin Howell, b. 19th da, 8th mo, 1710, d. 24th da, 8th mo, 1710; Hannah Howell, b. 23rd da, 12th mo, 1711, d. 10th da, 1st mo, 1711/12; John Howell, b. 12th da, 12th mo, 1712; Jacob Howell, b. 13th da, 5th mo, 1715; Sarah Howell, b. 5th da, 12th mo, 1716; Joseph Howell (twin), b. 6th da, 12th mo, 1718; Samuel Howell (twin), b. 6th da, 12th mo, 1718; Isaac Howell, b. 17th da, 3rd mo, 1722; Joshua Howell, b. 7th da, 6th mo, 1726; Mary Howell (twin), b. 5th da, 12th mo, 1728, d. 12th da, 12th mo, 1728; Martha Howell (twin), b. 5th da, 12th mo, 1728, d. 14th da, 12th mo, 1728.

Sarah Howell, wife of Jacob, d. 13th da, 11th mo, 1750, age 70.

Jacob Howell, minister and clerk of the Quarterly Meeting, d. 17th da, 3rd mo, 1768.

Evan and Sarah Howell. Children: Esther Howell, b. 30th da, 1st mo, 1714; Abraham Howell, b. 19th da, 9th mo, 1716; Jonathan Howell, b. 5th da, 6th mo, 1719; Isaac Howell, b. 19th da, 9th mo, 1721; Mary Howell, b. 3rd da, 1st mo, 1723/4.

Samuel and Ann Howell. Children: Abigail Howell, b. 23rd da, 10th mo, 1745; Hugh Howell, b. 18th da, 2nd mo, 1747; Jacob Howell, b. 14th da, 3rd mo, 1749; Sarah Howell, b. 1st da, 1st mo, 1750/1, d. 3rd da, 1st mo, 1752 N.S.; Ann Howell, b. 2nd da, 9th mo, 1753; Samuel Howell, b. 11th da, 1st mo, 1755; Debbie Howell, b. 28th da, 3rd mo, 1757.

Isaac and Mary Howell. Children: James Howell, b. 9th da, 8th mo, 1746, s. 12th da, 9th mo, 1748; Elizabeth Howell, b. 9th da, 1st mo, 1748/9; Eliza Howell, b. 3rd da, 7th mo, 1751; Sarah Howell, b. 21st da, 4th mo, 1754.

Mary Howell, wife of Isaac, d. 16th da, 10th mo, 1756, age 29.

Stephen and Frances Hugh of Springfield Twp. Child: Martha Hugh, b. 11th da, 3rd mo, 1684.

Stephen Hugh of Springfield Twp, d. 21st da, 11th mo, 1683.

William and Hannah Iddings. Children: Jane Iddings, b. 15th da, 3rd mo, 1772; Hannah Iddings, b. 3rd da, 9th mo, 1773; William Iddings, b. 6th da, 11th mo, 1775, d. 23rd da, 12th mo, 1786; Phebe Iddings, b. 7th da, 5th mo, 1778; Samuel Iddings, b. 5th da, 8th mo, 1780; Thomas Iddings, b. 5th da, 11th mo, 1782; Tamer Iddings, b. 20th da, 3rd mo, 1784; Ruth Iddings, b. 16th da, 1st mo, 1791.

Hannah Iddings of Middletown, d. 28th da, 9th mo, 1826, age 77, buried at Middletown.

Ephraim and Rachel Jackson. Children: John Jackson, b. 26th da, 1st mo, 1697; Joseph Jackson, b. 19th da, 6th mo, 1698, d. 6th da, 9th mo, 1698; Joseph Jackson, b. 13th da, 7th mo, 1699; Nathaniel Jackson, b. 17th da, 6th mo, 1701; Josiah Jackson, b. 20th da, 11th mo, 1702, d. 1st da, 1st mo, 1714/5; Samuel Jackson, b. 13th da, 12th mo, 1704; Ephraim Jackson, b. 7th da, 11th mo, 1706; Mary Jackson, b. 3rd da, 4th mo, 1708; Rachel Jackson, b. 10th da, 5th mo, 1710, d. 11th da, 2nd mo, 1749.

Ephraim Jackson, Sr., husband of Rachel, d. 11th da, 1st mo, 1732, age 74.

Rachel Jackson, widow of Ephraim, d. 1742.

Aaron and Elizabeth James. Children: Thomas James, b. 20th da, 4th mo, 1700; Mary James, b. 15th da, 5th mo, 1702; Sarah James, b. 1st da, 7th mo, 1704; Aaron James, b. 9th da, 11th mo, 1706; Joseph James, b. 29th da, 1st mo, 1709; Ann James, b. 24th da, 3rd mo, 1711.

George and Ann James. Children: Sarah James, b. 28th da, 9th mo, 1699; Mary James, b. 28th da, 6th mo, 1702; Mordecai James, b. 6th da, 12th mo, 1705, d. 15th da, 12th mo, 1776, buried in East Nottingham Twp; Jane James, b. 28th da, 9th mo, 1707; Hannah James, b. 17th da, 3rd mo, 1711; Ann James, b. 18th da, 2nd mo, 1714; Elizabeth James, b. 11th da, 7th mo, 1717.

Thomas and Mary James. Children: John James, b. 16th da, 7th mo, 1713; Thomas James, b. 24th da, 12th mo, 1714/5; Joseph James, b. 9th da, 9th mo, 1717; Benjamin James, b. 11th da, 10th mo, 1720.

Andrew and Elizabeth Job. Children: Benjamin Job, b. 13th da, 8th mo, 1693, d. 1st da, 9th mo, 1693; Jacob Job, 26th da, 5th mo, 1694; Thomas Job, b. 22nd da, 9th mo, 1695; Mary Job, b. 23rd da, 1st mo, 1696/7; Enoch Job, b. 9th da, 7th mo, 1698; Enoch Job, b. 6th da, 11th mo, 1700; Abraham Job, b. 22nd da, 6th mo, 1702; Caleb Job, b. 26th da, 5th mo, 1704.

Joseph and Esther Jobson of Upper Providence Twp. Child: Samuel Jobson, b. 22nd da, 7th mo, 1779.

Thomas and Gwen John. Children: Mary John, b. 10th mo, 1706; Susanna John, b. 21st da, 11th mo, 1714; Sarah John, b. 16th da, 1st mo, 1716; Rebecca John, b. 8th da, 7th mo, 1720.

Samuel and Margaret John. Children: Mary John, b. 19th da, 12th mo, 1709; Samuel John, b. 22nd da, 11th mo, 1710; Margaret John, b. 2nd da, 1st mo, 1713; David John, b. 30th da, 11th mo, 1715; Ellen

John, b. 26th da, 2nd mo, 1718; Daniel John, b. 12th da, 2nd mo, 1720.

Griffith and Ann John. Children: Ann John, b. 3rd da, 9th mo, 1715; Rachel John, b. 28th da, 12th mo, 1718.

Thomas and Ann Jones. Children: David Jones, b. 20th da, 7th mo, 1698; Mary Jones, b. 14th da, 4th mo, 1700; Peter Jones (twin), b. 12th da, 1st mo, 1703; Martha Jones (twin), b. 12th da, 1st mo, 1703.

Rees and Hannah Jones. Child: Sarah Jones, b. 25th da, 7th mo, 1690.

Samuel and Hannah Jones. Children: Rachel Jones, b. 25th da, 7th mo, 1715; Francis Jones, b. 10th da, 5th mo, 1714; Hannah Jones, b. 25th da, 9th mo, 1718; Samuel Jones, b. 29th da, 7th mo, 1720.

Cadwalader and Elinor Jones. Children: John Jones, b. 19th da, 8th mo, 1711; Mary Jones, b. 20th da, 12th mo, 1713; Sarah Jones, b. 6th da, 2nd mo, 1715; Rebecca Jones, b. 31st da, 8th mo, 1718.

David Jones, d. 4th da, 1st mo, 1707.

Susanna Jones, d. 18th da, 1st mo, 1707.

Thomas and Mary Kindall. Children: Jane Kindall, b. 3rd da, 9th mo, 1709; Mary Kindall, b. 28th da, 11th mo, 1712; Thomas Kindall, b. 23rd da, 3rd mo, 1715; John Kindall, b. 28th da, 9th mo, 1719.

Edward and Mary Kinneson. Children: Edward Kinneson, b. 1st da, 7th mo, 1705; Mary Kinneson, b. 14th da, 10th mo, 1707; William Kinneson, b. 13th da, 1st mo, 1711; James Kinneson, b. 10th da, 12th mo, 1712; Charles Kinneson, b. 1st da, 12th mo, 1715; Hannah Kinneson, b. 19th da, 2nd mo, 1718.

Joshua and Mary Lawrence of Marple Twp. Children: John Lawrence, b. 20th da, 12th mo, 1786; Isaac Lawrence, b. 12th da, 4th mo, 1789; Hannah Lawrence, b. 6th da, 8th mo, 1793; Henry Lawrence, b. 16th da, 3rd mo, 1796.

John Lea of Chester and his 1st wife, Hannah. Child: Jacob Lea, b. 11th da, 5th mo, 1740, d. 10th da, 1st mo, 1756/7.

Hannah Lea, wife of John of Chester, d. 24th da, 12th mo, 1750/1.

John Lea of Chester and his 2nd wife, Mary. Children: Hannah Lea, b. 31st da, 3rd mo, 1753; Ann Lea, b. 14th da, 4th mo, 1755; Thomas Lea, b. 22nd da, 5th mo, 1757.

John Lea of Chester, husband of Mary and widower of Hannah, d. 8th da, 4th mo, 1759.

Samuel and Hannah (Stretch) Levis. Child: Samuel Levis, b. 21st da, 8th mo, 1711, d. 7th da, 11th mo, 1717.

John and Mary Levis of Springfield Twp. Children: Kitty Ann Levis, b. 1st da, 10th mo, 1798; Margaretta Levis, b. 19th da, 4th mo, 1800;

Henrietta Levis, b. 15th da, 5th mo, 1805; Sarah Pancoast Levis, b. 26th da, 11th mo, 1806; John Ewin Levis, b. 12th da, 4th mo, 1811; Elizabeth Garrett Levis, b. 18th da, 6th mo, 1814; Thomas S. Levis, b. 1st da, 2nd mo, 1816.

Joseph and Sarah Levis of Springfield Twp. Children: David Levis, b. 7th da, 8th mo, 1789; Mary Levis, b. 22nd da, 11th mo, 1791; Joseph Levis, b. 9th da, 9th mo, 1795; Deborah Levis, b. 12th da, 5th mo, 1798; Sarah Ann Levis, b. 4th da, 8th mo, 1803.

Lewis and Mary Lewis. Children: Ann Lewis, b. 2nd da, 8th mo, 1701; Phineas Lewis, b. 29th da, 2nd mo, 1703; David Lewis, b. 29th da, 4th mo, 1705; Lydia Lewis, b. 5th da, 2nd mo, 1708; Lewis Lewis, b. 20th da, 1st mo, 1709/10; Deborah Lewis, b. 27th da, 8th mo, 1712; Jabez Lewis, b. 6th da, 2nd mo, 1715; Mary Lewis, b. 25th da, 9th mo, 1717; Agnes Lewis, b. 15th da, 10th mo, 1720; Elizabeth Lewis, b. 29th da, 7th mo, 1723.

Evan and Mary Lewis. Children: Hannah Lewis, b. 6th da, 3rd mo, 1707; Esther Lewis, b. 24th da, 8th mo, 1710, d. 29th da, 7th mo, 1720; Mordecai Lewis, b. 4th da, 3rd mo, 1713; Jonathan Lewis, b. 12th da, 2nd mo, 1717, d. 2nd da, 8th mo, 1720; Gwen Lewis, b. 5th da, 2nd mo, 1720; Esther Lewis, b. 25th da, 10th mo, 1721.

Evan Lewis, husband of Mary, arrived from Wales 6th da, 7th mo, 1677, d. 1735.

William and Gwen Lewis. Children: Nathan Lewis, b. 21st da, 9th mo, 1705, d. 5th da, 2nd mo, 1788; William Lewis, b. 23rd da, 8th mo, 1708; Jeptha Lewis, b. 27th da, 3rd mo, 1711; Enos Lewis, b. 19th da, 6th mo, 1714.

Gwen Lewis, wife of William, d. 18th da, 8th mo, 1716.

William and Lowrey Lewis. Child: Joseph Lewis, b. 4th da, 3rd mo, 1719.

Samuel and Phebe Lewis. Children: Elizabeth Lewis, b. 28th da, 1st mo, 1713; Hannah Lewis, b. 17th da, 10th mo, 1715; Priscilla Lewis, b. 5th da, 7th mo, 1716; Josiah Lewis, b. 12th da, 7th mo, 1719; Phebe Lewis, b. 26th da, 2nd mo, 1722; Samuel Lewis, b. 26th da, 6th mo, 1724; Jane Lewis, b. 31st da, 10th mo, 1726; Joshua Lewis, b. 14th da, 12th mo, 1730/1; Hannah Lewis, b. 1st da, 1st mo, 1732.

John and Jane Lewis of Springfield. Children: Jane Lewis, b. 25th da, 5th mo, 1772; Franklin Lewis, b. 3rd da, 9th mo, 1774; John Lewis b. 22nd da, 7th mo, 1776; Mary Lewis, b. 1st da, 6th mo, 1778.

John and Ann Lewis. Children: Sarah Lewis, b. 7th da, 12th mo, 1784; Lewis Lewis, b. 16th da, 5th mo, 1786; George Lewis, b. 15th da, 5th mo, 1788; Mordecai Lewis, b. 8th da, 11th mo, 1789; Sidney Lewis, b. 18th da, 6th mo, 1793.

William Lewis, husband of Ann, d. 9th da, 12th mo, 1707/8.

Ann Lewis, widow of William, d. 15th da, 12th mo, 1707/8.

Seborn Lewis, dau. of William and Ann, d. 16th da, 4th mo, 1707.

Samuel and Mary Lightfoot. Children: Benjamin Lightfoot, b. 28th da, 6th mo, 1726; Thomas Lightfoot, b. 7th da, 2nd mo, 1728; Samuel Lightfoot, b. 7th da, 1st mo, 1729/30; William Lightfoot, b. 20th da, 1st mo, 1731/2.

Mary Lightfoot, wife of Samuel, d. 20th da, 6th mo, 1732.

James and Susanna Lownes. Children: Joseph Lownes, b. 30th da, 1st mo, 1693; Hannah Lownes, b. 13th da, 11th mo, 1695; James Lownes, b. 3rd da, 1st mo, 1697/8.

George and Mary Lownes. Children: Jane Lownes, b. 10th da, 1st mo, 1702; Esther Lownes, b. 2nd da, 7th mo, 1703; Ann Lownes, b. 1st da, 8th mo, 1707, d. 17th da, 12th mo, 1780; George Lownes, b. 28th da, 2nd mo, 1709.

Hugh and Rebecca Lownes of Springfield Twp. Joseph Lownes, b. 17th da, 1st mo, 1787; Benanuel Lownes, b. 19th da, 2nd mo, 1790; Elizabeth Lownes, b. 18th da, 1st mo, 1793; Sidney Lownes, b. 13th da, 1st mo, 1796.

John and Lydia McIlvain. Children: Judith McIlvain, b. 18th da, 5th mo, 1762; John McIlvain, b. 19th da, 8th mo, 1763; Lydia McIlvain, b. 6th da, 12th mo, 1764; Jeremiah McIlvain, b. 29th da, 6th mo, 1767; James McIlvain, b. 12th da, 2nd mo, 1769; Margaret McIlvain, b. 14th da, 2nd mo, 1771; Richard McIlvain, b. 15th da, 12th mo, 1772; Hugh McIlvain, b. 19th da, 5th mo, 1775.

Jeremiah and Elizabeth McIlvain of Ridley. Children: Lydia McIlvain, b. 4th da, 10th mo, 1795; Elizabeth McIlvain, b. 13th da, 1st mo, 1798; Spencer McIlvain, b. 27th da, 3rd mo, 1803; John Spencer McIlvain, b. 24th da, 9th mo, 1805; Jeremiah McIlvain, b. 1st da, 2nd mo, 1808; Ann McIlvain, b. 4th da, 5th mo, 1810.

Randall Malin and his 1st wife, Elizabeth. Children: Isaac Malin, b. Latter end of the 5th mo, 1681; Jacob Malin, b. 7th da, 7th mo, 1686.

Elizabeth Malin, wife of Randall, d. Beginning of the 7th mo, 1687.

Randall Malin and his 2nd wife, Mary. Children: Hannah Malin, b. 6th da, 12th mo, 1693/4, d. 26th da, 3rd mo, 1695; Hannah Malin (2nd), b. 7th da, 1st mo, 1695/6; Rachel Malin, b. 24th da, 5th mo, 1702.

Gideon Malin, son of Jacob and Susanna, d. 26th da, 11th mo, 1796, age 71

Phebe (Bowman) Malin, widow of Gideon, Sr., dau. of Henry and Hannah Bowman of Monyash, Darbyshire, England, d. 21st da, 2nd mo, 1810, age 75.

Isaac and Elizabeth Malin. Children: David Malin, b. 3rd da, 11th mo, 1703; Thomas Malin, b. 3rd da, 10th mo, 1705; Isaac Malin, b. 8th da, 1st mo, 1708; Elizabeth Malin, b. 21st da, 12th mo, 1709; Alice Malin, b. 29th da, 9th mo, 1711; Randal Malin, b. 17th da, 4th mo, 1714, d. 7th da, 1st mo, 1715; Randal Malin (2nd), b. 30th da, 1st mo, 1716.

Elizabeth (Jones) Malin, wife of Isaac, dau. of David Jones, d. 14th da, 7th mo, 1717.

Thomas and Grace Malin. Children: Abner Malin, b. 14th da, 7th mo, 1781; Phebe Malin, b. 28th da, 3rd mo, 1783; Thomas Malin, b. 11th da, 2nd mo, 1785, d. 17th da, 8th mo, 1785; Jacob Malin, b. 23rd da, 8th mo, 1786; Minshall, b. 29th da, 7th mo, 1788; Agnes Malin, b. 1st da, 7th mo, 1790; Ann Malin, b. 16th da, 3rd mo, 1792; Elizabeth Malin, b. 3rd da, 7th mo, 1795; William Malin, b. 22nd da, 1st mo, 1797; Margaret Malin, b. 13th da, 4th mo, 1799, d. 24th da, 4th mo, 1802; Randal Malin, b. 15th da, 6th mo, 1802.

Grace Malin, wife of Thomas, d. 5th da, 2nd mo, 1811, age 52.

William and Elizabeth Malin of Upper Providence Twp. Child: Jacob Malin, b. 23rd da, 3rd mo, 1749 O.S., d. 24th da, 12th mo, 1814.

George and Rebecca Malin. Children: Aaron Malin, b. 27th da, 5th mo, 1795; Elizabeth Malin, b. 8th da, 6th mo, 1797; Preston Malin, b. 30th da, 3rd mo, 1799; Orpah [Orpha] Malin, b. 9th da, 3rd mo, 1802; Rebecca Malin, b. 8th da, 11th mo, 1805, d. 10th da, 12th mo, 1828; Esther Malin, b. 5th da, 11th mo, 1807.

Joel and Elizabeth Malin. Children: Pusey Malin, b. 3rd da, 9th mo, 1797; Susanna Malin, b. 2nd da, 2nd mo, 1800; Hannah Malin, b. 11th da, 8th mo, 1802; Mary Malin, b. 22nd da, 10th mo, 1803; Lydia Malin, b. 3rd da, 7th mo, 1805; Harvey Malin, b. 3rd da, 4th mo, 1808; Samuel Malin, b. 17th da, 8th mo, 1811; Sarah Ann Malin, b. 8th da, 2nd mo, 1815.

John Martin came for Edgcott, Berkshire, England, and settled in Middletown Twp. He and his wife, Elizabeth, left but one child, Thomas.

Elizabeth Martin, wife of John, d. 4th da, 12th mo, 1713/4.

Thomas Martin and his wife, Mary (Knight) Martin, dau. of Gyles and Mary Knight. Children: Alice Martin, b. 4th da, 2nd mo, 1709, d. 18th da, 10th mo, 1759; John Martin, b. 10th da, 12th mo, 1713/4; Ann Martin, b. 2nd mo, 1724, d. 20th da, 11th mo, 1780.

Mary (Knight) Martin, wife of Thomas, d. age 73 years, 3 months and 3 weeks.

Thomas and Margery Martin. Child: Moses Martin, b. 9th da, 1st mo, 1685/6.

Moses and Margaret Martin. Children: Adam Martin, b. 5th da, 10th mo, 1716; John Martin, b. 3rd da, 1st mo, 1718; Hannah Martin, b. 15th da, 3rd mo, 1720; Mary Martin, b. 29th da, 3rd mo, 1722; Margaret Martin, b. 21st da, 10th mo, 1729.

Joseph and Hannah Martin of Providence Twp. Children: Joshua Martin, b. 24th da, 8th mo, 1789; John Martin, b. 16th da, 9th mo, 1792; Elizabeth Martin, b. 25th da, 8th mo, 1796, d. 27th da, 2nd mo, 1817; Ruth Martin, b. 6th da, 10th mo, 1799; Orpah Martin, b. 31st da, 3rd mo, 1802; Samuel Martin, b. 18th da, 3rd mo, 1805; Hirium Martin, b. 22nd da, 1st mo, 1808; Caleb Martin (twin), b. 3rd da, 11th mo, 1810; Jacob Martin (twin), b. 3rd da, 11th mo, 1810.

George Maris, Sr., d. 15th da, 11th mo, 1703, age about 73.

John and Susannah Maris. Children: George Maris, b. 31st da, 6th mo, 1694; Sarah Maris, b. 31st da, 1st mo, 1696/7; Alice Maris, b. 11th da, 1st mo, 1699, d. same day; Mary Maris, b. 9th da, 1st mo, 1701/2; Hannah Maris, b. 8th da, 8th mo, 1702; Susanna Maris, b. 6th da, 5th mo, 1704; Jane Maris, b. 9th da, 6th mo, 1705; Katherine Maris, b. 8th da, 5th mo, 1707; John Maris, b. 15th da, 11th mo, 1709; James Maris, b. 28th da, 2nd mo, 1711; Elizabeth Maris, b. 12th da, 12th mo, 1713.

George Maris, Jr., and his wife, Jane. Children: Mordecai Maris, b. 22nd da, 7th mo, 1691; George Maris, b. 25th da, 9th mo, 1694, d. 8th da, 3rd mo, 1696; Hannah Maris, b. 17th da, 12th mo, 1698; Esther Maris b. 24th da, 2nd mo, 1703.

George Maris, Jr., husband of Jane, d. 1705.

Jane Maris, wife of George, Jr., d. 28th da, 6th mo, 1705.

Richard and Elizabeth Maris. Child: Jonathan Maris, b. 16th da, 1st mo, 1701/2.

Jesse Maris and his 1st wife, Rebecca. Children: Hannah Maris, b. 9th da, 11th mo, 1755; Owen Maris, b. 6th da, 5th mo, 1758; George Maris, b. 29th da, 3rd mo, 1761.

Jesse and his 2nd wife, Jane. Child: Rebecca Maris, b. 12th da, 9th mo, 1774.

Jonathan and Judith Maris. Child: Jesse J. Maris, b. 18th da, 6th mo, 1793, d. 15th da, 12th mo, 1860.

Judith Maris, widow of Jonathan, d. 2nd da, 3rd mo, 1843, age 81.

John and Jane Maris of Springfield. Children: John Maris, b. 28th da, 12th mo, 1779; Ann Maris, b. 11th da, 7th mo, 1781; Asa Maris, b. 8th da, 1st mo, 1783; Lydia Maris, b. 4th da, 10th mo, 1784; George Maris, b. 20th da, 1st mo, 1786; Ellis Maris, b. 4th da, 1st mo, 1788.

Elizabeth Maris, d. 9th da, 8th mo, 1720.

James Maris, d. 15th da, 8th mo, 1720.

Jane Maris, d. 21st da, 8th mo, 1720.

Thomas and Phebe Massey. Children: Esther Massey, b. 30th da, 8th mo, 1693 at about 7 in the evening; Mordecai Massey, b. 9th da, 6th mo, 1695 about 2 in the morning, d. 1748; James Massey, b. 13th da, 7th mo, 1697 about 4 in the morning; Hannah Massey, b. 9th da, 6th mo, 1699 about 4 in the afternoon; Thomas Massey, b. 21st da, 11th mo, 1701 about 1 in the afternoon, d. 13th da, 6th mo, 1784; Phebe Massey, b. 20th da, 2nd mo, 1705, d. 5th da, 2nd mo, 1719; Mary Massey, b. 3rd da, 12th mo, 1707.

Thomas Massey, Sr., husband of Phebe, d. 18th da, 9th mo, 1708 in the 45th year of his age.

Mordecai and Rebeckah Massey. Child: Hannah Massey, b. 7th da, 12th mo, 1731/2.

James and Mary Massey. Child: Hannah Massey, b. 20th da, 3rd mo, 1794.

Richard and Sarah Mather. Children: George Mather, b. 14th da, 4th mo, 1797; Martha Mather, b. 14th da, 3rd mo, 1699; Lydia Mather, b. 4th da, 12th mo, 1803; Sarah Ann Mather, b. 3rd da, 1st mo, 1807; McIlvain Mather, b. 16th da, 1st mo, 1809.

Aaron and Mary Matson of Edgmont. Children: John Matson, b. 8th da, 6th mo, 1799; Eli Matson, b. 27th da, 2nd mo, 1801; Hannah Matson, b. 23rd da, 4th mo, 1803; Jane Matson, b. 21st da, 4th mo, 1805; Mary Matson, b. 4th da, 11th mo, 1808.

John Medford, d. 16th da, 3rd mo, 1689.

Robert and Phebe Mendenhall of Concord. Child: John Mendenhall, b. 29th da, 4th mo, 1748.

John Mendenhall of Edgmont Twp, son of Robert and Phebe, and his wife,Tabitha, dau. of Nathaniel and Esther Newlin of Concord. Children: Cyrus Mendenhall, b. 25th da, 12th mo, 1781; Martha Mendenhall, b. 18th da, 4th mo, 1784; Esther Mendenhall, b. 5th da, 6th mo, 1786; Anne Mendenhall, b. 23rd da, 12th mo, 1789; John Mendenhall, Jr., b. 27th da, 5th mo, 1793.

Tabitha (Newlin) Mendenhall, widow of John, b. 4th mo, 1755.

Thomas Mercer, d. 22nd da, 9th mo, 1694.

Moses Meredith, d. 10th da, 11th mo, 1799.

Henry and Sarah Miller. Children born in the parish of Bradwell, Devonshire, England: John Miller, b. 5th da, 4th mo, 1704; Dorothy Miller, b. 16th da, 5th mo, 1706. Children born in the parish of Dunster, Somersetshire, England: Sarah Miller, b. 19th da, 4th mo, 1708; Henry Miller, b. 2nd da, 12th mo, 1710. Child born in the Town of Chester: George Miller, b. 19th da, 7th mo, 1716.

George and Phebe Miller. Children: Sarah Miller, b. 6th da, 11th mo, 1765, d. 22nd da, 4th mo, 1792; John Miller, b. 7th da, 5th mo, 1768, d. 21st da, 12th mo, 1783; Phebe Miller, b. 5th da, 9th mo, 1770; George Miller, b. 30th da, 12th mo, 1772.

Phebe Miller, wife of George, d. 21st da, 8th mo, 1789 at age 62.

George and Mary Miller of Upper Providence. Children: Phebe Miller, b. 28th da, 1st mo, 1795; Isaac Miller, b. 26th da, 3rd mo, 1796; George Miller, b. 30th da, 10th mo, 1797; John Miller, b. 7th da, 10th mo, 1799; Samuel Miller, b. 2nd da, 6th mo, 1801; Sarah Miller, b. 23rd da, 8th mo, 1803; Levis Miller, b. 16th da, 7th mo, 1806; Mary Miller, b. 9th da, 5th mo, 1812; Ann Levinia Miller, b. 3rd da, 6th mo, 1814, d. 19th da, 2nd mo, 1832, buried at Providence.

Thomas and Margaret Minshall. Child: Jacob Minshall, b. 1st da, 4th mo, 1685; Rebecca Minshall, b. 1st da, 4th mo, 1685; Moses Minshall, b. 14th da, 10th mo, 1687, d. 17th da, 1st mo, 1706. "Moses Minshall was taken sick the 8th day of the 1st month and died on the 17th of the same month, 1706, age 18 years 3 months. Testimony of his character and last expressions was prepared (12 pages) and signed by the following: His parents, Thomas Minshall and Margaret Minshall; his unkles and aunts, Bartholomew Coppuck, Margaret Coppuck, Robert Vernon, Eleanor Vernon; his brothers, Isaac Minshall, Jacob Minshall; his brother-in-law and sister, Bartholomew Coppuck and Rebecca Coppuck; his cousins, Randle Malin, Jacob Vernon, Isaac Vernon and Phebe Pickow; the friends that came to visit him or were with him in the time of his sickness, Griffith Owen, John Lea, Jacob Symcock, George Ashbridge and Sarah Vernon."

Margaret Minshall, wife of Thomas, d. 27th da, 3rd mo, 1727 age 34.

Rebecca Minshall, d. 5th da, 4th mo, 1682 at sea.

Isaac and Rebeccah Minshall. Children: Aaron Minshall, b. 10th da, 8th mo, 1708; Rebecca Minshall, b. 1st da, 4th mo, 1710; Griffith Minshall, b. 1st da, 11th mo, 1712; Isaac Minshall, b. 26th da, 8th mo, 1718; Samuel Minshall, b. 26th da, 8th mo, 1724; Edward Minshall, b. 28th da, 4th mo, 1727; Jacob Minshall, b. 10th da, 5th mo, 1729.

Jacob and Sarah Minshall. Children: Thomas Minshall, b. 3rd da, 1st mo, 1707/8, d. 12th da, 9th mo, 1783 at 8:30 PM; Sarah Minshall, b. 21st da, 5th mo, 1711; Margaret Minshall, b. 28th da, 10th mo, 1713; John Minshall, b. 21st da, 8th mo, 1716, d. 8th da, 1st mo, 1784; Moses Minshall, b. 26th da, 6th mo, 1718; Ann Minshall, b. 13th da, 11th mo, 1727/8.

Jacob Minshall, husband of Sarah, d. 15th da, 5th mo, 1734.

Sarah Minshall, widow of Jacob, dau. of Griffith and Sarah Owen, d. 28th da, 12th mo, 1756.

Jacob and Ann Minshall. Child: Hannah Minshall, b. 28th da, 1st mo, 1782.

Samuel and Jane Minshall. Child: Isaac Minshall, b. 4th da, 5th mo, 1752.

Aaron Minshall, d. 9th da, 6th mo, 1699.

John and Sarah Minshall. Children: Mary Minshall, b. 28th da, 4th mo, 1741; Jane Minshall, b. 5th da, 1st mo, 1742/3; Sarah Minshall, b. 16th da, 2nd mo, 1745; Thomas Minshall, b. 17th da, 12th mo, 1747/8; Moses Minshall, b. 5th da, 5th mo, 1751; Ann Minshall, b. 13th da, 8th mo, 1753.

Sarah Minshall, widow of John, d. 18th da, 4th mo, 1801, age 84, buried at Middletown on the 19th.

Jacob and Rebeccah Minshall. Child: Rebecka Minshall, b. 1st da, 4th mo, 1685.

Thomas and Agnes Minshall of Middletown. Children: Jacob Minshall, b. 15th da, 12th mo, 1738/9; Margaret Minshall, b. 19th da, 4th mo, 1741; Hannah Minshall, b. 24th da, 11th mo, 1742/3; Phebe Minshall, b. 26th da, 11th mo, 1744/5; Agnes Minshall, b. 4th da, 12th mo, 1746/7, d. 26th da, 1st mo, 1760; John Minshall, b. 4th da, 4th mo, 1749, d. 10th da, 1st mo, 1760; Ann Minshall, b. 12th da, 1st mo, 1752 N.S.; Owen Minshall, b. 26th da, 3rd mo, 1754, d. 26th da, 1st mo, 1760; Mary Minshall, b. 15th da, 2nd mo, 1757; Grace Minshall, b. 15th da, 11th mo, 1759.

Agnes Minshall, widow of Thomas, d. 14th da, 1st mo, 1813, age 98.

John and Rebecca Morgan of Edgmont. Children: Elizabeth P. Morgan, b. 5th da, 9th mo, 1786; Isaac Morgan, b. 8th da, 10th mo, 1788, d. 5th da, 10th mo, 1841; Anna Morgan, b. 19th da, 1st mo, 1791, d. 9th da, 3rd mo, 1855; William P. Morgan, b. 28th da, 6th mo, 1793, d. 3rd da, 12th mo, 1847; Mary Morgan, b. 18th da, 8th mo, 1795; Hannah Morgan, b. 30th da, 7th mo, 1798; John Morgan, b. 18th da, 8th mo, 1801, d. 11th da, 9th mo, 1859 in his 58th year.

Blanch Morgan, d. 11th da, 3rd mo, 1718.

Jonathan and Alice Morris. Children: Cadwalader Morris, b. 2nd da, 10th mo, 1758; Ann Morris, b. 1st da, 8th mo, 1760; Jonathan Morris, b. 16th da, 11th mo, 1762; Samuel Morris, b. 19th da, 2nd mo, 1768; Catharine Morris, b. 15th da, 6th mo, 1765; Evan Morris, b. 2nd da, 3rd mo, 1770; Hannah Morris, b. 3rd da, 1st mo, 1774; Thomas Morris, b. 26th da, 2nd mo, 1776; Alice Morris, b. 23rd da, 5th mo, 1779.

Thomas and Frances Norbury. Children: Stephen Norbury, b. 5th da, 8th mo, 1685; Jacob Norbury, b. 30th da, 9th mo, 1687; Deborah Norbury, b. 26th da, 11th mo, 1688; Thomas Norbury, b. 24th da, 6th mo, 1690; John Norbury, b. 11th da, 2nd mo, 1692; Philip Norbury, b. 23rd da, 4th mo, 1693; Mary Norbury, b. 9th da, 2nd mo, 1695; Hannah Norbury, b. 4th da, 2nd mo, 1696; Sarah Norbury, b. 15th da, 6th mo, 1698; Rachel Norbury, b. 24th da, 11th mo, 1701.

Jacob and Alice Norbury. Children: Sarah Norbury, b. 27th da, 6th mo, 1722; Hannah Norbury, b. 25th da, 6th mo, 1724.

David and Martha Ogden. Children: Jonathan Ogden, b. 19th da, 2nd mo, 1687; d. 6th mo, 1727; Martha Ogden, b. 23rd da, 5th mo, 1689; Sarah Ogden, b. 3rd da, 9th mo, 1691; Nehemiah Ogden, b. 15th da, 10th mo, 1693; Samuel Ogden, b. 30th da, 10th mo, 1695; John Ogden, b. 4th da, 5th mo, 1698; Aaron Ogden, b. 31st da, 3rd mo, 1700; Hannah Ogden, b. 22nd da, 6th mo, 1702; Stephen Ogden, b. 12th da, 11th mo, 1705, d. 16th da, 9th mo, 1760.

David Ogden, husband of Martha, d. 22nd da, 8th mo, 1705.

Stephen and Hannah Ogden. Children: Nehemiah Ogden, b. 12th da, 12th mo, 1744/5, d. 28th da, 8th mo, 1752; John Ogden, b. 31st da, 10th mo, 1746; Stephen Ogden, b. 8th da, 7th mo, 1748; Mary Ogden, b. 11th da, 8th mo, 1750; Hannah Ogden, b. 21st da, 6th mo, 1752; Aaron Ogden, b. 9th da, 7th mo, 1754; Martha Ogden, b. 20th da, 10th mo, 1756; Abigail Ogden, b. 27th da, 10th mo, 1760.

Hannah Ogden, widow of Stephen, d. 10th da, 10th mo, 1783 in Springfield Twp.

John and Sarah Ogden. Children: Elizabeth Ogden, b. 17th da, 1st mo, 1774; Mary Ogden, b. 28th da, 8th mo, 1775, d. 1842 age 66; James Ogden, b. 29th da, 2nd mo, 1778; Eloisa Ogden, b. 31st da, 10th mo, 1779; Hannah Ogden, b. 5th da, 12th mo, 1781; Martha Ogden, b. 12th da, 11th mo, 1783.

Sarah Ogden, wife of John, d. 23rd da, 8th mo, 1822, age 74.

William Paist of Middletown and his 1st wife, Sarah. Child: Elizabeth Paist, b. 22nd da, 2nd mo, 1795.

Sarah Paist, wife of William of Middletown, d. 1st da, 3rd mo, 1775, age 36.

William Paist and his 2nd wife, Alice. Children: Jonathan Paist, b. 23rd da, 10th mo, 1806; Sarah Paist, b. 19th da, 2nd mo, 1809.

James and Elizabeth Paist of Upper Providence Twp. Children: Mary Paist, b. 30th da, 11th mo, 1788; Charles Paist, b. 1st da, 10th mo, 1790; James Paist, b. 23rd da, 1st mo, 1793; Jacob Paist, b. 13th da, 2nd mo, 1795; Ann Paist, b. 1st da, 5th mo, 1797; Orpha Paist, b. 19th da, 6th mo, 1799; Elizabeth Paist, b. 15th da, 12th mo, 1801; James Paist (2nd), b. 17th da, 2nd mo, 1804, d. 12th mo, 1832 in Upper Providence Twp, buried in Springfield Twp; William Paist, b.9th da, 4th mo, 1806; Susan Paist, b. 21st da, 3rd mo, 1809; Sarah D. Paist, b. 14th da, 7th mo, 1810.

Elizabeth Paist, wife of James, d. 14th da, 10th mo, 1814 at age 50 years, 10 months, 26 days.

Samuel and Mary Pancoast of Marple Twp. Children: John Pancoast, b. 31st da, 5th mo, 1783; William Pancoast, b. 29th da, 1st mo, 1785; Samuel Pancoast, b. 12th da, 7th mo, 1787; Rebecca Pancoast, b. 24th da, 8th mo, 1789; Seth Pancoast, b. 24th da, 6th mo, 1792.

Mary Pancoast, wife of Samuel of Marple Twp, d. 2nd da, 2nd mo, 1817.

Samuel Pancoast of Marple Twp, widower of Mary, d. 1834, age 84.

Richard and Jemima Parsons. Children: Mahlon Parsons, b. 4th da, 7th mo, 1762; Joshua Parsons, b. 27th da, 6th mo, 1764; Naomi Parsons, b. 13th da, 2nd mo, 1766; Rebecca Parsons, b. 7th da, 2nd mo, 1768, d. 29th da, 4th mo, 1817 in Marple Twp, age 52; Jemima Parsons, b. 16th da, 7th mo, 1770; Mary Parsons, b. 10th da, 4th mo, 1772, d. 15th da, 7th mo, 1773; Mary Parsons (2nd), b. 27th da, 5th mo, 1774; William Parsons, b. 4th da, 9th mo, 1776, d. 14th da, 4th mo, 1821; Richard Parsons, b. 20th da, 2nd mo, 1782.

Jemima Parsons, wife of Richard, d. 26th da, 10th mo, 1804.

Richard Parsons, widower of Jemima, d. 6th da, 4th mo, 1828, age 97 years, 3 months, 17 days.

Mahlon Parsons of Lower Providence Twp, son of Richard and Jemima, and his wife, Mary. Children: Jemima Parsons, b. 8th da, 7th mo, 1786; Phebe Parsons, b. 24th da, 8th mo, 1788, d. 10th da, 3rd mo, 1791; Nathaniel Parsons, b. 14th da, 10th mo, 1790; Joseph Parsons, b. 21st da, 12th mo, 1792; Mary Parsons, b. 7th da, 1st mo, 1795, d. 2nd da, 9th mo, 1816; Sarah Parsons, b. 19th da, 12th mo, 1797, d. 5th da, 7th mo, 1799; Samuel Parsons, b. 27th da, 3rd mo, 1800, d. 21st da, 8th mo, 1807 in Providence Twp, age 7, buried in

Providence Twp; Mahlon Parsons, b. 30th da, 11th mo, 1802, d. 26th da, 3rd mo, 1821; George Parsons, b. 25th da, 7th mo, 1805; Israel Parsons, b. 17th da, 4th mo, 1808; Hannah Parsons, b. 12th da, 11th mo, 1811.

Sidney Parsons, d. 14th da, 4th mo, 1820 age 24.

Thomas and Margaret Paschall. Child: Margaret Paschall, b. 6th da, 8th mo, 1718.

William and Grace Paschall. Child: Grace Paschall, b. 26th da, 4th mo, 1721.

Grace Paschall, wife of William, d. 3rd da, 5th mo, 1721.

Thomas and Margery Pearson. Children: Robert Pearson, b. 3rd da, 12th mo, 1683; Thomas Pearson, b. 23rd da, 10th mo, 1685, d. 1st mo, 1705; Lawrence Pearson, b. 20th da, 10th mo, 1687; Enoch Pearson, b. 12th da, 3rd mo, 1690; John Pearson, b. 1st da, 10th mo, 1692; Abel Pearson, b. 9th da, 2nd mo, 1695; Sarah Pearson, b. 8th da, 2nd mo, 1697; Benjamin Pearson, b. 1st da, 12th mo, 1698; Mary Pearson, b. 20th da, 5th mo, 1701; Margery Pearson, b. 23rd da, 9th mo, 1703.

William and Mary Pearson. Child: Mary Pearson, b. 20th da, 5th mo, 1701.

Lawrence and Esther Pearson. Children: Hannah Pearson, b. 25th da, 3rd mo, 1712; Thomas Pearson, b. 9th da, 7th mo, 1714; Mordecai Pearson, b. 23rd da, 8th mo, 1716; Sibilla Pearson, b. 24th da, 8th mo, 1717; Phebe Pearson, b. 2nd da, 10th mo, 1719.

Roger and Rebecca Pedrick of Marcus Hook. Children: Rebecca Pedrick, b. 14th da, 7th mo, 1678; Thomas Pedrick, b. 14th da, 2nd mo, 1681.

Hannah Pennell, wife of Robert, d. 4th da, 12th mo, 1711, age 71.

Joseph and Alice Pennell. Children: Hannah Pennell, b. 4th da, 11th mo, 1702; Robert Pennell, b. 20th da, 6th mo, 1704; Joseph Pennell, b. 3rd da, 6th mo, 1706; Alice Pennell, b. 2nd da, 8th mo, 1709; Ann Pennell, b. 2nd da, 8th mo, 1711; Mary Pennell, b. 1717, d. 1727/8.

Joseph Pennell of Edgmont Twp, widower of Alice, d. 30th da, 9th mo, 1756.

Alice Pennell, wife of Joseph, d. 13th da, 7th mo, 1748.

William and Mary Pennell. Children: Thomas Pennell, b. 3rd da, 9th mo, 1712, d. 14th da, 2nd mo, 1745; Hannah Pennell, b. 9th da, 7th mo, 1714; James Pennell, b. 21st da, 6th mo, 1717; Phebe Pennell, b. 7th da, 6th mo, 1719; Ann Pennell, b. 26th da, 11th mo, 1721; Robert Pennell, b. 16th da, 9th mo, 1723; William Pennell, b. 27th da, 11th mo, 1725, d. 5th da, 9th mo, 1783.

Thomas and Mary Pennell. Children: Abigail Pennell, b. 30th da, 4th mo, 1740; Joseph Pennell, b. 2nd da, 1st mo, 1741/2; William Pennell, b. 3rd da, 8th mo, 1743, d. 1745; John Pennell, b. 20th da, 11th mo, 1745/6; Mary Pennell, b. 15th da, 6th mo, 1749.

James and Jemima Pennell. Children: Hannah Pennell, b. 28th da, 7th mo, 1742; William Pennell, b. 30th da, 7th mo, 1744; Edith Pennell, b. 12th da, 2nd mo, 1746; Rebecca Pennell, b. 6th da, 10th mo, 1747; James Pennell, b. 28th da, 4th mo, 1749; Thomas Pennell, b. 2nd da, 11th mo, 1751; Ruth Pennell, b. 18th da, 10th mo, 1752; Nathan Pennell, b. 7th da, 7th mo, 1754; Timothy Pennell, 14th da, 3rd mo, 1756; Jonathan Pennell, b. 27th da, 4th mo, 1761.

William and Mary Pennell. Children: Abraham Pennell, b. 9th da, 4th mo, 1753, d. 25th da, 9th mo, 1840; Robert Pennell, b. 14th da, 7th mo, 1755; Dell Pennell, b. 12th da, 1st mo, 1758; Samuel Pennell, b. 12th da, 4th mo, 1760, d. at sea; Rachel Pennell, b. 1st da, 8th mo, 1762; Esther Pennell, b. 13th da, 7th mo, 1765; William Pennell, b. 29th da, 11th mo, 1767; Aaron Pennell, b. 19th da, 12th mo, 1769; Jesse Pennell, b. 1st da, 8th mo, 1772; Mary Pennell, b. 3rd da, 10th mo, 1775.

William Pennell, husband of Mary (Dell), b. 27th da, 11th mo, 1725/6, d. 5th da, 9th mo, 1783.

Mary (Dell) Pennell, widow of William, dau. of Thomas and Rachel Dell, b. 16th da, 9th mo, 1734, d. 5th da, 10th mo, 1801. William and Mary m. 25th da, 2nd mo, 1751.

Abraham and Hannah Pennell. Children: Mary Pennell, b. 25th da, 6th mo, 1777; Joseph Pennell, b. 3rd da, 12th mo, 1778, d. 11th da, 5th mo, 1849; William Pennell, b. 6th da, 10th mo, 1783; Hannah Pennell, 12th da, 2nd mo, 1788.

Joseph and Sarah Pennell of Aston Twp. Children: Hannah Pennell, b. 17th da, 12th mo, 1770, d. 27th da, 6th mo, 1775; Moses Pennell, b. 23rd da, 3rd mo, 1772, d. 22nd da, 6th mo, 1775; Susanna Pennell, b. 5th da, 9th mo, 1773; Robert Pennell, b. 24th da, 9th mo, 1775; Alice Pennell, b.28th da, 8th mo, 1778; Sarah Pennell, b. 19th da, 11th mo, 1780; Joseph Pennell, b. 14th da, 10th mo, 1782; Mary Pennell, b. 7th da, 10th mo, 1785; Meredith Pennell, b. 26th da, 7th mo, 1788.

Joseph and Mary Phipps. Children: Samuel Phipps, b. 22nd da, 10th mo, 1697; Joseph Phipps, b. 26th da, 2nd mo, 1700; Nathan Phipps, b. 1st da, 9th mo, 1702; George Phipps, b. 12th da, 8th mo, 1705; John Phipps, b. 27th da, 12th mo, 1711; Aaron Phipps, b. 28th da, 5th mo, 1716.

Thomas and Rose Pilkington of Maiden Creek. Children: Joseph Pilkington, b. 26th da, 10th mo, 1745; Thomas Pilkington, b. 5th da, 7th mo, 1751; Abraham Pilkington, b. 25th da, 11th mo, 1755.

Rose Pilkington, widow of Thomas, d. 6th da, 3rd mo, 1793.

Jane Poolah, d. 1st da, 6th mo, 1720, age about 30.

Thomas Powell, son of Thomas, d. 17th da, 5th mo, 1682, buried at sea.

Joseph and Esther Powell. Child: Thomas Powell, b. 27th da, 3rd mo, 1686.

Thomas and Sarah Powell. Child: Susanna Powell, b. 10th da, 10th mo, 1714.

John and Amelia Powell. Children: Isaac Powell, b. 4th da, 10th mo, 1789; Margaret Powell, b. 14th da, 9th mo, 1790.

Amelia Powell, 1st wife of John, d. 29th da, 3rd mo, 1791, age 27.

John Powell and his 2nd wife, Amelia. Children: George Powell, b. 10th da, 4th mo, 1804; John Powell, b. 5th da, 12th mo, 1805; Elizabeth Powell, b. 12th da, 7th mo, 1807; Sarah Powell, b. 9th da, 2nd mo, 1812, d. 30th da, 4th mo, 1833; James Powell, b. 4th da, 5th mo, 1817.

James and Mary Preston. Child: Jonas Preston, b. 25th da, 1st mo, 1760.

Caleb and Ann Pusey. Children: Ann Pusey, b. 12th da, 1st mo, 1684/5; Lydia Pusey, b. 4th da, 7th mo, 1789.

Ann Pusey, wife of Caleb and Ann of Chester, d. about the middle of the 12th mo, 1682/3.

William and Elizabeth Pusey. Children: John Pusey, b. 16th da, 5th mo, 1708; William Pusey, b. 5th da, 1st mo, 1710/11; Lydia Pusey, b. 16th da, 6th mo, 1713; Joshua Pusey, b. 9th da, 11th, 1714.

Joseph and Abigail Pyle. Child: Naomi Pyle, b. 24th da, 11th mo, 1800; Martha Pyle, b. 7th da, 3rd mo, 1802; William Pyle, b. 25th da, 12th mo, 1803; John Pyle, b. 28th da, 9th mo, 1805, 9th da, 10th mo, 1805; Sarah Pyle, b. 22nd da, 11th mo, 1806; Anderson Pyle, b. 25th da, 10th mo, 1810; Gardiner Pyle, b. 5th da, 6th mo, 1814..

Lewis and Grace Rees. Children: Mary Rees, b. 16th da, 7th mo, 1706; Rebecca Rees, b. 7th da, 1st mo, 1709; David Rees, b. 21st da, 9th mo, 1711; Elinor Rees, b. 7th da, 10th mo, 1715; Hannah Rees, b. 27th da, 2nd mo, 1719.

Henry and Prudence Reynolds of Marcus Hook. Child: Margaret Reynolds, b. 25th da, 5th mo, 1682.

Joseph and Abigail Rhoads. Children: John Rhoads, b. 22nd da, 8th mo, 1703; Mary Rhoads, b. last da, 8th mo, 1705; Elizabeth Rhoads, b. 11th da, 6th mo, 1708; Abigail Rhoads, b. 6th da, 9th mo, 1710;

Rebecca Rhoads, b. 3rd da, 2nd mo, 1713; Joseph Rhoads, b. 3rd da, 9th mo, 1715; Jane Rhoads, b. 3rd da, 12th mo, 1717; Benjamin Rhoads, b. 25th da, 12th mo, 1719; James Rhoads, b. 15th da, 5th mo, 1722.

Owen and Mary Rhoads of Springfield Twp. Children: John Rhoads, b. 25th da, 8th mo, 1786; Elizabeth Rhoads, b. 17th da, 2nd mo, 1788; Susanna Rhoads, b. 26th da, 3rd mo, 1790, d. 23rd da, 8th mo, 1814; James Rhoads, b. 4th da, 2nd mo, 1793; Samuel Rhoads, b. 16th da, 8th mo, 1795; Hannah Rhoads, b. 22nd da, 8th mo, 1800; Owen Rhoads, b. 22nd da, 10th mo, 1802, d. 20th da, 12th mo, 1879 in Springfield Twp.

Joseph Rhoads and his wife, Mary (Ashbridge). Children: James Rhoads, b. 12th da, 3rd mo, 1781; d. 3rd da, 4th mo, 1819; George Rhoads, b. 18th da, 2nd mo, 1784, d. 24th da, 3rd mo, 1858; Joseph Rhoads, b. 2nd da, 1st mo, 1787, d. 16th da, 1st mo, 1861; Elizabeth Rhoads (twin), b. 29th da, 9th mo, 1789, d. 15th da, 9th mo, 1844; Rebecca Rhoads (twin), b. 29th da, 9th mo, 1789, d. 29th da, 1st mo, 1861; Phebe Rhoads, b. 24th da, 11th mo, 1793; William Rhoads, b. 2nd da, 4th mo, 1797.

Hannah Rhoads, wife of Isaac, dau. of Thomas Minshall, d. 2nd da, 2nd mo, 1767.

Mary Rhoads, wife of Owen of Springfield Twp, d. 6th da, 10th mo, 1813, age 48.

Joseph Rhoads, d. 5th da, 5th mo, 1829 in Marple Twp, age 60 years, 5 months, 2 days.

Mary Rhoads, widow of Joseph, d. 9th da, 2nd mo, 1830, age 71 years, 4 months, 27 days.

John and Esther Riley. Children: Rebecca Riley, b. 8th da, 10th mo, 1793; Thomas Riley, b. 24th da, 7th mo, 1795; Sarah Riley, b. 27th da, 6th mo, 1798.

Lawrence and Ann Routh of Weston on Chester. Children: Thomas Routh, b. 9th da, 6th mo, 1685; Lawrence Routh, b. 16th da, 1st mo, 1687, d. 16th da, 6th mo, 1690; Rachel Routh, b. 29th da, 10th mo, 1688; Francis Routh, b. 21st da, 10th mo, 1690.

Lawrence Routh, husband of Ann, d. 16th da, 6th mo, 1691.

Mary Salsby, b. at the beginning of the 12th mo, 1641/2.

John and Agnes Salkeld. Children born in Chester Twp: Joseph Salkeld, b. 27th da, 9th mo, 1706, d. 3rd da, 11th mo, 17448/9; Mary Salkeld, b. 30th da, 2nd mo, 1708, d. 2nd da, 2nd mo, 1800, age 91 years 9 months 3 days; John Salkeld, b. 12th da, 10th mo, 1709, d. 24th da, 1st mo, 1777; Thomas Salkeld, b. 24th da, 9th mo, 1711, d.

17th da, 7th mo, 1749; Agnes Salkeld, b. 25th da, 10th mo, 1714, d. 14th da, 1st mo, 1813, age 98 years 9 days (allowing 11 days for new style; Edmond Salkeld, b. 2nd da, 11th mo, 1716/7, 6th da, 5th mo, 1726; William Salkeld, b. 6th da, 12th mo, 1718/9, d. 30th da, 11th mo, 1742; David Salkeld (trip), b. 1st da, 1st mo, 1720/1, d. 6th mo, 1749; Samuel Salkeld (trip), b. 1st da, 1st mo, 1720/1, d. 9th da, 6th mo, 1721; Jane Salkeld (trip), b. 1st da, 1st mo, 1720/1, d. 27th da, 3rd mo, 1778; Jonathan Salkeld, b. 7th da, 1st mo, 1722/3, d. same night.

John Salkeld of Chester, husband of Agnes, son of Thomas Salkeld of the County of Cumberland, England, d. 20th da, 9th mo, 1739, age 67, buried 22nd da.

Agnes Salkeld, widow of John Salkeld, d. 12th da, 11th mo, 1748, age 70 years 10 months 26 days, buried 14th da.

David Salkeld, son of John and Agnes, d. 5th mo, 1749.

John and Elizabeth Salkeld. Children: Sarah Salkeld, b. 29th da, 4th mo, 1733, d. 10th da, 8th mo, 1742; John Salkeld, b. 2nd da, 4th mo, 1735; Agnes Salkeld, b. 5th da, 1st mo, 1736/7, d. 17th da, 12th mo, 1769; Mary Salkeld, b. 3rd da, 10th mo, 1739, d. 25th da, 6th mo, 1746; Joseph Salkeld, b. 10th da, 11th mo, 1741/2, d. 30th da, 7th mo, 1742; Isaac Salkeld, b. 24th da, 6th mo, 1743; Elizabeth Salkeld, b. 31st da, 8th mo, 1745; Ann Salkeld, b. 27th 9th mo, 1747; Sarah Salkeld, b. 9th da, 1st mo, 1749/50; Thomas Salkeld, b. 19th da, 12th mo, 1753, d. 10th da, 1st mo, 1759; Peter Salkeld (twin), b. 28th da, 3rd mo, 1755; James Salkeld (twin), b. 28th da, 3rd mo,1755, d. 12th mo, 5th da, 1757.

Geoffrey Sharpless of Blakenhall, Cheshire, England, d. 15th da, 10th mo, 1661.

John and Jane Sharples from South Bonsall. Children: Phebe Sharples, b. 20th da, 10th mo, 1663, d. 2nd da, 4th mo, 1685; John Sharples, b. 16th da, 11th mo, 1666, d. 9th da, 7th mo, 1747; Thomas Sharples, b. 10th da, 11th mo, 1668, d. 17th da, 5th mo, 1682, buried at sea; James Sharples, b. 5th da, 1st mo, 1670/1; Caleb Sharples, b. 22nd da, 7th mo, 1673, d. 17th da, 7th mo, 1686; Jane Sharples, b. 13th da, 6th mo, 1676, d. 28th da, 3rd mo, 1685; Joseph Sharples, b. 28th da, 5th mo, 1678, d. Spring of 1757, age 79. Snedling's copy of English records say Thomas was born 11th mo, 2nd da, and Joseph born in the 9th mo.

Lydia Sharples, wife of James (son of John and Jane), d. 1763.

Jane Sharples, wife of John, the elder, d. 1st da, 9th mo, 1722.

John Sharples, husband of Jane, d. 11th da, 4th mo, 1685.

John and Hannah Sharples. Children: Caleb Sharples, b. 27th da, 7th mo, 1693, d. 29th da, 2nd mo, 1720; Jane Sharples, b. 24th da, 12th mo, 1695/6; Hannah Sharples, b. 5th da, 8th mo, 1697; John Sharples, b. 16th da, 8th mo, 1699, d. 17th da, 8th mo, 1769; Phebe Sharples, b. 9th da, 11th mo, 1701/2; Rebecca Sharples, b. 17th da, 12th mo, 1703/4; Margaret Sharples, b. 21st da, 4th mo, 1706; Ann, b. 23rd da, 6th mo, 1708; Daniel Sharples, b. 24th da, 12th mo, 1710/1.

Hannah Sharples, wife of John, d. 31st da, 10th mo, 1721.

James Sharples, husband of Mary (Lewis), son of John and Jane, b. 5th da, 1st mo, 1670/1 in Hadderton, Cheshire, England.

Mary (Lewis) Sharples, wife of James, dau. of Ralph and Mary Lewis, b. 10th da, 5th mo, 1674 in Glamorganshire, North Wales, d. 17th da, 2nd mo, 1698.

James and Mary (Lewis) Sharples. Children: Lydia Sharples, b. 20th da, 12th mo, 1701; Mary Sharples, b. 27th da, 2nd mo, 1702; James Sharples, b. 6th da, 9th mo, 1703; Rachel Sharples, b. 9th da, 5th mo, 1708; Sarah Sharples, b. 27th da, 1st mo, 1710; Thomas Sharples, b. 6th da, 8th mo, 1712, d. 2nd da, 8th mo, 1713; David Sharples, b. 24th da, 4th mo, 1715; Esther, b. Not recorded.

Joseph and Lydia Sharples. Children: Susanna Sharples, b. 18th da, 12th mo, 1705; Joseph Sharples, b. 8th da, 7th mo, 1707, d. 4th da, 1st mo, 1769; Benjamin Sharples, b. 26th da, 11th mo, 1708/9, d. 16th da, 3rd mo, 1785; Samuel Sharples, b. 17th da, 12th mo, 1710/1, d. 24th da, 11th mo, 1790; Lydia Sharples, b. 7th da, 3rd mo, 1713; Nathan Sharples, b. 2nd da, 9th mo, 1715; Jane Sharples, b. 4th da, 12th mo, 1718; Abraham Sharples, b. 7th da, 5th mo, 1720; Jacob Sharples, b. 14th da, 10th mo, 1722; William Sharples, b. 31st da, 3rd mo, 1725.

Daniel and Sarah Sharples. Children: Thomas Sharples, b. 29th da, 8th mo, 1738; Rebecca Sharples, b. 22nd da, 10th mo, 1740; Phebe Sharples, b. 11th da, 6th mo, 1744, d. 30th da, 7th mo, 1746; Abigail Sharples, b. 29th da, 9th mo, 1746; Daniel Sharples, b. 12th da, 4th mo, 1751, d. 20th da, 6th mo, 1816.

John Sharples and his 1st wife, Mary. Child: Hannah Sharples, b. 13th da, 11th mo, 1726/7.

Mary Sharples, 1st wife of John, d. 24th da, 10th mo, 1747.

John Sharples and his 2nd wife, Elizabeth. Mary Sharples, b. 17th da, 2nd da, 1730; Margaret Sharples, b. 7th da, 7th mo, 1731; Elizabeth Sharples, b. 25th da, 6th mo, 1734; John Sharples, b. 26th da, 5th mo, 1736; George Sharples, b. 14th da, 5th mo, 1738.

Elizabeth Sharples, 2nd wife of John, d. 18th da, 12th mo, 1767, age 58.

Benjamin Sharples and his 1st wife, Edith. Children: Joseph Sharples, b. 19th da, 12th mo, 1737/8, d. 1st da, 9th mo, 1763; Benjamin Sharples, b. 26th da, 10th mo, 1740, d. 18th da, 6th mo, 1780; Edith Sharples, b. 30th da, 10th mo, 1742.

Edith Sharples, 1st wife of Benjamin, d. 13th da, 6th mo, 1744.

Benjamin Sharples and his 2nd wife, Martha. Children: Joshua Sharples, b. 28th da, 12th mo, 1746/7; Isaac Sharples, b. 16th da, 5th mo, 1748, d. 23rd da, 1st mo, 1780; Rebecca Sharples, b. 29th da, 10th mo, 1749, d. 9th da, 2nd mo, 1780; Martha Sharples, b. 28th da, 10th mo, 1751, d. 7th da, 9th mo, 1763; Ann Sharples, b. 1st da, 7th mo, 1754, d. 4th da, 9th mo, 1763; Aaron Sharples, b. 26th da, 8th mo, 1756, d. 25th da, 8th mo, 1798; Amy Sharples, b. 17th da, 11th mo, 1758; Enoch Sharples, b. 15th da, 9th mo, 1760, d. 15th da, 9th mo, 1763; Infant, b. 3rd mo, 1763, d. 3rd da, 4th mo, 1763; Hannah Sharples, b. 9th da, 4th mo, 1764, d. 11th da, 4th mo, 1795; Esther Sharples, b. 21st da, 5th mo, 1767; Sarah Sharples, b. 25th da, 9th mo, 1769; Samuel Sharples, b. 25th da, 11th mo, 1770, d. 8th da, 9th mo, 1796.

Samuel and Jane Sharples of Middletown. Children: Mary Sharples, b. 20th da, 3rd mo, 1737; John Sharples, b. 26th da, 7th mo, 1738, d. 16th da, 6th mo, 1805; Thomas Sharples, b. 26th da, 12th mo, 1739/40, d. 24th da, 11th mo, 1811; Lydia Sharples, b. 24th da, 4th mo, 1742; Abigail Sharples, b. 5th da, 1st mo, 1743/4; Samuel Sharples, b. 17th da, 11th mo, 1745/6, d. 11th mo, 1746/7; Hannah Sharples, b. 14th da, 11th mo, 1747/8; Susanna Sharples, b. 21st da, 11th mo, 1749/50; Phebe Sharples, b. 25th da, 5th mo, 1752, d. 28th da, 7th mo, 1826; Rachel Sharples, b. 3rd da, 6th mo, 1754; Samuel Sharples, b. 3rd da, 9th mo, 1756, d. 7th mo, 1764; Joel Sharples, b. 28th da, 11th mo, 1760, d. 25th da, 9th mo, 1795

Jane Sharples, wife of Samuel, d. 28th da, 11th mo, 1798.

Joseph and Mary Sharples. Children: Jacob Sharples, b. 21st da, 4th mo, 1741; Joseph Sharples, b. 31st da, 3rd mo, 1743; Daniel Sharples, b. 30th da, 5th mo, 1745; Hannah Sharples, b. 20th da, 12th mo, 1747, d. 2nd da, 10th mo, 1823; Caleb Sharples, b. 12th da, 3rd mo, 1750; William Sharples, b. 4th da, 10th mo, 1752; Mary Sharples, b. 2nd da, 9th mo, 1756; Amos Sharples, b. 7th da, 4th mo, 1759; Nathan Sharples, b. 27th da, 9th mo, 1761; Benjamin Sharples, b. 7th da, 8th mo, 1764; Jonathan Sharples, b. 17th da, 10th mo, 1767.

Daniel Sharples and his 1st wife, Hannah. Children: Isaac Sharples, b. 10th da, 4th mo, 1776; John Sharples, b. 31st da, 9th mo, 1778, d. 12th da, 3rd mo, 1854; Enos Sharples, b. 1st da, 3rd mo, 1781; Sarah Sharples, b. 17th da, 4th mo, 1783; Daniel, b. Not recorded.

Daniel Sharples and his 2nd wife, Sarah. Children: Henry Sharples, b. 11th da, 11th mo, 1790, d. 1853; Beulah Sharples, b. 19th da, 4th mo, 1793; Hannah Sharples, b. 7th da, 7th mo, 1796.

Abraham and Ann Sharples. Children: Mary Sharples, b. 6th da, 5th mo, 1752; Phebe Sharples, b. 15th da, 11th mo, 1755; Abraham Sharples, 16th da, 10th mo, 1758; Lydia Sharples, b. 18th da, 8th mo, 1760; Grace Sharples, b. 9th da, 3rd mo, 1762; Rebecca Sharples, b. 26th da, 9th mo, 1768.

Joel and Hannah Sharples. Children: Samuel Sharples, b. 14th da, 11th mo, 1785; Joshua Sharples, b. 30th da, 10th mo, 1790; Lydia Sharples, b. 9th da, 12th mo, 1792; Beulah Sharples, b. 24th da, 4th mo, 1796, d. 16th da, 10th mo, 1797.

Hannah Sharples, wife of Joel, d. 5th da, 11th mo, 1797.

Nathan and Rachel Sharples. Children: Isaac Sharples, b. 16th da, 12th mo, 1788; Anne Sharples, b. 24th da, 3rd mo, 1793; Aaron Sharples, b. 18th da, 7th mo, 1799.

Rachel Sharples, wife of Nathan, d. 9th da, 6th mo, 1802.

Joseph and Mary Sharples. Child: Edith Sharples, b. 8th da, 2nd mo, 1797.

Jacob and Alice Simcock. Children: John Simcock, b. 23rd da, 7th mo, 1685, d. 23rd da, 4th mo, 1773; Jacob Simcock, b. 25th da, 7th mo, 1686, d. 1716/7; Mary Simcock, b. 4th da, 11th mo, 1688; Benjamin Simcock, b. 10th da, 9th mo, 1690; Hannah Simcock, b. 25th da, 5th mo, 1692, d. 2nd da, 12th mo, 1743, age 50 years 5 months, buried at Abington; Sarah Simcock, b. 18th da, 7th mo, 1696.

Alice Simcock, wife of Jacob, d. 10th da, 10th mo, 1726.

John and Mary Simcock. Children: Alice Simcock, b. 28th da, 12th mo, 1707; Jacob Simcock, b. 15th da, 3rd mo, 1710.

John Simcock, d. 7th da, 1st mo, 1702/3.

George and Ruth Simpson. Children: Lydia Simpson, b. 18th da, 11th mo, 1707/8; George Simpson, b. 26th da, 1st mo, 1710; Stephen Simpson, b. 29th da, 9th mo, 1712; Henry Simpson, b. 9th da, 7th mo, 1715.

George and Sarah Smedley. Thomas Smedley, b. 15th da, 2nd mo, 1687, d. 9th da, 3rd mo, 1758; Mary Smedley, b. 3rd da, 2nd mo, 1690; George Smedley, b. 2nd da, 1st mo, 1692/3; Sarah Smedley, b. 2nd da, 8th mo, 1695; Alice Smedley, b. 2nd da, 3rd mo, 1696.

Sarah Smedley, widow of Thomas, d. 14th da, 3rd mo 1765, age 84.
Sarah Smedley, wife of George, d. 16th da, 3rd mo, 1709.
George Smedley and his 1st wife, Jane. Children: Caleb Smedley, b.
26th da, 4th mo, 1721, d. 4th da, 7th mo, 1725; Joshua Smedley, b.
30th da, 8th mo, 1723.
Jane Smedley, wife of George, d. 29th da, 6th mo, 1725.
George Smedley and his 2nd wife, Mary. Children: William Smedley, b.
19th da, 9th mo, 1728, d. 15th da, 2nd mo, 1760; Joseph Smedley, b.
17th da, 7th mo, 1730, d. 10th da, 5th mo, 1746; Caleb Smedley, b.
20th da, 9th mo, 1732; Jane Smedley, b. 16th da, 12th mo, 1734/5;
Sarah Smedley, b. 18th da, 11th mo, 1737; Samuel Smedley, b. 3rd
da, 7th mo, 1740, d. 12th da, 4th mo, 1762; Thomas Smedley, b. 25th
da, 1st mo, 1742; Ambrose Smedley, b. 19th da, 11th mo, 1745;
Joseph Smedley, b. 13th da, 7th mo, 1748, d. 15th da, 2nd mo, 1760;
James Smedley, b. 20th da, 2nd mo, 1752 N.S.
Mary Smedley, widow of George, d. 18th da, 2nd mo, 1774, age 64.
William and Elizabeth Smedley. Children: Peter Smedley, b. 28th da,
1st mo, 1754; Mary Smedley, b. 21st da, 10th mo, 1755; George
Smedley, b. 11th da, 3rd mo, 1758.
Ambrose and Mary Smedley. Children: Elizabeth Smedley, b. 22nd da,
4th mo, 1769; James Smedley, b. 9th da, 2nd mo, 1772, d. 25th da,
1st mo, 1783 about 9 AM; Sarah Smedley, 28th da, 2nd mo, 1774;
Mary Smedley, b. 28th da, 1st mo, 1776; George Smedley, b. 20th
da, 2nd mo, 1778, d. 29th da, 9th mo, 1786 about 9 PM; Phebe
Smedley, b. 30th da, 12th mo, 1779, d. 16th da, 1st mo, 1801, age 21
years 16 days 7 1/2 hours, unmarried; Ambrose Smedley, b. 14th da,
3rd mo, 1782; Joshua Smedley, b. 18th da, 1st mo, 1784.
Mary Smedley, wife of Ambrose, d. 23rd da, 2nd mo, 1788.
William and Elizabeth Smedley. Children: Joseph Smedley, b. 22nd da,
4th mo, 1761; Samuel Smedley, b. 28th da, 6th mo, 1763, d. 15th da,
1st mo, 1791; William Smedley, b. 9th da, 8th mo, 1765, d. 10th da,
4th mo, 1839.
Elizabeth Smedley, widow of William, d. 22nd da, 2nd mo, 1789, age 59.
William and Deborah Smedley. Children: Joseph Smedley, b. 12th da,
9th mo, 1794, d. 25th da, 7th mo, 1795; George Smedley, b. 25th da,
7th mo, 1796, d. 18th da, 7th mo, 1855; Samuel Smedley, b. 9th da,
4th mo, 1798, d. 19th da, 10th mo, 1834; William Smedley, b. 6th da,
12th mo, 1799, d. 27th da, 4th mo, 1866; Jacob Smedley, b. 31st da,
12th mo, 1801.

Ambrose and Elizabeth Smedley. Children: Samuel Smedley, b. 12th da, 6th mo, 1791 about 10:30 AM; Ahinoam Smedley, b. 29th da, 8th mo, 1795, d. 22nd da, 8th mo, 1857.

George Smedley of Middletown, d. 20th da, 11th mo, 1766.

George Smedley, son of George and Jane of Willistown, d. 1st da, 12th mo, 1765.

William Smedley, d. 29th da, 2nd mo, 1772, age 20.

Thomas Smedley, d. 22nd da, 1st mo, 1791.

Grace Stanfield, wife of Francis, d. 10th mo, 1691.

Francis Stanfield, d. about 1692.

Joseph Stedman, d. 23rd da, 12th mo, 1698.

Benjamin and Ann Stokes, formerly of Haverford Monthly Meeting. Children: Susanna Stokes, b. 25th da, 8th mo, 1793; Sarah Stokes, b. 8th da, 5th mo, 1795; Benjamin Stokes, b. 21st da, 5th mo, 1797; John Stokes, b. 9th da, 3rd mo, 1799.

James and Elizabeth Swaffer. Children: Elizabeth Swaffer, b. 12th da, 11th mo, 1686; James Swaffer, b. 23rd da, 3rd mo, 1691; William Swaffer, b. 22nd da, 9th mo, 1693.

William and Mary Swaffer. Children: Rebecca Swaffer, b. 20th da, 1st mo, 1696/7; Jacob Swaffer, b. 2nd da, 3rd mo, 1699; Joseph Swaffer, b. 4th da, 4th mo, 1701; Mary Swaffer, b. 8th da, 7th mo, 1703.

William and Mary Swaffer. Children: Hannah Swaffer, b. 29th da, 8th mo, 1718; Hannah Swaffer, 3rd da, 7th mo, 1720.

William Swaffer, d. 17th da, 2nd mo, 1720.

William Swaffer of Chester, d. 7th da, 11th mo, 1793.

Thomas and Mary Swayne. Children: Phebe Swayne, b. 9th da, 3rd mo, 1750; George Swayne, b. 15th da, 5th mo, 1752 N.S.; Elizabeth Swayne, b. 1st da, 2nd mo, 1754, d. 12th da, 3rd mo, 1766.

Elizabeth Swift, dau. of Henry and Mary, d. 5th da, 1st mo, 1702/3.

Elizabeth Swift, dau. of Henry and Mary, d. 5th da, 9th mo, 1703.

William Taylor of Providence Twp, d. 6th da, 1st mo, 1682/3.

Margaret Taylor, wife of William, d. 3rd da, 1st mo, 1682/3.

Peter and Sarah Taylor. Children: Peter Taylor, b. 20th da, 3rd mo, 1686; John Taylor, b. 1st da, 12th mo, 1687; Sarah Taylor, b. 6th da, 5th mo, 1690; William Taylor, b. 19th da, 4th mo, 1694; Samuel Taylor, b. 13th da, 12th mo, 1696/7.

Isaac and Sarah Taylor. Children: Isaac Taylor, b. 28th da, 6th mo, 1690; John Taylor, b. 27th da, 7th mo, 1692; Joseph Taylor, b. 11th da, 11th mo, 1694/5, d. 1791; Mary Taylor, b. 21st da, 10th mo, 1697; Benjamin Taylor, b. 18th da, 7th mo, 1700; Sarah Taylor, b. 9th da,

1st mo, 1703; Elizabeth Taylor, b. 9th da, 4th mo, 1705; Josiah Taylor, b. 7th da, 4th mo, 1708.

Jonathan and Martha Taylor. Children: Hannah Taylor, b. 12th da, 7th mo, 1703; Thomas Taylor, b. 21st da, 1st mo, 1705; Jonathan Taylor, b. 7th da, 1st mo, 1707; Mary Taylor, b. 21st da, 4th mo, 1709.

Peter and Elizabeth Taylor. Children: Mordecai Taylor, b. 7th da, 12th mo, 1713; Nathan Taylor, b. 29th da, 1st mo, 1715; Sarah Taylor, b. 2nd da, 12th mo, 1718.

Nathan and Ruth Taylor. Children: Rachel Taylor, b. 7th da, 7th mo, 1747, d. 17th da, 9th mo, 1750; Enoch Taylor, b. 10th da, 4th mo, 1749; Evan Taylor, b. 18th da, 4th mo, 1751; Hannah Taylor, b. 19th da, 4th mo, 1753; Ruth Taylor, b. 15th da, 10th mo, 1755; Rachel Taylor, b. 5th da, 6th mo, 1758.

Ruth Taylor, wife of Nathan, d. 12th da, 6th mo, 1761, age 36.

Peter and Elizabeth Taylor. Child: Mary Taylor, b. 5th da, 7th mo, 1749.

Mordecai and Frances Taylor. Children: Mary Taylor, b. 14th da, 9th mo, 1798; Benjamin Taylor, b. 13th da, 10th mo, 1800; Ann Taylor, b. 14th da, 2nd mo, 1803; Frances Taylor, b. 27th da, 2nd mo, 1806

Joseph and Abigail Thatcher of Aston. Children: Enos Thatcher, b. 14th da, 3rd mo, 1786, d. 22nd da, 5th mo, 1819; Thomas Thatcher, b. 28th da, 6th mo, 1787; William Thatcher, b. 20th da, 9th mo, 1789; Sidney Thatcher, b. 17th da, 3rd mo, 1792; Beulah Thatcher, b. 21st da, 9th mo, 1794; Sarah Thatcher, b. 24th da, 4th mo, 1797; Joseph Thatcher, b. 24th da, 12th mo, 1799; Abigail Thatcher, b. 8th da, 5th mo, 1802; John W. Thatcher, b. 16th da, 6th mo, 1805, d. 8th da, 3rd mo, 1892 in Philadelphia.

Joseph and Ann Thomas. Children: Abishai Thomas, b. 14th da, 6th mo, 1784; Sarah Thomas, b. 7th da, 6th mo, 1786; Mary Thomas, b. 12th da, 8th mo, 1787; John Thomas, b. 14th da, 1st mo, 1791; Samuel Thomas, b. 12th da, 8th mo, 1793.

Ann Thomas, d. 11th da, 11th mo, 1707.

Martha Thomas, d. 5th da, 3rd mo, 1746.

John Chew Thomas of Ridley, d. 20th da, 5th mo, 1836, age 72.

Joseph and Martha Townsend. Children: William Townsend, b. 26th da, 5th mo, 1712; Mary Townsend, b. 16th da, 8th mo, 1713; Joseph Townsend, b. 8th da, 4th mo, 1715; John Townsend, b. 2nd da, 12th mo, 1716; Hannah Townsend, b. 9th da, 6th mo, 1718.

Peter and Judith Trego. Children: Jacob Trego, 7th da, 8th mo, 1687; James Trego, b. last of the 4th mo, 1690; William Trego, b. 3rd da,

6th mo, 1693; John Trego, b. 15th da, 12th mo, 1696; Ann Trego, b. 28th da, 8th mo, 1702, d. 2nd da, 12th mo, 1791.

Jacob and Mary Trego. Children: John Trego, b. 6th da, 5th mo, 1715; Rachel Trego, b. 27th da, 7th mo, 1719.

Jacob Trego, d. 10th da, 4th mo, 1720.

Hannah Trego, dau. of Jacob, d. 10th da, 4th mo, 1720.

John and Elizabeth Turner. Child: Mary Turner, b. 25th da, 12th mo, 1694, d. 1st da, 1st mo, 1694/5.

Elizabeth Turner, wife of John, d. 3rd da, 1st mo, 1694/5.

James Turner, d. 6th da, 2nd mo, 1791, age 85.

Elijah and Martha Tyson. Children: Eliza Tyson, b. 24th da, 12th mo, 1796/7; Sarah Tyson, b. 1st da, 4th mo, 1799/1800; Edward Tyson, b. 19th da, 12th mo, 1800/1; Rebecca Tyson, b. 15th da, 11th mo, 1802/3; William Tyson, b. 23rd da, 9th mo, 1805; Mary Tyson, b. 18th da, 6th mo, 1808; Jonathan Tyson, b. 13th da, 10th mo, 1810.

Thomas Vernon, d. 25th da, 10th mo, 1698/9.

John and Sarah Vernon. Children: Moses Vernon, b. 26th da, 6th mo, 1703; Rachel Vernon, b. 27th da, 9th mo, 1704.

Sarah Vernon, wife of John, d. 16th da, 12th mo, 1706/7.

Hester Vernon of Cheshire, d. 1st da, 4th mo, 1675, buried same day.

Elizabeth Vernon, mother of Thomas, d. 24th da, 3rd mo, 1714.

Thomas and Lydia Vernon. Children: Thomas Vernon, b. 23rd da, 5th mo, 1703, d. same day; Lydia Vernon, b. 13th da, 1st mo, 1706; Jonathan Vernon, b. 3rd da, 4th mo, 1707; Jonathan Vernon, b. 11th da, 6th mo, 1708; Nathan Vernon, b. 10th da, 7th mo, 1710; Esther Vernon, b. 10th da, 8th mo, 1712; Nathaniel Vernon, b. 5th da, 12th mo, 1714; Hannah Vernon, b. 3rd da, 1st mo, 1716/7; Mordecai Vernon, b. 3rd da, 2nd mo, 1720.

Joseph and Lydia Vernon. Child: Joseph Vernon, b. 14th da, 5th mo, 1717.

Jacob and Elinor Vernon. Children: Robert Vernon, b. 31st da, 6th mo, 1713; David Vernon, b. 9th da, 9th mo, 1715; Jonathan Vernon, b. 9th da, 11th mo, 1717/8; Elinor Vernon, b. 28th da, 6th mo, 1720.

Elinor Vernon, widow of Robert [Jacob], d. 24th da, 7th mo, 1720.

Sarah Vernon, wife of Randall, d. 18th da, 12th mo, 1718.

Randall Vernon, widower of Sarah, d. 18th da, 8th mo, 1725, age 85.

Joseph Vernon, d. 6th da, 6th mo, 1747, age 76.

Thomas Vernon, d. 4th da, 11th mo, 1754, age 84.

John Weaman, d. 5th mo, 1682, buried at sea.

Isaac and Sarah Weaver of Nether Providence. Children: Thomas Dell Weaver, b. 27th da, 9th mo, 1751; Joshua Weaver, b. 28th da, 12th mo, 1753/4, d. 2nd da, 6th mo, 1827; Isaac Weaver, b. 1st da, 3rd mo, 1756; Elizabeth Weaver, b. 27th da, 7th mo, 1758; Baldwin Weaver, b. 20th da, 11th mo, 1760; James Weaver, b. 25th da, 3rd mo, 1763; Richard Weaver, b. 17th da, 7th mo, 1765; William Weaver, b. 25th da, 1st mo, 1768; Abraham Weaver, b. 31st da, 3rd mo, 1770; Sarah Weaver, b. 21st da, 9th mo, 1774.

William West, d. 11th da, 2nd mo, 1720.

Samuel and Mary West of Chester. Children: Pusey West, b. 22nd da, 4th mo, 1793, d. 10th da, 6th mo, 1793; Mary West, b. 11th da, 7th mo, 1795; Hannah West, b. 31st da, 10th mo, 1796; William West, b. 12th da, 9th mo, 1798; Anne West, b. 20th da, 4th mo, 1800, d. 9th da, 7th mo, 1801; Sarah Ann West, b. 11th da, 1st mo, 1802; Joshua P. West, b. 20th da, 6th mo, 1804, d. 11th da, 8th mo, 1831.

Thomas and Elizabeth West of Ridley Twp. Children: Sarah West, b. 8th da, 6th mo, 1791, d. 14th da, 1st mo, 1844; Eliza West, b. 29th da, 9th mo, 1792; Elizabeth West, b. 28th da, 7th mo, 1796; Mary West, b. 17th da, 4th mo, 1798, d. 7th da, 4th mo, 1832; Caleb D. West, b. 7th da, 7th mo, 1801; Thomas H. West, b. 17th da, 1st mo, 1804.

Ellis and Mary Williams. Children: Robert Williams, b. 29th da, 6th mo, 1715; Esther Williams, b. 2nd da, 2nd mo, 1718.

Daniel and Mary Williamson. Children: Robert Williamson, b. 3rd da, 10th mo, 1686; Daniel Williamson, b. 6th da, 8th mo, 1688; John Williamson, b. 11th da, 7th mo, 1690; Mary Williamson, b. 25th da, 7th mo, 1692; Thomas Williamson, b. 10th da, 10th mo, 1694; Joseph Williamson, b. 25th da, 2nd mo, 1697; Margaret Williamson, b. 12th da, 12th mo, 1698; Abigail Williamson, b. 16th da, 7th mo, 1702, d. 1775.

John and Sarah Williamson. Children: Mary Williamson, b. 2nd da, 10th mo, 1715; Sarah Williamson, b. 28th da, 5th mo, 1717; Margaret Williamson, b. 17th da, 10th mo, 1719.

Thomas and Ann Williamson. Children: Margaret Williamson, b. Oct 29, 1718; Ann Williamson, b. Dec 22, 1720; Thomas Williamson, b. July 3, 1723, d. 20th da, 8th mo, 1804; Mary Williamson, b. May 29, 1726; Daniel Williamson, b. Oct 8, 1728; William Williamson, b. Aug 5, 1731; Robert Williamson, b. July 9, 1738.

Thomas and Jane Wilson. Child: George Wilson, b. 10th da, 6th mo, 1777.

Cornelius and Mary Wood of Middletown. Children: Isaac Wood, b. 19th da, 8th mo, 1763; John Wood, b. 17th da, 8th mo, 1765; Jane Wood, b. 16th da, 1st mo, 1767; Hannah Wood, b. 22nd da, 3rd mo,

1773; Lydia Wood, b. 22nd da, 3rd mo, 1775; Mary Wood, b. 24th da, 5th mo, 1778.

James and Sarah Wood, Jr. Children: Joseph Wood, b. 29th da, 3rd mo, 1777, d. 7th da, 7th mo, 1798; Jacob Wood, b. 29th da, 3rd mo, 1779, d. same day; James Wood, b. 14th da, 4th mo, 1780; Ann Wood, b. 22nd da, 10th mo, 1782; Aaron Wood, b. 21st da, 11th mo, 1785; Joseph Wood, b. 13th da, 10th mo, 1788, d. 5th da, 9th mo, 1792; Mary Wood, b. 21st da, 4th mo, 1791; Frederick D. Wood, b. 27th da, 12th mo, 1792; John Wood, b. 23rd da, 9th mo, 1795; Sarah Wood, b. 19th da, 5th mo, 1798; Mahlon Wood, b. 29th da, 11th mo, 1800; William Wood, b. 12th da, 4th mo, 1806.

Richard and Jane Woodward. Children: William Woodward, d. 17th da, 9th mo, 1705; Joseph Woodward, d. 28th da, 9th mo, 1710.

Richard Woodward, Sr., d. 7th da, 10th mo, 1706, age about 70.

Edward and Abigail Woodward. Children: Margaret Woodward, b. 22nd da, 12th mo, 1705; Edward Woodward, b. 28th da, 10th mo, 1707; Abigail Woodward, b. 24th da, 5th mo, 1710, d. 1795; Mary Woodward, b. 25th da, 6th mo, 1712; Hannah Woodward, b. 2nd da, 5th mo, 1715.

Abigail Woodward, wife of Edward, d. 27th da, 9th mo, 1716.

Richard and Mary Woodward. Child: Susannah Woodward, b. 10th da, 11th mo, 1718.

John and Frances Worrall of Edgmont. Child: John Worrall, b. 26th da, 7th mo, 1685, d. 18th da, 12th mo, 1705.

Frances Worrall, wife of John of Edgmont, d. 13th da, 10th mo, 1712.

John Worrall, widower of Frances, d. 4th da, 2nd mo, 1742 in his 85th year.

John and Sarah Worrall. Children: Elizabeth Worrall, b. 29th da, 1st mo, 1715; Mary Worrall, b. 27th da, 4th mo, 1717; John Worrall (twin), b. 26th da, 8th mo, 1719; Peter Worrall (twin), b. 26th da, 8th mo, 1719, d. 7th da, 5th mo, 1772; Sarah Worrall, b. 19th da, 7th mo, 1722; Thomas Worrall, b. 21st da, 9th mo, 1724; Thomas Worrall, b. 29th da, 5th mo, 1728.

Peter and Abigail Worrall. Children: John Worrall, b. 31st da, 1st mo, 1758; Rachel Worrall, b. 24th da, 11th mo, 1759, d. 3rd da, 1st mo, 1760; Sarah Worrall, b. 16th da, 12th mo, 1760; Rachel Worrall, b. 17th da, 1st mo, 1763; Abigail Worrall, b. 29th da, 1st mo, 1766; Mary Worrall, b. 27th da, 9th mo, 1768; Elizabeth Worrall, b. 25th da, 7th mo, 1771.

William and Phebe Worrall. Children: Mary Worrall, b. 17th da, 10th mo, 1766; Nathaniel Worrall, b. 14th da, 8th mo, 1769; Ann Worrall, b. 17th da, 11th mo, 1771.

Nathaniel and Mary Worrall. Children: Jonathan Paul Worrall, b. 5th da, 9th mo, 1795; William Worrall, b. 29th da, 3rd mo, 1797; Edith Worrall, b. 1st da, 10th mo, 1798; Phebe Worrall, b. 19th da, 11th mo, 1800; Elizabeth Worrall, b. 10th da, 6th mo, 1802.

Thomas and Ruth Worrall of Middletown. Children: Caleb Peirce Worrall, b. 11th da, 11th mo, 1791, d. 26th da, 2nd mo, 1798; Sarah Worrall, b. 5th da, 4th mo, 1794; Ann Worrall, b. 20th da, 3rd mo, 1799; Mary Peirce Worrall, b. 9th da, 4th mo, 1802; Elizabeth Worrall, b. 30th da, 1st mo, 1805; Thomas Worrall, b. 11th da, 11th mo, 1807.

John and Hannah Worrall of Middletown. Children: Sarah Worrall, b. 15th da, 6th mo, 1781, d. 15th da, 3rd mo, 1861; Peter Worrall, b. 10th da, 12th mo, 1782; Abigail Worrall, b. 23rd da, 4th mo, 1786, d. 7th da, 9th mo, 1886; Hannah Worrall, b. 14th da, 5th mo, 1794; Rachel Worrall, b. 20th da, 11th mo, 1796; John Worrall, b. 17th da, 9th mo, 1800; Richard Thatcher Worrall, b. 23rd da, 1st mo, 1804, d. 13th da, 7th mo, 1847.

Francis and Hannah Yarnall. Children: Sarah Yarnall, b. 28th da, 5th mo, 1687; John Yarnall, b. 24th da, 10th mo, 1688; Peter Yarnall, b. 20th da, 8th mo, 1690; Moses Yarnall, b. last week of 10th mo, 1692; Francis Yarnall, b. 24th da, 12th mo, 1694; Joseph Yarnall, b. 13th da, 5th mo, 1697; Amos Yarnall, b. 28th da, 1st mo, 1700, d. 4th da, 12th mo, 1789; Daniel Yarnall, b. 1st da, 7th mo, 1703; Mordecai Yarnall, b. 11th da, 7th mo, 1705.

Philip and Dorothy Yarnall. Children: John Yarnall, b. 5th da, 1st mo, 1694/5, d. 5th da, 7th mo, 1749; Philip Yarnall, b. 29th da, 9th mo, 1696; Job Yarnall, b. 28th da, 1st mo, 1698; Sarah Yarnall, b. 25th da, 8th mo, 1700; Benjamin Yarnall, b. 20th da, 8th mo, 1702; Thomas Yarnall, b. 10th da, 6th mo, 1705; Nathan Yarnall, b. 27th da, 12th mo, 1707, d. 10th da, 1st mo, 1780; Samuel Yarnall, b. 12th da, 2nd mo, 1710.

Philip and Mary Yarnall. Children: Grace Yarnall, b. 24th da, 5th mo, 1721; Philip Yarnall, b. 22nd da, 5th mo, 1723; David Yarnall, b. 21st da, 6th mo, 1725; Abraham Yarnall, b. 31st da, 5th mo, 1728; Jane Yarnall, b. 19th da, 11th mo, 1730/1; Elizabeth Yarnall, b. 1st da, 9th mo, 1733; Esther Yarnall, b. 19th da, 1st mo, 1735; Dorothy Yarnall, b. 24th da, 11th mo, 1738/9; Mary Yarnall, b. 12th da, 7th mo, 1744.

Philip and Dorothy Yarnall. Children: Rebecca Yarnall, b. 6th da, 6th mo, 1712; Mary Yarnall, b. 23rd da, 8th mo, 1718.

Nathan and Rachel Yarnall. Children: Ephraim Yarnall, b. 6th da, 5th mo, 1733; Nathan Yarnall, b. 2nd da, 4th mo, 1736; Benjamin Yarnall, b. 5th da, 4th mo, 1738; John Yarnall, b. 8th da, 12th mo, 1739; Edith Yarnall, b. 13th da, 3rd mo, 1743; Joel Yarnall, b. 15th da, 6th mo, 1745, d. 20th da, 3rd mo, 1768; Samuel Yarnall, b. 29th da, 3rd mo, 1748.

Rachel Yarnall, wife of Nathan, d. 11th da, 2nd mo, 1749.

Thomas and Martha Yarnall. Children: Margaret Yarnall, b. 25th da, 6th mo, 1736; William Yarnall, b. 1st da, 10th mo, 1737, d. 9th da, 8th mo, 1807; Job Yarnall, b. 7th da, 10th mo, 1742; Caleb Yarnall, b. 14th da, 8th mo, 1744, d. 3rd da, 8th mo, 1800; Joseph Yarnall, b. 1st da, 9th mo, 1747; Hannah Yarnall, b. 15th da, 8th mo, 1749; Sarah Yarnall, b. 12th da, 1st mo, 1751.

John and Abigail Yarnall. Children: Mary Yarnall, b. Sept 21, 1722, d. 1792; Thomas, b. Feb 27, 1724/5, d. 1759; Ann Yarnall, b. Nov 30, 1729, d. 1797; Isaac Yarnall, b. Aug 3, 1732; Abigail Yarnall, b. No date recorded; Hannah Yarnall, b. Dec 4, 1741, d. 29th da, 12th mo, 1818.

Nathan and Hannah Yarnall. Children: Eli Yarnall, b. 29th da, 3rd mo, 1753, d. 25th da, 8th mo, 1812; Joshua Yarnall, b. 16th da, 1st mo, 1755; Ellis Yarnall, b. 31st da, 1st mo, 1757; Robert Yarnall, b. 5th da, 4th mo, 1761.

Hannah Yarnall, wife of Nathan, d. 19th da, 8th mo, 1760.

Eli and Priscilla (Walker) Yarnall of Edgmont Twp. Children: Walker Yarnall, b. 31st da, 1st mo, 1784; Sarah Yarnall, b. 4th da, 1st mo, 1786; Eli Yarnall, b. 20th da, 9th mo, 1789, d. 28th da, 8th mo, 1812.

Priscilla (Walker) Yarnall, wife of Eli, d. 7th da, 6th mo, 1795.

Caleb and Phebe Yarnall of Edgmont Twp. Children: John Yarnall, b. 24th da, 11th mo, 1776; Owen Yarnall, b. 13th da, 1st mo, 1779; Agnes Yarnall, b. 3rd da, 6th mo, 1781; Caleb Yarnall, b. 20th da, 2nd mo, 1783; Thomas Yarnall, b. 6th da, 8th mo, 1785, d. 20th da, 10th mo, 1788; Phebe Yarnall, b. 26th da, 4th mo, 1788.

Ezekiel and Sarah Yarnall. Children: Thomas Yarnall, b. 28th da, 11th mo, 1784, d. 11th da, 9th mo, 1799; Mary Yarnall, b. 1st da, 3rd mo, 1787; Alice Yarnall, b. 6th da, 3rd mo, 1789; Phebe Yarnall, b. 21st da, 1st mo, 1793, d. 25th da, 6th mo, 1815; John Yarnall, b. 2nd da, 2nd mo, 1795; Sarah Yarnall, b. 19th da, 6th mo, 1801.

Ezekiel Yarnall of Edgmont, d. 15th da, 4th mo, 1814, age 51.

James and Jane Yarnall. Children: Mary Yarnall, b. 19th da, 3rd mo, 1780; Isaac Yarnall, b. 10th da, 4th mo, 1783; Sidney Yarnall, b. 2nd da, 8th mo, 1785; Rachel Yarnall, b. 27th da, 10th mo, 1787; James Yarnall, b. 17th da, 11th mo, 1789; Albin Yarnall, b. 10th da, 7th mo, 1797, d. 12th da, 10th mo, 1836; Reuben Yarnall, b. 18th da, 5th mo, 1800.

William and Mary Yarnall of Middletown. Children: Israel Yarnall, b. 6th da, 2nd mo, 1792; Eliza Yarnall, b. 8th da, 11th mo, 1794; Mary Yarnall, b. 24th da, 11th mo, 1798.

Thomas and Margeret (Hill) Yarnall of Thornbury. Children: William Yarnall, b. 3rd da, 9th mo, 1755; Sarah Yarnall, b. 20th da, 9th mo, 1756.

William and Sarah Yarnall of Thornbury. Children: Mary Yarnall, b. 6th da, 2nd mo, 1782; d. 11th da, 3rd mo, 1857; Elizabeth Yarnall, b. 22nd da, 5th mo, 1785; Sarah Yarnall, b. 13th da, 10th mo, 1792, d. 7th mo, 1842; Margaret Yarnall, b. 3rd da, 3rd mo, 1794.

Jane Yarnall, wife of Nathan, d. 25th da, 5th mo, 1775.

Hannah Yarnall, dau. of Benjamin and Martha Sharples, d. 11th da, 4th mo, 1795.

CHESTER MONTHLY MEETING MARRIAGE CERTIFICATES

John Allin of Newtown Twp, Chester Co., and Alice Smedley, dau. of George Smedley of Willistown Twp, same county, m. 18/12/1718/9.

James Arnold of Springfield Twp, Chester Co., son of David Arnold, late of Gloucester Twp and County, New Jersey, dec'd, and Martha Ogden, dau. of Stephen Ogden, late of Springfield Twp, Chester Co., dec'd, m. 5/4/1787.

David Ashbridge, son of John Ashbridge, late of Goshen Twp, Chester Co., and Mary Powell, dau. of David Powell, late of Marple Twp, same county, m. 26/4/1769.

George Ashbridge of Edgmont Twp, Chester Co., and Mary Malin of Upper Providence Twp, same county, m. 23/8/1701.

George Ashbridge of Goshen Twp, Chester Co., son of George Ashbridge of the borough of Chester, same county, and Jane Hoopes, dau. of Daniel Hoopes of Westtown Twp, same county, m. 21/8/1730.

Joshua Ashbridge, son of George Ashbridge of Goshen Twp, Chester Co., dec'd, and Mary Davis, dau. of Lewis Davis of Haverford Twp, m. 4/11/1773.

William Ashque [Askew] and Sarah Yarnall, dau. of Francis Yarnall, late of Willistown Twp, Chester Co., m. 13/9/1729.

Thomas Babb of Newark Twp, New Castle Co. upon Delaware, yeoman, and Elizabeth Booth of Middletown Twp, Chester Co., widow., m. 25/3/1720.

Daniel Baily, son of Joel Baily of Marlborough Twp, Chester Co., yeoman, and Olive Harris, dau. of Hugh Harris, late of Birmingham Twp, same county, yeoman, dec'd, m. 16/1/1720/21.

Aaron Baker of Marlborough Twp, Chester Co., son of Joseph and Martha Baker of Edgmont Twp, same county, and Mary Edwards, dau. of John and Mary Edwards, m. 23/9/1727.

Aaron Baker, son of John Baker of Middletown Twp, Chester Co., and Ruth Taylor, dau. of Nathan Taylor of Upper Providence Twp, m. 19/5/1774.

John Baldwin, Jr., of the borough of Chester, Chester Co., yeoman, and Hannah Johnston of the same place, spinster, m. 11/4/1719.

John Baldwin of Newtown Twp, Chester Co., and Rebekah Register of Edgmont Twp, same county, m. 10/6/1779.

Robert Barber of the borough of Chester, Chester Co., and Hannah Tidmarsh of the same place, m. 17/5/1718.

Thomas Barnard of Aston Twp, Chester Co., carpenter, and Sarah Carter, dau. of Jeremiah and Mary Carter of Chester Twp., same county, m. 14/1/1722/3.

Abraham Barton, son of Isaac Barton, late of Chester, Chester Co., cordwainer, dec'd, and Lydia Simpson, spinster dau. of George Simpson of the same place, m. 5/12/1729.

James Bartram, son of William Bartram, late of Darby, Chester Co., dec'd, and Elizabeth Maris, dau. of Richard Maris of Springfield Twp, same county, m. 30/7/1725.

John Bartram of Darby, Chester Co., yeoman, and Mary Maris, dau. of Richard and Elizabeth Maris of Springfield Twp, same county, m. 25/2/1723.

John Bartram, Jr., son of John and Ann Bartram of Kingsess, Philadelphia Co., and Elizabeth Howell of Marple Twp, Chester Co., dau. of Isaac and Mary Howell of Philadelphia, she dec'd, m. 9/5/1771.

James Batten of Marple Twp, Chester Co., and Mary Moor, dau. of Thomas Moor of the same place, m. 19/2/1733.

John Beeson, son of Edward Beeson of Newcastle on the Delaware [New Castle Co., Delaware], and Alice Martin, dau. of Thomas Martin of Middletown Twp, Chester Co., m. 13/10/1732.

John Bennett of Birmingham Twp, Chester Co., and Sarah Maris of Springfield Twp, same county, dau. of John Maris, m. 17/7/1719.

Davis Bevan, son of Awbrey and Ann Bevan of the borough of Chester, Chester Co., she dec'd, and Agnes Cowpland, dau. of David and Isabell Cowpland of the same borough, m. 12/6/1760.

Edward Bezer of Bethel Twp, Chester Co., yeoman, and Margrett Cowpland, dau. of William Cowpland of Chester Twp, same county, m. 9 Nov 1727.

John Bezer of Chester Co., merchant, and Jane Cummings of Chester Co., dau. of Enoch Cummings of Lewes, Sussex Co., PA [DE], m. 6/9/1746.

John Birchall, son of Caleb Birchall, late of the City of Philadelphia, dec'd, and Lydia Pedrick of the borough of Chester, Chester Co., dau. of Phillip Pedrick, late of Chichester, Chester Co., dec'd, m. 12/4/1759.

John Birchall of Chester Twp, Delaware Co., son of Caleb and Rebecca Birchall, she dec'd, and Elizabeth Crozer of Springfield Twp, same county, dau. of James and Rachel Crozer, m. 13/9/1792.

Edward Bonsall of City of Philadelphia, son of Richard Bonsall, late of Darby Twp, then Chester Co., now Delaware, dec'd, and his wife

Sarah, and Hannah Gibbons, dau. of John and Martha Gibbons of borough of Chester, Delaware Co., m. 29/3/1797.

Isaac Bonsall, son of Enoch Bonsall of Chester Co. and Hannah Powell, dau. of Joseph Powell of Marple Twp, same county, m. 19/9/1754.

Joseph Bonsall, son of Obadiah Bonsall of Darby, Chester Co., and Hannah Lea, dau. of John Lea of Springfield Twp, same county, m. 23/4/1726.

Philip Bonsall of borough of Wilmington, New Castle Co. upon Delaware, son of Vincent Bonsell of said borough, and Catherine Harrison, dau. of Caleb Harrison of Middletown Twp, Chester Co., m. 10/6/1772.

Philip Bonsall of the borough of Wilmington, New Castle Co., Delaware, son of Vincent Bonsall of said borough, and Hannah Ogden, dau. of Stephen Ogden of Marple Twp, Delaware Co., m. 6/5/1790.

Vincent Bonsall of Middletown Twp, Chester Co., son of Obadiah Bonsall, and Grace Yarnall, dau. of Philip Yarnall of Edgmont Twp, same county, m. 9/2/1747.

Jesse Jacob Bourne of Calvert Co., MD, yeoman, and Alice Maris of Springfield Twp, Chester Co., seamstress, one of the daus. of John and Susannah Maris of the same place, m. 10/6/1721.

Richard Bradley, son of John Bradley of Yorkshire in Great Britain, dec'd, and Elizabeth Sharpless, dau. of John Sharpless of Providence Twp, Chester Co., m. 15/5/1755.

William Bromwell of Philadelphia, son of Jacob Bromwell, late of Talbot Co., Maryland, dec'd, and Beulah Hall, dau. of David Hall of Marple Twp, Chester Co., 1/4/1779.

David Broom, son of Daniel Broom, late of Marple Twp, Chester Co., dec'd, and Judith Calvert, dau. of John Calvert, late of Upper Providence Twp, same county, dec'd, m. 8/10/1725.

John Cain, son of John Cain, late of New Garden Twp, Chester Co., yeoman, dec'd, and Rachell Mealin [Melin], dau. of Randall and Mary Mealin [Melin] of Upper Providence Twp, same county, m. 7/9/1722.

John Calvert, son of Daniell and Elizabeth Calvert of Providence Twp, Chester Co., she dec'd, and Hannah Vernon, dau. of Thomas and Liddia Vernon of Providence Twp, same county, m. 12/2/1744.

Henry Camm, son of John Camm of Providence Twp, Chester Co., and Margaret Coppock, dau. of Bartholomew Coppock of Marple Twp, same county, m. 5/4/1728.

Edward Carter, son of Jeremiah Carter, of Chester Twp, Chester Co., and Mary Camm, dau. of John Camm of Providence Twp, same county, m. 4/9/1731.

James Carter, son of John Carter, late of East Bradford Twp, Chester Co., dec'd, and Ann Sharples, dau. of Jacob Sharples, late of Concord Twp, same county, m. 17/1/1782.

John Carter, son of John and Isabell Carter of Aston Twp, Chester Co., and Barbara Ruth, dau. of Francis and Barbara Ruth of Chichester Twp, same county, she dec'd, m. 25/3/1749.

Joseph Chamberlin, son of Robert and Mary Chamberlin of Concord Twp, Chester Co., yeoman, and Susannah Sharples, dau. of Joseph and Lydia Sharples of Middletown Twp, same county, m. 19/2/1726.

Goldsmith Chandlee of Frederick Co., VA, son of Benjamin and Mary Chandlee of Cecil Co., MD, and Hannah Yarnall, dau. of Thomas and Martha Yarnall, late of Edgmont, Chester Co., dec'd, m. 28/10/1784.

George Chandler, son of George Chandler, late of Chichester, Chester Co., dec'd, and Esther Taylor, dau. of Thomas Taylor of Springfield Twp, same county, m. 24/10/1724.

William Cloud of the borough of Wilmington, New Castle Co., Delaware, son of Mordecai and Ann Cloud, the latter dec'd, and Susannah Pennell, dau. of Joseph and Sarah Pennell of Aston Twp, Delaware Co., m. 5/3/1795.

Thomas Coates, son of Moses Coates of Charlestown, Chester Co., and Sarah Miller, dau. of Henry Miller of Providence Twp, same county, m. 21/3/1741.

Joseph Coebourn, son of Thomas Coebourn, and Susannah Churchman, both of Chester Twp., Chester Co., m. 26/9/1690.

Joseph Coebourn of Chester, Chester Co., and Sarah Fallowfield of the same place, m. 5/1/1717/8.

Joseph Coebourne of Chester Twp, Chester Co., husbandman, son of Thomas Coebourne of the same place, yeoman, and Mary Langham, dau. of Robert Langham, formerly of Chichester Twp, same county, yeoman, m. 17/4/1725.

Joseph Coeburn, Jr., of Chester Twp, Chester Co., and Lydia Carter, Jr., of Aston Twp, same county, m. 22/3/1718.

Caleb Cowpland of Chester, Chester Co., and Mary Tidmarsh of the same place, m. 14/1/1716/17.

Caleb Cowpland of Chester Co. and Sarah Edge of Providence Twp, same county, widow of Jacob Edge, dec'd, m. 10/11/1721/2.

David Cowpland, son of William Cowpland of Chester, Chester Co., cooper, and Isabell Bell, dau. of George Bell, late of the kingdom of Ireland, dec'd, m. 21/10/1730.

David Cowpland, son of David and Isabella Cowpland of the borough of Chester, Chester Co., and Hannah James, dau. of Samuel and Johanna James, she dec'd, m. 11/6/1772.

Joshua Cowpland, son of David and Isabella Cowpland of the borough of Chester, Chester Co., and Ann Evans, dau. of Cadwalader and Ann Evans of Edgmont Twp, same county, m. 24/10/1765.

Lawrance Cox of Willistown Twp, Chester Co., yeoman, and Sarah Edge, dau. of John Edge, late of Upper Providence Twp, same county, dec'd, m. 5/2/1739.

Caleb Cresson of the City of Philadelphia, merchant, son of James and Sarah Cresson, dec'd, and Jane Evans of Edgmont Twp, Delaware Co., dau. of John and Mary Cox and the widow of Thomas Evans, dec'd, m. 2/7/1795.

Samuel Crockson, son of Randale Crockson of Providence Twp, Chester Co., and Mary Baker, dau. of Robert Baker, late of Middletown Twp, same county, dec'd, m. 18/8/1733.

Samuel Crosley, son of Charles Crosley of Middletown Twp, Chester Co., dec'd, and Mary Woodward, dau. of Edward Woodward, late of the same place, dec'd, m. 17/10/1754

Thomas Cummings of the town of Chester, Chester Co., shoemaker, and Alice Burrow of the same place, m. 31/5/1729.

Jesse Darlington of Thornbury Twp, Chester Co. son of Thomas and Hannah Darlington, and Amy Sharples of Middletown Twp, same county, dau. of Benjamin and Martha Sharples, the former dec'd, m. 4/10/1787.

John Darlington, son of Abraham Darlington of Birmingham Twp, Chester Co., and Esther Dicks, dau. of Peter Dicks of the same place, m. 17/3/1751.

Lewis David of Haverford, Chester Co., and Rebecca Yarnall of Ridley Twp, same county, m. 21/2/1743.

Moses David, son of Meredith David, late of Plymouth, Philadelphia Co., dec'd, and Mary Pennell, dau. of Joseph Pennell of Edgmont Twp, Chester Co., m. 11/2/1739.

Daniel Davies of Providence Twp, Chester Co., and Mary Swaffer, dau. of William Swaffer, late of Providence Twp, same county, dec'd, m. 24/4/1726 [1736 probably intended].

John Davis of Whitpane Twp, Philadelphia Co., and Susannah James of Springfield Twp, Chester Co., m. 30/8/1746.

John Davis, son of James and Deborah Davis, formerly of Chichester, Delaware Co., dec'd, and Rebecca Hayworth, dau. of George and Patience Haworth of Haverford, m. 9/6/1796.

Nathan Davis, son of Lewis Davis of Haverford, Chester Co., and Hannah Griffith, dau. of John Griffith of Marple Twp, same county, m. 25/4/1765.

Nehemiah Davis of the borough of Chester, son of Daniel and Mary Davis, late of Blockley, Philadelphia Co., she dec'd, and Eleanor Stephens, dau. of Richard and Dorothy Stephens of Chichester, Chester Co., m. 1/7/1762.

Jonathan Dawes, son of Edward Dawes of the borough of Wilmington, New Castle Co., Delaware, and Hannah Woodward, dau. of Edward Woodward, Jr., late of Middletown Twp, Chester Co., dec'd, m. 9/10/1760.

Thomas Dell, son of Thomas Dell of Ridley Twp, Chester Co., and Rachel Sharples, dau. of James Sharples of Providence Twp, same county, m. 17/8/1728.

John Dicken, son of James Dicken of Merion Twp, Philadelphia Co., and Martha his wife, dec'd, and Ann Low, dau. of John and Jennet Low of Ridley Twp, Chester Co., m. 10/2/1739.

Joseph Dicks, son of Peter Dicks of Providence Twp, Chester Co., and Ann Engle, dau. of Fredrick Engle, late of Middletown Twp, same county, dec'd, m. 20/5/1745.

Nathan Dicks, son of Peter Dicks of Providence Twp, Chester Co., and Sarah Sharpless, dau. of James Sharpless of same twp, m. 7/2/1748.

Peter Dicks of Providence Twp, Chester Co., and Sarah Swaffer, dau. of William and Mary Swaffer of Providence Twp, same county, she dec'd, m. 17/3/1750.

Richard Dilworth of the City of Philadelphia, son of Charles and Mary Dilworth of borough of West Chester, Chester Co., and Sarah Pennell, dau. of Joseph and Sarah Pennell of Aston Twp, Delaware Co., m. 31/7/1800.

Christopher Dingee of Chester Twp, Chester Co., and Elizabeth Swaffer of the same place, widow, m. 30/11/1775.

Jacob Dingee, son of Christopher and Ruth Dingee of Chester Co., latter dec'd, and Elizabeth Maris, dau. of Richard and Ann Maris of Marple Twp, same county, m. 9/5/1787.

Joseph Downing of East Caln Twp, Chester Co., son of Richard and Mary Downing, Sr., and Ann Worrall of Ridley Twp, Delaware Co., dau. of William and Phebe Worrall, m. 4/5/1791.

Richard Downing, son of Thomas Downing of East Caln Twp, Chester Co., and Mary Edge, dau. of John Edge, late of Upper Providence Twp, same county, dec'd, m. 21/3/1741.

Jacob Dunn, son of Phillip amd Susannah Dunn of Newtown Twp, Chester Co., yeoman, and Mary Taylor, dau. of Mordecai Taylor, late of Upper Providence Twp, dec'd, and Esther his wife, m. 21/10/1762.

Richard Dutton, son of Thomas Dutton, late of Aston Twp, Chester Co., dec'd, husbandman, and Mary Martin, dau. of Thomas Martin of Middletown Twp, same county, m. 17/8/1733.

John Eblen, son of Hance Michal Eblen of Jarmantown [Germantown], Philadelphia Co., and Mary Warner of Marple Twp, Chester Co., dau. of Isaac Warner, dec'd, m. 25/2/1745.

George Edge, son of John Edge, late of Providence Twp, Chester Co., dec'd, and Ann Pennel, dau. of William Pennell of Middletown Twp, same county, m. 19/9/1741.

Benjamin Ellis, son of Ellis Ellis, late of Haverford, Chester Co., dec'd, and Ann Swafor, dau. of William Swafor, formerly of Nether Providence Twp, same county, m. 1/3/1735.

Evan Ellis of Easttown Twp, Chester Co., bachelor, and Sarah Yarnall of Edgmont Twp, same county, spinster, m. 21/2/1726.

Vincent Emmerson, son of John and Unity Emmerson of Murderkill [Motherkiln] Hundred, Kent Co., on Delaware, and Mary Pennell, dau. of John and Martha Pennell, Jr., of Chester Co., m. 26/11/1759.

Frederick Engle, son of Frederick Engle, late of Middletown Twp, Chester Co., dec'd, and Abigail Vernon, dau. of Moses Vernon of Nether Providence Twp, same county, m. 6/12/1753.

Isaac Engle of Chester, Delaware Co., son of Frederick and Abigail Engle, he dec'd, and Abigail Roberts, dau. of Reuben and Margaret Roberts of Nether Providence Twp, same county, latter dec'd, m. 3/10/1792.

Cadwalader Evans of the City of Philadelphia, and Ann Pennell, dau. of Joseph Pennell of Edgmont Twp, Chester Co., m. 10/10/1730.

John Evans, son of David Evans of Merion Twp, Philadelphia Co., and Phebe Musgrove, dau. of William Musgrove of Springfield Twp, Chester Co., dec'd, m. 30/10/1760.

Thomas Evans of Goshen Twp, Chester Co., and Elizabeth Atherton, m. 26/1/1719.

Thomas Evans, son of Cadwaldder and Ann Evans, he dec'd, late of Edgment Twp, Chester Co., and Jane Cox, dau. of John and Mary Cox of Chester Twp, same county, m. 14/6/1770.

Isaac Eyre of borough of Chester, Chester Co., son of William and Mary Eyre, late of Bethel Twp, same county, he dec'd, and Ann Preston, dau. of Jonas and Jane Preston of Chester Twp, also Chester Co., she dec'd, m. 26/6/1766.

John Eyre of the borough of Chester, Chester Co., son of William and Mary Eyre of Bethel Twp, same county, and Rebekah Sharpless, dau. of Daniel and Sarah Sharpless of Nether Providence Twp, also Chester Co., m. 13/12/1759.

Frederick Fairlamb, son of John Fairlamb, dec'd, and Susannah his wife of Middletown Twp, Chester Co., and Mary Pennell, dau. of Robert and Hannah Pennell of the same place, m. 10/12/1767.

John Fairlamb, son of Nicholas Fairlamb, late of Middletown Twp, Chester Co., dec'd, and Susanna Engle, dau. of Frederick Engle, late of the same place, dec'd, m. 13/11/1742/3.

Nicholas Fairlamb, son of John and Susanna Fairlamb of Middletown Twp, Chester Co., he dec'd, and Hannah Preston, dau. of Jonas and Jane Preston of Chester Twp, same county, she dec'd, m. 31/3/1768.

Robert Fairlamb, son of Frederick and Mary Fairlamb of Middletown Twp, Delaware Co., and Mary Harry, dau. of Jonathan and Alice Harry of White Marsh Twp, Montgomery Co., latter dec'd, m. 9/6/1791.

Richard Farr of Edgmont Twp, Chester Co., and Alice Norbury of Middletown Twp, same county, widow, m. [no date given, listed between 23rd da, 9th mo, and 14th da, 10th mo, 1727].

Edward Fell of Marple Twp, Chester Co., and Mary Musgrove of the same place, m. 15/3/1735.

William Fell, son of Thomas Fell of Springfield Twp, Chester Co., and Rebecca Coppock, dau. of Bartholomew Coppock of Marple Twp, same county, m. 8/9/1744.

Ziba Ferris of the borough of Wilmington, New Castle Co. upon Delaware, son of John Ferris, late of the same place, recently dec'd, and Edith Sharpless, dau. of Benjamin Sharpless of Middletown Twp, Chester Co., m. 12/1/1769.

Daniel Few of Kennett Twp, Chester Co., and Esther Howel, dau. of Evan Howel of Edgmont Twp, same county, m. 23/3/1734.

John Flower and Elizabeth Beethom of the town of Chester, Chester Co., m. 16/5/1776.

William Foulke, son of Levi and Ann Foulke of Gwynedd Twp, Montgomery Co., and Margaret McIlvain, dau. of John McIlvain, late of Ridley Twp, Chester Co., now Delaware Co., dec'd, and Lydia his wife, m. 6/11/1793.

Joseph Garratt, son of Samuell Garrat of Darby Twp, Chester Co., and Mary Sharples, dau. of James Sharples, yeoman, m. 25/2/1722.

David Garrett, son of Jesse Garrett, Chester Co., and Esther Pennell, dau. of William Pennell, late of Middletown Twp, m. 16/4/1789.

Nathan Garrett, son of Nathan and Ann Garrett of Darby, Chester Co., and Hannah Rhoades, dau. of James Rhoades, late of Marple Twp, same county, dec'd, and Elizabeth his wife, m. 6/7/1780.

Nathan Garrett, son of William Garrett of Willistown Twp, Chester Co., and Rebeccah Green, dau. of Robert Green, late of Birmingham Twp, Delaware Co., dec'd, m. 30/3/1797.

Thomas Garrett, son of Nathan and Ann Garrett of Darby Twp, Chester Co., and Margaret Levis, dau. of Samuel and Mary Levis of Springfield Twp, same county, m. 18/11/1773.

William Garrett of Goshen Twp, Chester Co., son of Thomas Garrett, dec'd, and Abigail Yarnall of Edgmont Twp, same county, widow of John Yarnall, dec'd, m. 9/5/1754.

George Gilpin of Birmingham Twp, Chester Co. and Sarah Woodward of Middletown Twp, same county, widow of Edward Woodward, Jr., m. 9/4/1760.

James Gillingham, son of Yeamans Gillingham of Oxford Twp, Philadelphia Co., and Sarah Wood, dau. of James Wood of Providence Twp, Delaware Co., m. 3/10/1792.

John Gleave of Springfield Twp, Chester Co., and Elizabeth Miller of the same place, m. 16/11/1706/7.

Richard Goodwin, son of Thomas Goodwin of Goshen Twp, Chester Co., and Lydia Potter, dau. of Abraham Potter, late of Sussex Co. PA [DE], dec'd, m. 8/12/1757.

Samuel Gray of Chester, Chester Co., sadler, and Lydia Coebourn, dau. of Joseph Coebourn, m. 18/1/1724.

Enoch Griffith, son of William and Hannah Griffith of Aston Twp, Delaware Co., he dec'd, and Rachel Webster, dau. of Joseph and Rebeccah Webster of Middletown Twp, same county, m. 17/4/1794.

John Griffith, formerly of Bristol Twp, Philadelphia Co., bachelor, and Mary Bevan of Newtown Twp, Chester Co., widow, m. 14/12/1716/7.

John Griffith, son of Benony Griffith, late of Willistown Twp, yeoman, dec'd, and Jane Yarnall, dau. of Philip Yarnall, late of Edgmont Twp, both Chester Co., yeoman, dec'd, m. 20/5/1762.

William Griffith, son of William and Hannah Griffith of Aston Twp, Delaware Co., and Sarah Smedley, dau. of Ambrose and Mary Smedley of Middletown Twp, same county, m. 6/6/1793.

Samuel Grubb, son of John Grubb, late of Chichester Twp, Chester Co., dec'd, and Mary Billerby, dau. of Isaac Bellerby, late of New Castle Co., Delaware, dec'd, m. 26/7/1745.

David Hall, son of Matthew Hall of Marple Twp, Chester Co., and
Deborah Fell, dau. of Edward Fell of Springfield Twp, same county,
m. 21/12/1758.

John Hall of Springfield Twp, Chester Co., yeoman, son of Samuell Hall
of the same place, and Mary Hodges of Ridley Twp, same county,
seamstress, dau. of Thomas Hodges, late of Bristol, Philadelphia Co.,
dec'd, m. 22/9/1721.

John Hall, son of John Hall of Springfield Twp, Chester Co., and
Susannah Maris, dau. of George Maris of the same place, m.
4/11/1756.

Mathew Hall of Buckingham, Buck Co., and Rebecca Massey of
Chester Co., widow of Mordecai Massey, m. 13/7/1750.

Thomas Hall, son of Samuel Hall of Springfield Twp, Chester Co., and
Mary Kendale, dau. of Thomas Kendale of the same place, m.
6/4/1728.

Thomas Hall of Goshen Twp, Chester Co. and Alice Farr of Edgmont
Twp, same county, widow of Richard Farr, m. 3/5/1746.

Thomas Hall, son of Thomas Hall, of Willistown Twp, and Mary
Minshall, dau. of John Minshall of Middletown Twp, both of Chester
Co., m. 17/6/1762.

Samuel Hampton, son of Simon Hampton, Thornbury Twp, Chester
Co., and Sarah Smedley, dau. of George and Mary Smedley of
Middletown Twp, same county, m. 10/5/1753.

Caleb Harrison, son of Caleb and Hannah Harrison of Middletown
Twp, Chester Co., yeoman, and Eloner Fairlamb, dau. of Nicholas
Fairlamb, late of the same county, dec'd, and Catherine his wife, m.
3/4/1743.

Joshua Harrison, son of Caleb and Eleanor Harrison of Middletown
Twp, Delaware Co., and Eliza Pancoast, dau. of Seth and Ann
Pancoast of Springfield Twp, same county, m. 7/4/1791.

Peter Hatton, son of Peter and Sarah Hatton of Concord, Concord
Twp, Chester Co., and Phebe Malin, dau. of Gideon and Phebe
Malin of Upper Providence Twp, same county, m. 3/4/1783.

John Haycock, son of Jonathan and Ann Haycock of Marple Twp,
Chester Co., and Sarah Taylor, dau. of Peter and Elizabeth Taylor of
Providence Twp, same county, m. 19/7/1739.

John Hendricks of Conistogoe, Chester Co., and Rebeckah Worley, also
of Conistogoe, same county, m. 30/2/1718.

Isaac Hibberd, son of Josiah Hibberd, late of Darby, Chester Co., dec'd,
and Mary Lownes, dau. of George Lownes, late of Springfield Twp,
same county, dec'd, m. 22/9/1744.

Isaac Hibberd, son of Isaac and Mary Hibberd of Darby, Delaware Co., and Ann Hill, dau. of John and Mary Hill of Middletown Twp, same county, m. 14/10/1790.

Josiah Hibberd, son of Benjamin Hibberd of Willistown, Chester Co., and Susanna Owen, dau. of John Owen, late of Chester Co., dec'd, m. 25/10/1764.

Thomas Holcombe, son of Jacob Holecombe of Buckingham Twp, Bucks Co., PA, and Hannah Pennell, dau. of William Pennell of Middletown Twp, Chester Co., m. 24/7/1741.

Henry Holland of Springfield Twp, Chester Co., and Lydia Fell, dau. of Thomas Fell of the same place, m. 27/6/1741.

Joseph Hoopes, son of Joshua Hoopes, dec'd, and Hannah his wife of Westow, Chester Co., and Mary Smedley, dau. of William Smedley, dec'd, and Elizabeth his wife of Middletown Twp, same county, m. 17/5/1781.

Nathan Hoops, son of Daniel Hoops of Westtown Twp, Chester Co., and Margaret Williamson, dau. of Thomas Williamson of Edgmont Twp, same county, m. 6/8/1737.

Edward Horne, son of William and Elizabeth Horne, late of Darby, Chester Co., he dec'd, and Mary Ogden, dau. of Stephen and Hannah Ogden of Springfield Twp, same county, he dec'd, m. 29/6/1775.

William Horne, son of William and Elizabeth Horne of Darby, Chester Co., and Phebe Swayne, dau. of Thomas and Mary Swayne of Ridley Twp, same county, she dec'd, m. 4/10/1770.

Joseph Hoskins of Chester, Chester Co., and Jane Fenn of the same place, m. 26/8/1738.

Joseph Hoskins, son of John and Mary Hoskins of the City of Burlington, Burlington Co., New Jersey, and Mary Graham, dau. of Henry Hale Graham, late of Chester Twp, Delaware Co., dec'd, and Abigail his wife, m. 12/6/1793.

Raper Hoskins, son of John and Mary Hoskins of the City of Burlington, Burlington Co., New Jersey, and Eleanor Graham, dau. of Henry Hale Graham of the borough and county of Chester, by Abigail his wife, m. 2/5/1781.

Henry Howarth of Upper Providence Twp, Chester Co., and Hannah Sharples, dau. of John Sharples of Ridley Twp, same county, spinster, m. 11/6/1720.

Israel Howel of the City of Philadelphia, son of Evan Howel of Edgmont Twp, Chester Co., dec'd, and Mary Hall, dau. of John Hall of Springfield Twp, Chester Co., dec'd, m. 12/11/1761.

Evan Howell, son of John Howell of the City of Philadelphia, and Sarah Ogden, dau. of David Ogden of Middletown Twp, Chester Co., m. 21/9/1711.

Isaac Howell, son of Jacob and Sarah Howell of Chester Co., and Mary Bartram, dau. of James Bartram of Marple Twp, same county, m. 21/9/1745.

Israel Howell, son of Evan Howell of Edgmont Twp, and Elizabeth Swayne, dau. of William Swayne of East Marlborough Twp, dec'd, m. 11/2/1751.

Jacob Howell of Chester, Chester Co., son of John Howel of Philadelphia, and Sarah Vernon, dau. of Randal Vernon of Providence Twp, same county, m. 17/6/1709.

Jacob Howell of Chichester, Chester Co., son of Thomas Howell, late of the same place, dec'd, and Ann Martin of Middletown, same county, dau. of Thomas Martin, late of the same place, dec'd, m. 24/1/1765.

John Howard, son of Henry Howard of Edgmont Twp, Chester Co., and Elizabeth Peary, dau. of Christopher Peary, late of the City of Philadelphia, dec'd, m. 22/8/1747.

Benjamin Hubbard, son of Josiah Hubbard of Darby, Chester Co., husbandman, and Phebe Sharpless, dau. of John Sharpless of Ridley Twp, same county, m. 25/2/1732.

William Hunter, son of John Hunter, late of Newtown Twp, Chester Co., and Hannah Woodward, dau. of Edward Woodward of Newtown Twp, same county, m. 11/10/1740.

John Hurford, son of John Hurford, shopkeeper in Aston, Chester Co., and Hannah Farelamb, dau. of Nicholas and Cathrine Farelamb, dec'd, m. 11/3/1732.

John Hutton of Springfield Twp, Chester Co., son of James Hutton of Maiden Creek Twp, Berks Co., PA, dec'd, and Massey Marshall of Springfield Twp, Chester Co., dau. of William Marshall of Union Co., South Carolina, m. 27/11/1788.

William Iddings, son of William Iddings of Robeson Twp, Berks Co., PA, and Hannah Sharples, dau. of Samuel Sharples of Middletown Twp, Chester Co., m. 23/5/1771.

John Iden of Falls Twp, Buck Co., PA, cordwainer, and Hannah Simcock, dau. of Jacob and Alice Simcock of Ridley Twp, Chester Co., m. 15/1/1721.

Ephraim Jackson, son of Ephraim Jackson, late of Edgmont Twp, Chester Co., dec'd, and Mary Regester, dau. of David Regester of the same place, m. 21/9/1733.

Joseph Jackson, son of Ephraim and Rachel Jackson of Edgmont Twp, Chester Co., and Hannah Pennell, dau. of Joseph and Alice Pennell of the same place, m. 18/8/1722.

Thomas Jacobs, son of Isaiah Jacobs of Providence, Philadelphia Co., and Lydia Pennell, dau. of Robert Pennell of Middletown Twp, Chester Co., m. 13/4/1780.

Ezekiel James, son of John James of Willistown, Chester Co., dec'd, and Keziah Henry, dau. of Job Henry of New Castle Co. on Delaware, dec'd, m. 9/3/1775.

Frederick James, son of Joseph James of Upper Providence Twp, Delaware Co., dec'd, and Rebekah Starr, dau. of James Starr, m. 30/11/1797.

John James, son of Thomas James of Willistown Twp, Chester Co., and Ann Baker, dau. of Robert Baker, late of Middletown Twp, same county, dec'd, m. 11/10/1735.

Joseph James, son of Samuel and Joanna James, he dec'd, and Mary Engle, dau. of Frederick and Abigail Engle, m. 4/2/1773.

Thomas James of Willistown Twp, Chester Co., and Mary Goodwin, dau. of Thomas and Elizabeth Goodwin of Edgmont Twp, same county, m. 21/8/1712.

Benjamin Johnson, son of Robert and Margaret Johnson of Newgarden Twp, Chester Co., and Mary Jackson, dau. of Ephraim and Rachell Jackson of Edgmont Twp, same county, m. 5/9/29.

Charles Jones, son of John and Elizabeth Jones of the City of Philadelphia, and Sarah Howell, dau. of Jacob Howell of the borough and county of Chester, m. 20/9/1740.

John Jones of Gwynedd Twp, Philadelphia Co., widower, and Margret Hillborn of Aston Twp, Chester Co., widow, m. 10/2/1718.

Richard Jones of Merion Twp, Philadelphia Co., and Rebeckah Garratt of Willistown Twp, Chester Co., m. 20/9/1718.

William Jones, son of David Jones of Plymouth Twp, Philadelphia Co., and Rebecca Yarnall, dau. of Philip Yarnall, late of Edgmont Twp, Chester Co., dec'd, m. 20/1/1739.

Benjamin Kendale of borough and county of Chester, and Grace Howard, dau. of Henry Howard of Edgmont Twp, same county, m. 24/11/1739.

John Kendale, son of Thomas Kendale of Springfield Twp, Chester Co., and Mary his wife, dec'd, and Rebeccah Collier, dau. of Isaac and Ruth Collier of the same place, m. 15/9/1739.

Thomas Kendall, son of Thomas Kendall of Springfield Twp, Chester Co., and Mary, his wife, dec'd, and Sarah Pilkington, dau. of Edward Pilkington of Middletown Twp, same county, m. 13/9/1740.

James Kenny, son of Alexander Kenny, late of Uwchlan Twp, Chester Co., yeoman, dec'd, and Mary Speakeman of Chester, same county, dau. of Isaac Speakman of the county of Wilts in England, dec'd, m. 3/12/1767.

William Larkin, son of John and Esther Larking, and Jane Smedley, dau. of George and Mary Smedley of Middletown Twp, Chester Co., m. 7/10/1756.

Henry Lawrance, Jr., son of Henry Lawrance of Haverford, Chester Co., and Hannah Massey, dau. of Mordecai Massey of Marple Twp, same county, dec'd, m. 4/2/1751.

Henry Lawrence of the City of Philadelphia, merchant, son of Henry and Hannah Lawrence of Marple Twp, Delaware Co., and Mary Pennell, dau. of William and Mary Pennell of Middletown Twp, Delaware Co., former dec'd, m. 27/4/1797.

Thomas Laycock of Darby Twp, Delaware Co., son of William and Hannah Laycock, formerly of Great Britain, and Martha Arnold, dau. of Stephen and Hannah Ogden of Springfield Twp, same county, dec'd, m. 27/11/1800.

John Lea of Chester, Chester Co., joiner, and Hannah Edge of the same place, spinster, m. 18/9/1736.

John Lea of the borough of Chester, Chester Co., widower, and Mary Pennell, widow of Thomas Penell, late of Middletown Twp, same county, dec'd, m. 7/5/1752.

Isaac Levis, son of Samuel and Mary Levis of Springfield Twp, Chester Co., and Phebe Pancoast, dau. of Seth Pancoast of Marple Twp, same county, m. 17/4/1766.

Samuel Levis, son of Samuel and Hannah Levis of Springfield Twp, Chester Co., and Mary Thomson, dau. of Joshua and Margaret Thompson of Ridley Twp, same county, m. 12/6/1742.

William Levis of Newark Twp, Chester Co., son of William and Elizabeth Levis of Kennett Twp, same county, and Jane Ogden, dau. of Samuel and Esther Ogden of Springfield Twp, same county, m. 21/6/1746.

William Levis of Upper Darby Twp, Delaware Co., son of Samuel and Elizabeth Levis of the same place, and Esther Pancoast of Springfield Twp, same county, dau. of Seth and Ann Pancoast of the same place., former dec'd, m. 11/10/1798.

Abraham Lewis, son of Abraham and Mary Lewis of Haverford, Chester Co., and Ann Rees of Springfield Twp, dau. of David and Elizabeth Rees, she dec'd, m. 28/1/1751.

Evan Lewis of Newtown Twp, Chester Co., bachelor, son of William Lewis of Haverford, same county, and Mary Hayes, dau. of Jonathan Hayes of Marple Twp, same county, spinster, m. 28/9/1704.

Jehu Lewis of Darby, Chester Co., son of Evan Lewis, late of Caln Twp, Chester Co., dec'd, and Alice Maris, dau. of George Maris of Springfield Twp, same county, m. 11/3/1749.

John Lewis of the City of Philadelphia, biscuit baker, son of Samuel Lewis, carpenter, and Girzzel his wife of Haverford Twp, Chester Co., and Alice Harvey, dau. of Joseph and Mary Harvey of Ridley Twp, same county, m. 20 March 1734.

John Lewis of Springfield Twp, Chester Co., son of Amos Lewis of Philadelphia, dec'd, and Ann Davis, dau. of Lewis Davis of Haverford Twp, Chester Co., m. 13/12/1781.

Nathan Lewis, son of David and Rachel Lewis, she dec'd, and Sarah Carter, dau. of Marlin and Jane Carter of Chester Twp, m. 7/11/1787.

Samuel Lewis, son of Ralph Lewis of Darby(?), and Phebe Taylor, dau. of Josiah Taylor, late of Marple Twp, Chester Co., dec'd, m. 17/4/1712.

Samuel Lewis of Edgmont Twp, Chester Co., and Mary Bickham of Newtown Twp, same county, m. 3/11/1744/5.

Thomas Lewis, son of John and Rebecca Lewis of Springfield Twp, Chester Co., and Sarah Pancoast, dau. of Seth and Hester Pancoast of Marple Twp, same county, m. 8/12/1763.

Samuel Litler of Nottingham Twp, Chester Co., and Mary Rooks of Providence Twp, same county, m. 22/6/1735.

Samuell Littler of Nottingham Twp, Chester Co., husbandman, and Rachel Taylor of Edgmont Twp, widow of Thomas Taylor and dau. of John Minshall of Great Britain, m. 31/5/1707.

Daird Llewellyn, son of Daird Llewellyn of Haverford Twp, Chester Co., and Ann Maris, dau. of Richard Maris of Springfield Twp, same county, m. 24/3/1739.

Robert Long of Edgmont Twp, Chester Co., and Rachell Taylor of the same place, widow, m. 14/1/1721/2.

Hugh Lownes, son of Benamuel Lownes of Springfield Twp, Chester Co., dec'd, and Rebecca Rhoads, dau. of James Rhoads of Marple Twp, same county, dec'd, m. 21/10/1784.

John Lownes, son of Joseph and Sarah Lowns of the City of Philadelphia, and Agness Cowpland, dau. of Caleb and Sarah Cowpland of the borough of Chester, Chester Co., m. 27/8/1753.

Joseph Lynn, son of John and Mary Lynn of Philadelphia, and Ann Morris, dau. of Jonathan and Alice Morris of Marple Twp, Chester Co., m. 17/6/1784.

George Malin, son of William and Elizabeth Malin of Upper Providence Twp, Delaware Co., she dec'd, and Rebeccah Ogden, dau. of Aaron and Esther Ogden, he dec'd, m. 30/5/1794.

Gideon Malin, son of Jacob Malin, late of Providence Twp, Chester Co., yeoman, and Susannah his wife, dec'd, and Phebe Bowman, dau. of Henry Bowman, late of Monyash, Derbyshire, England, dec'd, and Hannah his wife, m. 28/3/1754.

Jacob Malin, son of William and Elizabeth Malin of Upper Providence Twp, Chester Co., yeoman, and Susannah Bishop, dau. of Thomas Bishop of the same place, m. 16/12/1773.

Jacob Malin, son of William and Elizabeth Malin of Upper Providence Twp, Chester Co., and Ann Minshall, dau. of Thomas Minshall of Middletown Twp, same county, m. 15/4/1784.

Joel Malin, son of William and Elizabeth Malin of Upper Providence Twp, Delaware Co., she dec'd, and Elizabeth Taylor, dau. of Isaac and Mary Taylor, same county, she dec'd, m. 28/3/1793.

Thomas Malin of Upper Providence Twp, Chester Co., son of William and Elizabeth Malin of the same county, and Grace Minshall, dau. of Thomas and Agnes Minshall of Middletown Twp, same county, m. 8/5/1780.

George Maris, son of John Maris of Springfield Twp, Chester Co., and Sarah Levis, dau. of Samuell Levis of the same place, m. 19/3/1720.

George Maris, son of John Maris of Springfield Twp, Chester Co., and Ann Lowns, dau. of George Lowns of the same place, m. 14 Sep 1732.

Jesse Maris, son of George Maris of Springfield Twp, Chester Co., and Rebecca Owen, dau. of John Owen, late of the same place, dec'd, m. 22/8/1754.

Jonathan Maris, son of Richard Maris of Springfield Twp, Chester Co., and Jane Lownes, dau. of George Lownes of the same place, m. 19/4/1726.

Jonathan Maris of Gwynedd Twp, Montgomery Co., son of George Maris of the same place, and Judith McIlvan, dau. of John McIlvan, late of Ridley Twp, formerly Chester Co., now Delaware Co., m. 7/9/1791.

Joseph Maris, son of Richard and Elizabeth Maris of Springfield Twp, Chester Co., and Ann Shipley of Ridley Twp, same county, dau. of William Shipley of Wilmington, Christiana Hundred, Newcastle Co., Delaware, m. 21/11/1741/2.

Richard Maris, son of Jonathan Maris of Marple Twp, Chester Co., and Ann Swaffer, dau. of Joseph and Elizabeth Swaffer of Chester Twp, same county, m. 8/6/1758.

Abraham Marshall, son of John and Joanna Marshall of Darby, Chester Co., she dec'd, and Elizabeth Lea, dau. of Isaac and Sarah Lea of the borough of Chester, same county, m. 22/9/1744.

Humphrey Marshall, son of Abraham and Mary Marshall, late of West Bradford Twp, Chester Co., dec'd, and Margaret Minshall, dau. of Thomas and Agnes Minshall of Middletown Twp, same county, the former dec'd, m. 10/1/1788.

Abraham Martin of Aston Twp, Chester Co. and Susannah Ruth, dau. of Francis Ruth, of the same place, m. 1/5/1782.

John Martin, son of Thomas Martin of Middletown Twp, Chester Co., yeoman, and Lydia Sharples, dau. of Joseph Sharples of the same place, yeoman, m. 21/8/1736.

Jonathan Martin, son of Thomas and Mary Martin of Middletown Twp, Chester Co., and Martha Squibb, dau. of Robert and Mary Squibb of Chester Twp, she dec'd, m. 9/4/1752.

Joseph Martin, son of Caleb and Hannah Martin of Upper Providence Twp, Chester Co., and Hannah Malin, dau. of William and Elizabeth Malin of Chester Co., m. 8/5/1788.

George Massey of Willistown Twp, Chester Co., son of Levi and Catherine Massey of the same county, latter dec'd, and Hannah Mattson of Aston Twp, Delaware Co., dau. of Levi and Sarah Mattson of Delaware Co., m. 5/6/1800.

Joseph Massey, son of Thomas Massey of Willistown, Chester Co., and Ann Morgan of Springfield Twp, same county, dau. of Henry Morgan, dec'd, m. 12/11/1766.

Mordecai Massey, son of Thomas Massey of Marple Twp, Chester Co., dec'd, and Rebekah Roods [Roades], dau. of Joseph Roades of same place, m. 22 April 1731.

John Matson of Edgmont Twp, Chester Co., and Hannah Norbury, dau. of Jacob Norbury, late of Middletown Twp, dec'd, m. 5/9/1741.

Solomon Mercer, son of Daniel Mercer of East Marlborough Twp, Chester Co., and Abigail Sharpless, dau. of Daniel Sharpless of Nether Providence Twp, same county, dec'd, m. 8/5/1782.

John Meredith, son of Moses and Mary Meredith of Edgmont Twp, Chester Co., and Hannah Harrison, dau. of Caleb and Elinor Harrison of Middletown Twp, same county, m. 25/11/1773.

Joseph Miflin, son of John Miflin of Philadelphia, and Deborah Richardson, dau. of Francis Richardson of the borough of Chester, Chester Co., m. 10/6/1773.

George Miller, Jr., son of George Miller of Upper Providence Twp, Delaware Co., and Mary Levis, dau. of Isaac Levis of Middletown Twp, same county, m. 10/4/1794.

Thomas Miller of the City of Philadelphia, victualler, and Elizabeth Hatton of the borough of Chester, Chester Co., m. 6/2/1721.

Samuel Milner, son of James Milner of Christiana Hundred, New Castle Co., Delaware, and Mary Yarnall, dau. of Philip Yarnall, late of Edgmont Twp, Chester Co., dec'd, m. 26/1/1741.

Jacob Minshall, son of Thomas and Agnes Minshall of Middletown Twp, Chester Co., and Ann Heacock, dau. of John and Sarah Heacock of the same place, she dec'd, m. 6/11/1777.

John Minshall, formerly of Hartshaw [Hardshaw-West] Monthly Meeting, county of Lancaster, England, now of the borough of Chester, Chester Co., cordwainer, and Hannah Saunders, formerly of the City of Philadelphia, now also of the borough of Chester, spinster, m. 14/6/1718.

Thomas Minshall, son of Jacob and Sarah Minshall, late of Middletown Twp, Chester Co., he dec'd, and Agnes Salkeld, dau. of John and Agnes Salkeld of Chester, m. 18/3/1738.

John Moor, son of Richard Moor, late of Radnor, Chester Co., dec'd, and Rachel Coppock, dau. of Jonathan Coppock, late of Springfield Twp, same county, dec'd, m. 22 Sep 1737.

James Morgan, son of John Morgan of Bucks Co., and Ann Heacock, dau. of Jonathan Heacock of Marple Twp, Chester Co., m. 23/3/1745.

John Morgan, son of James and Ann Morgan of Rockhill Twp, Bucks Co., PA, and Rebekah Porter, dau. of William and Elizabeth Porter, late of Little Creek Hundred, Kent Co., MD, dec'd, m. 2/6/1785.

Thomas Morgan of the town of Chester, Chester Co., and Hannah Carter, dau. of Jeremiah Carter of the same place, m. 17/3/1722.

Jonathan Morris of East Marlborough Twp, Chester Co., son of Jonathan Morris, and Alice Evans, dau. of Cadwalader Evans of Edgmont Twp, same county, m. 15/12/1757.

Isaac Moss of the City of Philadelphia, son of Abraham Moss, dec'd, and Mary Howard, dau. of Henry Howard of Edgmont Twp, Chester Co., m. 27/2/1749.

Joseph Newlan of Birmingham Twp, Chester Co., and Phebe Lewis, dau. of Samuel Lewis of Edgmont Twp, same county, 22/3/1740.

Cyrus Newlin of Brandywine Hundred in Newcastle Co. upon Delaware, son of Nathaniel Newlin, late of Concord, Chester Co., dec'd, and Abigail Pennell, dau. of Robert Pennell of Middletown Twp, m. 4/4/1776.

Nathaniel Newlin, son of Thomas and Joanna Newlin of Concord Twp, Delaware Co., she dec'd, and Mary Worrall, dau. of William and Phebe Worrall of Ridley Twp, same county, m. 4/11/1789.

Nicholas Newlin, son of Thomas Newlin and Joanna his wife, the latter dec'd, of Middletown Twp, Delaware Co., and Sarah Smith, dau. of John and Martha Smith, both dec'd, of the borough of Chester, same county, m. 29/12/1790.

Thomas Norbury of Greenwich Twp, Gloucester Co., New Jersey, labourer, and Susannah Beckham, dau. of Richard and Jane Beckham of the same place, spinster, m. 4 Oct 1722.

Thomas Norbury of Chester Co. and Ann Crockson, dau. of Randle Crockson of Providence Twp, same county, m. 14/4/1744.

Charles Norris of the City of Philadelphia, son of Isaac and Mary Norris, dec'd, and Mary Parker, dau. of Joseph Parker of the borough of Chester, Chester Co., and Mary his wife, dec'd, m. 21/6/1759.

David Ogden of Springfield Twp, Chester Co., son of Samuel Ogden, and Alice Eachus of the same place, m. 20/9/1746.

George Ogden, son of Samuel Ogden of Springfield Twp, Chester Co., dec'd, and Mary Low, dau. of John Low, late of Ridley Twp, same county, dec'd, m. 25/2/1751.

John Ogden, son of Stephan Ogden, late of Springfield Twp, Chester Co., dec'd, and Sarah Crozer, dau. of James Crozer of Springfield Twp, same county, m. 15/4/1773.

Samuel Ogden, son of David Ogden, late of Middletown Twp, Chester Co., dec'd, and Esther Lownes, dau. of George Lownes of Springfield Twp, same county, m. 26/3/1720.

John Owen, son of Robert Owen, formerly of Merion Twp, Philadelphia Co., yeoman, and Hannah Maris, dau. of George Maris of Springfield Twp, Chester Co., m. 20/8/1719.

Enos Painter of East Bradford Twp, Chester Co., son of James and Jane Painter of the same place, and Hannah Minshall of Middletown Twp, Delaware Co., dau. of Jacob and Ann Minshall of the same place, m. 8/5/1800.

William Paist of Springfield Twp, Delaware Co., son of William Paist of the same place, and Sarah Davis of the same place, dau. of Henry Davis, dec'd, m. 3/4/1794.

Asher Palmer, son of John and Hannah Palmer of Concord, Chester Co., and Alice Malin, dau. of Gideon and Phebe Malin of Upper Providence Twp, same county, m. 17/10/1782.

Jonathan Palmer of Makefield Twp, Bucks Co., PA, yeoman, son of John and Christian Palmer of the same place, and Sarah Simcock of Ridley Twp, Chester Co., widow, m. 27/12/1721/2.

Moses Palmer, son of Moses and Abigail Palmer of Concord Twp, Delaware Co., he dec'd, and Hannah Pennell, dau. of Joseph and Sarah Pennell of Aston Twp, same county, m. 2/2/1792.

Samuel Pancoast of Marple Twp, Chester Co., son of Seth Pancoast of Springfield Twp, Chester Co., and Mary Levis, dau. of John Levis of the same place, m. 18/4/1782.

Seth Pancoast, son of William Pancoast of Mansfield Twp, Burlington Co., New Jersey, and Esther Coppock, dau. of Bartholomew Coppock of Marple Twp, Chester Co., m. 21/3/1741.

Seth Pancoast of Marple Twp, Chester Co., son of William Pancoast, dec'd, and Ann Woolley of the same place, dau. of Thomas Woolly, dec'd, m. 20/3/1766.

William Pancoast, son of William Pancoast of Mansfield Twp, Burlington Co., NJ, and Mary Cowpland, dau. of William Cowpland of Chester, Chester Co., m. 31/10/1730.

Thomas Parke, son of Thomas Parke, late of Concord, Chester Co., dec'd, and Rebecca his wife, and Jane Edge, dau. of Jacob and Sarah Edge, formerly of Providence Twp, same county, m. 26/2/1739.

Joshua Parsons, son of Richard and Jemimah Parsons of Nether Providence Twp, Chester Co., and Rebecca Evans, dau. of John and Phebe Evans of Upper Providence Twp, Chester Co., m. 15/12/1786.

William Parsons of Nether Providence Twp, Delaware Co., son of Richard and Jemima Parsons of the same place, and Ann Paist of Springfield Twp, same county, dau. of William and Ann Paist of the said place, m. 17/10/1799.

Thomas Paschall, son of Thomas Paschall of Blockley Twp, Philadelphia Co., yeoman, and Margret Jones, spinster dau. of Rees Jones, late of Merion Twp in the same county, yeoman, dec'd, m. 6/10/1716

William Paschall, son of Thomas Paschall of Blockley Twp, Philadelphia Co., bachelor, and Grace Hoopes, dau. of Daniell Hoopes of Westtown, Chester Co., spinster, m. 21/2/1720.

Augustine Passmore of Milford Hundred, Cecil Co., MD, son of John Passmore of Chester Co., PA, and Hannah Howard, dau. of Henry Howard of Edgmont Twp, Chester Co., m. 28/1/1754.

Lawrence Pearson of Marple Twp, Chester Co., tailor, son of Thomas Pearson of the same place, yeoman, and Esther Massey, spinster dau. of Thomas Massey, late of Marple Twp, same county, yeoman, dec'd, m. 24/3/1711.

Thomas Pedrick, one of the sons of Philip and Elizabeth Pedrick, late of Chichester, Chester Co., dec'd, and Mary Cummings, one of the daus. of Enoch and Hannah Cummings, late of Broad Kiln [Broadkill] in the county of Sussex, PA [DE], she dec'd, m. 14/5/1752.

John Peirce, son of Caleb and Ann Peirce of Thornbury Twp, Chester Co., and Jane Dicks, dau. of Peter and Sarah Dicks, the former dec'd, of Lower Providence Twp, same county, m. 17/11/1786.

Joseph Peirce, son of Caleb Peirce of Thornbury Twp, Chester Co., and Sarah Pyle, dau. of Isaac Pyle of Bethel Twp, same county, 27/4/1785.

John Pennal, son of John and Mary Pennal of Aston Twp, Chester Co., and Martha Martin, dau. of Thomas and Mary Martin of Middletown Twp, same county, m. 12/4/1740.

Abraham Pennell, son of William Pennell of Middletown Twp, Chester Co. and Hannah Sharpless, dau. of Joseph Sharpless, late of the same place, m. 9/5/1776.

Dell Pennell, son of William Pennell, late of Middletown Twp, Chester Co., dec'd, and Mary his wife, and Hannah Hill, dau. of John and Mary Hill of the same place, m. 20/10/1785.

Joseph Pennell, son of Robert and Hannah Pennell of Middletown Twp, Chester Co., she dec'd, and Sarah Meredith, dau. of Moses and Mary Meredith of Edgmont Twp, same county, m. 5/4/1770.

Nathan Pennell, son of James Pennell, late of Middletown Twp, Chester Co., dec'd, and Susanna Talbot, dau. of Joseph Talbot of Aston Twp, same county, m. 10/4/1776.

Robert Pennell of Middletown Twp, Chester Co., and Susannah Fairlamb of the same place, widow, m. 9/11/1769.

Robert Pennell, son of Joseph and Sarah Pennell of Aston Twp, Delaware Co., and Ann Gibbons, dau. of Joseph and Margery Gibbons, dec'd, of Springfield Twp, same county, m. 27/4/1797.

Samuell Pennell, son of William Pennell of borough and county of Chester, tanner, and Sarah Norris, spinster dau. of Humphrey and Rachell Norris of Philadelphia, she dec'd, m. 6/7/1750.

Thomas Pennell, son of William Pennell of Chester Co., yeoman, and Mary Yarnall, dau. of John Yarnall of Edgmont Twp, same county, yeoman, m. 5/2/1739.

William Pennell of Middletown Twp, Chester Co., son of Robert and Hannah Pennell of the same place, and Mary Mearcer, dau. of Thomas and Mary Mearcer of Thornbury Twp, same county, m. 26/8/1710.

William Pennell, Jr., son of William Pennell of Middletown Twp, Chester Co. and Mary Dell, dau. of Thomas Dell, late of Ridley Twp, same county, dec'd, m. 25/2/1751.

Christopher Penrose, son of Robert and Mary Penrose of the City of Philadelphia, cooper, and Ann Hunter, dau. of Peter and Jane Hunter of Middletown Twp, Chester Co., m. 7/3/1719.

Robert Penrose, son of Robert Penrose of Marple Twp, Chester Co., and Mary Haycock, dau. of Jonathan Haycock, m. 13 Sep 1733.

Caleb Perkins of Concord Twp, Chester Co., blacksmith, and Ann Beakes, dau. of Margaret Todhunter of Westtown Twp, same county, daughter of Abraham Todhunter, dec'd, m. 20/2/1721. [Should be "stepdaughter of Abraham Todhunter." See Chester Minutes 25/11/1713.]

William Poole of borough of Wilmington, New Castle Co. on Delaware, miller, son of William and Elizabeth Poole, late of the same place, dec'd, and Sarah Sharpless, dau. of Benjamin and Martha Sharpless of Middletown Twp, Delaware Co., former dec'd, m. 5/5/1791.

David Powell of Newtown Twp, Chester Co., and Ann Hayes of the same place, m. 25/8/1718.

John Powell of Ridley Twp, Chester Co., son of John Powell of Goshen Twp, same county, and Amelia Vaughan, dau. of Isaac Vaughan of Haverford Twp, Chester Co., dec'd, m. 6/11/1788.

Jonas Preston of Chester Twp, Chester Co., and Mary Lea of the borough of Chester, same county, widow of John Lea, m. 14/4/1763.

Caleb Pusey, Jr., and Prudence Carter, dau. of Robert Carter, yeoman, m. 5/9/1712.

Joshua Pusey of London Grove Twp, Chester Co., and Hannah Canby of borough of Chester, same county, m. 6/11/1782.

William Pusey of Chester Twp, Chester Co., weaver, and Elizabeth Bowater, dau. of Francis Bowater of Middletown Twp, same county, m. 5/9/1707.

Benjamin Pyle of Darby Twp, Chester Co., mason, son of Jacob and Jane Pyle of Thornbury Twp, same county, and Sarah Haycock, dau.

of Joseph and Hannah Haycock of Marple Twp, same county, she dec'd, m. 8/12/1774.

Isaac Pyle of Bethel Twp, Delaware Co., son of Joseph and Sarah Pyle of the same place, latter dec'd, and Sarah Ogden of the same place, m. 5/9/1799.

Robert Pyle of Bethel Twp, Chester Co., and Susannah Turner of Providence Twp, same county, widow, m. 30/10/1720.

Robert Pyle, son of Daniel Pyle, late of Bethel Twp, Chester Co., dec'd, and Rebecca Hampton, dau. of Simon Hampton of Thornbury Twp, same county, m. 8/11/1753.

Morris Reese of Nottingham Twp, Chester Co., and Sarah Butterfield, dau. of Thomas Butterfield of Providence Twp, same county, m. 19/1/1718.

Joseph Regester, son of David and Margeret Regester of Edgmont Twp, Delaware Co., the former dec'd, and Sarah Russell, dau. of William and Susannah Russell of the same place, latter dec'd, m. 1/5/1798.

Joseph Reyners of the town of Chester, Chester Co., cordwainer, and Mary Johnston of the same place, dau. of Joshua and Mary Johnston, spinster, m. 24/9/1720.

Jacob Reynolds, son of Henry Reynolds of West Nottingham Twp, Cecil Co., Maryland, dec'd, and Sarah Lownes, dau. of Benanuel Lownes, late of Springfield Twp, Chester Co., dec'd, m. 14/5/1789.

Isaac Rhoads of Marple Twp, Chester Co., son of John and Elizabeth Rhoads of the same place, he dec'd, and Hannah Minshall, dau. of Thomas and Agnes Minshall of Middletown Twp, Chester Co., m. 17/4/1766.

James Rhoads, son of Joseph Rhoads, and Elizabeth Owen, dau. of John Owen of Springfield Twp, Chester Co., m. 22/6/1745.

Owen Rhoads, son of James Rhoads, late of Marple Twp, Chester Co., dec'd, and Mary Hall, dau. of John Hall of Springfield Twp, same county, m. 20/10/1785.

Samuel Richards, son of Samuel and Hannah Richards of Philadelphia, latter dec'd, and Mary Worrall, dau. of Peter and Abigail Worrall, late of Middletown Twp, Delaware Co., former dec'd, m. 18/5/1791.

Joshua Richardson, son of Joseph and Mary Richardson of Middletown Twp, Bucks Co., PA, yeoman, and Sarah Preston, dau. of Jonas Preston of Chester Twp, Chester Co., miller, and Jane, his wife, dec'd, m. 16/4/1761.

Nathaniel Ring of Chester Twp, Chester Co., son of Nathaniel Ring, late of Bradford Twp, Chester Co., dec'd, and Lydia Vernon, dau. of

Thomas Vernon of Providence Twp, same county, yeoman, m. 6/4/1728.

Ellis Roberts, son of Reuben Roberts of Lower Providence Twp, Delaware Co., and Ann Shaw, dau. of Joseph Adkinson, late of Bristol Twp, Bucks Co., dec'd, m. 2/5/1792.

Jonathan Robeson, son of John Robeson of Lower Merion Twp, Montgomery Co., PA, and Hannah Levis, dau. of Samuel Levis of Springfield Twp, Chester Co., m. 17/11/1785.

Nicholas Rogers of the City of Philadelphia, and Mary Pearson, dau. of Thomas Pearson of Marple Twp, Chester Co., m. 22/7/1720.

James Rushton of Middletown Twp, Chester Co., weaver, and Ann Trego, dau. of Peter and Judith Trego of the same place, m. 11/6/1725.

William Russell, son of William and Mary Russell, dec'd, of Edgmont Twp, Delaware Co., and Lydia Sharpless, dau. of Samuel Sharples, dec'd, and Jane his wife of Middletown Twp, same county, m. 2/6/1791.

David Salkeld, son of John Salkeld, late of Chester Twp, Chester Co., dec'd, and Mary Serman, dau. of William Serman of Middletown Twp, same county, m. 29/10/1743.

John Salkeld, Jr., son of John and Agnes Salkeld of the town of Chester, Chester Co., and Elizabeth Worrall, spinster, m. 13/11/1731.

William Salkeld of Middletown Twp, Chester Co., son of David and Mary Salkeld, late of Chester, he dec'd, and Sarah Hampton of Upper Providence Twp, same county, dau. of Samuel and Sarah Hampton, late of Philadelphia, he dec'd, m. 17/11/1774.

John Scholler of Springfield Twp, Chester Co., yeoman, and Jane Coppock of Springfield Twp, same county, widow, m. 9/7/1719.

John Scott, son of James Scott of Cast Town, Chester Co. and Elizabeth Maris, dau. of Joseph Maris, late of Springfield Twp, dec'd, m. 3/11/1774.

Daniel Sharples, son of John Sharples of Ridley Twp, Chester Co., and Sarah Coppock, dau. of Bartholomew Coppock of Marple Twp, same county, m. 15/2/1736.

Isaac Sharples, son of Benjamin and Martha Sharples of Middletown Twp, Chester Co., and Elizabeth Talbot, dau. of Joseph and Hannah Talbot of Aston Twp, same county, she dec'd, m. 13/2/1777.

James Sharples of Nether Providence Twp, Chester Co., yeoman, and Mary Edge, dau. of John Edge of the same place, m. 3/1/1697.

James Sharples, son of James Sharples of Providence Twp, Chester Co., and Elizabeth Taylor, dau. of Isaac Taylor of Springfield Twp, same county, m. 12/4/1729.

John Sharples of Ridley Twp, Chester Co., and Hannah Pennell, dau. of Robert Pennell of Middletown Twp, same county, m. 23/9/1692.

William Sharples, son of Joseph Sharples of Middletown Twp, Chester Co., and Mary Martin, dau. of Jonathan Martin of the same place, m. 4/6/1778.

Amos Sharpless, son of Joseph and Mary Sharpless, former dec'd, and Lydia Hill, dau. of John and Mary Hill, all of Middletown Twp, Delaware Co., m. 17/10/1793.

George Sharpless of Philadelphia, son of John Sharpless of Lower Providence Twp, Chester Co., and Mary Lewis, dau. of John Lewis of Ridley Twp, same county, m. 19/11/1761.

Joshua Sharpless of Middletown Twp, Chester Co., son of Benjamin Sharples of the same place, and Edith Yarnall, dau. of Nathan Yarnall of Edgmont Twp, same county, m. 15/12/1768.

Nathan Sharpless, son of Joseph Sharpless, dec'd, of Middletown Twp, Chester Co., and Rachel Pennell, dau. of William Pennell, dec'd, of the same place, m. 7/4/1785.

Thomas Sharpless, son of Daniel and Sarah Sharpless of Nether Providence Twp, Chester Co., and Martha Preston, dau. of Jonas and Jane Preston of Chester, same county, she dec'd, m. 23/6/1763.

Anthony Shaw of borough of Chester, Chester Co., shoemaker, son of John and Rebeckah Shaw of Kendall, [county of Westmoreland], England, she dec'd, and Mary Salkeld, spinster dau. of John and Agnes Salkeld of Chester Twp, Chester Co., m. 29/2/1731.

Joseph Shipley, son of Thomas Shipley of borough of Wilmington, New Castle Co. on Delaware and Mary his wife, dec'd, and Mary Levis, dau. of Samuel and Mary Levis of Springfield Twp, Chester Co., m. 19/10/1775.

William Shipley of Ridley Twp, Chester Co., yeoman, and Elizabeth Lewis, dau. of Samuel Levis of Springfield Twp, same county, m. 30/4/1728.

Jacob Simcock of Ridley Twp, Chester Co., yeoman, and Alice Maris of Holmhouse, same county, m. 15/11/1684.

Ambrose Smedley of Middletown Twp, Chester Co., son of George and Mary Smedley, late of Middletown Twp, he dec'd, and Mary Taylor, dau. of Peter and Elizabeth Taylor of Upper Providence Twp, same county, m. 23/6/1768.

Francis Smedley, son of Thomas Smedley of Willistown Twp, Chester Co., and Ann Hunter, dau. of Jonathan Hunter, late of Middletown Twp, same county, dec'd, m. 24/4/1742.

George Smedley, Jr., of Middletown Twp, Chester Co., yeoman, and Jane Sharples, dau. of John and Hannah Sharples of Ridley Twp, same county, m. 2/3/1717.

George Smedley of Middletown Twp, Chester Co., and Mary Hammans, dau. of William and Margaret Hammans of Upper Providence Twp, same county, m. 14/10/1727.

Peter Smedley, son of William Smedley, late of Middletown Twp, Chester Co., dec'd, and Elizabeth his wife, and Phebe Sharples, dau. of Samuel and Jane Sharples of the same place, m. 6/6/1782.

Thomas Smedley of Upper Providence Twp, Chester Co., son of George Smedley and Mary his wife late of Middletown Twp, dec'd, and Elizabeth Rhoads, dau. of John Rhoads, late of Marple Twp, same county, dec'd, and Elizabeth his wife, m. 20/6/1776.

Thomas Smedley, son of Thomas and Lydia Smedley of Willistown Twp, Chester Co. and Abigail Yarnall, dau. of Isaac and Mary Yarnall, late of Edgmont Twp, Chester Co., now Delaware Co., m. 3/6/1790.

William Smedley of Middletown Twp, Chester Co., son of George Smedley, and Elizabeth Taylor, dau. of Peter Taylor, late of Upper Providence Twp, same county, dec'd, m. 5/10/1753.

William Smedley, son of William and Elizabeth Smedley, late of Middletown Twp, Chester Co., now Delaware Co., dec'd, and Deborah Lightfoot, dau. of Joseph and Deborah Lightfoot, late of Maiden Creek Twp, Berks Co., PA, dec'd, m. 5/12/1793.

John Smith, formerly of Dartmouth in New England, son of Eliezer and Ruth Smith of the same place, and Ann Pusey, dau. of Caleb Pusey of Chester, Chester Co., m. 5/1/1706/7.

John Smith of Lower Chichester Twp, Chester Co., and Dorothy Graham of borough of Chester, same county, dau. of William Graham, late of said borough, dec'd, by Eleanor his wife, m. 3/12/1783.

Tristram Smith of the borough of Chester, Chester Co., son of John and Elizabeth Smith, late of Lower Chichester Twp, same county, she dec'd, and Lydia Beakes of the same place, dau. of Steney [Stephen] Beakes and Mary his wife, late of Trenton, New Jersey, dec'd, m. 5/4/1770.

Nathaniel Squibb, son of Robert Squibb of Chester Twp, Chester Co., and Mary his wife, dec'd, and Margery Person, dau. of Enoch

Pearson, dec'd, and Mary his wife of the same county, m. 15/11/1759.

Robert Squibb of Chester Twp, Chester Co., labourer, and Mary Coebourn, dau. of Thomas Coebourn of the same place, spinster, m. 19/8/1721.

Edward Stabler of Petersburg, VA, merchant, son of Edward Stabler of the City of York, Yorkshire, England, and Mary Robinson, dau. of William Robinson, late of Chester, Chester Co., dec'd, m. 3/11/1757.

Acquilla Starr, son of James Starr of Middletown Twp, Delaware Co., and Abigail James, dau. of Joseph James, dec'd, of Upper Providence Twp, m. 9/6/1796.

James Starr of Charlestown Twp, Chester Co., and Sarah Minshall, dau. of John Minshall of Middletown Twp, same county, m. 13//4/1769.

Jeremiah Starr, son of John Starr, formerly of Cavan Co., Ireland, now of Berks Co., PA, and Hannah Sharpless, dau. of John Sharpless of Chester Co., m. 24/4/1760.

Thomas Steel of Upper Providence Twp, Delaware Co., son of Andrew and Mary Steel, former dec'd, and Mary Hill, dau. of John and Mary Hill of Middletown Twp, same county, m. 6/11/1794.

William Surman of Middletown Twp, Chester Co. and Sarah Howell of Edgmont Twp, same county, m. 10/10/1741.

William Swaffer of Nether Providence Twp, Chester Co., husbandman, and Mary Caudwell of Ridley Twp, same county, dau. of Rebeccah Caudwell, widow, m. -/6/1694.

William Swaffer of the borough of Chester, Chester Co., and Abigail Worrall of Middletown Twp, same county, widow, m. 8/9/1774.

Francis Swaine, Marlborough Twp, Chester Co., and Esther Dicks of Providence Twp, same county, m. 10/4/1724.

William Swaine, son of Francis and Elizabeth Swaine of Marlborough Twp, Chester Co., and Elizabeth Dell, dau. of Thomas and Mary Dell of Ridley Twp, same county, m. 29/7/1720.

Thomas Swayne, son of William and Elizabeth Swayne of East Marlborough, Chester Co., she dec'd, and Mary Sharpless, dau. of John and Elizabeth Sharpless of Ridley Twp, same county, m. 18/3/1749.

Jacob Talbot, son of Joseph Talbot of Middletown Twp, Chester Co., and Susannah Sharples, dau. of Samuel Sharples of the same place, m. 22/11/1770.

Joseph Talbot, son of Joseph Talbot of Middletown Twp, Chester Co.,
and Hannah Pennall, dau. of James Pennall of the same place, m.
13/1/1762.

Joseph Tanyer and Rebecca Vernon of Ridley Twp, Chester Co., m.
16/11/1752.

Evan Taylor, son of Nathan Taylor of Upper Providence Twp, Chester
Co., and Amy Moore, dau. of Thomas Moore of the same place, m.
18/3/1772.

Isaac Taylor of Thornbury Twp, Chester Co., son of John Taylor, late
of Pennsborough, same county, dec'd, and Sarah Baker, dau. of
Jesse Baker of Thornbury Twp, Chester Co., m. 12/2/1784.

Joseph Taylor, son of Isaac Taylor, formerly of Springfield Twp,
Chester Co., and Mary Maris, dau. of John Maris of the same place,
m. 29/9/1722. [Year supplied by the minutes.]

Mordecai Taylor, son of Peter Taylor of Providence Twp, Chester Co.,
and Esther Sharples, dau. of James Sharples of the same county, m.
18/3/1738.

Peter Taylor, son of Peter Taylor, late of Upper Providence Twp,
Chester Co., dec'd, and Elizabeth Hall, dau. of John Hall of
Springfield Twp, same county, yeoman, m. 17/2/1746.

Philip Taylor of Thornbury Twp, Chester Co., yeoman, son of Francis
Taylor, and Ann Conway of Upper Providence Twp, same county,
dau. of Thomas and Mary Conway, he dec'd, m. 6/10/1705.

Robert Taylor, son of Josiah Taylor of Marple Twp, Chester Co.,
doctor, and Jane Schollar of Springfield Twp, same county, widow,
m. 21/3/1724.

Thomas Taylor, son of Thomas Taylor, late of Springfield Twp, Chester
Co., dec'd, and Mary Adams, dau. of William Adams of Fallowfield
Twp, Chester Co., m. 11/4/1730.

William Temple, son of Thomas Temple of Pennsbury Twp, Chester
Co., and Alice Lownes, dau. of Benamuel Lownes, late of Springfield
Twp, same county, dec'd, m. 5/12/1776.

Joseph Thatcher, son of William and Sarah Thatcher of Thornbury
Twp, Chester Co., and Abigail Worrall, dau. of Peter Worrall, late of
Middletown Twp, Chester Co., dec'd, m. 27/4/1785.

Benjamin Thomas of City of Philadelphia, sadler, son of Richard
Thomas, late of Warrington Twp in Bucks Co., PA, dec'd, and
Susannah Yarnell, dau. of Job Yarnall, late of Ridley Twp, Chester
Co., dec'd, m. 12/9/1765.

Joshua Thomas of Marple Twp, Chester Co., and Sarah Taylor, dau. of Peter and Elizabeth Taylor of Upper Providence Twp, same county, m. 16/5/1788.

Peter Thomas, son of Peter Thomas of Willistown Twp, Chester Co., and Margaret Taylor, dau. of Peter Taylor, late of Providence Twp, same county, dec'd, m. 14/2/1742.

Thomas Thomas, son of Jacob and Sarah Thomas of Newtown Twp, Delaware Co., dec'd, and Mary Minshall, dau. of Thomas and Agnes Minshall of Middletown Twp, same county, the former dec'd, m. 7/4/1791.

William Thomas, son of Thomas Thomas of Newtown Twp, Chester Co., and Rebecca Camm, dau. of Henry Camm of Providence Twp, same county, m. 11/3/1749.

Edward Thompson, son of Henry and Prudence Thompson, now dwelling in Upper Providence Twp, Chester Co., weaver, and Mary Barrett, dau. of Giles and Mary Barrett, dec'd, m. 6/11/1713.

John Thomson, son of Joshua Thomson of Ridley Twp, Chester Co., and Ann Yarnall, dau. of John Yarnall of Edgmont Twp, same county, m. 10/10/1747.

Mordecai Thomson, son of Joshua Thomson of Ridley Twp, Chester Co., and Hannah Collier, dau. of Isaac and Ruth Collier of Springfield Twp, same county, m. 22/8/1741.

John Tomlinson of Gloucester Twp and County, New Jersey, and Mary Fairlamb, dau. of Nicholas Fairlamb, late of Chester, dec'd, m. 9/10/1736.

Joseph Tomlinson, son of Joseph Tomlinson, late of the town of Gloucester, Gloucester Co., New Jersey, dec'd, and Elizabeth his wife, and Catherine Fairlamb, dau. of Nicholas Fairlamb, late of Middletown Twp, Chester Co., dec'd, m. 8/4/1738.

Francis Townsend, son of Joseph Townsend of East Bradford, Chester Co., dec'd, and Rachel Talbot, dau. of Joseph Talbot of Middletown, same county, m. 8/7/1762.

Peter Trego, son of Peter and Judith Trego of Middletown Twp, Chester Co., and Ann Whiteaker, dau. of Charles and Hannah Whiteaker of Ridley Twp, same county, m. 5/11/1726/7.

Morris Truman, son of James and Mary Truman of Philadelphia, and Mary Sharples, dau. of Joseph Sharples, late of Middletown Twp, Chester Co., dec'd, and Mary his wife, m. 5/7/1781.

Joseph Tucker, son of Thomas and Mary Tucker, late of Chester Twp, Delaware Co., dec'd, and Margaret Sankey of Nether Providence

Twp in the same county, dau. of Giles and Margaret Sankey, she dec'd, m. 10/10/1794.

George Valentine, son of Robert and Rachel Valentine, late of East Caln Twp, Chester Co., dec'd, and Phebe Ashbridge, dau. of George and Rebekah Ashbridge, late of Goshen Twp, same county, dec'd, m. 20/11/1788.

Aaron Vernon, son of John Vernon, formerly of Providence Twp, Chester Co., and Margaret Woodward, dau. of Edward Woodward of Middletown Twp, same county, m. 23/12/1732.

Abraham Vernon, son of Jacob and Ann Vernon of Thornbury Twp, Chester Co., and Lydia Sharples, dau. of James and Mary Sharples of Providence Twp, same county, m. 14/10/1726.

Jacob Vernon, son of Robert Vernon of Providence Twp, Chester Co., doctor, and Elinor Owen, dau. of Thomas Owen of Whiteland, Chester Co., m. 5/4/1712.

Jonathan Vernon, son of Thomas and Lydia Vernon of Providence Twp, Chester Co., yeoman, and Ann Engle of Middletown Twp, same county, widow, m. 19/8/1738.

Moses Vernon, son of John Vernon of Providence Twp, Chester Co., and Abigail Woodward, dau. of Edward Woodward of Middletown Twp, same county, m. 23/10/1730.

Nathaniel Vernon, son of Thomas and Liddia Vernon of Providence Twp, Chester Co., and Mary Salkeld, widow of William Salkeld, late of Chester, same county, m. 13/7/1744.

Thomas Vernon of Nether Providence Twp, Chester Co., and Lydia Ralfe, m. 13/8/1702.

Enoch Walker of Tredyffrin Twp, Chester Co., son of Joseph and Sarah Walker, the latter dec'd, and Phebe Miller, dau. of George and Phebe Miller, dec'd, of Upper Providence Twp, Delaware Co., m. 9/6/1797.

William Waln of Ridley Twp, Chester Co., son of Nicholas and Jane Waln of Northern Liberties, Philadelphia Co., and Ann Hall of Springfield Twp, Chester Co., dau. of Samuell and Mary Hall, also of Springfield Twp, m. 18/11/1721/2.

Nathaniel Walter of Concord Twp, Delaware Co., son of William and Rachel Walter of the same place, and Rachel Sharples of Middletown Twp, same county, dau. of Samuel and Jane Sharples of the same place, m. 10/4/1800.

John Warner, son of Isaac Warner of Blockley Twp, Philadelphia Co., and Sarah Norbery, dau. of Jacob Norbery, late of Middletown Twp, Chester Co., dec'd, m. 20/3/1742.

Joshua Way of Edgmont Twp, Chester Co., son of Robert Way, late of Edgmont Twp, same county, dec'd, and Elizabeth Lewis, dau. of Samuel and Phebe Lewis of the same place, m. 18/9/1731.

Isaac Weaver, son of Richard and Elizabeth Weaver of the borough of Chester, Chester Co., tanner, and Sarah Dell, dau. of Thomas Dell, Jr., of Ridley Twp, same county, m. 20/7/1750.

William Webb, Jr., son of William and Rebeckah Webb of Kennet Twp, Chester Co., and Elizabeth Hoopes, dau. of Daniell and Jane Hoopes of Westtown Twp., also Chester Co., m. 23/9/1732.

William Webster of Marlborough Twp, Chester Co., and Sarah James, dau. of George James, late of Springfield Twp, same county, dec'd, m. 4/11/1720.

William Webster of Middletown Twp, Delaware Co., son of Joseph and Rebecca Webster, former dec'd, and Lydia Sharples of the same county, dau. of Joseph and Mary Sharples, dec'd, m. 4/12/1800.

John Weldon of Chester Twp, Chester Co., and Sarah Coebourn of Aston Twp, same county, m. 17/1/1725.

Thomas West, son of Thomas West of Concord, Chester Co., and Susannah Powell, dau. of Thomas Powell, late of Upper Providence Twp, same county, dec'd, m. 21/3/1736.

Thomas West of the City of Philadelphia, cordwainer, son of Thomas West, late of Concord Twp, Chester Co., dec'd, and Sarah Yarnall, dau. of Job Yarnall, late of Ridley Twp, Chester Co., dec'd, m. 10/5/1764.

William West of Concord Twp, Chester Co., yeoman, and Deborah Coppock, dau. of Bartholomew Coppock of Springfield Twp, same county, m. 12/8/1709.

John Wharton of Chester, sadler, son of Thomas Wharton, late of the City of Philadelphia, dec'd, and Rachel his wife, and Mary Dobbins of Chester, dau. of James Dobbins, late of Philadelphia, dec'd, m. 2/9/1727.

James Wickersham of East Marleborough, Chester Co., and Ann Eachus of Springfield Twp, same county, m. 22/2/1736.

William Willkins of Donfield, Gloucester Co., New Jersey, son of William Willkins, dec'd, and Mary Beckam, dau. of Richard Beckham, weaver, of Greenwich Twp in the same county, m. 4/9/1724. [Spelled Wilkins in minutes.]

John Willson, formerly of Ireland, now of Birmingham Twp, Chester Co., chapman, and Ruth Hinde, dau. of James Hinde of Chester Twp, same county, m. 3/11/1720.

Thomas Wilson of Ridley Twp, Chester Co., and Jane Larkin, widow of Upper Providence Twp, same county, m. 27/4/1775.

Cornelius Wood, son of Nathan and Hannah Wood of Wilmington, New Castle Co., Delaware, and Mary Sharpless, dau. of Samuel and Jane Sharpless of Middletown, Chester Co., m. 11/11/1762.

James Wood, son of James and Mary Wood of Ridley Twp, Chester Co., and Sarah Dicks, dau. of Joseph and Ann Dicks of Nether Providence Twp, same county, m. 14/12/1775.

Edward Woodward, son of Richard Woodward, and Abigail Edge, dau. of John and Jane Edge of Providence Twp, Chester Co., m. 24/3/1705.

Edward Woodward, son of Edward Woodward of Middletown Twp, Chester Co., and Sarah Sharples, dau. of James Sharples of Providence Twp, same county, m. 21/1/1733.

Edward Woodward of Newtown Twp, Chester Co., and Elizabeth Tayler of Providence Twp, same county, m. 15/4/1743.

Jesse Woodward, son of Thomas Woodward of Ridley Twp, Chester Co, and Jane Kendell, dau. of Thomas Kendell of Springfield Twp, same county, m. 5/9/1730.

Richard Woodward of Springfield Twp, Chester Co., and Mary Brittan of the same place, widow, m. 5/1/1717/18.

John Worral, son of Peter Worrall of Marple Twp, Chester Co., and Hannah Taylor, dau. of Jonathan Taylor, formerly of the same place, m. 20/4/1723.

Benjamin Worrall, son of Peter Worrall of Marple Twp, Chester Co., and Phebe Edwards, dau. of John Edwards of Middletown Twp, same county, m. 23/4/1743.

Elisha Worrall, son of Joseph and Margaret Worrell of Upper Providence Twp, Chester Co., and Mary Maris of Springfield Twp, same county, dau. of Joseph Maris, late of the same place, dec'd, and Ann his wife, m. 6/6/1765.

James Worrall, son of Peter Worrall of Marple Twp, Chester Co., and Hannah Calvert of Upper Providence Twp, same county, m. 24/5/1735.

James Worrell of Marple Twp, Chester Co., son of Peter Worrell, dec'd, and Ann Edge of the borough of Chester, same county, widow of George Edge, m. 11/1/1759.

John Worrall of Edgmont Twp, Chester Co., and Sarah Goodwin, dau. of Thomas Goodwin of the same place, m. 9/4/1714.

John Worrall, son of John Worrall of Edgmont Twp, Chester Co., and Priscilla Lewis, dau. of Samuel Lewis of the same place, m. 18/4/1741.

Joshua Worrall, son of John Worrall, late of Marple Twp, Chester Co., dec'd, and Margaret Spoonly, dau. of Lewis Spoonly of the same place, m. 23/1/1727.

Thomas Worrall, son of John Worrall, late of Middletown, Chester Co., dec'd, and Hannah his wife, and Lydia Vernon, dau. of Jonathan and Ann Vernon of Lower Providence Twp, same county, m. 4/3/1762.

John Worrelow, yeoman, son of Thomas Worrelow, and Ann Maris, dau. of George Maris of Springfield Twp, Chester Co., m. 14/8/1690.

John Yarnal of Willistown, Chester Co. yeoman, and Mary Edge of Upper Providence Twp, same county, widow, m. 7/9/1739.

Thomas Yarnal of Edgmont Twp, Chester Co., and Martha Hammans, dau. of William Hammans of Providence Twp, same county, m. 21/9/1734.

Caleb Yarnall, son of Thomas and Martha Yarnall, late of Edgmont Twp, Chester Co., he dec'd, and Phebe Minshall, dau. of Thomas and Agnes Minshall of Middletown Twp, same county, m. 8/12/1774.

Ezekiel Yarnall, son of William and Mary Yarnall of Edgmont Twp, Chester Co., and Sarah Hall, dau. of Samuel and Sarah Hall of Goshen, same county, m. 6/5/1784.

John Yarnall, son of Philip Yarnall of Edgmont Twp, Chester Co., bachelor, and Abigail Williamson, dau. of Daniell Williamson of Newtown Twp, same county, spinster, m. 11/9/1719.

Mordecai Yarnall of Philadelphia, son of Francis Yarnall, late of Springfield Twp, Chester Co., dec'd, and Ann Maris of Springfield Twp, Chester Co., dau. of William Shipley of Wilmington in New Castle Co., m. 3/3/1768.

Nathan Yarnall, son of Philip and Dorothy Yarnall of Edgmont Twp, Chester Co., and Rachel Jackson, dau. of Ephraim Jackson of the same place, m. 13/8/1731.

Nathan Yarnall of Edgmont Twp, Chester Co., and Jane Bazer of Chester, same county, widow of John Bazer of the same county, m. 5/1/1769.

Peter Yarnall of Concord Twp, Chester Co., son of Mordecai Yarnall, late of Springfield Twp, dec'd, and Hannah Sharples, dau. of Benjamin Sharples of Middletown Twp, Chester Co., m. 5/9/1782.

Philip Yarnall, son of Philip Yarnall of Edgmont Twp, Chester Co., bachelor, and Mary Hoopes, dau. of Daniell Hoopes of Westtown Twp, same county, spinster, m. 24/2/1720.

Samuel Yarnall, son of Nathan Yarnall of Concord Twp, Delaware Co., and Mary Harrison, dau. of Caleb Harrison of Chester Twp, same county, m. 3/7/1793.

William Yarnall, son of William and Mary Yarnall of Edgmont Twp, Delaware Co., and Mary Porter, dau. of William and Elizabeth Porter, late of Little Creek Hundred, Kent Co. on Delaware, MD, dec'd, m. 31/3/1791.

Following is additional information on a few Quakers who married out:

Virgil Eaches and Bethsheba Webb m. 4 Jan 1791 at St. Michael's and Zion Lutheran Church, Philadelphia Co.

John Mather and Mary Hopkins, dau. of John and Ruth, m. 27 Feb 1730 at St. Paul's in Chester.

Samuel Levis, son of Samuel and Hannah, and Hannah Stretch m. 15th da, 10th mo, 1709 in Philadelphia. Wit: Peter and Margery Stretch.

Esther Vernon, dau. of Thomas and Lydia, m. 1st on 24 June 1741 James Milner at Swedes Church, Delaware; m. 2nd Abraham Ashton.

Thomas Worrall and Ruth Pennell m. Jan 4, 1791, at St. Michael's and Zion Lutheran Church in Philadelphia Co.

Eli Yarnall and Priscilla Walker, dau. of Joseph and Sarah Walker, m. 26th da, 7th mo, 1783 at Great Valley.

CHESTER MONTHLY MEETING MINUTES

*Appearing on the first page of the old book after the fly leaf
and just before the minutes which commence on the second page is the
following entry, an acknowledgment by William Clayton. The date is
gone; however, as Prudence Reynolds was married before Chester
Monthly Meeting was established this was probably presented to
Burlington Monthly Meeting.*

"15 day of the 7 month in the year ... I will: Clayton the ellder
doe in the fear and dread of the Lord and in the hewmillity of my Soull
acknowledg that I did sin agayens god and frindes and broak the good
order of truth in consenting to the marriage of my daster prudent to
hendry Runolls hee beeing noot a faythful frind hoping that you my
frindes of the montyly meeting will as freely forgivf mee as i hawfe
freely confesed the same and as you for Christ sake woolld have god to
forgivfe you"

*The following names were subscribers, ca. 1690/1691, for the
building of the meeting house in Chester:* Thomas Powell; Thomas
Brassey; Randall Varnon; Thomas Varnon; John Sharples; Walter
Faucet; John Hoghkins; Caleb Pusey; Robert Barber; Joshua Hastings;
John Baldwin; John Broomall; John Bristow; John Simcocke; William
Woodmansee; Jacob Simcock; James Sharples; Andrew Job; James
Whittacree; Mordecai Maddock; John Simcock, Jr.; Robert Taylor;
Edward Walter; Edward Carter; John Beall; Charles Brookes; William
Browne; Thomas Vernon, yongr.; Francis Worly; Willm. Coborne;
Joseph Coborne; John Edge; John Corsby; John Parker; John Martin;
Thomas Martin; Nathan Evans; John Churchman; Henry ---; Thomas
Coebourne; John Worall; Randell Maillen; Robert Vernon; Thomas
Minshall; Peter Tailler; Joseph Vernon and Jacob Vernon; John
Hoskins, jonnt.[?]; James Swaford; William Swaford; Henry Worly;
John Powell; Thomas Joans; Lawrance Rooth; George Churchman.

MEN'S AND WOMEN'S COMBINED MINUTES

10/11/1681. A Monthly Meeting of Friends belonging to Marcus Hook,
alias Chichester (and Upland) Meeting, was held at the house of
Robert Wales, William Clayton, Jr., and Elizabeth Bezor of
Chichester.

2/8/1682. John Bales to marry Mary Clayton.

6/9/1682. John Grist and Ann Butt granted permission to marry.

3/7/1683. John Langworthy to marry Jane Cool.

5/9/1683. John Worrall to marry widow [Frances] Taylor; John was required to clear himself of some reports of him from England.

2/2/1684. A difference has arisen between George Gleve and John Nickson.

6/8/1684. William Brown of Chichester to marry Ann Mercer.

3/9/1684. A difference has arisen between Nathaniel Evans and Charles Brooks.

1/10/1684. John Kingsman to marry Hannah Simcock. Thomas Norbery to marry Frances Hough. [He to bring up her child as his own and to pay quit rent for that land in Newtown being head land taken up by the child's father.]

2/1/1685. James Swafor to marry Elizabeth Hoolstone; he to bring a certificate. Peter Taylor to marry Sarah Hoolston. William Gregory to marry Rebeckah Hoolston.

2/4/1685. Peter Lester to marry Mary Duncalf.

7/7/1685. Daniell Williamson to marry Mary Smith.

1/9/1685. Hugh Durborow to marry Elizabeth Taylor.

4/11/1685/6. Thomas Cartwright of this county, husbandman, to marry Jane Langley. David Ogden of Chester Co. to marry Martha Holston of the same.

1/1/1686. A difference has arisen between Joseph Richards and Hugh Durborow. William Cobourn to marry Mary Baker. Peter Thomas to marry Sarah Stedman.

7/4/1686. William Malin of Providence to marry Mary Stephenson. Anthony Weaver to marry Ann Richards of Northly; though Anthony owns himself to be none of us, he is willing to submit to the order of Friends.

6/7/1686. Francis Yarnall of Darby Monthly Meeting to marry Hannah Baker. Thomas Bowater to marry Sarah Edge.

6/9/1686. William Woodmanson acknowledged that he spoke foolishly when he compared Joseph Richards to a London pickpocket.

3/10/1686. Jonathan Lively of the town of Dublin in Philadelphia Co. to marry Rachell Taylor, he to bring a certificate.

7/1/1687. Charles Whitacer to marry Sarah Backer (Baker).

6/4/1687. A difference arose between Thomas Holingsworth and John Calvert about dividing their lands in the township of Upper Providence.

4/5/1687. Josiah Taylor and Mary Williamson, wife of Daniell Williamson, reported for some unsavory and disorderly carriages.

7/9/1687. George Gleves to marry Esther Powell [widow of Joseph Powell]. George Gleves promised to make over his land to the orphans court to pay Joseph Powell's children's portions according to the will.

2/11/1687. Henry Hams intends to take Rebecah Finch to wife. [No further mention.]

4/12/1687. John Cooke of Bucks Co. to marry Mary Simcock of Chester Co.

4/4/1688. Robert Brothers and Rebecah Bracey were asked by the Meeting to desist and proceed no further.

2/5/1688. Subscribing to a position against giving, trading or selling liquor to the Indians: Robert Taylor, John Worrall, Edward Keninson, John Simcock, Andrew Job, John Bristoll, Thomas Bracy, John Hasting, Randall Vernon, Jacob Simcock, Thomas Vernon, Joshua Hastings, Caleb Pusey, William Woodmanson, John Bailes, Thomas Martin, James Kenerly, Richard Few, Walter Faucit, Robert Vernon, Joseph Baker, [Ep]hraim Jackson, [Ra]ndall Malin, Joseph Richards, Thomas Minshall, William Edwards, Peter Chaler [Taylor?], John Edge, Joseph Edge, John Bowater, James Swaford, George Maris, Bartho: Coppock, Robert Peniell, John Worrilow, Henry Worley, Joseph Peniell, Peter Thomas, Paul Sanders, Daniell Hoopes, Aron James, Elis David, Robert Williams, John Sharples, Joseph Carter, Bartho: Coppock, Senr., Joseph Jervis, Francis Yearnall, Thomas Woodward, George Smedley, Cadwalader Ellis, Peter Dix, Joseph Baker, Jr., Edward Carter, Joseph Cookson, Thomas Powell, Thomas Dross, David Ogden, John Martin, Robert Baker, George Gleave, Henry Hains, William Swaford, Richard Barnet, Charles Brooks, Thomas Vernon, John Churchman, Thomas Massey, Rice Hinton, James Sirrell, George Asbridg, David Jones, William Cobourn, Philip Yearnall, John Lee.

10/7/1688. Robert Carter to marry Liddia Walley.

3/10/1688. William Edwards of Middletown to marry Jane Attkinson of Ridley.

4/1/1688/9. A difference arose between Thomas Lively and John Hodgkins about a lot in Philadelphia. Benjamin Mendinghall to marry Ann Pennill of Chichester Monthly Meeting.

1/2/1689. Isaack Few proposes to marry Jane Theacher, dau. of Richard Theacher of Chichester Monthly Meeting. John Baldwin proposed his intentions of marriage with Katherin Turner, widow of Philadelphia.

John Medford to marry Martha Cobourn; Mary Cobourn, wife of William Cobourn and Mary Cobourn, dau. of Thomas Cobourn, to inquire into her clearness.

1/5/1689. Isaac Taylor, son of Robert Taylor, proposed his intentions to marry Sarah Broadwell, dau. of Mary Broadwell of Dublin Monthly Meeting in Philadelphia Co.

8/7/1689. John Worrall and Richard Barnet reported for reaping on First Day. John Howell and his wife reported for absenting themselves from meetings.

6/11/1689. James Stanfield published his intentions to marry Mary Hutcheson, dau. of George Huchenson of Burlington. William Cureton, son of Richard and Margret Cureton of Haverford Monthly Meeting, and Mary Cobourn, dau. of Thomas Cobourn, expressed their intentions to marry, he to bring a certificate and his parents' consent.

3/1/1690. Josiah Taylor to marry Elizabeth Pennell, their parents being present gave their consent. On the differences between William Gabetas and Mary Pennell regarding her son, William Gabetas instructed to give Mary Pennell 20 shillings and a new pair of shoes for the lad for his services and Gabetas should deliver the boy to his mother along with all her husband's tools in his custody.

7/2/1690. Josiah Taylor to marry Elizabeth Pennell. David Merideth of Radnor to marry Mary Jones.

2/4/1690. Thomas Thomson, son of John Thomson of Elsenburg, West Jersey, to marry Rebecah Bracy, dau. of Thomas Bracey.

4/6/1690. George Maris, son of George Maris, to marry Jane Maddock, dau. of Henry Maddock.

1/7/1690. Edward Walter to marry Mary Pennell, widow. James Whiteacer to marry Mary Martin.

13/8/1690. Robert Barber to marry Hannah Ogden.

1/4/1691. Joseph, Elizabeth and Mary Taylor reported for neglect in attending meetings.

12/8/1691. Joseph Ware to marry Esther [Hester] Gleave.

7/10/1691. Walter Fawcit and Elizabeth Simcock proposed marriage; however, the Meeting understands that her father is against the marriage and therefore asks that they reconsider.

7/1/1691/2. William Huntly of Brumingham [Birmingham Twp], member of Concord Monthly Meeting, to marry Mary Stanfield, dau. of Francis Stanfield of Marple Twp, he to bring a certificate. William Malin of Upper Providence Twp intends marriage with Ann Laxford of Darby Monthly Meeting.

2/3/1692. Robert Burrows reportedly has removed to Philadelphia.

6/4/1692. Ralph Fishbourn of Talbot Co., Maryland, to marry Elizabeth Simcock, dau. of John Simcock.

3/8/1692. The widow Rudman has need of relief. Andrew Jobe to marry Elizabeth Vernon. Thomas Masey to marry Phebe Taylor, dau. of Robert. Henry Lewis to marry Mary Taylor, dau. of Robert, he of Haverford Monthly Meeting.

7/9/1692. James Lowns to marry Susanna Richards.

2/11/1692. Randall Malin of Upper Providence Twp, widower, intends to marry Mary Conaway, dau. of Valentine Hollingsworth of New Castle Co., and requested a certificate.

6/1/1692/3. Francis Worley to marry Mary Brasey.

11/7/1693. John Maris proposed marriage with Susannah Lewis of Haverford. John Goulding to marry Elthew Roberts.

4/10/1693. Humphrey Johnson to marry Ann Routh, widow; the estate of Ann's late husband will be divided for her children.

5/1/1693/4. Joseph Phips, son of Joseph [and Sarah] Phips of Chettenham, Philadelphia Co., to marry Mary Woodear, dau. of George Woodear. Philip Yarnall to marry Dorethy Baker.

2/2/1694. Walter Faucit intends to marry Rebecah Fearn, dau. of Elizabeth Fearn, widow, of Darby Meeting. John Turner to marry Elizabeth Woodear, dau. of George and Elizabeth Woodear.

7/11/1694/95. An attempt will be made to dissuade Mary Taylor, dau. of William, from marrying Samuell Robinet, he not being a member.

4/12/1694/95. William Collet of Chichester Monthly Meeting to marry Jane Worrelow, dau. of Thomas Worrelow.

1/5/1695. Henry Hollingsworth reported setting up a house at Chester formerly laid out by the Court and Grand Jury for the county's use and also cutting the eves of the new prison. Mary Neeld is to be visited about her taking John Neeld to be her husband who was not a member of the Society.

2/7/1695. John Simcock, Jr., is to be spoken to regarding his loose and disorderly walking in his conversation.

5/6/1695. Moses Musgrave to marry Grace Roberts.

30/9/1696. Richard Parker to marry Susana Tunclift. Thomas Joans [Jones] to marry Ann Elott.

25/11/1696/7. Martha Taylor's miscarriage reported. Martha Woodwors miscarriage reported.

22/12/1696/7. Meeting informed of several misdemeanors, i.e., unseemly actions committed by Thomas, Jonathan, Jacob and Martha Taylor, children of Mary Taylor of Marple Twp, widow.

30/1/1696. Jeremiah Langly in a distressed condition, languishing under great affliction of body, is to be moved to Thomas Vernon's house as soon as a person is found to look after him.

27/2/1696. Randall Vernon to pay his brother Thomas 40 shillings, it being in full to this time for Jeremiah Langly's attendance and diet, and also 2 weeks of Robert Williams' diet.

28/7/1696. John Churchman expressed his intentions to marry Hannah Sary, dau. of Sarah Busby of Philadelphia Co., and requested a certificate.

26/8/1696. Daniel Hoops of Makefield, Bucks Co., to marry Jane Worrellow of Chester Monthly Meeting.

30/9/1696. Richard Parker of Darby Monthly Meeting to marry Susannah Tunnicliff. A difference has arisen between Walter Faucit of Chester Monthly Meeting and Edward Prichard about a plantation bought by Walter; matter referred to a committee whose decision they agree to abide by.

22/12/1696/7. Thomas Hope to marry Elizabeth Stanfield. Peter Britton to marry Mary Coppeck, dau. of Bartholomew, Sr. Meeting informed of misdemeanors committed by Thomas, Jonathan, Jacob and Martha Taylor, sons and daus. of Mary Taylor of Marple, widow. [Thomas pleaded innocent, but the rest acknowledged their offenses.]

27/7/1697. Thomas Jones and his wife and Joseph Phips and his wife were ordered to come to the next Meeting to give an account of their going to the marriage of Edward Paver and Ruth Calvert.

27/10/1697. Friends were appointed to speak to Elizabeth Prichet concerning her disorderly appearing in Meeting.

28/11/1697/8. Moses Musgrave requested a certificate to marry Patience Hussy, dau. of John Hussy of New Castle Co., Delaware. Moses to bring his mother's consent.

28/1/1698/9. Samuell Garrett of Darby Monthly Meeting to marry Jean [Jane] Pennell, dau. of Robert Pennell, he to bring his certificate.

29/6/1698. Richard Maris to marry Elizabeth Hays. George James to marry Ann Woodworth.

27/7/1698. Charles Whitacer to marry Hannah Hoskins. John Hoskins and Ruth Atkins granted liberty to proceed with their marriage.

27/12/1698. Isaac Few to marry Hannah Stanfield.

29/3/1699. Thomas Minshall complained that Elizabeth Vernon accused his wife of murthering [murdering, smothering] her child on shipboard as also of being a whore. Upon careful investigation, the Meeting finds these charges to be utterly false.

31/5/1699. John Blunston of Darby Monthly Meeting and Margret Stedman of this Meeting expressed their intentions to marry.

30/8/1699. Edward Pritchett withdrew his accusation that John Simcock took 8 acres of his land.

27/9/1699. Edward Prichard disowned for disunity. Henry Worley to marry Mary Vernon. Henry and Mary acknowledged their error in becoming engaged before informing their parents.

25/10/1699. James Sharples proposes to marry Mary Lewis, dau. of Ralph Lewis of Haverford Monthly Meeting.

29/11/1699/1700. John Edwards requested a certificate to marry Mary Ingram, dau. of Mary Ingram, a member of Burlington Monthly Meeting, West Jersey.

25/1/1700. Margret Stedman, being removed from this Meeting, requested a certificate.

29/2/1700. Thomas England requested a certificate signifying his clearness in marriage.

26/6/1700. George Woodier [Woodyar] to marry Mary Hoskins. Thomas Taylor condemned his taking too much liberty in drinking, riding, unnecessary discourse and taking his wife contrary to discipline. Jonathan Taylor, brother of Thomas Taylor cited in this Meeting, condemned his being overtaken in drink. John Parker, now removed to Philadelphia, has requested a certificate.

31/7/1700. Thomas Taylor requested a certificate to marry Rachel Minshall of Philadelphia.

24/12/1700/01. Joseph Selby to marry Mary Taylor.

28/2/1701. Friends to speak with Mary Worley.

25/3/1701. Jacob Vernon to marry Ann Yoursley. Stephen Jackson requested a certificate to marry Elizabeth Clemmens of Philadelphia, widow.

28/5/1701. George Lowns to marry Mary Bowers.

25/6/1701. Thomas Taylor advised to leave off his vain course of life.

29/7/1701. A certificate was requested for Rachell Elis.

24/9/1701. Lidia Wade left the Meeting a legacy of £30 in her will. Randall Mellin and Peter Taylor appointed as overseers of Lower Providence [Preparative] Meeting.

29/10/1701. Edward Dawes and Joseph Selby appointed overseers for Springfield [Preparative] Meeting; Robert Barber and John Sharples appointed overseers for Chester Monthly Meeting. Jean Edgg and Feby Freckow chosen overseers for Providence Women's Meeting; Sarah Smedely and Martha Ogden for the women's Meeting at the house of John Bowater; Elizabeth Fishborn and Elizabeth Job appointed overseers for Chester Women's Meeting; Ann Hays and Hannah Yarnall for Springfield Women's Meeting. A certificate was requested for Ann Vernon. Randall Vernon requested a certificate to Concord for his son Jacob. Thomas Worrolow, removing to Philadelphia, requested a certificate signifying his clearness in marriage.

26/11/1701/2. Randall Coxton requested a certificate to marry Sarah Garrett, dau. of William Garrett of Darby Monthly Meeting. Joseph Pennell requested a certificate to marry Alice Garrat [Garrett], dau. of William Garrat [Garrett] of Darby Meeting.

25/12/1701. Thomas Bowater requested a certificate to marry Frances Barnet of Chichester Monthly Meeting, widow.

30/1/1702. Alexander Mode requested a certificate to remove to Bucks Co. and to take Ellin Dunken, dau. of William Dunken [of Byberry], in marriage.

27/2/1702. Jonathan Taylor to marry Martha Hugh. Susana Marris and Elizabeth Davies chosen overseers for Springfield Women's [Preparative] Meeting.

28/7/1702. John Vernon granted a certificate to marry Sarah Pile.

30/9/1702. Frances Worrall and Sarah Smedley chosen as overseers for Middletown Women's [Preparative] Meeting.

25/11/1702. Isaac Malin to marry Elizabeth Jones. John Wolford [John Hurfort of Dublin Monthly Meeting] to marry Elizabeth Brown.

22/12/1702. Elizabeth Brown's certificate received from England. Mordica Maddock intends to go to Old England and requested a certificate.

25/1/1703. Mary Morgin requested a certificate in order to marry.

5/2/1703. Thomas Hoops requested a certificate to remove into the limits of another Meeting. George Simpson reported for keeping his hat on when George Simcock was in prayer and reflecting on his testimony as dead and dry stuff.

31/3/1703. Thomas Bartlet requested a certificate to remove from Chester to Talbot Co., Maryland.

28/4/1703. John Worrall of Edgmont Twp complained of Joseph Carter not paying his debts. Benjamin Barrett requested a certificate to marry Mary Hanson of Philadelphia Co.

26/5/1703. Benjamin Barrett's certificate granted, having inquired of several of his neighbors in Old England.

30/6/1703. Susana Painter requested a certificate in order to marry.

27/7/1703. Nickolas Farelamb of Philadelphia to marry Katherin Crosby, he producing a certificate and consent of his father, mother and brother.

29/9/1703. Edward Kinneson proposes to marry Mary Green, servant to William Branton of Concord Monthly Meeting.

31/11/1703/4. David Ogden condemned his speaking defaming words against John Worrall at the smith's shop in Edgmont.

28/12/1703/4. Thomas Garrett to marry Rebecca Vernon. Thomas Oldham to marry Susana Few. Friends appointed to deal with Joseph Jervis concerning a report of his pretended vision or sighting of [the ghost of] Samuell Buckley, dec. Joseph Jervis reported for selling rum to the Indians.

27/1/1704. Samuell Tomlinson to marry Mary Sanders. Joseph Sharples expressed his intentions to marry Lidia Lewis, dau. of Ralfe Lewis of Haverford Monthly Meeting.

24/2/1704. Thomas Woodward, son of Richard, intending to remove, requested a certificate to Chichester Monthly Meeting. Thomas Jones reported for unlawfully taking some corn from Joseph Jervis at his mill. David Jones reported for working his neighbors' creatures without the knowledge of their owners.

29/3/1704. William Story to marry Ann James.

26/4/1704. Bartholomew Coppock to marry Rebecca Minshall. Thomas Garrett brought a certificate from Darby in order for his removal to Goshen Meeting. John Worrall is allowed to take his course with Joseph Carter at law.

28/6/1704. Thomas Woodward, son of Richard Woodward, and Rachell Martin, dau. of Thomas Martin, granted liberty. Robert Barber requested a certificate to go to England.

25/7/1704. Hannah David produced a certificate from Merron [Merion] received. Thomas Woodward requested a certificate for himself and his wife, Rachell, to Concord Meeting. Nathan Faucit being removed to Philadelphia, requested a certificate signifying clearness in marriage.

30/8/1704. Henry Hollingsworth, in idle conversation with Ralfe Fishbourn and his wife, defamed the family of Randall Vernon by saying that the family is guilty of having a bastard child, and stated that he might take them to the grave and show them the bones of it. [disowned].

26/1/1705. Charles Booth to marry Elizabeth Conaway. Edward Hardiman requested a certificate to Philadelphia.

Last day/2/1705. Joseph Jervis reported for debts by James Sorrell.

28/3/1705. William Huntly [and his wife] requested a certificate to remove to the north side of the Brandywine [River].

30/5/1705. Thomas Martin, son of John Martin, to marry Jean [Jane] Kent, dau. of Rice and Ann Kent.

29/8/1705. In a visit with Jean Kent, she stated that she could not love Thomas Martin well enough to take him to be her husband; she was sorry she had proceeded so far with him. Members to inventory the possessions of Jeremiah Langly, dec.

31/10/1705. William Smith of Darby to marry Elizabeth Prichett of Crumbereck in the township of Ridley. Philip Taylor's marriage reported accomplished in good order.

28/11/1705/6. Grace Crook's certificate from England received. John Simcock, son of Jacob and Alice Simcock, proposed to marry Mary Waln, dau. of Nicholas Waln of Philadelphia Co. Robert Pearson, son of Thomas and Margery Pearson, requested a certificate to Haverford Monthly Meeting to marry Katherin Thomas, dau. of Margret Thomas, widow.

25/12/1705/6. Elizabeth Holford being removed to Chichester, requested a certificate. [It was ordered along with a certificate for her husband.] Alexander Ross requested a certificate to Chichester and Concord Monthly Meeting to marry Katherine Chambers of Chichester Meeting. John Hurford requested a certificate to Chichester and Concord.

26/1/1706. Elizabeth Job and Hannah Churchman being removed, a certificate was requested for each of them to Concord Monthly Meeting [with their husbands' certificates: Andrew Job and John Churchman]. Ann Taylor requested a certificate to the same. Philip Prichard requested a certificate to Darby to marry Sarah Smith, dau. of William Smith of Darby.

29/2/1706. John Smith of Springfield Meeting requested a certificate to Falls to marry Mary Worrall, widow.

27/3/1706. Agness Salkild's certificate received from England. Certificates from Radnor Monthly Meeting received for Ann Lewis, Mary Lewis, Elizabeth Howell, Mary Lewis, Mary Beven, Gwin Lewis.

24/4/1706. Philip Taylor and his wife granted a certificate to Chichester and Concord Monthly Meeting.

26/6/1706. A general certificate was received for the following Friends from Merion Monthly Meeting: William Lewis, Sr., Lewis Lewis, Evan Lewis, William Lewis, Rice Howell, William Bevan, William Thomas and Peter Thomas as members of the Newtown Meeting.

28/8/1706. John Rimington produced a certificate.

25/9/1706. John Smith produced a certificate from Dartmouth Monthly Meeting in New England. Jacob Minshall proposed to marry Sarah Owen, dau. of Griffith Owen of Philadelphia.

30/10/1706. John Worrallow reported for not attending meetings. Edward Hardman, who formerly resided within the limits of the Chester Monthly Meeting and attended meetings of worship, requested a certificate to certify his clearness in marriage.

27/11/1706/7. John Wood of Darby to marry Rebecca Faussett of Chester Meeting; her children to be protected according to their father's will. George Simpson of Chester to marry Ruth Hollingsworth, dau. of Henry Hollingsworth. Paul Sanders requested a certificate to Chichester and Concord Meeting.

24/12/1706/7. Mary Baratt about to remove, a certificate is requested. Benjamin Barret of Springfield requested a certificate to Frankford Monthly Meeting, Philadelphia Co. Thomas Martin, son of John of Middletown, requested a certificate to marry Mary Knight, dau. of Giles Knight of Byberry Meeting.

31/1/1707. Evan Lewis, son of Ralph Lewis of Haverford Monthly Meeting, to marry Ann David, formerly of Darby, dau. of John David of Great Valley; she being a stranger to the Meeting, a certificate was requested and her parents' consent; he also to bring a certificate. Certificate signed for Thomas Martin who was absent at Dublin Monthly Meeting, but his father, Nicholas Fairlamb, and William Pennell declared the continuation of his intentions.

28/2/1707. A shift was to be procured for widow Readman before the next Meeting.

28/5/1707. Sarah Minchall's certificate from Philadelphia was received.

25/6/1707. Isaac Minshall, son of Thomas and Margaret of Providence, requested a certificate to marry Rebecca Owen, dau. of Griffith Owen of Philadelphia.

29/7/1707. Lidia Painter requested a certificate to Philadelphia.

27/8/1707. Kathern Owen requested a certificate to Haverford Monthly Meeting. William Thomas of Newtown acknowledged going to the burial of one of his neighbor's children, "one of the separates" and when one of them went to pray, he inadvisedly took off his hat with them.

26/11/1707/8. David Brintnall requested a certificate to Philadelphia Monthly Meeting.

23/12/1707/8. Michall Blunston of Derby to marry Phebe Peceo of Springfield. Robert Wharton of Haverford to marry Jean [Jane]

Kent, dau. of Rees Kent. Elizabeth Davis requested a certificate to Haverford. Rebecca Minchall's certificate from Philadelphia was received. Joseph Edge by his brother John requested a certificate to Concord signifying clearness of marriage. John Crockson requested a certificate to Philadelphia.

31/3/1708. Friends to inquire into Francis Bowater and her daughter's clearness in order for a certificate.

26/5/1708. Joseph Phips acknowledged his quarreling with Christopher Clayton.

30/6/1708. Joseph Harvey of Darby to marry Mary Simcock, dau. of Jacob and Alice Simcock; he produced a certificate from Darby. Joseph Carter accomplished his marriage contrary to discipline: disowned. John Cadwallader produced a certificate from Radnor Monthly Meeting.

27/7/1708. William Phillips of Newtown to marry Elizabeth Williams, dau. of Robert Williams of Goshen. Robert Wharton and Rees Kent with Jean [Jane], his dau., gave satisfaction as to why they did not proceed in their intended marriage which was by reason of Robert being in loose company and overtaken by drink. They have released each other from all covenants and promises. William Thomas reported for not coming to the Newtown Meeting.

25/8/1708. Edward Davis, being removed within the limits of Haverford Monthly Meeting, requested a certificate. Joseph Harvey's marriage reported accomplished in good order.

29/9/1708. John Faucet, son of Walter Faucett, dec'd, to marry Grace Crook of Springfield, spinster, both belonging to this Meeting. Thomas Mercy being deceased, John Maris was appointed in his place to inquire concerning Edward Davis. Jonathan Coppock requested a certificate in order to marry Jane Owen, dau. of Griffith Owen of Philadelphia.

27/10/1708. William Thomas reportedly has joined the Baptists. Thomas Dell produced a certificate from Reading Monthly Meeting in Berkshire, England. Isaac Few, having removed into the limits of Newark Monthly Meeting, requested a certificate.

31/11/1708/9. Friends to inquire into Hannah Few's clearness to marry.

28/12/1708/9. David David, son of Ellis David, to marry Jean [Jane] Jones, dau. of Rees and Hannah Jones, he dec'd. William Sinkler to marry Phebey Gleave [Phebey Glave]. Lidia Carter requested someone accompany her to Concord Monthly Meeting to request that she become a member of this Meeting. Thomas Gooding produced a certificate from Rudholt Particular Meeting, he being engaged to the ship could not stay until the Monthly Meeting. Robert Carter requested to be a member of Chester Particular Meeting [from Chichester and Concord Monthly Meeting, which was eventually approved].

28/1/1709. Joseph Baker, son of Joseph Baker of Edgmont, to marry Mary Worrallow, dau. of John Worrallow. John Smith of Elk River, Maryland, to marry Jean [Jane] Kent, dau. of Rees Kent of Newtown. In a visit to Elizabeth Prichett, she said that she received Friends' love and that she would not leave the man. Thomas Kendall has taken a wife out of unity [disowned].

25/2/1709. David David's marriage reported accomplished in good order.

30/3/1709. Joseph Baker's marriage reported accomplished in good order. John Smith's marriage went pretty well. Joshua Cavlert requested a certificate to Newark Monthly Meeting to marry Deborah Harling, dau. of George Harling.

27/4/1709. Friends to inquire into Susana Oldham's life and conversation.

25/5/1709. Rebeckah Powell condemned her behavior in taking her late husband out of the way of Truth.

29/6/1709. John Edgg, son of John of Providence, to marry Mary Smedly, dau. of George Smedly of Westtown. Lewis Rees produced a certificate from Merion Monthly Meeting. Lewis Rees and his wife Grace granted a certificate. Marriage of Jacob Howell reported accomplished in good order. John Scot of Chester Meeting requested a certificate to Philadelphia to marry Mary Humphrey. Jonathan Hays, Jr., requested a certificate to Merion Monthly Meeting to marry Jane Rees, dau. of Edward Rees of Merion. Joseph Baker, Jr., requested a certificate to Concord Monthy Meeting.

26/7/1709. Samuel Levis, son of Samuel Lewis of Springfield, requested a certificate to Philadelphia to marry Hannah Stretch. Thomas Vernon, son of Robert Vernon, offered an acknowledgment.

31/8/1709. West's and Edge's marriages reported accomplished in good order. John Vernon reported for keeping evil company and drinking too much.

28/9/1709. Robert Baker, son of Joseph Baker, requested a certificate to Philadelphia to marry Susannah Paker, dau. of Robert Paker [Packer] of Philadelphia. Jacob Trigoe, son of Peter Trigo, requested a certificate to Darby Monthly Meeting to marry Mary Cartlidge, dau. of widow Cartlidge of Derby.

30/11/1709/10. William Hudson to marry Hannah Barber. James Morris, son of Anthony Morris of Philadelphia, to marry Margaret

Cooke, dau. of John Cooke of Frankford in Philadelphia County, but she of Chester Monthly Meeting. Friends to speak to Elizabeth Calvert concerning her outgoing in marriage. John Worrall intends to go to Old England and requested a certificate. Elizabeth Calvert to be visited regarding her marriage to one not of the Society [disowned].

27/1/1710. John Earsly of Concord and Chichester Monthly Meeting to marry Sarah Conaway; he is to bring a certificate. Bartholomew Coppock, widower, to marry Pheby Massey, widow. Thomas Jones disowned.

29/3/1710. Earsley's marriage reported accomplished in good order. Robert Williams reported that he is willing to sell his plantation in order to pay his debts.

24/4/1710. Robert Williams reported by Edward Roberts for not paying a just debt. Evan Lewis, Jr., reported for neglecting meetings. Newark Monthly Meeting requested a fresh certificate for Joshua Calvert.

26/4/1710. Representatives. Chester: Susana Lowns and Sarah Howell; Springfield: Margritt Coppock and Elmer Coppock; Providence: Eliner Vernon and Sarah Crockson; Middleton: Frances Worrall and Mary Baker; Goshen: Mary Asbridge; Newtown: Mary Lewis and Elizabeth Philips. Peter Britain and his wife Mary requested a certificate to Newark. Isack Vernon of Providence to marry Hannah Williams of Chester.

31/5/1710. James Middleton produced a certificate from Lurgan Monthly Meeting in Ireland.

28/6/1710. Jacob Malin, son of Randall of Upper Providence, to marry Susana Jones, dau. of David Jones of Whiteland, dec'd. Thomas Smedley, son of George Smedley of Willistown, to marry Sarah Baker, dau. of Joseph Baker of Edgmont. James Thomas of Whiteland to marry Martha Ogden, widow of David Ogden; the rights of the widow's children to be secured. John Pyle, son of Robert and Ann Pyle of Bethel, to marry Lidia Thomas, dau. of Peter and Sarah Thomas, he to bring a certificate from Chichester and Concord. [The marriages were accomplished.] Isaac Vernon's marriage reported accomplished in good order. Thomas Jacob produced a certificate from Friends in Cork, Ireland, and one from Darby where he has resided most since he came into these parts. Thomas Jacob of Providence Meeting requested a certificate to Newark Monthly Meeting to marry Mary Robinson, dau. of George Robinson.

30/8/1710. Marriages of Thomas Smedley and James Thomas reported accomplished in good order. Joseph Brown, son of William Brown of Nottingham, to marry Margret Sinkler of Chester Meeting, he to produce a certificate from Concord and Chichester.

27/9/1710. Thomas Vernon and Nicholas Fairlamb to accompany Joshua Calvert to the widow Cartright to know if she met Joshua on the Queens road between New Castle and Christien Ferry and to find out if Christian Stillman [Steelman] followed him. John Pyle's marriage reported accomplished in good order.

25/10/1710. Friends asked Mary Malin to tell her dau. Sarah Yearsly that the meeting wants her to write something to clear herself. Meeting was informed that the marriage of Jacob Malin and Susana Jones was not accomplished as scheduled. Friends appointed to learn the reason. Joseph Brown's marriage reported accomplished in good order.

9/11/1710. Jacob Malin's marriage reported accomplished in good order.

26/12/1710. Mary Pennell produced a certificate from Concord. Elizabeth Hains produced a certificate from Chesterfield. Jean Thomas produced a certificate from Philadelphia. Thomas Smith of Chester to marry Jean [Jane] Thomas, formerly of Philadelphia. Nathaniel Newlin, Jr., of Concord to marry Jean [Jane] Woodward of Middletown, he to bring a certificate. Susana Malin appeared and said she was heartily sorry for what she had done and that the marriage was not accomplished at the day appointed. A paper of condemnation was received concerning John Yearsly and his wife condemning their defiling their marriage bed. Joshua Calvert disowned. Thomas Mearcer, Jr., of Thornbury to marry Hannah Taylor of Middletown; he produced a certificate from Concord and was requested to have his father and mother with him. A letter of condemnation was received from John Yearsley and his wife Sarah. Thomas Taylor continues his practice of drinking and keeping evil company.

26/1/1711. Mary Dell produced a certificate from Reading Monthly Meeting, county of Berks, England; one came with her husband but did not mention her, so she has now brought another. Friends to speak with Martha Tayler and Deberow Norbery to know why they consented to put up their paper in order for marriage contrary to the advice of Friends. John Peall of Chester proposed to remove to the compass of Duck Creek Monthly Meeting.

30/2/1711. A certificate being prepared for Margritt Brown. John Pew to marry Jean Rees. Peter Thomas, Jr., to marry Elizabeth Goodwin

[Goodin], Jr. Jean Newlin and Mary Newlin requested a certificate to Concord Monthly Meeting. Thomas Smith's marriage reported accomplished in good order; also Nathaniel and John Newlin's marriages; also Thomas Massey's marriage. John Pugh to marry Jane Rees, having frequented the meetings. Middletown Meeting has given its permission for Francis Yarnall to join with Newtown Meeting.

28/3/1711. Lawrence Pearson's marriage reported accomplished in good order. Jacob Simcock, Jr., requested a certificate to Philadelphia to marry Sarah Waln, dau. of Nicholas Waln.

25/4/1711. Lidia Pile requested a certificate. Kathern Baldin produced a certificate from Concord and Chichester Monthly Meeting. John Pugh's marriage reported accomplished in good order. John Baldwin produced a certificate from Concord and Chichester. John Hains produced a certificate from Newton Monthly Meeting in West Jersey.

30/5/1711. Susana Baker produced a certificate from Philadelphia. Jean Pooly produced a certificate from Kendall [Kendal] Monthly Meeting in Westmoreland in Old England. Certificate signed for Lidia Pile. John Scott requested a certificate to Philadelphia to marry Mary Humphreys. Newtown Meeting reported that William Phillipes had joined the Baptists.

27/6/1711. Hannah Mercer requested a certificate to Newark Monthly Meeting. William Brown of Nottingham to marry Mary Mathis [Matthews], formerly of Philadelphia, he to bring a certificate from Concord, she from Philadelphia. John Beals, Jr. to marry Sarah Bowater, he to bring a certificate. A certificate was signed for Hannah Mercer. James Hendrixson has gone to Philadelphia to see his brother who is very sick.

24/7/1711. Mary Mathis produced a certificate from Philadelphia. John Bailes, Jr., of Nottingham to marry Sarah Bowater, dau. of Thomas, he to bring a certificate from Concord and Chichester and his father's consent. William Brown's marriage reported accomplished in good order.

26/9/1711. The marriage of John Bailes reported accomplished in good order. William Bailes being removed within the limits of Concord and Chichester, requested a certificate. Alexander Baines produced a certificate from Radnor Monthly Meeting. Joseph Helsby produced a certificate from Newtown Monthly Meeting in Cheshire in Great Britain.

31/10/1711. Mary Jacobs from Newark Monthly Meeting. John Smith expressed his intention to go to sea and requested a certificate. Rees Henton proposed to remove down to Elk River and requested a certificate to Newark Monthly Meeting. Evan Lewis of Edgmont declines to attend meetings.

28/11/1711/2. Abraham Darlington to marry Deborah Carter. Friends spoke with Mary Williamson about going to her daughter's marriage contrary to Friends' orders. Thomas Taylor disowned. John Owen requested a certificate to Great Britain.

25/12/1711. Jean Hays brought a certificate from Merion. Susanna Lowns requested a certificate with her husband to Philadelphia. Kathern Pairson condemned her attending the marriage of Mary Williamson. Friends appointed to prepare a paper to signify that John Pugh never was deemed a member. Robert Pearson, Enoch Pearson and Daniel Williamson, Jr., acknowledged themselves to blame for going to the marriage of Mirack Davies and are sorry. Peter Taylor, Jr., requested a certificate to Haverford Monthly Meeting to marry Elizabeth Jermon. James Lownes has removed to the limits of Philadelphia Monthly Meeting and requests a certificate.

13/1/1712. Elizabeth Hatton brought a certificate from Frandly Monthly Meeting, Cheshire, England. James Lowns granted a certificate to Philadelphia for himself and his wife. Evan Lewis reported for neglecting meetings. Abraham Darlington's marriage reported accomplished in good order.

28/2/1712. Certificates prepared for Mary Brown and Sarah Beals. Cadwalleder [Cadwalader] Elis to marry Margrit Edwards. John Salkeld appeared and signified his disappointment with his voyage to the Islands. Inion Williams requested through Chester Meeting that he be permitted to go to law with the executors of Ralph and Elizabeth Fishbourn. Jonathan Hayes acknowledged going to a marriage of those not in unity with Friends.

26/3/1712. Cadwalet [Cadwalader] Elis and Margritt Edwards were asked to forbear at present until Friends can be satisfied as to her behavior.

20/4/1712. Hannah Coborn was condemned for going from Friends to marry one not of the Society. The Meeting sent Mary Edwards 20 shillings for the use of her mother. Jacob Vernon's marriage reported accomplished in good order. John Baldwin reported for looseness in drinking to excess. Thomas James produced a certificate from Merion Monthly Meeting. Edward Thompson produced a certificate from Lurgan Monthly Meeting in Ireland and also one from Newark Monthly Meeting. Cadwalleder [Cadwalader] Ellis reported for going to the marriage of Ellis Williams who took his wife contrary to the Rules of discipline.

28/5/1712. Hannah Boldin was condemned for marrying outside our Society. Mary Kendall requested that Friends forgive her. William Phillips is inclined to join the Seventh Day Baptist Church. Cadwalleder Ellis married by a Justice. Jacob Edge requested a certificate to Merion Monthly Meeting to marry Sarah Jones.

25/6/1712. Henery Wood of West Jersey to marry Mary Cookson.

29/7/1712. Hannah Hodges produced a certificate from Philadelphia Monthly Meeting. Margritt Morris requested a certificate. Sarah and Martha Hays produced a certificate from Newtown Monthly Meeting in Cheshire in Old England. Benjamin Simcock to marry Hannah Hodges. Jonathan Hayes, Jr., produced a certificate from Newtown Monthly Meeting in Cheshire in Great Britain, signifying the consent of Friends with him his brother and sisters coming for these parts as also their parents consent ..." Joseph Woodward requested a certificate to Concord Monthly Meeting to marry Elizabeth Mearcer.

27/8/1712. Susana Woodworth produced a certificate from Philadelphia. Certificate signed for Margritt Morris. Henry Wood's marriage reported accomplished in good order. John Holland produced a certificate from Newtown Monthly Meeting in Cheshire in Great Britain and also one from Darby. John Holland proposes to go to Great Britain and requested a certificate.

24/9/1712. Elthew Goldin and Sarah Minshall to speak to Sarah Phiphs concerning her going contrary to friends in marrying one not a member. Hannah Williamson condemned her marriage. Thomas Kendall acknowledged taking a wife contrary to order. The marriage of Benjamin Simcock reported accomplished in good order. Samuel Worthington produced a certificate from the Monthly Meeting of Moate greenage in Ireland signifying his clearness in marriage.

29/10/1712. Hannah Cookson will be asked to come to next meeting to give Friends the reason why she consented to put up a paper in order for marriage contrary to Friends' advice. John Worrall produced a certificate by Ephraim Jackson from Newtown Monthly Meeting in Cheshire in Great Britain.

26/11/1712/3. Sarah Holstone condemned for marrying contrary to Friends' orders and advice. Sarah Edgg produced a certificate from Merion. John Worrall reported Joseph Jervis for non-payment of money due upon a bond.

28/12/1712/3. Sarah Powell, formerly Sarah Hays, was asked to come to the next meeting to see what she can say for herself in marrying outside of our Society.

30/1/1713. Hannah Clowd, formerly Cookson, said she was sorry; Friends asked her to withdraw at present. James Lowns by Chester Meeting complained of John Scott for debt. John Worrall complained of Daniell Cookson for not paying due upon a bond, she being security for his brother, Joseph Jervis. Alexander Baine requested a certificate to Haverford to marry Jane Moore.

25/3/1713. Kathren Heald condemned her marrying contrary to Friends' orders. John Smith, intending to settle within the limits of Newark Monthly Meeting, requested a certificate. Ann Smith requested a certificate jointly with her husband to Newark. Feby Lewis desires a certificate to Harford Monthly Meeting.

29/4/1713. Elizabeth Tayler produced a certificate from Merion. Thomas John to marry Gwin Cadwalader.

27/5/1713. Hannah Jones produced a certificate from Philadelphia. It appears that John Baldwin was made drunk by rum mixed with cider contrary to his knowledge; he promised to be more careful in the future. Samuel Jones produced a certificate from Philadelphia for himself and his wife.

31/6/1713. Thomas John's marriage reported accomplished in good order. Richard Fletcher requested a certificate to Newark Monthly Meeting to marry Mary Huntley. Francis Jones produced a certificate for himself and family from Redstone Monthly Meeting in Pembrokeshire, South Wales.

28/7/1713. Kathren Ross requested a certificate to Radnor. Caleb Harrrison to marry Hannah Vernon. Hannah Vernon submitted a letter stating she had "entertained a love for Caleb Harrison as to give him incorrougment to marridge without my parents consent and by friends labour of love is maid sencibell that it is contrary to the disapline of friends ..." Alexander Ross being settled within the compass of Radnor Meeting, requested a certificate.

26/8/1713. Mary Jacob requested a certificate to Newark. Kathren Ross's certificate was deferred on her husband's account. Nathan Gibson produced a certificate from Kendall [Kendal] Monthly Meeting in Westmoreland in Great Britain. Thomas Jacob requested a certificate to Newark Monthly Meeting.

30/9/1713. Caleb Harrison's marriage reported accomplished in good order. Elizabeth Woodward produced a certificate from Concord. Philip Pethirick (Pedrick) to marry Elizabeth Cobourn. Mary Jacob granted a certificate jointly with her husband. Caleb Harrison's marriage reported accomplished in good order. Ellis Williams condemned his outgoing in marriage. William Tidmarsh signified to the meeting that his uncle, John Hyett, left his three daughters, Mary, Rose and Sarah Tidmarsh, £5 each in his will and is advised from his executors to get a certificate from the meeting stating that the money is already secured to his said daughters and money may be paid unto his order in England.

28/10/1713. Sarah Followfield produced a certificate from Great Strickland Monthly Meeting in the county of Westmoreland in Old England. David Wilson produced a certificate from Kendall [Kendal] Monthly Meeting in Westmoreland in Great Britain. David Gibson produced a certificate from Great Strickland Monthly Meeting in Westmoreland in Great Britain.

25/11/1713. Grace Lloyd from Philadelphia. Kathern Ross and her husband granted a certificate to Harford. Margarett Todhunter condemned her outgoings in marriage. Philip Pedrick's marriage reported accomplished in good order. David Lloyd produced a certificate from Philadelphia Monthly Meeting. John Davis produced a certificate for himself and his brother David from Namptwich Monthly Meeting in Cheshire in Great Britain. Joseph Parker produced a certificate from Coldbeck Monthly Meeting in the county of Cumberland in Great Britain.

22/12/1713. Moses Martin to marry Margarett Battin. John Worrielow reported overtaken with strong drink.

29/1/1714. Thomas Boldin (Baldwin, Jr.) to marry Helchew (Elthey) Hendrickson. Elinor Cook produced a certificate from Frandly Monthly Meeting in the county of Chester in Old England. Mary Edward's mother will be given cloth enough to make her mother two shifts. Hugh Davis produced a certificate from Radnor.

26/2/1714. Moses Martin's marriage is delayed because of his ill health.

31/3/1714. Marriages of Moses Martin and Thomas Boldin reported accomplished in good order. Jean Bean produced a certificate from Harford Monthly Meeting.

26/5/1714. Caleb Pusey, Jr., and his wife to Newark Monthly Meeting. Prudence Frewsey [Pewsey] requested a certificate to Newark. John Turner to marry Sarah Shakraff. John Fincher to marry Eliner Cook; her children's estate to be secured to them. Griffith John to marry Ann Williams; "desiring that none may be concerned in relation to marriage so young for the future as she is." Isaac Haines produced a certificate from Newtown Monthly Meeting in West

Jersey. John Williamson acknowledged his regret for running a horse race at Chester Fair. Samuel Thomlinson has neglected meetings.

30/6/1714. Prudence Pewsey and her husband granted a certificate. Isaac Hains to marry Kathren David. Thomas Williamson to marry Ann Malin.

27/7/1714. The marriages of John Turner and John Fincher reported accomplished in good order. Ann Malin produced consent from her father-in-law and her mother. Robert Chamberlin, Jr., to marry Sarah Woodward, he to bring certificate from Concord. Thomas Lancaster produced a certificate from Kendall Monthly Meeting in Westmoreland in Great Britain.

25/8/1714. Marriages of Haynes and Williamson reported accomplished in good order. Sarah Woodward is ill. Eliner Thomas produced a certificate from Philadelphia. Mary Holland produced a certificate from Hartshaw [Hardshaw] Monthly Meeting in Lancashire in old England; also for John Holland. Caleb Cowpland produced a certificate from Sedberg [Sedgbergh] Monthly Meeting in Yorkshire in Great Britain. Daniel Williamson, Jr., acknowledged wild and unseemly carriage at Chester Spring Fair, having taken too much drink.

29/9/1714. John and Patience Wright produced a certificate from Hartshaw [Hardshaw] Monthly Meeting; also from Philadelphia Monthly Meeting for himself, wife and children. Tobias Holloway produced a certificate from Bristol Monthly Meeting in Great Britain. Middletown informed of a difference between the widow Cookson, her son Daniel and John Dyer, a Friend lately come from England.

27/10/1714. The marriages reported accomplished in good order. Friends to visit John Edwards to see how it was with their mother. Sarah Miller produced a certificate from Milverton Monthly Meeting in Somersetshire, England. John Williamson to marry Sarah Smedley. Henry Miller produced a certificate from Minehead Monthly Meeting in Great Britain for himself and his wife. Thomas Coebourn produced a certificate from Cashell Monthly Meeting in Ireland.

31/11/1714. Francis Joans [Jones] requested a certificate to move with his family to Duck Creek.

28/12/1714. Marriage reported accomplished in good order. Peter Yarnall to marry Alice Worrolow.

28/1/1715. John Scarlett to marry Eliner Martin. Randle Croxton condemned his being overtaken with strong drink at the burial of

Thomas Powell. James Pew [Pugh] produced a certificate from Haverford Monthly Meeting.

25/2/1715. Lydia Tarbuck produced a certificate from Hartshaw [Hardshaw] Monthly Meeting, Lancashire in Old England. Sarah Harris produced a certificate from Newgarden Monthly Meeting, Carlow County, Ireland. Peter Yarnall's marriage reported accomplished in good order. John Williamson reported for being one of the chief actors in dressing a man pretending him to be a dead man or corpse at Daniell Calvert's and bringing of him into the house to frighten the people; he being by some of them there reproved for it and was asked how he would answer for it to the Monthly Meeting to which he replied it was but giving in a paper and they might get a box and call it Williamson's box for which presumptuous action and slight answer this Meeting taking into consideration. Aaron Mendinghall requested a certificate to Concord Monthly Meeting. Jacob Minshall of Middletown reported for scandalous behavior towards the wife of John Holston.

30/3/1715. Alice Pennell [apparently means Yarnall] spoke concerning the report of uncivil carriage, which fell out at the time of her marriage after she went home, in taking of her garters which is a practice not allowed by Friends, and she said she was sorry. John Scarlett's marriage was reported accomplished in good order. Mary Barritt produced a certificate from Philadelphia; James Barrat produced a certificate from Philadelphia for himself and his wife. John Scarlet's marriage reported accomplished in good order. Papers from the Quarterly Meeting concerning Charles Whitacre's loss by fire.

27/4/1715. It was reported that Peter Taylor and his wife Sarah reported for giving their consent to their son William to take a wife outside of the Society. [It appears that Peter Taylor spoke to the Justice to marry his son and kept the wedding dinner at his house.] Sarah Barton produced a certificate from Philadelphia. William Tidmarsh produced a certificate from Whitney Monthly Meeting in Oxfordshire in Great Britain. Isaac Barton produced a certificate from Killcomenber Monthly Meeting in Ireland. Sarah Harris produced a certificate from Newgarden Monthly Meeting in Ireland for her dec'd husband Roger Harris, herself and children.

25/5/1715. Jean Woodard and Sarah Chamberlain requested certificates to Concord. Thomas Fell and his wife Lidia produced a certificate from Hartshaw Monthly Meeting, Lancashire in old England. John Minshall produced a certificate from Hartshaw Monthly Meeting,

Lancashire in Great Britain. James Sorrell requested that he and his wife might become members.

29/6/1715. Jean Woodard and her dau. Sarah Chamberlain granted a certificate to Concord. Jean Smith to Dartmouth Monthly Meeting in New England. Joseph Rednap requested a certificate to Philadelphia Monthly Meeting to marry Elizabeth Jarman. Joseph Renear requested a certificate to York [Yorkshire, England] to see his brother and sister and thinking to winter there. Daniel Williamson, Jr., reported for some ill behavior at Chester Fair. Thomas Smith proposed to settle in New England with his father and requested a certificate.

26/7/1715. Kathren Richardson produced a certificate from Hartshaw Monthly Meeting, Lancashire, England. Jean Smith and her husband granted a certificate to Dartmouth. John Worrall complained of Robert Baker concerning a mortgage of Robert's plantation to him.

31/8/1715. James Baly to marry Sarah Person; she is desired to bring a certificate. Jean Hays requested a certificate to Haverford. Hugh David to marry Ann Richard. Joseph Vernon reported for keeping a woman in the house with him when concerned with her relationship to him. Samuel Worthington requested a certificate to England. There was a reported need to assist John Edwards in maintaining his mother-in-law, Mary Ingram.

28/9/1715. Sarah Person is now well. William Pusey requested a certificate to Newark Monthly Meeting for himself and family. Elizabeth Pewsey requested a certificate to Newark. Ann Richards produced a certificate from Merion. Sarah Person produced a certificate from Salem Monthly Meeting. Richard Prichard requested a certificate to Concord Monthly Meeting to marry Elizabeth Arnold. Joseph Vernon has removed the young woman.

26/10/1715. Sarah Person is still ill. Hugh David's marriage was reported accomplished in good order. Elizabeth Pewsey and her husband granted a certificate to Newark. Friends appointed to visit Peter Yarnall's wife to speak with her concerning her coming [with child] before her time.

30/11/1715. Daniel Williamson, Jr., disowned. James Baley to marry Sarah Pearson. Richard Prichard's certificate deferred because of his practice of cursing and swearing. John Redmell married a woman not of the Society.

27/12/1715. It is believed that Peter Yarnall's child was born before its time. James Baly's marriage was reported accomplished in good order. Joseph Vernon to marry Lydia Tarbuck. David Wilson requested a certificate to remove to Bucks Co. John Davis requested a certificate for himself and brother David to Gwynedd Monthly Meeting.

26/1/1716. John Carter requested a certificate to Middletown Monthly Meeting, Bucks Co., to marry Isabell Attkinson.

30/2/1716. Friends appointed to speak with Hannah Malin about her keeping company with a young man reportedly against her parents' consent. Eliner Fincher and John Fincher requested a certificate to Newark. Daniel Worsly to marry Sarah Harriss, he to produce a certificate; her children's portions to be secured. Joseph Vernon's marriage reported accomplished in good order.

28/3/1716. Sarah Miller produced a certificate from Minehead Monthly Meeting, Somersetshire in Old England. Eliner Fincher and husband granted a certificate to Newark. Elizabeth Woodard requested a certificate to Concord.

26/4/1716. Daniel Worsley's marriage reported accomplished in good order. Sarah Worsly requested a certificate to Newark. John Saul has removed to within the verge of Falls Monthly Meeting, Bucks Co.

30/5/1716. David Gibson to marry Sarah Followfield. Mary Camm produced a certificate from Philadelphia. Joseph Jervis neglects to pay a debt to Joseph Kirkbride. David Powell produced a certificate from Haverford Monthly Meeting.

27/6/1716. David Gibson reported deceased. Joseph Jervis contemptuously left when his business was commenced and went to England and Barbadoes without notifying Friends. William Tidmarsh requested a certificate to Philadelphia to marry Hannah Emblin. Thomas Paschall, Jr., produced a certificate from Darby, clear from marriage engagements. Abraham Darlington requested a certificate to Middletown Monthly Meeting, Bucks Co., to marry Elizabeth Hilbourn, dau. of Thomas and Elizabeth Hilbourn. Randall Croxton reported for dishonestly taking things from several persons, namely, John Sharplis, Jacob Edge and others.

29/8/1716. Jean Benson of Uwchlan Meeting condemned her outgoing in marriage. Sarah Simcock disowned for fornication with Samuel Worthington before their marriage.

31/10/1716. Thomas Paschall's marriage reported accomplished in good order. [Annotation: Thomas Garrett, one of the overseers, died about the 12th month in this year.] John Welding produced a certificate from Kilcomon Monthly Meeting in Ireland for himself and his wife. James Trego reported for being married by a priest to one not of the Society.

28/11/1716. Benjamin Head produced a certificate from Cherlevell Meeting in Ireland. William Tidmarsh requested a certificate to Philadelphia Monthly Meeting. Joseph Jervis and Daniel Cookson complain of William Coebourn for debt.

25/12/1716. Friends were apponted to speak with Mary Scot concerning her keeping company in order for marriage with one not of our Society. Elizabeth Prichet produced a certificate from Concord. Elizabeth Philips is understood to have left Friends and intends to go to the Baptists along with her husband, Joseph Ringer. James Barrat reported for neglecting meetings. Thomas Pearson appointed overseer in place of Isaac Taylor, dec.

25/1/1717. Ruth Hind produced a certificate from Ireland. Friends appointed to speak with Sarah Edwards concerning her keeping company in order for marriage with one not of the Society. Francis Yarnall to marry Mary Baker. Caleb Cowpland's marriage reported accomplished in good order. Francis Ferries requested a certificate to Concord to marry Rachel Newby. Daniel Cookson for not paying a debt to Edward Woodward [exec. of his brother Joseph]. Evan Howell reported for not paying a debt to William Kelley of Philadelphia. Jonathan Ogden reported for keeping company with a woman of ill report.

29/2/1717. Sarah Head produced a certificate from Ireland. Sarah Dicks, formerly Sarah Powell, gave a paper of condemnation concerning her going to a priest to be married.

27/3/1717. Friends were appointed to speak with Sarah Edwards, alias Prat. Francis Yarnall's marriage reported accomplished in good order. Sarah Edwards and Mary Scott have married men not of the Society.

25/4/1717. Kathren Hearld requested a certificate to Center [New Ark] Monthly Meeting. Rachell Coborn produced a certificate from Kilcommon Monthly Meeting, Ireland. Hannah Tidmarsh produced a certificate from London.

29/5/1717. Joseph Steadman complains of James Barrat for debt. William Trego reported for marrying a woman not of the Society.

26/6/1717. Ann Hunter produced a certificate from Ireland expressing her clearness in relation to marriage. Peter Hunter brought a certificate from Ballycame Monthly Meeting in Ireland. Jacob Thomas, son of Peter Thomas, requested a certificate to Haverford Monthly Meeting to marry Elizabeth Richards.

30/7/1717. Sarah Hodgson requested a certificate to Newark Monthly
Meeting. Mary Trego produced a certificate from Merion Monthly
Meeting. Robert Hutchingson being removed requested a certificate
to Newark Monthly Meeting for himself and family. Jacob Trego
produced a certificate from Merion Monthly Meeting for himself and
his wife.

28/8/1717. Ann Pewsey requested a certificate to Newark. Mary
Simcock requested a certificate to Abington. Friends appointed to
speak with Susana Baker who is keeping company in order for
marriage with one not of the Society. Margritt Helborn produced a
certificate from Middletown Monthly Meeting. Joseph Jervis excuses
former absence by the death of his brother-in-law. Caleb Pusey
being removed, requested a certificate to Newgarden Monthly
Meeting for himself and his wife. Peter Dicks produced a certificate
from Concord.

26/9/1717. Ann Pewsey and husband granted a certificate. Ann Weldin
produced a certificate from Killcommon Monthly Meeting in Ireland.
Richard Woodward produced a certificate from Philadelphia. David
Cadwallader requested a certificate to Concord to marry Mary
Swafford.

30/10/1717. Isabell Carter produced a certificate from Middletown
Monthly Meeting. Rachell Ferris produced a certificate from
Concord. Friends appointed to speak with Susana Baker about
putting out her children and advise her to break off with that man.
Paper of denial reported against Hannah Mallin, now Williamson, for
outgoing in marriage and without her parents' consent. Joseph
Jervis disowned. Henry Howard brought a certificate from Darby
Monthly Meeting. William Roberts brought a certificate from Radnor
Monthly Meeting for himself and his wife.

27/11/1717. Mary Britton [Britain] produced a certificate from Newark
Monthly Meeting. Richard Woodworth [Woodward] to marry Mary
Britton [Britain]. Friends appointed to draw up a paper of denial
against Sarah Person. Susanna Baker stated she never intends to
have any more to do with the man mentioned earlier. John Lea
produced a certificate from Concord for himself and his wife
[Hannah]. William Lewis requested a certificate to Gwynedd
Monthly Meeting to marry Lowry Jones.

24/12/1717. Jean Roberts produced a certificate from Radnor Monthly Meeting. John Joans (Jones) to marry Margritt Hilborn, he to bring a certificate [from Gwynedd]. William West and Elizabeth Levis granted a certificate.

31/1/1718. Rebeckah Starr produced a certificate from Carlow Monthly Meeting [Carlow Co.] in Ireland. Joseph Coborn, Jr., to marry Lydia Carter, Jr. Reported that Sarah Pearson has absconded. John Worrall complained of George Simpson for debt. William Levies being removed, requested a certificate to Newark Monthly Meeting.

28/2/1718. Margritt Joans requested a certificate to Gwynedd. Elizabeth Darlington produced a certificate from Middletown Monthly Meeting. Robert Thornton to marry Sarah Tayler, Jr. Mary James granted a certificate. George Maris requested a certificate to Haverford Monthly Meeting to marry Jane Hayes, widow.

26/3/1718. At John Hendrickson's marriage "things were indifferently well."

30/4/1718. Hannah Sanders produced a certificate from Philadelphia. Mary Thomlinson to Duck Creek. Joshua Low and his wife Sarah produced a certificate from Hartshaw Monthly Meeting in Old England; also one for Joshua from Flushing on Long Island. Sarah Low was asked to produce a certificate from Flushing. Inquiry into Robert Thornton's life and conversation does not recommend him. Samuel Thomblinson requested a certificate to Duck Creek Monthly Meeting.

28/5/1718. Robert Thornton reportedly plans to proceed in marriage out of the unity of Friends with Friend Peter Taylor's daughter [Sarah]. John Baldwin reported for being overtaken with drink.

25/6/1718. Sarah Low produced a certificate from Flushing. Sarah Taylor asked to attend Meeting regarding the disorderly proceeding in marriage of her daughter Sarah Taylor, Jr. John Cook requested a certificate to Newark Monthly Meeting to marry Elinor Landsdell and another to Newgarden for settlement. William Trotter requested a certificate to Abington Monthly Meeting. Joseph Thomas requested a certificate to Haverford Monthly Meeting to marry Gemima Davies.

29/7/1718. Esther Canby requested a certificate to Falls Monthly Meeting. Mary Cadwalader produced a certificate from Chichester Monthly Meeting. Ann Haycock produced a certificate from Wolverhamton Monthly Meeting, County of Stafford, Great Britain. John Waln brought a certificate from Philadelphia Monthly Meeting for himself and his wife Jean. Edward Fell brought a certificate from Hartshaw Monthly Meeting in Lancashire in Great Britain. Jonathan Haycock brought a certificate from Wolverhamton Monthly Meeting in Staffordshire in Great Britain.

27/8/1718. Ann Hay's marriage was delayed first because of their settlement and second because of an injury from a fall she had. A letter of denial reported against Sarah Norbery for marrying contrary to order and advice.

24/9/1718. Jean Marris produced a certificate from Merion. Samuel Lewis produced a certificate from Haverford Monthly Meeting for himself and his wife Pheby.

29/10/1718. John Alin (Allen) to marry Alice Smedly. Paper of denial reported against Sarah Beckham signed. Samuel Jones complained of Francis Worley for debt.

26/11/1718. Because the river was frozen, Sarah Beckham was unable to attend. Daniel Cookson reported for marrying one not of the Society.

23/12/1718. Hannah Barber reported for fornication before marriage. Nicholas Fairlamb reported for not paying a debt to Isaac Norris of Philadelphia. Nicholas Rogers requested to be a member (recommended to Springfield Meeting). Abel Pearson has married out of unity.

30/1/1719. John Camm brought a certificate from Philadelphia. John Jackson requested a certificate to Newgarden to marry Jane Swaine, dau. of Francis, and to settle there. William Cundill produced a certificate from Philadelphia. John Cadwalleder [Cadwalader] complained of Thomas Fell for debt.

27/2/1719. Jemima Thomas produced a certificate from Radnor. John Crosby married out of unity. Adam Treharn requested a certificate to Darby to marry Lucey Ellet.

25/3/1719. Sarah Reese requested a certificate to Newgarden. William Cundall requested a certificate to Abington Monthly Meeting to marry Elizabeth Tomlinson.

29/4/1719. Ann Lewis requested a certificate to Concord. Mary Barratt requested a certificate to Philadelphia.

27/5/1719. Ann Lewis's certificate delayed on her husband's account.

31/6/1719. John Mendenhall produced a certificate from Concord for himself and his wife Esther. Isaac Taylor requested a certificate to Darby to marry Sarah Smith. Evan Lewis of Edgmont requested a certificate to Concord.

28/7/1719. Jonathan Ogden requested a certificate to go trading in the Islands.

26/8/1719. Ann Lewis and husband granted a certificate to Concord.

30/9/1719. Sarah Bennett requested a certificate to Concord.

28/10/1719. John Hastings married out. John Worrall reported by Middletown Meeting for abusing his servants.

29/12/1719. Isaac Williams requested a certificate to Burlington Monthly Meeting to settle.

28/1/1720. Jean Fenn produced a certificate from Gwynedd Monthly Meeting. Nathan Gibson acknowledged committing fornication with Ann Blunston, widow, before marriage.

25/2/1720. Friend Lydia Carter requested a certificate to Newgarden for herself and her dau. Mary signifying her clearness on account of marriage. John Sharples to be overseer in the room of William Swarford, dec.

30/3/1720. Robert Benson to be overseer in the room of Joseph Helsby, dec'd. Jonathan Ogden produced a certificate from Bridgetown Monthly Meeting, Barbadoes, [West Indies]. Mary Wing, having been a considerable time amongst us, desires to return home and requested a certificate. Jonathan Hayes reported for loose conversation and marrying out.

27/4/1720. Grace Willson produced a certificate from Middletown Monthly Meeting. David Wilson produced a certificate from Middletown Monthly Meeting for himself and his wife. John Simcock acknowledged frequenting bad company and drinking houses. He also produced a paper from his neighbors in Abington for himself and his wife Mary and requested a certificate to Abington Monthly Meeting.

25/5/1720. Elizabeth Bab requested a certificate to Newark.

29/6/1720. Mary Simcock granted a certificate to Abington. Ann Williams produced a paper concerning her going from Friends to be married. Evan Howel reported for debt to John Worrall. Lewis Williams acknowledged outgoing in marriage with the daughter of James Thomas without consent of her father.

26/7/1720. Joseph Townsend produced a certificate from Concord for himself and his wife, Martha. Thomas Stubes requested a certificate to Newark to marry Mary Miner and settle there.

31/8/1720. Elizabeth Swain requested a certificate to Newgarden Monthly Meeting. There was a complaint made from Uwchlan Meeting against Elizabeth Cadwalader, dau. of John and Sarah Cadwalader of Uwchlan, for being overtaken with strong drink last harvest, dancing with a man's jacket on and acting unseemly with a man and in a manner not fit to be mentioned. Jonathan Ogden requested a certificate to marry Ann Robinson, dau. of George and Katherine Robinson of Newark Monthly Meeting. Joshua Cowpland brought a certificate from Sedberg Monthly Meeting, Yorkshire, Great Britain.

28/9/1720. The signing of a paper of denial reported against Elizabeth Cadwalader was delayed at the request of her father, John Cadwalleder, and his son, David. Jonathan Hayes disowned.

26/10/1720. Hesther Dicks produced a certificate from Concord. Paper of denial reported against Elizabeth Cadwaleder signed. Joshua Low reported for frequenting a disorderly house in Chester and behaving indecently towards women [the latter charged was dropped].

30/11/1720. Mary Minyard, formerly Coebourn, and Alice Coebourn, daus. of William Coebourn, engaged in loose conversation and married contrary to Friends orders with one not of our Society. William Davies produced a certificate from Merion Monthly Meeting.

27/12/1720. Sarah Webster requested a certificate to Newgarden. John Waln acknowledged taking too much strong drink. Griffith Lewis requested a certificate to Abington to marry Mary Busby.

27/1/1721. Kathren Mallin reported for keeping company in order for marriage with one not of the Society against the wishes of her parents. Paper of denial reported against Mary Minehead, dau. of William Coebourn, for marrying out and other disorders. John Musgrove complains of John Worrall for debt.

24/2/1721. Elizabeth Miller requested a certificate to Philadelphia. Mary Davis requested a certificate to Falls Monthly Meeting.

29/3/1721. Elizabeth Condal produced a certificate from Abington. Pheby Sinkler and husband requested a certificate to Concord. Providence Meeting informed that Kathern Mallin [dau. of Randall Malin], now Teat (Tate), was married by a priest. Oliff Baily requested a certificate to Newark. Thomas Oldman requested a certificate to Philadelphia. William Sinkler requested a certificate to Concord Monthly Meeting. William Davies requested a certificate to Darby. Samuel Taylor has married out.

26/4/1721. Pheby Sinkler's certificate deferred on her husband's account. Ann Ogden produced a certificate from Newark. Abraham and Elizabeth Darlington requested a certificate to Concord and Chichester Monthly Meeting. Isaac Lea requested a certificate to Darby.

31/5/1721. Hannah Iden requested a certificate to Falls. Richard Jones to be an elder in place of Ellis David, dec'd.

28/6/1721. Esther Ogden requested a certificate to Philadelphia. Isaac Lea's certificate deferred; he being sick, his father produced a paper from him acknowledging dancing at John Wade's house where he was in company of young folks and some music. John Edge reported for neglecting meetings, keeping loose company and drinking to excess. Daniel Hoopes requested a certificate to Great Britain. Stephen Beakes requested a certificate to Great Britain.

25/7/1721. Samuel Jones and his wife, Hannah, requested a certificate to Concord Monthly Meeting. Alice Bourn requested a certificate to the Monthly Meeting at the Clifts in MD. Ann Perkins reported as giving birth before her time or about 16 weeks after marriage. Samuel Ogden's wife requested a certificate to Philadelphia Monthly Meeting.

27/9/1721. Rachell Farries requested a certificate to Concord with her husband. Chester Meeting complained of Ann Howell, dau. of Henry and Mary Worly, for having a child within a week after her marriage to William Howell. Francis Ferres requested a certificate for himself and his wife to Concord Monthly Meeting.

25/10/1721. Ann Worly, now Howell, being removed towards Nottingham and the season being unsuitable for travel, a letter will be written to her regarding the evil she has committed. Ann Perkins disowned. William Coebourn requested a certificate to Concord for marriage. John Bond produced a certificate from Lavington Monthly Meeting in the county of Wilts in Great Britain.

29/11/1721/22. Hannah Iden produced a certificate from Falls Monthly Meeting. John Ogden brought a certificate from Philadelphia. John Iden produced a certificate for himself and his wife from Falls Monthly Meeting.

26/12/1721/22. Chester Monthly Meeting on this date consisted of the following meetings: Chester, Springfield, Providence, Middletown, Goshen, Newtown and Uwchlan. The marriage of Jonathan Palmer and Sarah Simcock was not completed by reason of the death of her father and brother.

26/1/1722. Thomas, son of Joseph Coebourn, requested a certificate to marry Elizabeth Cockfield, widow, dau. of William Hudson. Edward Woodward requested a certificate to Goshen to marry Alice Allin, widow, dau. of George Smedley. Barnabas Murfey has imposed upon Friends in preaching and praying contrary to their advice. Sarah Barton has married one not of the Society.

28/3/1722. Mary Trego requested a certificate to Darby signifying clearness. Elizabeth James and Sarah Smedly requested to join Goshen Monthly Meeting. Mary Garrat requested a certificate to Goshen.

25/4/1722. John Walne reported for being disordered with strong drink and refusing the council of Friends. Sarah Palmer requested a certificate to Falls Monthly Meeting. Springfield Meeting informed that Mary Norbery is like to come under the care of Friends for maintenance.

30/5/1722. Providence Meeting complained that John Edge has not attended meetings. Mary Norbery was visited; her brother-in-law Jacob Taylor is still willing to keep her at £10 per year. Ann Walln requested a certificate to Philadelphia. Susana Worly reported for having a bastard child.

27/6/1722. John Thomkins produced a certificate from Philadelphia for his mother and himself. Mary Tomkins produced a certificate from Philadelphia. Ann Coppock requested a certificate to Goshen.

24/7/1722. William Davies produced a certificate from Darby. William Hammons produced a certificate from Concord and Chichester for himself and his wife. Alice Woodworth produced a certificate from Goshen.

29/8/1722. John Bond requested a certificate to Abington. Samuel Worthington requested a certificate to Salem Monthly Meeting for himself and his wife Sarah. Joseph Jackson requested a certificate to Newgarden for himself and his wife Hannah. Mary Taylor, dau. of Thomas, condemned for having a bastard child. Margret Hamonds produced a certificate from Concord.

26/9/1722. John Walne still drinking to excess. Joseph Taylor and Mary Maris not yet married due to Mary's indisposition of body, being lame. Testimony reported against Ann Howell, dau. of Henry Worley and against Susannah Worley, dau. of Francis Worley. John Ogden requested a certificate to Philadelphia. David Powell requested a certificate to Haverford where he intends to settle. Nicholas Rogers requested a certificate for himself and his wife Mary to Philadelphia.

31/10/1722. Testimony reported against Ann Howell to be sent to Nottingham Meeting. John Wilson produced a few lines from Friends in Ireland concerning his clearness. Frances Burd requested a certificate to Philadelphia including her clearness in marriage. Mary Hastings requested to join; however, she once belonged to Newark Meeting and never produced a certificate.

28/11/1722. Copies of testimony reported against John Walne to be sent to him, and to Darby and Philadelphia. Meeting informed that Susannah Worly has removed from Conestogo and is now within the compass of Plymouth Meeting. David Powell renewed his request for a certificate to Haverford. John Hastings and his wife Mary acknowledged former offenses and requested to come under the care and inspection of Friends. Newark wrote that they no longer consider Mary Hastings a member of that meeting; this meeting accepted her paper so far.

25/12/1722. Thomas Woodward produced a certificate from Concord and Chichester for himself and family. Rachell Woodward produced a certificate from Concord. John Hastings and his wife Mary requested a certificate to Newgarden. Peter Dickes intends to go to Great Britain to settle some affairs in the county of Chester. John Hampton produced a certificate from Concord for himself and his wife Ann. Hannah Carter requested a certificate of clearness to Newgarden. Elizabeth Coborn produced a certificate from Philadelphia. Judith Calvert reported by Providence Meeting for defrauding Peter Dicks.

25/1/1723. Sarah Barnard requested a certificate to Concord. Mary Taylor, dau. of Sarah, reported by Springfield Meeting for having a bastard child. Martha McDaniell requested a certificate to Philadelphia signifying clearness in marriage. Hannah Williamson acknowledged committing fornication.

29/2/1723. James Hinde requested a certificate to Concord to marry Elizabeth Jones.

27/3/1723. Jacob Simcock acknowledged imprudent management of affairs and drinking too much. Rachell Norbury, being of age but not capable of managing the portion left her by her dec'd father, Thomas Norburry, Thomas Martin and Thomas Smedley were appointed to take care of her and manage her portion. Samuell Gray produced a certificate from Philadelphia. Hannah Williamson recommended by a few lines to Goshen at their request.

24/4/1723. James Hendrick and his wife and John Hendrick and his wife requested certificates to Newgarden Monthly Meeting. Lucy Hendrick and her dau.-in-law Rebeckah Hendrick requested a certificate to Newgarden. The Quarterly Meeting recommended contributions towards the loss by fire of James Moore and Thomas Clifford. Mary Bartram requested a certificate to Darby.

29/5/1723. Daniel Williamson produced a certificate from Goshen. Ann MacVitte produced a certificate from Newgarden.

26/6/1723. Daniel Hoopes produced a certificate from Norton Monthly Meeting in the county of Durham in Great Britain.

30/7/1723. Ruth Wilson requested a certificate to Concord. Elizabeth Hind produced a certificate from Concord. Deborah Dicks produced a certificate from Concord.

23/8/1723. David Wilson requested a certificate for himself and his wife Grace to Newtown Meeting, Bucks Co.

23/9/1723. Martha Hays reported for marrying contrary to advice of Friends.

30/10/1723. William Cowpland brought a certificate from Sedberg Monthly Meeting in Yorkshire in Great Britain for himself and family. Agness Cowpland produced a certificate from Sedberg Monthly Meeting in Yorkshire in Great Britain for herself and her daughter expressing her daughter's clearness from marriage engagements. Mary Norbery, being dec'd, John Handby will be asked for the time she was there and the charge of her burial.

30/1/1724. Samuel Ogden produced a certificate from Philadelphia for himself and his wife Esther. Ann Worralow, Jr., reported for having a bastard child.

27/2/1724. James Harker produced a certificate from Middletown, Bucks Co. John Gibbons requested a certificate to Concord and Chichester Monthly Meeting.

25/3/1724. Robert Penrose, Jr., produced a certificate from Dublin, Ireland. Peter Dicks, having returned from England, produced a certificate from Newton Monthly Meeting. William Robinson produced a certificate from Ballycaine, [Wicklow Co.], Ireland. Thomas Norbury requested a certificate to Goshen for himself and his wife Susana. Ruth Jones, a minister, produced a certificate from Goshen Monthly Meeting.

30/4/1724. Mary Taylor, dau. of Thomas Taylor, married out of unity by a priest. Elizabeth Talbot, widow of John Talbot, married Hugh Bowen out of the unity with Friends by a priest. Martha Hayes, dau. of Joseph Hayes of Great Britain, dec'd, married out of unity with Friends to --- Tannear, not of the Society. James Streator produced a certificate from Buckingham, Bucks Co., for himself and his wife Ann. Margaret and Bartholomew Coppock, executors of the estate of John Coppock, complained against Joseph Steadman for detaining part of the said estate.

27/5/1724. Thomas Goodwin offered acknowledgment for drinking and using unsavory language. Margret Elles produced a certificate from

Delobourn in Montgomeryshire, North Wales, signifying her clearness in marriage.

31/6/1724. Joseph Taylor requested a certificate to Newgarden Monthly Meeting for himself and his wife [Mary]. Testimony was read to Susannah Worley for adultery with a married man. Jane Hunter produced a certificate from the Monthly Meeting at Ballycaine, Wicklow County, Ireland.

28/7/1724. William Surman produced a certificate from Worcester Monthly Meeting in Great Britain for himself and his wife.

26/8/1724. Mary Sermon produced a certificate from Worcester Monthly Meeting in Great Britain. Esther Swain requested a certificate to Newgarden.

30/9/1724. Mary Wilkins, wife of William, requested a certificate to Haddonfield. Thomas Kendale acknowledged courting Rebecka Swarfar too soon after his wife's death. Rebecka Swarfar acknowledged her allowing Thomas Kendale to court her too soon after his wife's death and unknown to her mother.

28/10/1724. Isaac Lea obtained a certificate some time ago to Darby but for some time did not deliver it and now returns with an acknowledgment for fornication with his wife before marriage.

25/11/1724. Thomas Park produced a certificate from the men's Meeting of Carlow, [Carlow Co.], Ireland for himself and two sons, Jonathan and Thomas. Sarah Cowpland, dau. of William Cowpland, requested a certificate to Middletown Monthly Meeting; a few lines will be drawn from a certificate she had jointly along with her parents from England as she did not settle among this Monthly Meeting.

22/12/1724/5. Elizabeth Levis, Jr., and Jane Fenn wish to visit Friends in Barbadoes, New England, Rhode Island and Long Island; Elizabeth's parents consent, confirmed by her brother Samuel. Richard Beckham, Jr., requested a certificate to Haddonfield to marry Mary Wood, dau. of Henry Wood, dec'd.

29/1/1725. Jane James requested a certificate to Newgarden Monthly Meeting. Joshua Emlen requested a certificate to Philadelphia. George Deeble produced a certificate from Philadelphia. Susana Turner produced a certificate from Minehead Monthly Meeting in Somersetshire in Great Britain dated 21/11/1721.

28/2/1725. John Mendenhall requested a certificate to Newgarden Monthly Meeting for himself and his wife Esther.

31/3/1725. George Deeble requested a certificate to Abington. Mary Head requested a certificate to Newgarden signifying her clearness to marry. Thomas Massey and Sarah Taylor, dau. of Sarah Taylor, widow, first cousins belonging to Springfield Meeting, were married by a priest. Hannah Maris, now Harlin, condemned her committing fornication with him that is now her husband.

26/4/1725. Margaret Elis requested a certificate to Concord. Hannah Maris, dau. of John, condemned her having carnal knowledge with Michael Harlin, Jr., and for marrying by a priest. James Bartram produced a certificate from Darby.

26/5/1725. Mary Taylor, dau. of Isaac Taylor, dec'd, [and Sarah Taylor, his widow], requested a certificate to Abington Monthly Meeting. Rachel Cain, wife of John, requested a certificate to Newgarden.

30/6/1725. Esther Chandler requested a certificate to Concord. Ruth Jones requested a certificate to Goshen. Joseph Townsend requested a certificate to Concord [Abington] for himself, his wife Martha and family.

26/7/1725. John Sharples, Jr., requested a certificate to Concord to marry Mary Key, dau. of Moses Key. Judith Calvert reported for keeping company with intent to marry from Friends.

25/8/1725. James Streeter and his wife are likely to be objects of charity. John Rimington and his wife Sarah requested a certificate to Philadelphia. Thomas Coebourn, son of Thomas Coebourn, and Elizabeth Coebourn, widow, reported for keeping company with each other too soon after the death of her husband and for continuing indecently to cohabit. Deborah Dicks requested a certificate to Newgarden. Phebe Lewis was chosen overseer for Middletown Meeting along with Dorithy Yarnall instead of Jean Smedley who was removed by death. Mary Ross produced a certificate from Newgarden.

22/9/1725. Those appointed have agreed with Jacob Vernon of Providence to find James Streeter meat, drink, washing and lodging and the keeping of a horse for £9 for one year, and to find Ann, wife of said James Streeter, suitable meat, drink, washing and lodging with necessary attendance for one year if she lives so long for £15. Elizabeth Coebourn has since married Nathaniel Ring and a testimony was signed against her. George Maris, son of John Maris, and Hannah Massey, dau. of Thomas Massey, dec'd, to marry. Margaret Cowpland requested a certificate to Duck Creek.

27/10/1725. Margery Person, dau. of Thomas Person, reported by Springfield Meeting for marrying by a priest.

20/11/1725/6. George Maris and Hannah Massey reported for marrying by a Justice. John Pearson reported by Springfield Meeting for

drinking strong liquor and expressing abusive behavior. George
Turner requested a certificate to Newgarden. Susanna (Turner) Pyle
requested a certificate to Concord. Margery Person, now Tomson, to
be visited on account of her marriage by the priest.

28/12/1725/26. The reason George and Hannah Maris married as they
did is because they had carnal knowledge of each other, which they
acknowledged. Sarah Whiteacer, dau. of Charles Whiteacer, dec'd,
reported for keeping company in order for marriage with one not a
member. Mary Sharples produced a certificate from Concord.

28/1/1726. William Shipley produced a certificate for himself and his
wife. John Iden requested a certificate for himself and his wife
Hannah to Philadelphia.

25/2/1726. Margery Thompson, dau. of Thomas Pearson, acknowledged
marrying by a priest. A collection ordered to pay for necessities for
Henry Swift's wife. William Davis requested a certificate to
Philadelphia.

30/3/1726. Susannah Chamberlin requested a certificate to Concord.

27/4/1726. Friends to pay 2 shillings, 6 pence to James Barber for
digging Henry Swift's wife's grave. Thomas Massey and his wife
Sarah, being first cousins, acknowledge marrying by a priest and
having carnal knowledge before marriage. Thomas Parks requested a
certificate to Concord for himself and his sons. Mary Joans [Jones]
produced a certificate from Philadelphia.

25/5/1726. George Turner neglected to deliver his certificate to
Newgarden but now returns it and by Henry Miller requested one to
Concord.

29/6/1726. Nothing done in regard to selling James Streeter's effects as
he has been abroad mostly since last meeting and his wife is dec'd.
Sarah Ellis requested a certificate to Goshen. Joshua Low and his
wife Sarah requested a certificate to Newgarden [some obstruction].

27/7/1726. James Trego acknowledged disorderly walking.

31/8/1726. Katharine Maris, dau. of John, reported for marrying by a
priest to --- Willis. Jane Worrowlow [dau. of John Worrilow], now
Whippo, reported for fornication and marrying out. Susannah
Taylor, now Worolow, reported guilty of fornication and marrying by
a priest. Margret Cowpland produced a certificate from Duck Creek.
Elizabeth Welden, now South, reported for marrying out and has
since removed.

28/9/1726. Abraham Vernon not yet married by reason of sickness in
his father's family and the death of his sister. John Pearsons
reported for fornication, marrying out and drinking. Friends

appointed to prepare a memorial to Thomas Wilson, dec'd. Ann Sharples, dau. of John Sharples reported married to Samuel Bond, not a member of the Society, before a priest.

30/11/1726. Lidia Vernon, wife of Abraham, requested a certificate to Concord.

27/12/1726. Stephen Hoskens requested a certificate to Chester Monthly Meeting, MD, to marry Sarah Warnor, widow. John Iden produced a certificate from Philadelphia. Hannah Iden produced a certificate from Philadelphia.

27/1/1727. Mary Ross requested a certificate to Newgarden.

24/2/1727.Randale Malin requested a certificate to Goshen for himself and his wife Mary.

29/3/1727. Samuel Lightfoot produced a certificate from Newgarden for himself and his wife Mary. John Wright requested a certificate to Newgarden Monthly Meeting for himself and children: James, Susannah, Elizabeth and Patience. Richard Dobbs to marry Margaret Woodward [dau. of Edward Woodward]. Jacob Vernon acknowledged his drinking. Sarah Whiteaker and Roger Cairee reported for marrying before a priest. Margreat Thompson produced a certificate from Goshen. Lydia Booth requested a certificate to Goshen.

26/4/1727. Jonathan Worral, son of Peter, requested a certificate to North Wales Monthly Meeting to marry Mary Taylor, dau. of Jonathan, dec'd. Thomas Massey and his wife Sarah requested a certificate to Goshen. Thomas Griffith produced a certificate from Talcot Monthly Meeting in Radnorshire, to be recorded and after sent to Abington to his brother who is recommended in the same certificate. Samuel Jackson requested a certificate to Newgarden.

31/5/1727. Richard Dobbs and Margaret Woodward not married by reason of some disorder by him. Mordecai Madock produced a certificate from Nottingham Monthly Meeting in Great Britain for himself and his wife. Mary Billerby requested a certificate to Goshen. Hannah Jenkinson produced a certificate from Pardshaw Cragg in the county of Cumberland, England. Mary Richardson produced a certificate from Barbados. Sarah Maddock produced a certificate from Nottingham in Great Britain.

28/6/1727. Richard Dobbs was charged with cursing, swearing and calling for damnation on himself if ever he married Margaret Woodward; her father withdrew his consent, and Margaret does not intend to proceed in marriage.

30/8/1727. Richard Dobbs went out of the country before the
testimonial could be read to him. Thomas Worrilaw produced an
acknowledgment for himself and his wife Susanna for fornication and
marriage by a priest.
25/10/1727. Samuel Taylor requested a certificate to Newgarden to
marry Elizabeth Wright, dau. of John Wright. Ann James requested
a certificate to Goshen. Margarett Bezer requested a certificate to
Concord.
25/1/1728. Robert Barber, about to remove himself and family to
Conastoga, requested a certificate to Newgarden. Friends appointed
to inquire concerning Hannah Barber. Richard Lowdon requested a
certificate to Newgarden to marry Patience Wright, dau. of John
Wright. John Baker reported by Middletown Meeting for marrying
one not of the Society. Margaret Woodward has been delivered of a
bastard child.
29/2/1728. Margaret Woodward acknowledged fornication with Richard
Dobbs. Aaron Baker requested a certificate to Newgarden for
himself and his wife Mary. William Robinson reported for marrying
out.
27/3/1728. Hannah Bonsall, wife of Joseph Bonsall, requested a
certificate to Darby. Walter Worrilaw acknowledged having been
overtaken with drink. Hannah Williamson produced a certificate
from Goshen.
29/5/1728. Daniel Calvert with the consent of Springfield Meeting
requested to come under the care of Friends; also Hannah Calvert.
26/6/1728. John Low produced a certificate from Hartshaw Monthly
Meeting in Lancashire in Great Britain for himself, wife Jennet and
six children. Jonathan Marries reported for drinking to excess and
marrying out. Nathaniel Ring reported for fornication with his wife
Lydia before marriage; she was delivered of a child about 9 weeks
after marriage. Rebecah Flower produced a certificate from
Chichester Monthly Meeting. Mary Mercy reported for marrying by
a priest to William Musgrove.
30/7/1728. Elizabeth Calvert, wife of Daniel, acknowledged marrying
out. Mordecai Moor produced a certificate from Radnor. Mary
Musgrove, wife of William Musgrove, acknowledged marrying out.
Edward Fell to marry Jane Kendale. John Lea produced a
certificate from Concord and Chichester. Mary Belerby produced a
certificate from Goshen.
28/8/1728. Benjamin Weldon requested a certificate to Concord to
marry Hannah Hurford, dau. of John Hurford. John Beals produced

a certificate from Newgarden for himself, his wife Sarah and children. Mary Worrall produced a certificate from Gwynedd.

30/10/1728. John Gleave requested a certificate to Goshen Monthly Meeting to marry Elizabeth Eaches, widow of Robert Eaches. Jacob Vernon requested a certificate to Philadelphia for himself, his wife Elinor and children. The marriage of Edward Fell and Jane Kendale has not been accomplished; she signified that she does not love him well enough to marry him. Nathaniel Jackson has gone out of the country and left considerable debts.

27/11/1728/9. Robert Wilson produced a certificate from Great Strickland in the county of Westmoreland, England, for himself and his wife Ann. Thomas Butler produced a certificate from Middletown Monthly Meeting, Bucks Co. Hannah Jenkins [Jenkinson?] requested a certificate to West River Monthly Meeting.

24/12/1728/9. Nineveh Carter requested to join the Society.

1/31/1729. Richard Lowden requested a certificate to Newgarden Monthly Meeting for himself and family. John Sharples, Jr., requested a certificate to Goshen to marry Elizabeth Ashbridge, dau. of George Ashbridge. Mordecai Moor absconded from his creditors.

28/2/1729. Richard Barry produced a certificate from Concord [Goshen] for himself and his wife Mary. Martha Thomas produced a certificate from Goshen.

26/3/1729. Thomas Cummings produced a certificate from Lancaster Monthly Meeting. James Rushton requested a certificate to Goshen for himself and his wife Ann. Alice Borrow produced a certificate from Lancaster Monthly Meeting, England. Elizabeth Gleave produced a certificate from Goshen.

30/4/1729. Hannah Welden produced a certificate from Concord. Ann Trego requested a certificate to Goshen with her husband.

28/5/1729. Thomas Goodwin, Jr., requested a certificate to Goshen to marry Ann Jones, dau. of Richard Jones. Ann Trego not settling out of the verge of this meeting, her request for a certificate was dropped.

25/6/1729. John Philips to marry Deborah Britton, dau. of Peter Britton, dec'd, he to produce a certificate. John Norbury, unable to procure a competent livelihood, requested assistance. Elizabeth Sharples produced a certificate from Goshen.

29/7/1729. Moses Vernon acknowledged keeping company with Sarah Houlston at unseasonable hours and in an unbecoming and scandalous manner. Jane Brummer married Aaron Thompson before a priest. Isabell Bell produced a certificate from Ballendery [Ballinderry], Ireland.

26/8/1729. Sarah Coppock, dau. of Jonathan and Jean Coppock, dec'd, acknowledged her marriage to Thomas Wooly by a priest. Joseph Lees requested to come under the care of Friends.

24/9/1729. Mary Jonson, wife of Benjamin Jonson, requested a certificate to Newgarden. Deborah Philips requested a certificate to Gwynedd.

29/10/1729. Robert Penrose, Jr., acknowledged taking too much strong drink.

26/11/1729. Joseph Harvy, son of Job Harvy, requested a certificate to Darby. Mary Lowden requested a certificate to Newgarden.

23/12/1729. Peter Hunter requested a certificate to marry Esther Beson, widow of Edward Beson. Jonathan Booth requested a certificate to Concord. Hannah Owen, wife of John Owen, reported for kepting loose and vain company for some time past and of late has gone away with John Walker, a young man, without the knowledge of her husband. John Edge reported by Middletown Meeting for drinking to excess for some time. Sarah Askew, wife of William Askew, requested a certificate to Concord.

3/1/1730. Robert Penrose granted a certificate to Goshen. Joseph Parker requested a certificate to Haddonfield to marry Mary Ladd, dau. of John Ladd. David Newman to marry Esther Gleave, dau. of John Gleave, he to bring a certificate. Mary Adams requested to come under the care of Friends. Elizabeth Williams produced a certificate from Newgarden. Ann Goodwin produced a certificate from Goshen. Susana Marriss [Maris], alias James, reported by Springfield Meeting for marrying by a Justice contrary to her parents' wishes.

27/2/1730. Esther Gleave now states she does not love David Newman.

25/3/1730. Thomas Moor and his wife Mary request to come under the care of Friends. George Ashbridge produced a certificate from Goshen for himself and his wife Margaret. William Sankey produced a letter in place of a lost certificate from Pont y Moile in Great Britain for himself and his wife.

29/4/1730. Margaret Hodges granted a certificate to Falls Monthly Meeting. Dinah Coborn [alias Russell] reported by Chester Meeting for marrying by a priest.

27/5/1730. Aubery Bevan and William Gorsuch each acknowledged marrying by a priest. George Maris requested a certificate to Goshen to marry Mary Busby, widow of Joseph Busby. Susannah James reported with child before marriage.

31/6/1730. Jacob Simcock requested a certificate to Abington. William Bartram requested a certificate to NC in order to look after some estate. Robert Penrose has returned his certificate having greater encouragement for his trade in these parts. Joseph Camm plans to transport himself to Great Britain. Deborah Taylor sometime past went out in her marriage for which she now makes acknowledgment and joins herself to Goshen Monthly Meeting. Jean Kendall brought a paper of clearance from Edward Fell with which the meeting is satisfied.

28/7/1730. Susannah James, wife of Daniel James, acknowledged marrying out. Daniel Hoops, Jr. requested a certificate to marry Alice Taylor, dau. of Abiah Taylor. Jonathan Maris acknowledged drinking to excess and marrying one not of the Society. Henery Jones acknowledged marrying out and requested a certificate to Newgarden. Sarah Hoskins produced a certificate from Cecil Monthly Meeting in Maryland. Mary Parker produced a certificate from Haddonfield.

26/8/1730. Jane Ashbridge, wife of George Ashbridge, requested a certificate to Goshen. Dinah Russel, wife of Edward, acknowledged marrying by a priest. Peter Jones requested a certificate to Haverford to marry Ann Lewis, dau. of David Lewis. Esther Hunter produced a certificate from Newark.

30/9/1730. Joseph Lees requested a certificate to Darby. Samuel Whiteaker [Whitacre], son of Charles Whiteaker, requested a certificate to Wales Monthly Meeting.

28/10/1730. Thomas Morgan requested a certificate to Concord to marry Elizabeth Key, dau. of Moses Key. Thomas Butler requested a certificate to Middletown, Bucks Co., PA. Esther Gleave, dau. of John Gleave, married out of unity to John Crosier, not of the Society, and has joined a Presbyterian congregation. Ann Evans, wife of Kadwalder [Cadwalader] Evans, requested a certificate to Philadelphia. Hannah Baldwin requested a certificate to Philadelphia. Mary Mariss produced a certificate from Goshen. Mary Roads, now Powell, reported by Springfield Meeting for marrying by a Justice.

25/11/1730/31. John Rhodes requested a certificate to Goshen to marry Elizabeth Mallin, dau. of Isaac Mallin. Thomas Wooly requested to come under the care of Friends. Joshua Hoops, son of Daniel, requested a certificate to Goshen to marry Hannah Ashbridge, dau.

of George Ashbridge. Mary Pancoast granted a certificate to Burlington Monthly Meeting. Elizabeth Ives produced a certificate.

22/12/1730/31. Mary Rhodes, dau. of Joseph Rhodes, acknowledged marrying out to Robert Powel, not of the Society. Anthony Shaw produced a certificate from Abington. Obadiah Bonsall, Jr., requested a certificate to Darby. Susannah Pyle produced a certificate from Concord.

29/1/1731. Ninevah Carter, son of Jeremiah Carter, requested a certificate to Concord to marry Mary Clayton, dau. of William Clayton. James Hinde, being removed, requested a certificate to Darby for himself and family (wife Elizabeth). Mary Hoskins, dau. of John Hoskins, dec'd, married by a priest to John Mather, not of the Society.

26/2/1731. Ann Penrose, widow of Christopher Penrose, reported by Middletown Meeting for marrying by a priest to Thomas Wills, not of the Society. Joseph Hoskins requested a certificate to Barbadoes. Esther Hunter requested a certificate to Newark Monthly Meeting. Jane Elwell requested a certificate to the same place. Daniel Hoops, Jr., requested a certificate to Goshen.

31/3/1731. Frederick Engle and his wife requested to be taken under the care of Friends. Ann England requested to come under the care of Friends. Mary Harry requested to come under the care of Friends. Elizabeth Eachus produced a certificate from Goshen. Elizabeth Williams produced a certificate from North Wales. Jane Edwards, being by weakness incapable of helping as usual, an inquiry is to be made to see what Mary Edwards requires for her attendance.

28/4/1731. Joshua Way produced a certificate from Newark. Elizabeth Morgin produced a certificate from Concord.

26/5/1731. Jane Edwards, through some dislike, left the care of James Edwards to Henry Camms, who is to have £3 per annum for her attendance and house rent.

30/6/1731. Susannah Whiteaker [Whitacre], dau. of Charles Whiteaker [Whitacre], requested a certificate to Abington.

25/8/1731. Thomas Croxton reported by Providence Meeting for drinking to excess and lying [disowned].

27/10/1731. Thomas Pearson requested a certificate to Darby. Cadwalader Evans produced a certificate from Philadelphia for himself and his wife Ann. Mary Elbeck, under the notice of this meeting, married out by a Justice to Jonathan Oldfield, not of the Society.

28/12/1731/2. Robert Wilson requested a certificate to Concord for himself and his wife Ann. Mary Jones, wife of David Jones, reported for being overtaken with drink. Elizabeth Williams granted a certificate to North Wales, cleared from marriage engagements.

27/1/1732. John Mendenhall produced a certificate from Concord. Rebecca Flower reported for drinking to excess. Margaret Skelton reported for marrying out by a priest to Patrick Cartee, not of the Society. Elizabeth Coebourn, dau. of Thomas Coebourn, reported for marrying by a priest to Patrick Donovan, not of the Society.

24/2/1732. William Ives requested a certificate to Nottingham for himself and dau. Elizabeth. Susannah Coebourn, dau. of Joseph Coebourn, reported for marrying by a priest to Joseph Parsons. Mary Harry requested a certificate to Goshen, clear from marriage engagements. Susannah Coebourn said that she did not intend to marry other than among Friends.

29/3/1732. Phebe Hibberd, wife of Benjamin Hibberd, granted a certificate to Goshen. Hannah Hurford, wife of John Hurford, Jr., granted a certificate to Concord. Mary Worley granted a certificate to Nottingham, clear from marriage engagements. Martha McDaniel produced a certificate from Philadelphia, but owing to some scandalous reports, the women Friends were not willing to receive it; she has since delivered a bastard child. Friends appointed to deal with Rachall Norbery for having a bastard child.

26/4/1732. Ninevah Carter requested a certificate to Concord for himself and his wife Mary. Joshua Thompson and James Battin requested to come under the care of Friends. John Iden requested a certificate to Philadelphia for himself, wife Hannah Iden, a minisher, and their family.

31/5/1732. Thomas Powell requested to come under the care of Friends. Margaret Eaton produced a certificate from Darby. Elizabeth Powell, wife of Thomas Powell, requested to come under the care of Friends.

28/6/1732. John Parvin produced a certificate from the Monthly Meeting at the Moate in Ireland; he not intending to reside here long. Thomas Williamson reported for drinking to excess.

25/7/1732. James Battin expressed some intentions of going to Great Britain and requested a certificate. Abigail Bell produced a certificate from Cecil Monthly Meeting.

30/8/1732. William Hamman requested a certificate to Goshen to marry Lowry Lewis, widow of William Lewis. Mary Ashton, wife of Peter

Ashton, produced a certificate from Mountrath Monthly Meeting, Ireland.

27/9/1732. Francis Parvin produced a certificate from Newgarden.

25/10/1732. Alice Beeson granted a certificate to Newark Monthly Meeting. Abraham Hoops, son of Daniel Hoops, requested a certificate to Goshen to marry Mary Williamson, dau. of John Williamson.

29/11/1732. Elizabeth Webb, wife of William Webb, Jr., granted a certificate to Newark. John Lea requested a certificate to Barbadoes.

25/1/1733. Lowry Hammans produced a certificate from Goshen. Susanna Pyle granted a certificate to Concord. Richard Weaver requested a certificate for himself, wife Elizabeth and children, that they might come under the care of Friends. Ephraim Jackson, who served in entering the minutes and other papers, died and wished the papers to be taken from her custody.

30/2/1733. John Tompkins reported for marrying out to one not of the Society. Jacob Lightfoot produced a certificate from Newgarden. Joseph Coebourn reported for marrying by a priest and in seven weeks after the death of his wife.

28/3/1733. Sarah Beals, now Miles, dau. of John Beals, acknowledged marrying by a priest and disorderly conversation some years past when she lived in Chester; her father requested a certificate for her to Nottingham, she being removed to Mannockisey, which is in the verge of Nottingham Monthly Meeting. John Beals also requested a certificate to Nottingham for himself, his wife Sarah and children. Hannah Lea, widow of John Lea, requested a certificate to Darby. Robert Barber reported by a member of Newgarden Meeting for still neglecting to deliver his certificate to that meeting which he received from this meeting several years ago. Mary Broomer granted a certificate to Goshen.

25/4/1733. Edward Farr produced a certificate from Concord. Esther Bickerdike granted a certificate. Mary Lightfoot produced a certificate from Newgarden. Jane Farr produced a certificate from Goshen. Mary Hoops, wife of Abraham Hoops, produced a certificate from Goshen. Thomas Powell requested a certificate to Goshen for himself and his wife Elizabeth. Abigail Cowpland granted a certificate to Crosswicks.

30/5/1733. Mary Ashton, wife of Peter Ashton, granted a certificate to Concord. Esther Maris, dau. of George Maris, acknowledged marrying by a priest to Mordecai Taylor. Thomas Goodwin acknowledged taking too much strong drink.

27/6/1733. Joseph Harvey, Jr., reported married by a priest to one not of the Society. Acknowledgment from Ann Howell, now Reynolds. Margaret Williams requested to come under the care of Friends. Ann Jones requested a certificate to Haverford.

24/7/1733. Thomas Kendale requested a certificate to Wrightstown, Bucks Co., to marry Elizabeth Wilkinson, widow. Mordecai Maddock requested a certificate to Chichester to marry Dorothy Roman, widow. Ann Jones, widow of Peter Jones, granted a certificate. Rachel Jackson, executrix of Ephraim Jackson, reported by Aaron Baker of Middletown Meeting for a debt; she desires time. Hannah Britton acknowledged fornication. Thomas Williamson, reported for continuing to drink to excess.

29/8/1733. James Trego requested a certificate to Concord for himself, wife Elizabeth and dau. Mary. John Taylor and his wife Elizabeth acknowledged fornication before marriage. Sarah Crockson, Jr., reported for keeping disorderly company and drinking to excess.

26/9/1733. Mary Dutton, wife of Richard Dutton, granted a certificate to Concord.

31/10/1733. Francis Parvin requested a certificate to North Wales.

28/11/1733. John Williamson reported his brother in a disposition to be reclaimed and Thomas appearing here is returned to the care of Middletown Meeting.

25/12/1733/4. Benjamin Maddock, son of Mordecai, requested a certificate to Philadelphia to marry Elizabeth, dau. of John Hart.

25/1/1734. John Howell, son of Jacob, requested a certificate to Haddonfield to marry Katherine Ladd, dau. of John Ladd, and settle there. Anthony Shaw and his wife Mary requested a certificate to Newgarden. Elizabeth Kendale, wife of Thomas, produced a certificate from Buckingham.

29/2/1734. Edward Woodward requested a certificate for himself and his wife Alice to Goshen. Benjamin Hickman complained of William Surman for debt.

27/3/1734. John Weldon married out of unity to one not a member. Esther Mendenhall, wife of John, produced a certificate from Concord. George Lowns reported for refusing to refer a difference with Enoch Pearson. Robert Penrose and his wife Mary acknowledged fornication before marriage and drinking to excess on his part. Sarah Jackson granted a certificate to Philadelphia. Ephraim Jackson and his wife Mary requested a certificate to Goshen. Thomas Williamson still drinking to excess.

24/4/1734. Evan Howell was taken away by death soon after last meeting. Abraham Barton reported for absconding from his creditors and drinking to excess, now removing to Philadelphia. Robert Penrose and his wife Mary requested a certificate to Gwynedd. Hannah Britton requested a certificate to Gwynedd, clear of marriage engagements. Samuel Lewis appointed to take care at burials in place of Philip Yarnall, dec'd.

29/5/1734. William Surman has paid the greatest part of Benjamin Hickman's demand. Martha Petell produced a certificate from Boston in New England. Mary Lightfoot, dau. of Michael, requested a certificate to Newgarden.

26/6/1734. Thomas Vernon, son of Thomas, requested a certificate to Concord to marry Letice Chamberlain, widow of John Chamberlain, and settle. Joseph Sleigh produced a certificate from the Monthly meeting at Cork, Ireland.

30/7/1734. Alexander Bows admitted to membership by his request. Henry Howard granted a certificate to Great Britain by Middletown Meeting to settle some affairs. Esther Few, wife of Daniel, granted a certificate to Newark. Elizabeth Lowns, dau. of Mordecai Maddock, reported for marriage by a priest. [It appears by a letter of Agnes Salkeld that her son Joseph was courting Elizabeth Maddock and going every week to see her until 26/3/1734 when she told him she had been married near 3 months to George Lownes.]

28/8/1734. Richard Barry reported for commencing an action of law against Nathaniel Grubb, one under the notice of Friends. James Speary received into membership. Mary Woodward requested a certificate to Gwynedd, North Wales. Elizabeth Maddock, dau. of Mordecai Maddock, reported for marrying by a priest to George Lowns, Jr. Daniel Davis was admitted to membership by request.

25/9/1734. Benjamin Weldon requested a certificate to Concord to marry Sarah, widow of Thomas Barnard, and settle. Walter Worrilow reported for going away and leaving considerable debts unpaid. Samuel Croxton and his wife Mary acknowledged fornication before marriage.

30/10/1734. Kathren Willis, now Pusey, reported for marrying by a priest. Martha Petell requested a certificate to Boston, clear of marriage engagements. Thomas Hall requested a certificate for himself and his wife Mary to Goshen.

24/12/1734. James Hill received into membership.

31/1/1735. Jacob Lightfoot requested a certificate to Darby to marry Mary Bonsall, dau. of Obadiah Bonsall, dec'd. Susannah Mallin, dau.

of Jacob Mallin, dec'd, acknowledged fornication with and marriage to Philip Dunn. Alice Bell produced a certificate from Cecil Monthly Meeting signifying clearness to marry.

28/2/1735. Mary Jones, alias Butcher, reported for marriage by a priest.

26/3/1735. Benjamin Kendale requested a certificate to settle in the compass of the monthly meeting in Yorkshire. John Maris, son of John, requested a certificate to Concord to marry Katherine Heiden, widow of Andrew Heiden. Robert Pearson reported by Mordecai Maddock for debt. Mary Brooks produced a certificate from Newgarden clear of marriage engagements. Joshua Gill produced a certificate from Abington.

30/4/1735. Samuel Sharp requested a certificate to Choptank in Maryland. Thomas Minshall requested a certificate to Newgarden for himself, his wife and children. Margaret Paschall, dau. of Thomas Paschall, reported married out by the priest to William Mather, not of the Society, and was with child before marriage. Elizabeth Edwards, dau. of John Edwards, reported for going out of the Province and bearing a bastard child. Nathan Gibson requested a certificate to Darby. James Battin and his wife Mary requested a certificate to Haverford. John Worrall of Marple Twp acknowledged assisting Mary Jones, dau. of Thomas Jones of Providence, dec'd, to marry Matthew Boucher, not of the Society. Alice Lewis [wife of John] requested a certificate to Philadelphia. Ann Baker reported married by a priest.

28/5/1735. Elizabeth, wife of Benjamin Maddock, produced a certificate from Philadelphia. John and Thomas Hoops, sons of Daniel, requested a certificate to Goshen.

25/6/1735. Thomas Woodward requested a certificate to Goshen for himself, wife Rachell and daughters. Katherine Pusey, wife of John Pusey, acknowledged marrying by a priest.

27/8/1735. Mary Littler, wife of Samuel, granted a certificate to Nottingham.

24/9/1735. Ann Regester, dau. of David Regester, acknowledged marrying by a priest to Jesse Baker, not of the Society. Hannah Shepard reported for marrying out.

27/10/1735. Hannah Taylor, dau. of Thomas Taylor, acknowledged marrying out to William Shepperd.

26/11/1735. Samuel Bell produced a certificate from London dated 4/16/1725. Joseph Yarnall requested a certificate to Goshen to marry Mary Townsend, widow. Jonathan Haycock acknowledged being overtaken with strong drink. Ann Ellis, wife of Benjamin, granted a certificate to Haverford. Esther Vernon, dau. of Thomas Vernon, reported for bearing a bastard child and concealing the father. Ann Eaches produced a certificate from Newark.

29/1/1736. Samuel Sharples, son of Joseph, requested a certificate to marry Jane Newland, dau. of John Newland. Ann James, wife of John James, granted a certificate to Goshen. Hannah Vernon, dau. of Isaac, produced a certificate from Newark. In the sale of the Chester Meeting House to Edward Russell, Mordecai Maddock was asked to convey the lot, he being the only one living to whom the original lot was conveyed. Joshua Bispham some months earlier produced a certificate from Hartshaw [Hardshaw-West] Monthly Meeting but intending to return soon, it was given back to him. Sarah Coburn, now Harris, reported for marrying by a priest with one not of the Society.

26/2/1736. Springfield Meeting requested a certificate to Newark for Joshua Way and his wife Elizabeth. John Iden produced a certificate from Philadelphia for himself and his wife Hannah, a minister. James Tremble produced a certificate from Concord for himself and his wife Mary.

31/3/1736. Samuel Morris requested a certificate to Philadelphia. Mary Powell, wife of Robert Powell, granted a certificate to Goshen. Springfield Meeting requested a certificate to Goshen for Thomas Moor, his wife and children.

28/4/1736. Mary Yarnall, wife of Joseph, produced a certificate from Goshen. John Mendinghall requested a certificate to Newgarden. John Lea produced a certificate which he received from the meeting to Barbadoes some time past and requested to come under the care of Chester Monthly Meeting. William Surman requested a certificate to North Wales for himself, wife Mary and children. Jane Edwards reported dec'd. Sarah Harris reported unwell. Mary Moor requested a certificate to Goshen.

26/5/1736. Sarah Coebourn, dau. of Joseph Coebourn, acknowledged marrying by a priest to John Harris. Jane Smith, wife of John Smith of Opeckon, requested a certificate to Hopewell Monthly Meeting, she having appeared at Springfield Preparative Meeting. Ann Wickersham, wife of James Wickersham, granted a certificate to Newark. Sarah Simcock, alias Ruth [Routh], reported married by a priest.

27/7/1736. Jane Sharples, wife of Samuel, produced a certificate from Concord.

25/8/1736. John Maxfield requested a certificate to Haddonfield. Ephraim Jackson and his wife Mary produced a certificate from Goshen. Sarah Simcock, dau. of Benjamin Simcock, reported marrying out to Francis Routh, Jr., and was brought to bed about 6 months after marriage. Walter Outeloo produced a certificate from Horslydown Monthly Meeting, London, dated about 2 years earlier. Elinor Neail, now Stevenson, reported for being with child before marriage.

29/9/1736. Thomas Fawcet produced a certificate for himself, wife Lydia and three sons from Ballendery [Ballinderry] Monthly Meeting in the north of Ireland. John Minshall being dec'd, his widow Hannah returned the certificate he had from the meeting and neglected to deliver; a certificate will be prepared for her and her children to Newgarden. William Shipley and his wife Elizabeth granted a certificate to Newark. Mary Fearon requested to come under the care of Friends.

27/10/1736. Thomas Outerloo produced a certificate from Newgarden. Mary Tomlinson, wife of John, granted a certificate to Haddonfield. Thomas Williamson, son of Robert, reported for the practice of fighting and neglecting meetings.

31/11/1736/7. Esther Bickerdick granted a certificate to Mansfield Monthly Meeting, Burlington Co., NJ. Samuel Croxton requested a certificate to Goshen. Stephen Hoops requested a certificate to Goshen, being settled there. Mary Crookson requested a certificate to Goshen.

29/12/1736/7. Eleanor Nayle, dau. of John Nayle, formerly of Providence, acknowledged fornication with and marriage to Robert Stephenson. Walter Outerloo requested a certificate to West River. Susannah Woodward granted a certificate to North Wales, clear of marriage engagements. Benjamin Sharples, son of Joseph, requested a certificate to Concord to marry Edith Broom, dau. of James, dec'd.

25/2/1737. Susannah Woodward's certificate returned as she has since married Robert Crosier, not a member of the Society, by a priest. [An annotation seems to suggest that she was dau. of Richard and Mary (Coppock) Woodward.] Alexander Bows requested a certificate to Newark. Moses Martin requested a certificate to Goshen for himself, wife Margaret and seven children: George, Mary, John, Moses, Margaret, Rachel and Susannah. Hannah Crosley, wife of Charles Crosley, acknowledged marrying out. Ann Bond, wife of Samuel, granted a certificate to Nottingham.

39/3/1737. Daniel Williamson acknowledged drinking to excess. Hannah Martin, dau. of Moses Martin, now Smith [wife of John Smith], reported for marrying by a priest [to one not of the Society].

27/4/1737. Alexander Bows' conduct not so bad as represented; he does not intend to remove from Chester at present. Daniel Williamson requested a certificate to Concord for himself, wife [Hannah] and children (except Elizabeth). Mary Weaver, dau. of Richard Weaver reported for keeping company in order for marriage with one of another society.

27/5/1737. Jacob Howell, son of Jacob, requested a certificate to Haddonfield to marry Mary Cooper, dau. of Joseph Cooper. Mary Weaver, dau. of Richard Weaver, reported married by a priest to William Hays, not of the Society. Elizabeth Weaver has not been clear as to her daughter's marriage. Sarah Hoops reported for marrying by a priest.

29/6/1737. Job Yarnall, son of Philip, requested a certificate to Philadelphia to marry Rebecca Lownes, dau. of James Lownes. Joseph Sharples requested a certificate to Bradford for himself, wife Lydia and sons: Nathan, Abraham, Jacob and William. Rebecca Minshall having returned, produced a certificates from Cork Meeting, Dublin Meeting and Second Days Morning Meeting in London.

26/7/1737. Hannah Paschall, dau. of Thomas Paschall, granted a certificate to Philadelphia. Edith Sharples, wife of Benjamin, and Mercy Edwards produced a certificate from Concord. Benjamin Kendall, having returned from old England where he went to visit his relations, produced a certificate. Sarah Hoops reported unwell.

21/8/1737. William Sheppard received into membership at his request. Sarah Hoops, dau. of Daniel Hoops, acknowledged marrying by a priest to George Hall, not of the Society.

30/11/1737/8. Rebecca Yarnall, wife of Job Yarnall, produced a certificate from Philadelphia. Mary Griffith produced a certificate from Concord. James Hill reported by Middletown Meeting for marrying out to Jane Newlin and for keeping company as man and wife before marriage. Jonathan Maris acknowledged taking too much strong drink.

28/12/1737/8. Henry Maddock married out to one not a member. John Maddock reported for loose behavior and neglecting meetings. Samuel Britton sent acknowledgment from Opeckon with recommendations from some Friends of that meeting which was received and a certificate granted at his request to that meeting which will be sent if his creditors are satisfied. Jonathan Maris reported too familiar with women when drunk, considering his station as a minister, but the witnesses think there was nothing lewd or dishonest intended. Rachel Gleaves, now Crosser, reported for marrying by a priest but at the request of her mother-in-law, disownment will be deferred.

27/1/1738. Jane Albin acknowledged marrying out by a priest and without her mother's knowledge. Joseph Swaffer acknowledged marrying out. Griffith Minshall married his first cousin [Sarah], both by father and mother. Mary Howell, wife of Jacob, Jr., produced a certificate from Haddonfield. Rachel Crosier acknowledged fornication before marriage.

24/2/1738. Samuel Bell and Mary Reyneer, widow of Joseph Reyneer, reported for marrying out of unity by a priest. James Trimble and his wife of Providence Meeting requested a certificate to Concord.

29/3/1738. Jesse Woodward requested a certificate for himself and his wife Jane to Newark.

26/4/1738. Katherine Tomlinson, wife of Joseph, granted a certificate to Haddonfield. Elizabeth Neale, now Bonsall, acknowledged marrying by a priest.

31/5/1738. Joshua Gill requested a certificate to Salem.

29/6/1738. Elizabeth Bonsall, wife of Obadiah Bonsall, acknowledged marrying out. Thomas Outerloo reported for going away and leaving debts and not enough to satisfy them. John Levis, son of Samuel, requested a certificate to Darby to marry Rebecca Davis, dau. of John Davis. Jane Sharples, dau. of Joseph Sharples, granted a certificate to Concord clear of marriage engagements.

25/7/1738. Sarah Hammans, now Pugh, reported with child before marriage.

30/8/1738. John Calvert with consent of Chester Meeting complained of Thomas Dell who refused to refer a matter in dispute [to arbitration]. William Hammans requested a certificate to Duck Creek for himself, wife Lowery and children: William, Hannah, Thomas and Ambrose Lewis. Hannah Edwards reported married by a priest.

27/9/1738. Mary Barton produced a certificate from Concord clear of marriage engagements. Peter Worrall, son of John of Marple Twp, dec'd, requested a certificate to Sadsbury. Thomas Fawcet, son of Thomas, requested a certificate to Lisbourn [Lisburn] Meeting in Ireland. Joseph Slea requested a certificate to Newark.

25/10/1738. Alexander Seaton produced a certificate from Abington. Thomas Lewis produced a certificate from Goshen for himself and his wife Sarah (a minister).

29/11/1738. Susannah Sankey, dau. of William Sankey, granted a certificate to Haverford. Joseph Hoskins requested a certificate to Boston to settle some business. Rebecca Levis, wife of John Levis, produced a certificate from Darby. Kathrine Barry, now Bethel, reported for marrying by a priest.

26/12/1738/9. Mary Oldfield, wife of Jonathan, acknowledged fornication before marriage. John Needham produced a certificate from Nottingham Monthly Meeting in Great Britain for himself and his wife Elizabeth. Nathan Hoops requested a certificate to Goshen for himself and his wife.

26/1/1739. Isaac Collier requested that he, his wife Ruth and children: Hannah, Rebecca, Isaac, Elizabeth and James, be taken under the care of Friends. George Miller requested a certificate to Barbadoes, he intending to merchandise there and the vessel sailing soon. Goshen for Mary Broomer produced a certificate from Goshen. Margret Hoops requested a certificate to Goshen.

30/2/1739. Sarah Hammans [dau. of William Hammans], wife of Roger Pugh, acknowledge fornication before marriage. Hannah Harvey, wife of Job Harvey, Jr., acknowledged marrying by a priest. Elizabeth Bonsall, wife of Obadiah Bonsall, granted a certificate to Darby. Hannah Vernon, dau. of Isaac Vernon, granted a certificate to Goshen.

28/3/1739. Alexander Seaton requested a certificate to Newark. Samuel Simcock acknowledged fornication and marriage by a priest. John Dickin and his wife Ann requested a certificate to Newark. Jacob Durborow produced a certificate from Philadelphia for himself and his wife Ann. Joshua Gill produced a certificate from Salem. Jane Parke, wife of Thomas, granted a certificate to Bradford. Sarah Cox, wife of Lawrence, granted a certificate to Goshen. Mary David, dau. of Moses granted a certificate to Gwynedd. Elizabeth Tolbet produced a certificate from Darby.

25/4/1739. Elizabeth Talbot, wife of Benjamin Talbot, produced a certificate from Darby. Rebecca Minshall (a minister) requested a certificate to Philadelphia where she has gone to reside. Katherine Bethel, wife of Joseph Bethel, acknowledged marrying in another society.

30/5/1739. Mary Griffith granted a certificate to Darby. George Miller produced a certificate from Bridgetown Monthly Meeting in Barbadoes.

27/6/1739. Joseph Hoskins returned from Boston. Benjamin Rhodes, son of Joseph Rhodes, requested a certificate to Goshen to marry Katherine Pugh, dau. of Thomas Pugh, reported dec'd.

24/7/1739. Joseph Dobbins requested a certificate to Haddonfield. John Iden requested a certificate to Abington for himself [and his wife Hannah]. Joseph Newland requested a certificate to Concord. Hannah Iden requested a certificate to Abington. Jane Whippe reported in need of relief.

29/8/1739. Rebecca Minshall, Jr., granted a certificate to Philadelphia, clear of marriage engagements. Joseph Levis, son of Samuel Levis, requested a certificate to Philadelphia to marry Susannah Waln, dau. of Richard Waln. Mary Lightfoot, wife of Jacob, produced a certificate from Darby. Ann Llewelyn, wife of David Llewelyn, Jr., granted a certificate to Haverford. John Minshall, son of Jacob, dec'd, requested a certificate to Goshen to marry Sarah Smedley, dau. of Thomas Smedley.

26/9/1739. Jane Albin, wife of James, granted a certificate to Goshen. Martha Rumford (unmarried) produced a certificate from Gwynedd. James Maddock acknowledged marrying one of another society. Joseph Williamson acknowledged marrying out.

31/10/1739. As the stay of John Iden and his wife is uncertain, Abington Monthly Meeting indicated that they did not think a certificate necessary. Abraham Carter acknowledged marrying out. Mary Yarnall, wife of John, granted a certificate to Goshen.

28/11/1739/40. Margret Williams granted a certificate to Philadelphia. Nathan Edwards acknowledged marrying by a priest to one of another society. Ann Hunter requested to come under the care of Friends.

25/12/1739/40. John Scarlet requested a certificate to Oley for himself, wife Eleoner and children: Hannah and Eleoner. Nathaniel Ring requested a certificate to Concord. Samuel Bell requested a certificate to Philadelphia for himself, wife Mary and children: Hannah Reyneer and Rachel Reyneer. [Annotation: 3 young ch: Hannah, Rachel and Mary]

31/1/1740. Jane Hoskins, wife of Joseph, requested a certificate to visit Friends at the Yearly Meeting on Long Island. John Croxson reported for drinking to excess. John Matson requested to be received into membership: approved. Jane Owen, now West, reported for marrying by a priest. Martha Baker requested to come under the care of Friends: approved.

28/2/1740. Jane West, wife of Joseph West, acknowledged marrying out of unity. William Jefferis requested a certificate to Concord for himself, his wife Elizabeth, their children, and Elizabeth's dau. Jane Neal, clear of marriage engagements. Sarah Minshall, wife of John Minshall, produced a certificate from Goshen. Hannah Harlan, wife of Michall Harlan, granted a certificate to Newgarden. Katherine Pusey, wife of John Pusey, granted a certificate to Newgarden. Rebecca Jones, wife of William Jones, granted a certificate to North Wales. Jacob Durbra (Durborro) requested a certificate to Philadelphia for himself, wife Ann and children. Joseph Sharples, Jr., requested a certificate to Concord to marry Mary Pyle, dau. of Daniel Pyle.

26/3/1740. Joshua Gill requested a certificate to Newark. Susannah Couborn, now Doyle, married out.

30/4/1740. Sarah Pugh, wife of Roger Pugh, granted a certificate to North Wales. Martha Pennell, wife of John, granted a certificate to Concord. Grace Faucet granted a certificate to Haddonfield, clear of marriage engagements. Jonathan Maris acknowledged drinking too much. Adam Martin requested a certificate to Goshen.

28/5/1740. Nathaniel Ring charged by Esther Vernon, dau. of Thomas and sister to Nathaniel's late wife, with promising to marry her, and it is suspected that he has had some criminal conversation with her of which she does not clear him. Joseph Swafer acknowledged drinking to excess.

25/6/1740. Phebe Newland, wife of Joseph Newland, granted a certificate to Newark. Katherine Rhoads, wife of Benjamin Rhoads, produced a certificate from Goshen. Robert Williamson reported for drinking and being of a turbulent behavior. John Fawcet acknowledged marrying out by a Justice. David Sharples married by a priest.

29/7/1740. Jane Hoskins returned from Long Island. John Corsley, Jr., acknowledged marrying by a priest. George Warner requested a certificate to Cecil Monthly Meeting. Samuel Yarnall requested a certificate to Concord to marry Sarah Vernon, dau. of Jacob Vernon, dec'd, of Thornbury. Mary Sharples, wife of Joseph Sharples, Jr., produced a certificate from Concord.

27/8/1740. Susannah Lewis, wife of Joseph Lewis produced a certificate from Philadelphia.

24/9/1740. Henry Holland requested to become a member. John Gleave acknowledged being overtaken with strong drink.

29/10/1740. Thomas Swaffer requested a certificate to Salem.

26/11/1740. Thomas Swaffor's certificate not prepared as he has lived some time in Jersey and the weather has hindered the inquiries. Susannah Pile produced a certificate from Bradford. Charles Jones and his wife Sarah requested a certificate to Philadelphia. Joseph Salkeld reported for drinking to excess. Ann McCamish has married by a priest.

23/12/1740/1. Ann Rhoades, dau. of John Rhoades and wife of Patrick McCamish, condemned for marrying by a priest to one of another society. Joseph Howell, son of Jacob, requested a certificate to Philadelphia to marry Hannah Hudson, dau. of Samuell Hudson, dec'd, and settle there. Hannah Hunter, wife of William Hunter, granted a certificate to Goshen.

30/1/1741. Moses Minshall reported for marrying by a priest. [Annotation: m. 20 Sep 1740 to Jane Salkeld, Swedes Church, Wilmington.] Hannah Williamson, wife of Daniel Williamson, produced a certificate from Concord for herself, her children and for Sarah Yarnall, wife of Samuel.

27/7/1741. Richard Downing and Mary Edge may accomplish their marriage at Uwchlan Meeting House for their own convenience. Susannah Coebourn, dau. of Joseph Coebourn, reported for marrying one of another society. Richard Barry reported for going out of the country leaving debts unpaid; disowned. Mary Milner, wife of Samuel, granted a certificate to Newark Monthly Meeting. Mary Williams requested a certificate to Newark.

25/3/1741. Moses Minshall acknowledged committing fornication before marriage with his wife Jane. John Camaren requested to be received into membership. Mordecai Taylor of Springfield acknowledged marrying by a priest.

29/4/1741. Jane Pugh, wife of John Pugh, granted a certificate to Nottingham where she has lived a considerable time. Moses Edwards, son of John, requested a certificate to Newgarden. Mary Martin, dau. of Moses Martin, dec'd, acknowledged fornication with Richard Smith. Sarah Coates, wife of Thomas Coates, granted a certificate to Bradford.

27/5/1741. John Kendale and his wife Rebecah requested a certificate to Newark. William Haycock, son of William, requested a certificate to Gwynedd. Seth Pancoast and his wife Esther, requested a certificate to Newark. James Pennell, son of William, requested a

certificate to Goshen to marry Jemima Matlock. Mary Downing, wife
of Richard Downing, granted a certificate to Goshen. Ann McCamish,
wife of Patrick McCamish, granted a certificate to Darby.
26/6/1741. Samuel Howell produced a certificate from Nottingham.
James Lea produced a certificate from Darby for himself and his
wife Margret. Thomas Hodge reported for keeping loose and vain
company and being extravagant in his conduct and conversation.
Eleanor Mason, wife of John Mason, acknowledged marrying out to
one not a member by a priest. Alice Bell granted a certificate to
Philadelphia. Lydea Regester, dau. of David Regester, acknowledged
marrying by a priest to Nehemiah Baker, not a member. Jemima
Pennell, wife of James, produced a certificate from Goshen. Mary
Barton granted a certificate to Philadelphia, clear of marriage
engagements.
31/3/1742. Rachell Jackson reported deceased. Edward Fell requested a
certificate to Haverford for himself and his wife Mary. William
Shepperd has absconded from his creditors. Certificate received from
Newgarden for Thomas Salkeld but he has removed to Newark.
28/4/1742. Griffith Minshall and his wife Sarah acknowledged
fornication before marriage and marrying by a priest, being nearly
related. Jane Whippo, widow of George Whippo, reported for being
with child, which, when born, is likely to be a bastard.
26/5/1742. Sarah Lea, wife of Isaac Lea, produced a certificate from
Darby for herself and children; Isaac Lea already being under the
notice of the meeting. Sarah Warner, wife of John Warner, granted
a certificate to Philadelphia. Margaret Thomas, wife of Peter
Thomas, granted a certificate to Goshen. Mordecai Taylor appointed
to be elder in place of his father, Peter Taylor, dec'd.
30/6/1742. All representatives of the meetings appeared except William
Gorsuch who was absent because of the death of one of his children.
27/7/1742. William Surman requested a certificate to Crosswicks for
himself and his wife Sarah.
25/8/1742. Mary Bickham, widow of Richard Bickham, produced a
certificate from Haddonfield. Sarah Warner, dau. of George Warner,
dec'd, requested a certificate to Cecil Monthly Meeting. Dorothy
Yarnall granted a certificate to Newark. There is a difference
between John Crosley and Thomas Dell in that they have built a
forge on Crum Creek, the dam thereof overflows some part of said
Dell's land, the damage of which they have been unable to settle.
29/9/1742. Thomas and Joseph Williamson, two of the sons of Robert
Williamson, reported for marrying out to those of other societies.

Hannah Swaffer, dau. of William Swaffer, dec'd, granted a certificate to Haverford.

21/11/1742/3. Thomas Salkeld reported to be removed from Newark. John Knowles, who has lived as an apprentice with James Bartram, requested a certificate to Abington. Griffith Minshall requested a certificate to Newark for himself and his wife Sarah. Evan Lewis, son of Evan, produced a certificate from Bradford.

28/12/1742/3. Thomas Williamson acknowledged marrying out but also neglects meetings. James Lea requested a certificate to Darby for himself and his wife Margaret. Thomas Fawcet requested a certificate to Hopewell for himself, wife Lydia and son Richard.

28/1/1743. John Worrall of Marple Twp requested a certificate to Exeter. William Smith requested a certificate to Darby. Edward Farr requested a certificate to Goshen for himself and his wife Jane. Hannah Worrall requested a certificate to Owley.

25/2/1743. Thomas Salkeld produced a certificate from Newgarden. Mary Thomas, wife of Joseph Thomas, acknowledged marrying by a priest to one not of the society. [Annotation: Mary Fearn, dau. of Joshua Fearn, b. 21/9/1715 at Darby, m. Joseph Thomas and d. 3/3/175--.] Esther Bickerdike produced a certificate from Chesterfield, NJ, clear of marriage engagements. Samuel Levis and his wife Mary acknowledged fornication before marriage.

30/3/1743. Mary Barry, wife of Richard Barry and her children granted a certificate to Haverford. (Her dau. Margaret clear of marriage engagements.)

27/4/1743. Ann Smedley, wife of Francis Smedley, granted a certificate to Goshen. Joseph Coebourn of Chichester reported for fornication and marrying by a priest. Rebecah Burchley produced a certificate from Philadelphia, clear of marriage engagements.

25/5/1743. William Weldon reported for marrying out and other irregularities. Elizabeth Marris, wife of John Marris, acknowledged marrying out by a priest. Mordecai Taylor reported for fornication before marriage and other irregularities. John Needham requested a certificate to Philadelphia for himself, wife Elizabeth and daus. Ann and Mary.

29/6/1743. John Martin requested a certificate to Concord to marry Phebe, dau. of Thomas Masser (Mercer). Robert Regester requested a certificate to Goshen to marry Jane Williamson, dau. of John Williamson. David Salkeld produced a certificate from Nottingham where he was an apprentice. Sarah Dicks chosen overseer for the women's Providence Preparative Meeting instead of Elizabeth

Taylor, now Woodworth. Margaret Mathew, now Watson, reported for marrying by a priest, it being the second offense. [Annotation: Married July 24, 1743 at Christ Church, Philadelphia]

26/7/1743. Elizabeth Williams, wife of Rees, produced a certificate from Gwynedd for herself, dau. Elizabeth and younger children: Isaac, Ruth and Phebe. Katherine Williams, dau. of Rees, produced a certificate from Gwynedd. Margaret Mather, widow of William Mather, married Thomas Watson, not of the Society. Elizabeth Woodward, wife of Edward Woodward, granted a certificate to Goshen. Caleb Harrison, Jr., requested a certificate to Exeter for himself and his wife Elener. Thomas Shipley requested a certificate to Falls to marry Mary Merriot, dau. of Thomas Merriot.

31/8/1743. Joseph Coebourn acknowledged marrying out. John Edwards, Jr., reported for marrying out to one not a member and neglecting meetings.

28/9/1743. Jane Cummings, dau. of Enoch Cummings, produced a certificate from Duck Creek. James Read received into membership.

26/10/1743. William Weldon's acknowledgment to be read at Chester Meeting but his father-in-law, John Peters, to be first acquainted with it to raise any objection to its being received. John Edwards disowned. Phebe Martin, wife of John Martin, produced a certificate from Concord. Vincent Bonsall produced a certificate from Darby. John Edwards, Jr., reported for marrying out to one not a member and neglecting meetings.

30/11/1743/4. Thomas Fell requested a certificate to Darby to marry Elizabeth Hinds, widow of James Hinds, and to settle. John Calvert, son of Daniel Calvert, received into membership. Sarah Hoskins, wife of Stephen Hoskins, requested a certificate to Philadelphia. Jane Regester, now Scot, reported for marrying [to John Scott] by a priest. Mary Shipley produced a certificate from Falls Monthly Meeting.

26/12/1743/4. John Baldwin produced a certificate from Concord for himself and his wife Ann. Mary Shipley, wife of Thomas, produced a certificate from Falls. James Moor produced a certificate from Hartshaw Monthly Meeting in Lancashire in Great Britain. Martha Dickin granted a certificate to Goshen, clear of marriage engagements.

26/1/1744. Jane Regester produced a certificate from Goshen.

30/2/1744. Sarah Scott, wife of James Scott, acknowledged marrying by a priest to one not a member. Stephen Ogden and his wife Hannah Surman acknowledged fornication and marriage by a priest. Cathrin

Williams, now Boyrn, reported for marrying by a priest. Lydia
Vernon, dau. of Isaac, reported for having a bastard child and
concealing the father. Jane Regester of Middletown Meeting, now
wife of John Scott, reported for fornication and marrying by a priest.

28/3/1744. Ann Key, dau. of Moses Key, delivered a bastard child and
declared Mordecai Vernon, son of Thomas, to be the father.
Elizabeth Shipley, dau. of William Shipley, granted a certificate to
Newark, clear of marriage engagements. Sarah Taylor, [formerly
Worrall], now wife of John Taylor, Jr., of Thornbury, acknowledged
marrying by a priest.

25/4/1744. Benanuel Lowns requested a certificate to Goshen to marry
Alice Williamson, dau. of John Williamson.

30/5/1744. Ann Norbury, wife of Thomas, granted a certificate to
Goshen. Rees Williams, Jr., produced a certificate from Gwynedd.
Moses Meredith produced a certificate from Gwynedd for himself
and his wife Mary. Hannah Longacre and Rachall Jerson requested
to come under the care of Friends.

27/6/1744. Mary Martin, dau. of Moses, delivered a bastard child, being
the second offense and she has removed to a great distance.

24/7/1744. Hannah Coebourn, dau. of Joseph Coebourn, acknowledged
marrying out by a Baptist priest to Thomas Battin. Rachel Edge
granted a certificate to Goshen.

29/8/1744. Hannah Battin, wife of Thomas Battin, granted a certificate
to Bradford. Elizabeth Morris, wife of John Morris, granted a
certificate to Goshen. Aaron Watson requested a certificate to
Philadelphia. John Ebulon received into membership. Thomas
Bonsall produced a certificate from Darby for himself and his wife
Esther. Evan Lewis requested a certificate to Bradford.

26/9/1744. Alice Lowns, wife of Benanuel Lowns, produced a certificate
from Goshen. Mary Shaw produced a certificate from Sadsbury.
Abigail Taylor, wife of John Taylor of Chester, shoemaker,
acknowledged marrying out to one not of the Society. Rachell Moor,
wife of John Moor, granted a certificate to Haverford. Sarah Routh,
wife of Francis Routh, Jr., granted a certificate to Concord.

29/10/1744. Samuel Howell, son of Jacob, requested a certificate to
Haverford to marry Ann Evans, dau. of Hugh Evans of Merion.
Mary Hibberd, wife of Isaac Hibberd, granted a certificate to Darby.
Prudence Coebourn, dau. of Joseph Coebourn, granted a certificate
to Philadelphia. Isaac Minshall requested a certificate to Newark.
Thomas Pilkington produced a certificate from Darby for himself, his

wife Rose and for his apprentice Archibald Job. Abraham and Jacob Sharples produced a certificate from Bradford.

28/11/1744/5. Elizabeth Marshall, wife of Abraham Marshall, granted a certificate to Darby. Sarah Taylor, wife of John Taylor of Thornbury, granted a certificate to Concord. John Worrall of Marple Twp produced a certificate from Exeter for himself, his wife and children.

25/12/1744/5. Rees Williams, son of Rees, requested a certificate to North Wales to marry Rachell Starr, dau. of James Starr. Jonathan Haycock, son of Jonathan, requested a certificate to Richland. Thomas Yarnall, son of Thomas, reported married by a priest. Jonathan Maris acknowledged drinking and other disorders. Francis Swain, Jr., requested a certificate to Newgarden.

25/1/1745. Thomas Wooley, wife Sarah and children, requested a certificate to Philadelphia. George Smedley, Jr., requested a certificate to Goshen. John Moor requested a certificate to Haverford. Catharine Brownall received into membership.

29/2/1745. Lewis Davis produced a certificate from Haverford. Joseph Levis requested a certificate to Abington for himself and his wife Susannah. John Fawcett requested a certificate to Hopewell for himself and his wife Rebecca. Henry Holland requested a certificate to Goshen for himself and his wife Lydia. David Salkeld requested a certificate to Bradford for himself and his wife.

27/3/1745. Joseph Slaigh produced a certificate from Newgarden. Hannah Longacre, wife of Andrew Longacre, granted a certificate to Concord.

24/4/1745. Ann Howell, wife of Samuel, produced a certificate from Merion. Jacob Edge requested a certificate to Goshen. Thomas Yarnall acknowledged marrying out and without his parents' consent or knowledge.

29/5/1745. John Hall requested a certificate to Philadelphia to marry Mary Thomlinson, widow of Benjamin Thomlinson. Ann Morgan, wife of James Morgan, granted a certificate to Richland.

26/6/1745. Benjamin Kendale requested a certificate to Philadelphia for himself, his wife Grace and three apprentices: Peter Howard, John Cummings and Thomas Pederick. John Harrison, son of Caleb, requested a certificate to Goshen to marry Mary Thomas, dau. of Richard Thomas, dec'd. Reubin Roberts produced a certificate from Gwynedd.

30/7/1745. Rachel Williams, wife of Rees Williams, Jr. and dau. of James Starr, produced a certificate from Gwynedd. Randale Croxton reported for not paying a just debt to Thomas Pennall and for keeping a disorderly house by suffering people of ill fame to frequent it. [He shortly thereafter paid the debt and promised to keep a more orderly house.] Thomas Constable produced a certificate from Falmouth Monthly Meeting of the county of Cornwall in Great Britain.

28/8/1745. Rachell Fawcett, wife of Richard Fawcett, acknowledged fornication and marrying by a priest.

25/9/1745. Rowland Richards produced a certificate from Gwynedd for himself, his wife Sarah and three of their younger children: Aquilla, Samuel and Sarah. David Cowpland, son of Caleb Cowpland, has an inclination to go to sea in a vessel bound for Ireland with an intent to trade there, granted a certificate. Priscilla Taylor reported for marrying out to James McMickle, not of the Society. Thomas Pilkington reported for not paying John Pennall a just debt. George Turner produced a certificate from Newark Monthly Meeting.

30/10/1745. Richard Gormun received into membership. Rachell Fawcet, wife of Richard Fawcet, requested a certificate to Hopewell.

24/12/1745/6. Robert Pennell, son of William, requested a certificate to Concord to marry Hannah Chamberlin, dau. of Joseph. Esther Bonsall, widow of Thomas, requested a certificate to Darby.

31/1/1746. Mary Harrison, wife of John, produced a certificate from Goshen. Henry Miller reported for drinking to excess and for corrupt conversation. Ann Lewis, dau. of Thomas Lewis, dec'd, requested a certificate to Darby. Benjamin Sharples requested a certificate to Concord to marry Martha Mendinghall, dau. of Benjamin Mendinghall, dec'd.

28/2/1746. Rebeccah Burchall requested a certificate to Philadelphia.

23/3/1746. John Regester, son of David, accused by Margaret Boyd. Jane Lewis, dau. of Samuel Lewis, acknowledged fornication with Thomas Brinton. Susanna Billerby requested a certificate to Concord. Susannah Powell married out of unity.

30/4/1746. Since her application for a certificate to Philadelphia, Rebecca Burchall, school mistress, has received strong encouragement from the residents of Germantown to establish and run a school there. She, therefore, desires the certificate be directed to Abington Monthly Meeting. The children of Alice Farr by Norbury, her first husband, are of age and the widow has nothing to pay them, the estate being left to his brother. Rebecca Burn, wife of Daniel, produced a certificate from North Wales for herself and children, Caleb and Rachell. Susannah Williamson, dau. of Daniel Williamson, married David Powell out of unity; she chose to be disowned. Joseph Sharples produced a certificate from Bradford for himself and his wife Lydia.

25/5/1746. Samuel Evans produced a certificate from Sadsbury for himself, wife Ann and children. Nathan Taylor requested a certificate to Haverford to marry Ruth Evans, dau. of Evan Evans. Jane Levis, wife of William, requested a certificate to Newark. Alice Hall, wife of Thomas, requested a certificate to Goshen. Joseph Edwards and his wife Elizabeth acknowledged marrying by a priest.

29/7/1746. Mary Hall produced a certificate from Philadelphia. Hannah Pennell, formerly Hannah Chamberlin, produced a certificate from Concord. Benjamin Sharples requested a certificate to Concord to marry Martha Mendinghall, dau. of Benjamin, dec'd.

27/8/1746. John Crosley denied the charge yet he or someone for him has paid toward the maintenance of the child to stop prosecution.

24/9/1746. Laurance Cox produced a certificate from Goshen for himself, his wife Sarah and children: John, Martha and Rachel. Katherine Brownill married Thomas Williamson. Isaac Gleave, son of John, requested a certificate to Darby to marry Mary Hunt, dau. of James Hunt, dec'd.

29/10/1746. Henry Miller reported for drinking to excess. Nathan Taylor appointed overseer in the room of Edward Woodward, Jr., dec'd.

26/11/1746/7. Samuel Ogden reported for frequently being disordered by drinking to excess and being very unruly when so. Roger Pugh requested a certificate to Duck Creek for himself, his wife Sarah and children. Hannah Davis, wife of John, requested a certificate to North Wales.

23/12/1746/7. Katherine Rhodes, late widow of Benjamin Rhodes, acknowledged marrying out to James Traveller, not of the Society.

30/1/1747. Isaac Gleave requested a certificate to Philadelphia. John Thomson, son of Joshua, requested to be received into membership; approved. Josiah Lewis reported in cohabitation with Martha Allen as man and wife. Jane Norbury requested a certificate to Richland, Bucks Co. signifying clearness in marriage. Mary Pearson, now Janey, married out of unity.

27/2/1747. Josiah Lewis produced a few lines to demonstrate that he has married Martha Allen but did not disclose the date of the marriage, she not a member of the Society. Mary Gruff, wife of Samuel, requested a certificate to Concord. Mary Pearson, dau. of Robert Pearson, married out of unity to Able Jenney, Jr., and conceals the time of her marriage.

25/3/1747. Ruth Taylor, wife of Nathan Taylor, produced a certificate from Radnor. Richard Person produced a certificate from Philadelphia and requested a certificate to Hopewell [Virginia]; Friends appointed to inquire regarding his wife Sarah Person.

29/4/1747. Mary and Ann Cummings produced a certificate from Duck Creek, clear from marriage engagements.

28/7/1747. John Harrison requested a certificate to Exeter in Philadelphia Co with his wife Mary. Aaron Vernon requested a certificate to Goshen with his wife Margrat and children. Thomas Calvert, son of Daniel, reported for marrying out. Katherine Bethel, wife of Joseph, requested a certificate to Darby. Mary Giffing requested a certificate to Philadelphia.

30/9/1747. Katherine Traviller, wife of James, requested a certificate to Goshen.

29/10/1747. Hannah Neale requested a certificate to Philadelphia. Sarah Dicks, dau. of Peter Dicks, reported for being clandestinely married to, or living as the wife of, Thomas Elly (Eley).

29/11/1747/8. Christian Hoops, dau. of Daniel, requested a certificate to Newark. Alice Crosley, wife of John, acknowledged marrying out of unity. John Pennell produced a certificate from Concord for himself and his wife Martha. Joshua Garrett, son of William, requested a certificate to Abington. Samuel Ogden reported drinking to excess.

27/1/1749. Joseph Ashbridge requested a certificate to Goshen to marry Priscilla Davis, dau. of David. Jonathan Cowpland produced a certificate from Bridgetown, Barbadoes. Rebecca Bourn, wife of Daniel, requested a certificate to Gwynedd for herself and children: Caleb and Rachell. Patience Howell requested to come under the care of Friends.

24/2/1749. Mary Ogden, dau. of Samuel, dec'd, requested a certificate to Philadelphia.

29/3/1749. Isaac Weaver and his wife Mary acknowledged marrying out by a priest. Nathan Dicks and his wife Sarah acknowledged fornication before marriage. Thomas Goodwin requested a certificate to Goshen with his wife and children. Mary Moss, wife of Isaac, requested a certificate to Philadelphia. John Yarnall requested a certificate to Newark with his wife Abigail and children: Isaac, Abigail and Hannah.

26/4/1749. John Gracy produced a certificate from Exeter, Philadelphia Co., for himself and his wife Catharine. Mary Sharples, now Swain, requested a certificate to Newgarden.

31/5/1749. Mary Swayne, wife of Thomas, requested a certificate to Newgarden. Jonathan Worrall, son of John of Marple Twp, married out of unity to one not a member. Alice Lewis, wife of Jehu, requested a certificate to Derby. Rebecca Thomas, wife of William, requested a certificate to Goshen. Sarah Yarnall, widow of Samuel, requested a certificate to Newark. Jane Russell and children received into membership.

28/6/1749. Priscilla Ashbridge, wife of Joseph, produced a certificate from Goshen. Seth Pancoast produced a certificate from Newark for himself and his wife Esther. Robert Taylor reported for drinking to excess.

25/7/1749. Nathan Cowpland requested a certificate, he intending a trading voyage to Ireland. William Melin and his wife Elizabeth acknowledged marrying by a priest.

27/8/1749. A certificate was signed last 4th month for John Yarnall, Abigail his wife and three children, and since their removal to Wilmington, John died, and now the widow and children have returned the certificate with endorsement from Newark (Wilmington Preparative Meeting). John Crosby, Jr., neglected to pay a debt to Esther Bickerdike. Joshua Thomson, Jr. and Martha Ogden, dau.of Samuel, dec'd, married by a priest.

25/10/1749. Elias Neal produced a certificate from Concord for himself, his wife Grace and children. Margaret Bishop, wife of Thomas, acknowledged marrying by a priest. Israel Howell produced a certificate from Newgarden. Archibald Job requested a certificate to Nottingham. Daniell Calvert refuses to pay a debt to Peter Dicks.

29/11/1749/50. Benjamin Lightfoot, son of Samuel, requested a certificate to Barbadoes, intending to merchandise there. Rachel Martin produced a certificate from Goshen. Vincent Bonsall requested a certificate to Newark. Thomas Williamson, son of Thomas, acknowledged marrying by priest.

26/12/1749/50. Nathan Yarnall requested a certificate to Newgarden to marry Hannah Mendinghall, dau. of Benjamin Mendinghall, dec'd.

26/1/1750. Thomas Kendall requested a certificate with his wife Sarah and children to Warrington, York Co. Rebeccah Lea, dau. of Isaac, reported for fornication. Elizabeth Williams married by a priest to one not a member.

30/2/1750. Rees Williams, Jr., requested a certificate to Exeter for himself and his wife Rac---. John Baldwin requested a certificate to Concord Monthly Meeting for himself and his wife Ann. John Harry produced a certificate from Newark for himself and his wife Frances.

Martha Thompson, wife of Joshua, Jr., acknowledged marrying out.
Rebecca Lea, dau. of Isaac Lea, acknowledged fornication with
Samuel Vere. *[Annotation: Isaac C. Lea of New York in his 77th
year, wrote to Minshall Painter in 1863 for information about his
ancestry; says his father Samuel was born about 1750 but the family
record had been destroyed by fire years before; he also stated that
Samuel's father died when Samuel was an infant; Isaac claimed to
be a descendant of John Lea, the minister.]* Rachel Martin, dau. of
Moses Martin, dec'd, reported for marrying her first cousin Samuel
Battin. George Turner requested a certificate to marry Sarah Hays,
dau. of Jonathan. Thomas Worrall, son of John, dec'd, requested a
certificate to Concord to marry Mary Peirce, dau. of Caleb Peirce.
Jonathan Howell requested a certificate to Goshen to marry
Elizabeth Thomas, dau. of Richard Thomas, dec'd. Margery Thomson
reported for being of a loose disorder and conversation.
28/3/1750. Elizabeth Fishwater [late Williams] acknowledged marrying
out. Marjory Thompson of Springfield reported for keeping idle,
dissolute company to the scandal of her sex.
25/4/1750. Rebecca Lea refuses to be present at the reading of the
acknowledgment. Peter Dicks, Jr., acknowledged marrying by a
priest. Richard Gorman acknowledged marrying by a priest.
30/5/1750. Jesse Maris, son of George, produced a certificate from
Haverford. Thomas Moore produced a certificate from Goshen with
his wife Sarah and children. Hannah Yarnall, wife of Nathan,
produced a certificate from Newgarden. Rebecca Vernon produced a
certificate from Goshen. Hannah Lewis, dau. of Samuel, requested a
certificate to Wilmington.
27/6/1750. Robert Taylor reported for drinking to excess and for using
unbecoming and extravagant language. Ann Reese requested to
come under the care of Friends; approved.
24/7/1750. Reuben Roberts requested a certificate to North Wales.
29/8/1750. Edward Russell requested for himself and children to come
under the care of Friends. Joshua Mendinghall produced a certificate
from Newgarden. Elizabeth Fitgwater, wife of Thomas, requested a
certificate to Gwynedd. Elizabeth Howell, wife of Jonathan,
produced a certificate from Goshen. Mary Worrall, wife of Thomas,
produced a certificate from Concord. Elizabeth Swain, dau. of
William, dec'd, produced a certificate from Newgarden.
26/9/1750. Ann Lewis, dau. of Thomas, produced a certificate from
Darby. Hannah Evans, dau. of Cadwalader Evans, acknowledged

marrying Rowland Parry, not a member and without her parents' consent.

31/10/1750. Thomas Swain produced a certificate from Newgarden for himself and his wife Mary. Benjamin Lightfoot requested a certificate to Philadelphia. Samuel Lightfoot requested a certificate to Goshen with children: Thomas, Samuel and William.

28/11/1750/1. John Eblen requested a certificate to Darby for himself, his wife Mary and children. Jonathan Willis produced a certificate from Radnor for himself and his wife Dinah. John Cameron, who some time past requested to come under the care of Friends, has lately married to one not of the Society.

25/12/1750/1. Joseph Worrall of Providence requested a certificate for himself, his wife Mary and children to be received into membership; approved. John Cox requested a certificate to Goshen to marry Mary Farr. Samuel Hampton requested to be received into membership; approved. Abigail Edge requested a certificate to Bradford. Rebecca Hall requested a certificate to Buckingham. Robert Taylor still continues to drink to excess.

25/1/1751. George Simpson produced a certificate from Concord. David Yarnall, son of Philip, requested a certificate to Newark. Elizabeth Yarnall, dau. of Philip, requested a certificate to Newark. John Gracy requested a certificate to Newgarden to marry Ruth Miller, widow of James.

29/2/1751. Patience Howell, dau. of William, dec'd, requested a certificate to Sadsbury.

27/3/1751. Susannah Day, wife of James, produced a certificate from Haverford. Sarah Harris, formerly wife of John Harris, married out to John Coppock, not a member of the Society. Richard Bowman produced a certificate from Chesterfield Monthly Meeting in Derbyshire, England, for himself and his sister Phebe. Cornelius Bowman produced a certificate from Leek Monthly Meeting in Staffordshire, England.

24/4/1751. Isaac Lea requested a certificate to Wilmington with his wife Sarah and children: Hannah, Rebecca, Mary, Sarah, Ann, George and Rachaell. Susannah Bourn requested a certificate to Newark.

29/5/1751. Isaac Murry produced a certificate from the two weeks meeting in London. Mary Cox, wife of John, produced a certificate from Goshen. Joshua Mendinghall requested a certificate to Concord.

26/6/1751. Richard Crosby, a young man under notice of the meeting, has been charged with several scandalous reports, such as having had carnal knowledge of one or more young women and keeping rude and disreported company. Phebe Jervis, wife of William, acknowledged marrying out. Esther Ashton, wife of Abraham Ashton, acknowledged fornication with Nathaniel Ring.

30/7/1751. Grace Buckannan produced a certificate from Waltham Abbey Monthly Meeting giving her clearness to marry. Hannah Parry requested a certificate to Haverford. Pheby Jervis [wife of William] requested a certificate to Philadelphia. Abigail Williamson produced a certificate from Concord Monthly Meeting. Thomas Thompson married out to one of another persuasion. David Malin acknowledged marrying one not a member. Israell Howell requested a certificate to Concord for himself and wife Elizabeth.

28/8/1751. Jonathan Cowpland produced a certificate from hence with a few lines on the back thereof from Lurgan. Ruth Gracy, wife of John, produced a certificate from Newgarden. Samuel Minshall produced a certificate from Philadelphia.

25/9/1751. Agreed that friends within the compass of our yearly meeting should be concerned with the minute of the yearly meeting in London regarding the method of computing time as prescribed by a late act of Parliament, as followeth, viz., Agreed that as by the late act of Parliament for regulating the commencement of the year that it is ordered that the first day of the eleventh month next shall be deemed the first day of the year 1752 and that the month called January shall be successively called the first month of the year and not the month called March as heretofore hath been our method of computing.

That from and after the time above mentioned the eleventh month called January shall thence forward by deemed and reckoned the first month in every year and to be so styled in all the records and writings of Friends Instead of computing from the month called March according to our present practice and friends are recommended to go on with the names of the following months numerically according to our practice from the beginning so that the months may be called and written as follows. That named January to be called and written the first month and February to be called and written the second month and so on all other methods of computing and calling the months unavoidably leads into contradiction.

And whereas for the more regular computation of time the same act directs that in the month now called September which will be in the year 1752 after the second day of the said month eleven nominall days shall be omitted and that which would have been the third day shall be recorded and esteemed the fourteenth day of the said month and that which otherwise would have been the fourth day of the said month must be deemed the fifteenth and so on.

[Change from Julian to Gregorian calendar 31 October 1751 at midnight.]

27/1/1752. George Debble produced a certificate from Darby. Isaac Howell of Edgmont, carpenter, accused of fornication and begetting a child with Elizabeth Vaughan and was married out to another woman.

24/4/1752. Isaac Howell denied part of the charge. William Squibb requested a certificate to Warrington in order for settlement there.

30/3/1752. Lydia Minshall, wife of Isaac, produced a certificate from Wilmington. Joseph Coubourn, Jr., of Chester, acknowledged marrying out. Ephraim Jackson requested a certificate to Exeter with wife Mary and children. Susannah Day, wife of James Day, requested a certificate to Gloucester in Great Britain. Abraham Martin, son of Thomas, requested a certificate to Concord to marry Lydia [Hughs], widow of Isaac Hues [Hughs].

27/4/1752. John Harris requested a certificate to Darby for himself, his wife Frances and children. John Howard reported for being intoxicated with strong drink, going to David Wetherby's and drawing cider without leave, and neglecting meetings. Lydia Minchall [Minshall] requested a certificate to Goshen.

25/5/1752. Sarah Moore, widow of Thomas, Jr., requested a certificate to Goshen with children. Certificate produced from Philadelphia for Edward Carter, son of John, who is now settled in the verge of Wilmington Meeting, to which the certificate is now directed. Joseph Tanyer of Springfield requested to be taken under the care of Friends; approved. Joshua Lewis acknowledged marrying out to Abigail Williamson, dau. of Daniel Williamson.

27/7/1752. George Dibble reported for being frequently overtaken with strong drink, having dealt with him several times but unable to reclaim him.

31/8/1752. Hannah Holcombe produced a certificate from Abington. Esther Darlington, wife of John, requested a certificate jointly with her husband to Concord. Joseph Haycock, son of Jonathan, requested a certificate to Goshen to marry Hannah Massey, dau. of Thomas Massey.

25/9/1752. Abraham Dicks acknowledged marrying out to one of
another persuasion. Isaac Howell acknowledged undue and unlawful
liberty with Elizabeth Vaughan and marrying out to one of another
persuasion. Isaac Gleaves produced a certificate from Philadelphia
for himself and his wife Mary.

30/10/1752. Benjamin Maddock reported for drinking to excess,
breaking his promises to his creditors and neglecting meetings.
Abraham Martin requested a certificate to Concord.

27/11/1752. James Maris acknowledged marrying by a priest to Rachel
Evans.

25/12/1752. Jonas Preston produced a certificate from Middletown,
Bucks Co. for himself, his wife Sarah and children with her dau.
Sarah Carter. Richard Bradley produced a certificate from Settle
Monthly Meeting in Yorkshire, Great Britain. Susannah Day
returned from Great Britain. Grace Buckhannan requested a
certificate to Philadelphia.

29/1/1753. Elizabeth Maddock, wife of Benjamin, reported for drinking
to excess. Meeting informed by Friends of Chester that John Salkeld
hath for some time absented himself from their meeting and hath
frequented the worship of the Church of England, so called. James
Reed reported for joining the Society of the Presbyterians from
whence he came and going to reside in a remote part of York
County.

26/2/1753. Hannah Haycock, wife of Joseph, produced a certificate from
Goshen. William Pearson requested a certificate to Goshen. Samuel
Pennell acknowledged marrying out. [See Swedes Church, marriage
of Samuel Pennell and Rachel Cobourn 21 Nov 1752.] Susannah
Dunn, wife of Phillip, requested a certificate to Goshen for herself
and children (Sarah and Younger). Jonathan Maris requested a
certificate to North Wales to marry Ann Waln, dau. of Richard.
Randale Croxton reported for neglecting meetings and drinking to
excess. Rebeccah Hamton and Sarah her sister, requested to come
under the care of Friends.

26/3/1753. Peter Thompson, son of Peter, dec'd, requested a certificate
to Philadelphia. Thomas Wiley produced a certificate from Exeter in
Berks Co. for himself and his wife Rebeccah.

30/4/1753. Henry Camm requested a certificate to Goshen for himself,
his wife Margery. and children, Sarah and Esther.

28/5/1753. Jacob Lightfoot requested a certificate to Exeter. Isaac
Murrey requested a certificate to Devonshire Monthly Meeting in
London. Robert Carter married out of unity. Jonathan Howell

requested a certificate to Goshen for himself and his wife Elizabeth. Ninevah Carter granted a certificate for himself and his wife; certificate returned for not mentioning the minor children and a question of settling affairs. Cadwalader Evans reported for drinking to excess and charges were lodged by Hannah Holcomb against him for having criminal conversations with her; he denied the latter. Elizabeth Giferd [Gifford] requested to come under the care of Friends.

25/6/1753. Some accounts reported between Jane Hoskins and Isaac Murrey; he being gone into Maryland. Elizabeth Crosby, wife of Richard, acknowledged marrying out of unity. Hannah Holcomb's charges are false, by her own confession saying that Cadwalader Evans had gotten her with child.

30/7/1753. John Holton produced a certificate from Philadelphia for himself, his wife and children. Jesse Woodward produced a certificate from Goshen for himself and children. Sarah Clayton, wife of David, acknowledged marrying out of unity. Jacob Howell requested a certificate to Newgarden to marry Deborah Fred, widow of Benjamin Fred, and to settle there.

27/8/1753. Isaac Yarnall reported for marrying out to one of another Society and without his mother's consent. Jane Brooks has taken sick and is in need of assistance.

24/9/1753. Samuell Swayne requested a certificate to Newgarden. Ninevah Carter produced a certificate from Buckingham for himself and his wife Mary.

29/10/1753. William Eachus produced a certificate from Goshen for self, his wife Sarah and son Gainer Peirce. Ann Maris, wife of Jonathan produced a certificate from Gwynedd. Prudence Woodworth produced a certificate from Goshen jointly with her husband (Jesse). Elizabeth Holton produced a certificate from Philadelphia with husband and child.

26/11/1753. Agness Lowns, wife of John Lowns, granted a certificate.

28/1/1754. John Emblen produced a certificate from Darby for himself and his wife Mary.

25/2/1754. Hannah Passmore, wife of Augustine, requested a certificate to Nottingham. Rebecca Pyle, wife of Robert, requested a certificate to Concord.

26/3/1754. Daniel Eachus, son of Robert, requested a certificate to Newark. George Worrall, son of John, acknowledged marrying out to Priscilla David. Mary Grubb, wife of Adam, acknowledged marrying by a priest. Rachel Pennell, wife of Samuel Pennell, and Mary

Robinson, dau. of William Robinson, dec'd, and Elizabeth Roberts of Springfield, requested to come under the notice of Friends.

29/4/1754. William Eachus requested a certificate to Goshen with his wife Sarah and her son Gainer Peirce. Abraham Haydock [of Darby, Chester Co.], son of Robert of the county of Lancaster in England, and Elizabeth Roberts, to marry, he to bring certificate. Richard Bowman requested a certificate to Philadelphia. Joshua Lewis reported for debts to William Jones. Rachel Bunting, wife of William, acknowledged marrying out. Mary Robinson requested a certificate to Philadelphia. Eleanor Godferra produced a certificate from Ballinacris, Antrim Co., Ireland.

27/5/1754. Abigail Garrett, wife of William, requested a certificate to Goshen with two daus., Abigail and Hannah (Yarnall). Elias Neal acknowledged marrying by a priest to Sarah Green. Christian Vores produced a certificate from Goshen for himself, his wife Sarah and children. Abraham Yarnall acknowledged marrying out to Elizabeth James. Abraham Haydock and Elizabeth Roberts intend to marry; however, his certificate from Darby Monthly Meeting to be returned to him as it is thought that he is not in the proper condition, not appearing to be rational. Hannah Powell, dau. of Joseph, Jr., of Marple Twp, received into membership.

24/6/1754. Jesse Maris Emblen produced a certificate from Darby for himself and his wife Mary.

29/7/1754. Kirnelius [Cornelius] Bowman requested a certificate to Darby. William Edwards, son of James, requested a certificate to Goshen to marry Sarah Dunn, dau. of Philip. Pennell Evans, son of Cadwalader, requested a certificate to Exeter.

30/9/1754. Robert Rogers produced a certificate from North Wales for himself and his wife Ann. Sarah Claton, wife of David, requested a certificate to Concord.

28/10/1754. Lydia Mendinghall produced a certificate from Duck Creek. John Philips produced a certificate from Gwynedd for himself, his wife Deborah and their children, except Mary, but they now removed into the verge of Nottingham. Jonathan Howell and his wife Elizabeth having returned from the limits of Goshen, now return their certificate which they neglected to deliver to Goshen. Thomas Pilkington reported for neglecting to pay a debt to Nathan Edwards. Sarah Hall, widow of George, requested a certificate to Nottingham.

25/11/1754. John Phillips granted a certificate to Nottingham for himself, his wife and all of their children except Hannah. Edward

Fell produced a certificate from Haverford for himself and children, Deborah and Hannah. Elias Neal requested a certificate to Concord. Aaron Minshal reported for marrying out and drinking to excess. Joshua Lewis reported for debts to Robert Mendinghall.

29/12/1754. Jacob Lightfoot requested a certificate to Exeter. George Simpson requested a certificate to Concord. Elizabeth Fox married out of unity.

27/1/1755. Joshua Lewis absconded from these parts and thereby defrauded his creditors. Thomas Parvin produced a certificate from Goshen for himself and his wife Mary. Margaret Starr produced a certificate from Goshen for herself and her sons, Samuel and Moses. Elizabeth Williams, widow of Rees, requested a certificate to Newark with dau. Ph---. Isaac Williams, Jr., requested a certificate to Newark. Henry Lawrance, Jr., produced a certificate from Radnor. David Ogden reported for drinking to excess and absconding from his creditors. Elizabeth Fawkes acknowledged marrying by a priest [wife of William].

24/2/1755. Lawrance Cox requested a certificate to Goshen for himself, his wife Sarah and their children by said wife. Margaret Malin, wife of David, received into membership. Hannah Harris married out of unity.

24/3/1755. Cadwalader Evans reported for continuing to drink to excess.

28/4/1755. Isaac and James Collier reported for going into another province without paying or securing their debts, being given to an extravagance in conversation and some excess in drinking. John Cox requested a certificate to Goshen for himself, his wife Mary and children. Susannah Daugherty produced a certificate from Philadelphia.

26/5/1755. Esther Eachus, wife of Enoch, requested a certificate to Newark for herself and two children, William and Sarah.

30/6/1755. John Lea, Jr., of Wilmington reported for marrying out of unity. Thomas Starr produced a certificate from Goshen for himself, his wife Sarah and children.

28/7/1755. John Lea having gone to sea, his case continued. Certificate signed for Christian Vore and family. Isaac Starr produced a certificate from Goshen. Alice McCall, wife of William McCall (formerly Alice Bell) acquainted the meeting that several years ago she received a certificate from this meeting directed to Philadelphia Monthly Meeting but soon after was taken ill of a disorder and lost the certificate, and since had married a man not of our Society by a priest and which she has condemned. Jane Green, wife of Abel Green, acknowledged marrying out of unity. Hannah Phillips, dau. of John, requested a certificate to Nottingham. Richard Bradley requested a certificate to Goshen for himself and his wife Elizabeth. George Turner reported for setting up a separate meeting and preaching at them contrary to the Rules and Orders established among Friends.

25/8/1755. Ruth Collier reported for being of a turbulent and abusive behavior. Mary Crokson produced a certificate from Gwynedd. Samuel Crosley and his wife Mary acknowledged fornication before marriage and other faults.

29/9/1755. William Edwards acknowledged fornication before marriage. Hannah Ogden, dau. of Samuel, requested a certificate to Philadelphia.

27/10/1755. Jeremiah Carter, son of Neneveh, requested a certificate to Newgarden. Alice Ogden, wife of David, requested a certificate to Burlington for herself and 3 children. Margret Powell acknowledged marrying out of unity.

24/11/1755. Rachel Woodward, widow of Thomas, produced a certificate from Goshen.

29/12/1755. John Williamson, son of Daniel, reported for fornication before marriage and keeping evil and vain company. Hannah Harris, dau. of Daniel Williamson, acknowledged marrying out to John Harris. Thomas Williamson requested a certificate to Concord for himself, his wife and children.

26/1/1756. Friends appointed were of the opinion that the greatest of Hannah Harris's papers of acknowledgment was not truth. Aaron Minshall reported for drinking to excess and marrying out. Mary (Russell) Grubb, wife of Adam, requested a certificate to Concord. Sarah Scott, wife of James, requested a certificate to Goshen. Abigail Williamson and husband requested a certificate to Concord.

23/2/1756. John Williamson was reported as saying that he "thought it would be better for friends to deny him ..." Hannah Bonsall, wife of Isaac, requested a certificate to Darby. David Brooks produced a certificate from Newgarden for himself and his wife Eleanor, dated about 20 years earlier which he neglected to deliver but now acknowledged and requested a certificate to Darby. Samuel Crosley reported for debt to Samuel Howell.

31/3/1756. Jonas Preston requested a certificate to Haverford to marry Hannah Lewis, widow of William of Haverford. Thomas Shipley requested a certificate to Wilmington with his wife and children.

William Edwards acknowledged fornication before marriage.
Abraham Yarnall, son of Philip, requested a certificate to Newark.
John Hoopes, son of Abraham, acknowledged fornication before
marriage.

26/4/1756. Elizabeth Gleave, widow of John Gleave, dec'd, requested a
certificate to Newark Monthly Meeting. Hannah Williamson, wife of
Daniel, requested a certificate to Goshen. Elizabeth Key, widow of
Moses, produced a certificate from Concord. Thomas Musgrove
reported for drinking to excess and marrying out. James Sharpless
reported for refusing to refer a matter in dispute with Joel Willis.
Joseph Worrall reported for cursing and abusing the overseers.
Robert Edwards has signed articles with an intent to be engage in
military service but is undecided whether he will proceed any
further.

31/5/1756. Amos Edwards reported for drinking, quarreling and
neglecting meetings.

28/6/1756. Friends who visited Joseph Worrell stated that instead of
making any acknowledgment of his wrongs, he seemed to justify
himself and behaved at that time in a violent and rude manner
unbecoming a man of any civil society, fetching his gun with the
intent, as they thought, of shooting or at least frightening one of the
party concerned. Elizabeth Smith, wife of Samuel, produced a
certificate from Darby. Mary Robinson produced a certificate from
Philadelphia. Matthew Hall produced a certificate from Radnor with
his wife Rebecca and son David. John and Peter Worrall, sons of
John Worrall, reported for quarreling and fighting with their father
standing by encouraging them.

26/7/1756. William Pearson produced a certificate from Goshen.
Benjamin Davis produced a certificate from Darby for himself and
his wife Ann; they and their children were received. Esther Ashton,
wife of Abraham, requested a certificate to Newgarden. Thomas
Pilkington reported for refusing to refer a difference with Margaret
Carter [to arbitration of Friends].

30/8/1756. Thomas Cortney produced a certificate from Goshen.
Mahlon Hall produced a certificate from Falls.

27/9/1756. Patience Richardson produced a certificate from
Philadelphia. Elizabeth Weaver, widow of Richard Weaver, and her
children, who, with her husband some time ago, made application to
come under the care of Friends, of late have all (except Isaac) joined
the Church of England. James Broom married out to one not a
member. Hannah Carter, now Farraw, married out.

25/10/1756. Susannah Lea requested a certificate to Philadelphia. Mary Everson acknowledges marrying out of unity.

29/11/1756. Regarding the children of widow Weaver - she desires that Friends disjoin her; her son Valentine desires some time to consider and Jude was not spoken to. Joseph Parkers reported for being in the practice of personally administering the oath. Hannah Preston, wife of Jonas, produced a certificate from Haverford for herself and her dau. Ann Rogers produced a certificate from Gwynedd for herself and her daughter.

27/12/1756. Alice Lewis, wife of Jehu, produced a certificate from Concord; also one from Goshen for Sarah Calvert, wife of Thomas, and her children. Margaret Powell, wife of John, who was taken under the care of this meeting, has since married out to John Powell, not a member. A certificate was requested for Abraham Howell, son of Evan, who hath been settled for some time within the verge of Duck Creek Monthly Meeting.

31/1/1757. James Barton was received into membership. Samuel Pennell reported for drinking to excess and neglecting meetings. Priscilla Worrall, wife of George, produced a certificate from Merion. Jane Larkin, wife of William, requested a certificate to Concord.

28/2/1757. Mahlon Hall, son of Matthew, requested a certificate to Middletown Monthly Meeting to marry Jane Higgs, dau. of James. Isaac Gleave, George Ogden and Phebe Musgrove made acknowledgments. Thomas Yarnall, Jr., reported for fighting and using unbecoming language. Peter Worrall, son of John, dec'd, requested a certificate to Newark to marry Abigail Pile, dau. of John Pile.

28/3/1757. Ann Sival, wife of Samuel, produced a certificate from Concord for herself and her children.

25/4/1757. Phebe Musgrove reported for taking too much liberty with George Ogden. Mary Evanson, wife of George, acknowledged marrying out. Hannah Phillips, dau. of John, produced a certificate from Nottingham. Lydia Potter, dau. of Abraham, produced a certificate from Duck Creek. Mary Tomlinson, widow of Othniel, produced a certificate from Concord with his daughter. Meeting informed that Abigail Woodward was granted a certificate from Goshen to this meeting about two years ago but has not delivered it and has now married a man of another society; Friends in her area will be advised. Samuel Worrall acknowledged marrying out to one not of the Society. Agnes Minshall, wife of Thomas Minshall, and Sarah Minshall, wife of John Minshall, are proposed as Elders.

30/5/1757. Patience Rouse made an acknowledgment. Caleb Cowpland, Jr., returned from Barbadoes.

27/6/1757. Samuel Carter, son of John, married by a priest. Mary Lightfoot, wife of Jacob Lightfoot, and Grace, wife of John Fi---, returned from a religious visit. Sarah Surman produced a certificate from Chesterfield in the Jerseys. Richard Bradley produced a certificate from Goshen for himself and his wife Elizabeth. Amos Edwards reported for drinking to excess and fighting. Joshua Lewis and his wife reported for not living together and not performing their marriage covenant. William Williamson has married out to one too nearly related to him [*And from the women's minutes the following:*] Sarah Williamson has married by a Justice to her mother's 1st cousin. Samuel Crosley reported for suing Samuel Min--- without leave of the meeting. Barbara Carter reported for her loose conduct.

25/7/1757. Abigail Woodward [Woodworth], dau. of Thomas, dec'd, reported for marrying out to John Gillam of another society. John Eyre produced a certificate from Concord.

29/8/1757. Joshua Lewis and his wife promised to live together as soon as he can get a house. Jesse Woodward, requested a certificate to Wilmington for himself, his wife Prudence and children, they having removed some time ago. Nathan Newlin produced a certificate for Abigail Worrall, wife of Peter. Samuel Worrall seldom attends meetings. Abigail Huff, wife of Peter, reported for marrying out by a priest. Elizabeth Fawkes, wife of William, requested a certificate to Goshen. Samuel Richards, William Yarnall and Sarah Ritchits acknowledged attending a marriage before a priest.

26/9/1757. Edward Stapler and Mary Robinson did not appear at the meeting because Edward is living at a distance of 300 miles and at this time had business to transact. Elizabeth Cummings reported deceased. Lewis Davis requested a certificate to Darby to marry Hannah Lloyd, widow of Richard. Samuel Hampton reported for assisting at a marriage where one of the persons was not a member.

31/10/1757. Caleb Cowpland has died since last meeting; he had been clerk to the meeting for the past 30 years. Moses Minshall reported for undertaking to be commander of a privateer and engaging part time in this activity in the past; additional complaints were made against his wife for drinking spirituous liquors to excess. Daniel Thomson has married out of unity. David Brooks acknowledged marrying out of unity. Francis Hinklin produced a certificate from Concord. William Griffith produced a certificate from Goshen for himself and his wife Hannah. Elizabeth Key, widow of Moses, requested a certificate to Concord. Sarah Hampton, married woman, and her sister-in-law, Sarah Hampton, spinster, acknowledged attending a marriage by a Justice in which one of the parties was a Friend.

28/11/1757. David Brooks granted a certificate to follow David to Darby Monthly Meeting with a citation therein. Richard Stephens produced a certificate from Exeter from himself, his wife Dorothy and six children: Elizabeth, Eleanor, John, George, Susannah and Ann. Mahlon Hall requested a certificate to Philadelphia. Reuben Roberts produced a certificate from Gwynedd. Ann Pasmore produced a certificate from E. Nottingham. Nathan Yarnall, Jr., produced a certificate from Newark. Samuel Baker produced a certificate from Newgarden. Thomas Yarnall reported for nonpayment of a debt to James Pennell. Mary Stabler, wife of Edward, requested a certificate to Henrico Co., VA. Barbara Carter reported for fornication. Hannah Farrow, wife of Samuel Farrow, reported for marrying by a priest. Benjamin Yarnall and John Yarnall, sons of Nathan, requested certificates to Philadelphia. Lydia Sharples requested a certificate to Concord.

26/12/1757. Elizabeth Stephens, who came to Chester with her parents, was granted a certificate to Exeter. Thomas Worrolow reported for drinking to excess. Lydia Sharpless requested a certificate to Concord.

30/1/1758. Darby Meeting refused to receive David Brooks on certificate. George Sharpless, son of John, requested a certificate to Philadelphia. John Taylor reported for an unpaid debt to Joseph Maris. Alice Morris, wife of Jonathan, requested a certificate to Newgarden.

27/2/1758. Elizabeth Yarnall produced a certificate from Newark, clear of marriage engagements. Susanna Powell acknowledged marrying out; her children: Prudence, Benjamin, Mary and Samuel, received by her request. Sarah Bickerton acknowledged marrying out of unity. Thomas Smedley, son of George, requested a certificate to Concord. Agnes Salkeld [dau. of John Salkeld], now wife of [Simon] Gest, has married out [by a priest].

24/3/1758. Richard Bradley requested a certificate to Cane Creek, NC, for himself, his wife Elizabeth and child. Mary Evason, wife of George, requested a certificate to Concord.

24/4/1758. John Dicks acknowledged marrying by a priest. Samuel Richards requested a certificate to Philadelphia. Samuel Evans requested a certificate to Philadelphia for himself, his wife Ann and children: Mary, Moses, Deborah, Abigail, Samuel and Joshua. Sarah Hampton, wife of Samuel, requested a certificate for herself and her children: Mary, Sarah and Elizabeth.

29/5/1758. Sarah Sarman requested a certificate to Philadelphia; Lydia Goodwin to Goshen; Elizabeth Gifford to Concord. Hannah Davis, wife of Lewis, produced a certificate from Darby. Thomas Parvin requested a certificate to Exeter for himself, his wife Mary and child. Richard Gorman reported for an unpaid debt to Daniel Sharpless. John Cox produced a certificate from Goshen for himself, his wife Mary and children: Jane, Eleanor, John and Israel. Phillip Jones produced a certificate from Wilmington. Thomas Worrall requested a certificate to Philadelphia for himself, his wife Mary and children: Peter, Sarah and Mary. Richard Howard, son of Henry, requested a certificate to Philadelphia.

26/6/1758. Jane Maris, widow of George, requested a certificate to Haverford.

31/7/1758. John Little, son of Joshua, now an apprentice placed with Samuel Howell, produced a certificate from Wilmington. Hannah Ashbridge produced a certificate from Goshen. Hannah Smith, dau. of Moses Martin and wife of John Smith, requested a certificate to Cane Creek. Jeremiah Starr, son of John, and Jacob Starr, son of Isaac, produced certificates from Exeter. Richard Gorman reported for commencing several suits at law against David Sharpless. Friends in Ireland informed this meeting that Sarah Worrall died within the verge of their meeting while on a religious visit to England, Wales and Ireland.

28/8/1758. Tasey Bevan, dau. of Awbrey, wife of Thomas Proyer (Pryer) reported for marrying by a priest. Dorothy Graham requested to come under the care of Friends. Ephraim and Dorothy Yarnall reported for marrying by a priest, and they being 1st cousins. [*Annotation: Thomas Prior and Tacy Bewan of Chester County and Philadelphia married by license 24th June, 1758. Ephraim Yarnall and Dorothy Yarnall, m. June 3, 1758 at Christ Church.*]

18/9/1758. Friends appointed to treat with Robert Squibb, Sr., for suing Richard Gorman and taking his goods in execution. Jonathan Cowpland requested a certificate to Philadelphia to marry Mary Nicholas, dau. of Anthony Nicholas, dec'd. James Moore requested a certificate to Duck Creek. Certificate for Jesse Woodward and family not received by Wilmington Monthly Meeting because they think he ought to be dealt with for some misdemeanors.

23/10/1758. Samuel Howell requested a certificate to Philadelphia for himself, his wife Ann and children: Abigail, Hugh, Jacob, Ann, Samuel and Debbe and his apprentice, John Littler. Mary Carter, widow of Nineveh, requested a certificate to Concord. It appears that Jesse Woodward fraudulently removed his goods without paying his rent. Ann Pasmore requested a certificate to Nottingham. Mary Crookham requested a certificate to Goshen for herself and her children: James, Deborah and John.

17/11/1758. Mary Carter granted a certificate for herself and her dau. Mary. Eleanor Godfrey requested a certificate to Philadelphia. Caleb Harrison, Jr., produced a certificate from Exeter with his wife Elinor and 6 children: Hannah, Caleb, Catharine, Mary, Eleanor and Joshua. Richard Bond produced a certificate from Goshen. Thomas Calvert reported for being hired in the service of the War as armorer in the present expedition to the westward.

25/12/1758. Ann Fell, wife of Richard Lovelock, reported for marrying by a priest. Samuel Minshall requested a certificate to Philadelphia for himself and his son Isaac. Benjamin Sharpless, Jr.,requested a certificate to Philadelphia and Samuel Baker to Newgarden. Benjamin Sharpless appointed overseer instead of Philip Yarnall, dec'd. Prudence Woodward, wife of Jesse Woodward, requested a certificate to Wilmington for herself and her children: Jesse, Sarah and Jane, [his certificate being returned]. Chester Meeting represented some months ago that Hannah Carter, dau. of Nineveh Carter, dec'd, had joined the Church of England, so called, and been sprinkled in their way; she is now disowned. Elizabeth Roberts requested a certificate to Darby.

29/1/1759. Reported that after the overseers of James Worrall's marriage had left the house some members of this meeting behaved in a very disorderly manner.

26/2/1759. Thomas Swaine requested a certificate to Newgarden for himself, his wife Mary and children: Phebe, George and Elizabeth. William Worrall requested a certificate to Goshen to marry Phebe Grubb, dau. of Nathaniel Grubb. Elizabeth Roberts, contrary to her expectations, being removed to within the verge of this meeting only, has dropped her application for a certificate.

23/3/1759. It appears that at James Worrall's marriage Peter Worrall, being a person entrusted with the care of the liquor, had kept unseasonable hours and quarrelled with Lawrence Howard, and

Daniel Broom had also quarrelled and fought with the said Lawrence Howard and beat and abused him to a pretty great degree. [*Annotation: Lawrence Howard and Nanny James m. Dec 7, 1752 at Gloria Dei Church.*] Tacy Pryer, wife of Thomas Pryer, requested a certificate to Philadelphia. Elizabeth Talbot, wife of Benjamin, requested a certificate to Bradford with children: John, Joseph, Mary, Elizabeth, Benjamin and William. David Cowpland and Awbrey Bevan reported for quarreling and getting into an excessive passion, and David Cowpland was also reported for denying the fact and abusing the Friend appointed to treat with him. Robert Evans requested a certificate to Duck Creek. George Lowder received into membership. Margery Pearson requested to come under the care of Friends.

30/4/1759. Lydia Burchel, wife of John, requested a certificate to Philadelphia. A minute received from Philadelphia stated objection to receiving Eleanor Godfrey's certificate. Elizabeth Cameron, wife of Dugald, produced a certificate from Concord. Margery Pearson, dau. of Enoch, dec'd, received into membership. John Howard reported for an unpaid debt to Robert Valentine.

28/5/1759. Isaac Starr requested a certificate to Duck Creek. Mary Ellis, dau. of Benjamin, dec'd, produced a certificate from Goshen. William Starr produced a certificate from Philadelphia for himself and his wife Jane. Edward Smith reported for marrying by a priest and neglects meetings.

25/6/1759. Peter Worrall, instead of being more careful in his conversation as he had promised, suffered himself to be too free in the company of soldiers at the Square and behaved himself very disreputably amongst them. Daniel Broom reported guilty of several things: fighting, keeping loose company and neglecting meetings. Dugland Cameron produced a certificate from Goshen. Eleanor Graham, widow of William Graham, produced a certificate from London dated 1733.

30/7/1759. Mary Tomlinson requested a certificate to Wilmington for herself and her dau. Mary. Sarah Hampton requested a certificate to Philadelphia. Joshua Hoopes, Jr., produced a certificate from Goshen.

27/8/1759. Mary Norris, wife of Charles, requested a certificate to Philadelphia. Sarah Richards requested a certificate to Philadelphia. Thomas Morgan reported for going to sea in a vessel of war as an assistant. Samuel Crosley reported for an unpaid debt to Joseph Swaffer. Ann Lewis, now wife of James Betty, married by a priest.

21/9/1759. Mary Clayton, wife of Adam Clayton, acknowledged marrying by a priest to one not a member.

29/10/1759. Jane Rhoads requested a certificate to Goshen. Peter Dicks and John Lea were appointed some time ago to view the rough minutes and order them transcribed, but before anything was done, the said John Lea died. Abigail Woodworth, now Gilpin, acknowledged marrying out.

26/11/1759. Martha Pennell requested a certificate to Duck Creek for herself with her husband and two children.

31/12/1759. Mary Emerson, wife of Vincent Emerson, produced a certificate. Mary Ellis requested a certificate to Goshen. John Worrilow reported for marrying out, later absconding from these parts and joining with soldiers. Chester Meeting informed that the ground on which their meeting house was erected was conveyed by deed of 2/17/1736 to six trustees: Jacob Howell, Thomas Cummins, John Owen, Samuel Lightfoot, John Salkeld, Jr., and John Sharpless, Jr., and that by the declaration of trust it was provided that if any of these were disowned or deceased their places might be filled by appointment of the monthly meeting - John Owen, being deceased, and John Salkeld, Jr., being disowned, the meeting appointed Jonathan Cowpland and Joseph Ashbridge to succeed them. Phebe Worrall produced a certificate from Goshen Monthly Meeting. Something having hindered Martha Pennell's joint certificate, it is thought proper to let her daughter have one by herself and the same Friends are continued to treat with her.

28/1/1760. Aaron Vernon, Jr., produced a certificate from Goshen for himself and his wife Rachel. Mary Musgrove produced a certificate from Goshen. Middletown reports that Cadwalader Evans continues to drink to excess. Robert Rogers, Jr., produced a certificate from Gwynedd with a few lines stating that they had granted him a certificate to this meeting but he had not delivered it and had since married out.

25/2/1760. Sarah Taylor requested a certificate to Newark. Susannah Ruth produced a certificate from Concord. Valentine Weaver is much abroad in military service.

18/3/1760. John Wilson produced a certificate from Concord, and another was produced from Newgarden for his wife Dinah Wilson.

28/4/1760. Robert Rogers produced a certificate from Gwynedd which he has long kept. Jeremiah Starr requested a certificate to Exeter for himself and his wife Hannah. John Salkeld, Jr., requested a certificate to Wilmington. Jacob Starr requested a certificate to Duck

Creek. John Fincher requested a certificate to Exeter. Robert Edwards is again engaged in military service.

26/5/1760. John Sharpless, Jr., requested a certificate to Duns Creek Monthly Meeting in Bladen County, NC. Elisha Jones produced a certificate from Darby. Moses Vernon, Jr., reported for abusing a neighboring woman in a very brutish and shameful manner.

30/6/1760. Agnes Gest, wife of Simon, acknowledged marrying out. Reuben Roberts acknowledged marrying out by a priest; also his wife Margaret Sharpless, acknowledged the same. Gwen Jones, wife of Elisha, produced a certificate from Goshen. Jonathan Cowpland and Davis Bevan reported for trading in Negroes contrary to a late rule of our Yearling Meeting. Abigail Varnon reported for loose and disorderly conduct and dancing in a tavern at Chester Fair. Elizabeth Sharples, wife of James Sharples, reported for being disguised with strong liquor at the last fair in Chester and other misconduct. Mary Martin requested to come under the care of Friends.

7/28/1760. Thomas Worrall produced a certificate from Philadelphia for Thomas Worrall, his wife Mary and Samuel Starr.

25/8/1760. Jonathan Cowpland vindicates his practice and has lately purchased one or more Negroes. Robert Taylor requested a certificate to Abington. Isaac Gleave reported for unpaid debts to Jonathan Haycock. Samuel Wilcox produced a certificate from Goshen.

25/9/1760. Agnes Gest, wife of Simon, requested a certificate to Concord; also one for Hannah Phillips to Sadsbury; one for Sarah Gilpin, wife of George, to Concord with two of her children, Edward and Lydia Woodward.

27/10/1760. James Hill produced a certificate from Buckingham for himself and his wife Ann. Cornelius Wood produced a certificate from Concord. William Yarnall acknowledged marrying by a priest. [Annotation: *William Yarnall and Mary Chance, license dated Jan 30, 1760; married same date, St. Michaels and Zion Lutheran Church, Philadelphia.*]

24/11/1760. Jonathan Cowpland reported for administering the oath as magistrate. Israel Taylor reported for neglecting Meeting, for beating and abusing Daniel Broom, Jr. and suing him at law for an unpaid debt. Robert Squibb, the elder, acknowledged suing Richard Gorman. Mary Cowpland, now McClung, acknowledged marrying one of another society.

29/12/1760. Hannah Thomson reported for refusing to pay a demand to her father-in-law, Joshua Thomson. Moses Starr requested a certificate to Philadelphia. Daniel Broom, Jr., reported for drinking to excess and swearing. William Regester reported for marrying by a priest to Abigail Hoopes, dau. of Abraham. Rachel Edwards married by a priest to one not a member. Elizabeth Scotham acknowledged marrying out of unity.

26/1/1761. John, Mary, Sarah and Ann Edge, children of George Edge, dec'd, requested a certificate to Goshen. Lewis David of Haverford is proposed as an overseer in place of Isaac Howell who has removed to Philadelphia. A difference has arisen between Hannah Thomson and Joshua Thomson.

23/2/1761. A paper was received from John Sinclar stating that Isaac Gleave has made satisfaction. John McIlvain requested for himself and his two children, Isaac and Mary, to come under the care of Friends. Joshua Calvert reported for drinking to excess, fighting and swearing. Joseph Talbot requested for himself and children: Joseph, Rachel, Jacob, Elizabeth, Hannah and Susannah, to come under the care of Friends; the said Joseph the younger requesting for himself; Rachel also requesting for herself. Joseph Hoskins acknowledged signing a qualification with another magistrate sworn. Rachel Edwards charged with drinking to excess.

30/3/1761. William Russel, Jr., received into membership. Mary McClung, wife of Robert, acknowledges marrying out. Hannah Dawes, wife of Jonathan, requested a certificate to Wilmington. Joseph Talbot requested a certificate to Concord to marry Lydia Townsend, widow of Joseph. James Hill requested a certificate to Philadelphia for himself, his wife Ann and two children. George Stevens requested a certificate to Philadelphia. Susannah Ruth, dau. of Francis, and Ann Beavan [Bevan], dau. of Awbrey, dec'd, requested a certificate to Philadelphia. Rachel Edwards reported for marrying out and drinking to excess. Alice Norry, wife of John, reported for marrying out to one not a member. Abraham Hoopes, Jr. reported for accompanying members of this meeting to their marriage by a priest.

27/4/1761. Joshua Thomson reported removed at a distance. John Lewis produced a certificate from Philadelphia for himself, his wife Alice and children. Elizabeth Scothorn acknowledged marrying out. Philip Jones requested a certificate to Wilmington. Amy Lewis requested a certificate to Philadelphia. Sarah Richardson requested a certificate to Middletown Monthly Meeting. Rebekah Wiley requested a certificate to Wilmington for herself and her children: Vincent, Martha and Mary.

25/5/1761. Joshua Thompson reported deceased. Joseph Russel acknowledged marrying out. Ann Lovelock acknowledged marrying out.

29/6/1761. Elizabeth Yarnall, dau. of Philip, dec'd, requested a certificate to Abington. Samuel Wilcox requested a certificate to Goshen.

27/7/1761. Hannah Worrall, now Newson, married out to one of another society. Hannah Worrall, now Massey, married out.

31/8/1761. William Pearson requested a certificate to Goshen. Mary Spikeman produced a certificate from Goshen. Elizabeth Worrall, dau. of James, reported for fornication. John Ebelon reported for purchasing a Negro slave. Margaret Read married out.

25/9/1761. John McIlvain, who was lately taken under the care of the meeting, married his former wife's first cousin; disowned. George Sharpless and Mary Lewis to marry, he to bring certificate. John Marris requested a certificate to Gwynedd. Sarah Edwards, wife of William, produced a certificate from Goshen. Acknowledgments received from Hannah Massey, wife of James, and Hannah Nuzum [Newson], wife of Richard. Margaret, wife of Thomas Read, reported for marrying by a priest. James Howard, son of Henry, dec'd, requested a certificate to Nottingham to marry Alice Pasmore, dau. of Augustine. Deborah Thornton produced a certificate from Bradford.

26/10/1761. Lydia Talbot, wife of Joseph, produced a certificate from Concord and Rachel McCullough, wife of James, produced a certificate from Radnor. Mary Kirk [formerly Mary Brown], wife of Joshua, reported for marrying by a priest. Hannah Thomson reported for neglecting to comply with award of referees between her and the executor of her father-in-law, Joshua Thomson. John Cobourn requested a certificate to Concord to marry Elizabeth Larken, dau. of John Larken. Nathan Thomson reported for marrying by a priest. Nathan Vernon reported for marrying by a priest and to his 1st cousin. John Waily requested a certificate to Exeter.

30/11/1761. Jacob Howell, Jr., reported for drinking to excess. Robert Rogers reported for drinking to excess. Mary Bevan requested a certificate to Darby. Mary Martin requested a certificate to Goshen.

28/12/1761. Dugald Cameron produced a certificate dated the 6th month 1759 from Goshen which was not then received but is received now. Hannah Thomson, wife of Nathan, acknowledged marrying by a priest. George Turner requested a certificate to Goshen for himself, his wife Sarah and children.

25/1/1762. Wilmington Friends reported that Rachel Woodward, a member of Chester Monthly Meeting, through age and indisposition, is in need of assistance and cannot be removed; there will probably be a charged of 20 shillings a week or more. George Louther requested a certificate to Gwynedd.

22/2/1762. George Turner granted a certificate for himself, his wife and children, Gamaliel and Susanna. John Gracy requested a certificate to Haverford for himself, his wife Ruth and son Samuel. Patience Richardson and Mary Morgan requested certificates to Philadelphia; also Rebekah Howard and Mary Howell, wife of Israel, requested certificates to Philadelphia. Alice Lewis, wife of Jehu, requested a certificate to Fairfax [Virginia] for herself and three of her children: Joel, Hannah and Evan. Joseph Vernon reported for marrying out and drinking to excess. Nathan Yarnall, Jr., requested a certificate to Concord.

26/3/1762. Sometime ago Joseph Vernon fell into the practice of drinking to excess and before his case was brought to the monthly meeting he had married out, after which it was thought he had not the full use of his reason. Certificate received from Wilmington for William Milner, son of Samuel, dec'd, but he has already removed within the verge of Concord. Hannah Harris acknowledged marrying out, for which she was formerly disowned. John Wilson requested a certificate to Goshen for himself, his wife Dinah, and dau. Mary. Robert Cobourn acknowledged marrying out.

26/4/1762. Joseph Wilkinson produced a certificate from Wrightstown for himself, his wife Barbara and children, Jesse and Sarah, and an apprentice girl, Mary Ball. Jeremiah Starr produced a certificate from Exeter for himself, his wife Hannah and little dau. Mary. Daniel Yarnall reported for suing a member at law. Dugald Cameron acknowledged some passionate conduct towards Job Dicks. Jonathan Maris proposes to visit some back parts of Virginia; his brother-in-law James Bartram proposing to accompany him. Joshua Proctor requested to be taken under the care of Friends.

31/5/1762. John Ebelan acknowledged buying and selling a Negro. Hannah Harris requested a certificate to Goshen. Alice Howard, wife of James, produced a certificate from Nottingham. Alice Hughs produced a certificate from Concord. Job Ridgway produced a certificate from Burlington for himself, his wife Mary and six children: Elizabeth, Hannah, Ann, Lydia, Beulah and Daniel. George Hall reported for drinking to excess and keeping idle company. Jonathan Howell reported for drinking to excess and neglecting meetings. Sarah Morton married out. Esther Bickerdike, clerk of the women's meeting, is about to remove.

28/6/1762. Esther Bickerdike requested a certificate to Middletown Monthly Meeting, Bucks Co., for herself and her niece [cousin written above] Lydia Beakes. Mary Sharpless, wife of George, requested a certificate to Philadelphia. Sarah Morton, wife of William, reported for marrying before a priest. Deborah Thornton, wife of Samuel, who was recommended from Bradford about 9 mos. ago, requested a certificate; a few lines were added on the back of her old certificate.

26/7/1762. Jane Gest produced a certificate from Concord Monthly Meeting. Jane Griffith, wife of John, requested a certificate to Goshen. Diana Bryan produced a certificate from Richland, Bucks Co. Thomas Courtney requested a certificate to Goshen. Nathan Newlin requested a certificate to Cecil Monthly Meeting for himself, his wife Susannah and children. John Houlton acknowledged marrying out. Jacob Worrall acknowledged marrying out. Providence Meeting complained that Margaret Tremble [wife of Lewis] was married by a priest to one not a member.

30/8/1762. Benjamin Hance produced a certificate from Wilmington dated 7/12/1754 for himself, his wife and children; also a complaint was lodged against him for an unpaid debt to Esther Bickerdike. The said Benjamin to be dealt with for neglecting to deliver his certificate and not paying his debts. Rachel Townsend, wife of Francis, requested a certificate to Concord. Robert Rogers continues his practice of drinking to excess. John Howard reported for drinking to excess. Samuel Wilcox produced a certificate from Goshen.

24/9/1762. Abigail Graham acknowledged marrying out. Mary Hall, wife of Thomas, Jr., requested a certificate to Goshen. Patience McChaskey, wife of James McChaskey, reported for marrying out. Mary Johnson acknowledged marrying out. Sarah Hance neglected to produce her certificate from Wilmington.

10/25/1762. John Eblen requested a certificate to Fairfax [Virginia] for himself, his wife Mary and children: Hannah, Liza, Mary, Rachel, John and Isaac. Mary Hill [wife of John] produced a certificate from Concord. Rebekah Calvert requested a certificate to Philadelphia. Abraham Sharpless produced a certificate from Goshen for himself, his wife Ann and children: Mary, Phebe, Esther, Abraham, Lydia and Grace. Mary McClung requested a certificate to the forks of Gunpowder.

29/11/1762. Rachel Edwards, wife of Amos, reported for marrying out and drinking to excess; there appears to be no hope of amendment. Hannah Gleave, dau. of Isaac, requested a certificate to Philadelphia. Mary Johnson, wife of Abraham, reported for marrying before a priest. Meeting informed that Samuel Davis, son of Benjamin, who sometime past removed from Chester without a certificate to the lower part of New Castle Co. on Delaware and there set up a store and fell into the inordinate practice of drinking to excess, has of late absconded from his creditors. Ann Lovelock, wife of Richard, acknowledged marrying before a priest to one not a member. Joseph Swaffer reported for drinking to excess. William Taylor reported for marrying before a priest. Abigail Woodward, dau. of Edward the younger, reported for marrying before a priest to Vincent Gilpin, and it is thought that she was one of the persons who caused Richard Gorman to be sued at law. Martha Thompson requested a certificate to Philadelphia.

27/12/1762. Elizabeth Roberts requested a certificate to Goshen. Martha Thomson, wife of Joshua, requested a certificate to Philadelphia. Joseph Edwards reported for marrying before a priest to one not a member.

9/2/1763. Lydia McIlvain, wife of John, produced a certificate from Bradford. Ann Hayard produced a certificate from Philadelphia. Mary Ogden [widow of George] requested a certificate to Philadelphia for herself and children: Esther and Hugh. Susanna Day requested a certificate to Gloucester Monthly Meeting in old England.

28/2/1763. Joseph Cobourn, Jr., reported for drinking to excess and neglecting meetings; also for debt to Elisha Price, assignee of Esther Bickerdike. Susanna Day, wife of James of Springfield, requested a certificate to Glocestershire in Old England. Thomas Cobourn of Chichester acknowledged marrying by a priest to one not a member. Jacob Worrall reported for marriage by a priest. Vincent Pilkington requested a certificate to Wilmington. Thomas Worrall reported for not fulfilling a contract with his brother John Worrall.

25/3/1763. Jane Gest requested a certificate to Concord. Jonathan Willis, wife of Dinah [?] and children: John, Jonathan and David, requested a certificate to Philadelphia. James Worrall reported for neglecting meetings, drinking to excess and giving way to passion.

William Russell requests a certificate to Goshen to settle and marry Susannah Griffith.

25/4/1763. Sarah Hall [a later annotation suggests that she may have been the dau. of Thomas Taylor], wife of Richard, reported for marriage by a priest to one not a member. Ann Sival and children requested a certificate to Concord. Joseph Swaffer was reported still to be in the practice of drinking to excess. Job Dicks reported for not clearing himself of a scandalous report.

30/5/1763. It is reported that Job Dicks has for several years neglected to deliver his certificate, and, being removed to Wilmington, requested one directed there. Elizabeth Yarnall, dau. of Philip, produced a certificate from Abington.

31/10/1763. Richard Howard produced a certificate from Philadelphia. Sarah Wooly produced a certificate from Philadelphia for herself and two of her children, Robert and Ann. Benjamin Lacey produced a certificate from Wrightstown; Robert Evans from Gwynedd; and Jacob Sharpless, wife Ann and children: John, Nathan, Lydia, Joseph, Jesse and Ann, from Concord. Mary Barton, dau. of Abraham of Chester, reported for marriage by a priest to Peter Steel, not a member. Jonathan Howell continues in the practice of drinking to excess. William Carter, son of Abraham, requested a certificate to Philadelphia. Elisha Taylor, son of Thomas, reported for marrying by a priest to one not a member and neglecting meetings. Caleb Smedley reported for marrying by a priest to one not a member. Lydia Talbot, wife of Joseph, requested a certificate to Concord for herself and her youngest children: Elizabeth, Hannah and Susanna.

28/11/1763. Joshua Worrall, son of John, formerly of Marple, reported for drinking to excess and neglecting meetings. Elizabeth Smith, wife of Samuel, requested a certificate to Darby. Peter Worrall, son of John (formerly of Marple, dec.), reported for drinking to excess and neglecting meetings; in the past he has given several acknowledgments for misconduct. Robert Woolley reported for drinking to excess, marrying by a priest, and wholly neglecting to attend meetings. Jonathan Cowpland, who was appointed trustee for Chester Meeting on 31/12/1759, was disowned. Thomas Sharpless was appointed in his place.

26/12/1763. Ann Sival granted a certificate for herself and eight of her children: Joseph, Elizabeth, John, George, Mary, Enoch, Robert and Abraham. Rebekah Sharpless, now wife of Leonard Helm, reported for marrying by a priest to one not a member and being removed to

Maryland. David Cobourn reported for marrying by a priest to one not a member. Isaac Howell, son of Evan, dec'd, of Edgmont, reported for drinking to excess and neglecting meetings.

30/1/1764. Hannah Massey, wife of James, requested a certificate to Goshen. Mary Reed, wife of James, reported for marrying by a priest to one not a member. Joseph Slay reported for drinking to excess and removing without a certificate. John Calvert, son of Thomas, reported for fornication before marriage. Benjamin Simcock reported for being in the practice of drinking strong liquor to excess and slighting the care and counsel of Friends by removing from this meeting a long time ago without a certificate and not joining with any Monthly Meeting - disowned. Thomas Schofield produced a certificate from Buckingham for himself, Rebekah his wife and children: Nathan, Ann and Thomas; also Jonathan Scolfield produced a certificate from Wrightstown.

27/2/1764. James Yarnall requested a certificate to Philadelphia. Providence Friends reported that John Calvert still drinks to excess.

23/3/1764. Lydia Jackson requested a certificate to Exeter. Israel Howell produced a certificate from Philadelphia for himself, his wife Mary and their two children, Stephen and Esther. Moses Thomson requested a certificate to Goshen to marry Grace Hoopes, dau. of Stephen.

3/4/1764. Jane Ruth produced a certificate from Concord. John Woolley produced a certificate from Philadelphia. Ann Rogers requested a certificate to Gwynedd.

28/5/1764. Mary Grubb, wife of Adam, produced a certificate from Concord. Sarah West, wife of Thomas, requested a certificate to Philadelphia. Jacob Howell, the Elder, and his wife Deborah, produced a certificate from New Garden Monthly Meeting.

25/6/1764. Susanna Crukshank requested a certificate to Philadelphia.

30/7/1764. Thomas Starr requested a certificate to Philadelphia for himself, wife Jane and children: John, Elizabeth, Jane and Jacob; Samuel Starr; and Joseph Russell. Thomas Schofield requested a certificate to Goshen for himself, wife Rebecca and children: Nathan, Ann and Thomas. John Lewis reported by Springfield for selling a Negro woman. Caleb James produced a certificate from Concord for himself, wife Mary and son Aaron; also one for Elizabeth Garrison, their apprentice. Esther Ashton, wife of Abraham, produced a certificate from Newgarden for herself and her children, Joseph and Esther. Jane Pugh, dau. of Jesse Pugh, produced a certificate from Hopewell. Abigail Gilpin, wife of Vincent, acknowledged marrying out and neglecting to inform the meeting well in advance before commencing a suit against a member of the meeting. Deborah Gregg produced a certificate from Kennett. Elizabeth Garrison, dau. of Eliakim Garrison, produced a certificate from Concord.

27/8/1764. Thomas James produced a certificate from Wilmington. Isaac Eyre produced a certificate from Concord. Abraham Carter reported for drinking to excess. Joseph Rhoads requested a certificate to Haverford to marry Rachel Evans, dau. of Evan Evans of Radnor. Edith Pennel, dau. of James Pennel, now wife of William Bail, Jr., married by a priest.

21/9/1764. David Cowpland reported for striking and wounding a man and using profane language.

29/10/1764. Hannah Ashbridge requested a certificate to Duck Creek. Testimony against John Calvert, son of Daniel Calvert.

26/11/1764. Davis Bevan reported for administering the oath in his office as coroner. John Regester requested a certificate to Concord to marry Rebecca Green.

31/12/1764. Susanna Hibberd, wife of Isaac, requested a certificate to Goshen. Nathan Milner produced a certificate from Nottingham. George Miller requested a certificate to Goshen to marry Phebe Massey.

28/1/1765. Grace Thomson, wife of Moses, produced a certificate from Goshen.

25/2/1765. Benjamin Leasey requested a certificate to Wrightstown. George Taylor reported for marrying by a priest. Jacob Sharpless, son of Joseph of Middletown, requested a certificate to Kennett to marry Sarah Hames, dau. of Joseph. Mary Worrall, dau. of John of Edgmont, reported for marrying by a priest to Robert Thomson, not a member.

22/3/1765. John Maris produced certificate from Gwynedd. Meeting informed that Jane Russell, wife of William Russell, some years ago made application for herself and children to be taken under the care of Friends, she having a son who is deaf and dumb, and she has lately procured him to be married by a priest to a woman not a member. [None of her children living except James who may be accounted as members.]

29/4/1765. Rachel Rhoads, wife of Joseph, produced a certificate from Radnor. Joseph Thomson, son of Mordecai, reported for drinking. Edith Pennel, dau. of James, now wife of William Bail, Jr., reported for marrying by a priest.

27/5/1765. Mary Ball requested a certificate to Wrightstown. Joseph Worrall, son of Jonathan, reported for destroying a not of hand [promissory note] he had given for security of payment of a sum of money and refusing to pay the same and also being charged with being the father of a bastard child. Ann Worrall, dau. of Jonathan, now wife of Hugh Linn, Jr., reported for marrying by a priest. Jane Hoopes, dau. of Abraham, reported for having a bastard child and concealing the father's name. Elizabeth Maddock, dau. of Benjamin, now wife of Thomas Manley, reported for marrying by a priest. Veronica Neifren requests to come under the care of Friends [approved]. Jonathan Scholdfield requested a certificate to Buckingham. Mary Chamberlin, wife of John, produced a certificate from Concord. Thomas Worrall, son of John, formerly of Middletown, reported for drinking to excess and defaming his neighbor. The certificate for Ann Savill was refused. Jane Pugh requested a certificate to Hopewell. Lydia Talbot sometime ago requested a certificate to Concord with her husband and youngest children; they have returned.

24/6/1765. Phebe Miller, wife of George Miller, requested a certificate.

29/7/1765. Stephen and Esther Howell, children of Israel, dec'd, requested a certificate to Newgarden. Jacob Sharpless, Jr., requested a certificate to Concord. Elizabeth Worrall, dau. of John of Edgmont, now wife of Abraham Hoopes, Jr., reported for marrying by a Justice to one not a member.

26/8/1765. John Longstreth of Charlestown, son of Bartholomew, dec'd, of Bucks Co. and Jane Minshall, dau. of John of Middletown, to marry; he to bring certificate. William West produced a certificate from Philadelphia for himself and 5 of his children: John, James, William, Rebekah and Benjamin. Phebe Traviller, dau. of James Traviller, produced a certificate from Warrington. Hannah Yarnall, wife of David, produced a certificate from Kennett for herself and two children, Lydia and Sarah.

30/9/1765. Rebekah Regester, wife of John, produced a certificate from Concord.

28/10/1765. Sarah Taylor, dau. of Mordecai Taylor of Upper Providence, dec'd, now wife of William Robison, reported for marrying by a priest to one not a member. Mary Taylor, dau. of John, requested a certificate to Kennett. Joseph Hoskins requested a certificate to Middletown, Bucks Co., to marry Esther Bickerdike. Joshua Proctor reported for marrying by a priest to one not a

member. Dan Calvert, son of Thomas, reported for wholly neglecting to attend meetings and leaving these parts in a clandestine manner.
25/11/1765. Matthew Hall reported for drinking to excess and neglecting to pay a debt to Henry Lawrence, Jr. Susannah Stephens, dau. of Richard, requested a certificate to Exeter.
30/12/1765. Lydia Bartin, dau. of Abraham, now wife of Elisha Price, reported for marrying by a priest to one not a member. Alice Taylor, dau. of John, reported for marrying by a priest to Abel Way who is not a member. Susannah Day returned the certificate she obtained from the meeting nearly 3 years ago in order to settle in Glocestershire, England, and informed the meeting she has had no opportunity of delivering it; now has returned to settle within the verge of this meeting.
27/1/1766. Jane Hinkson, wife of John Hinkson produced a certificate from Coot Hill in Cavan County, Ireland. Benjamin Morgan requests that he, his wife Jane and children be received into membership; Ann Morgan also requests the same. Thomas Williamson, son of Daniel, requested a certificate to Kennett.
24/2/1766. Mary Worral, dau. of Jonathan, reported for marrying out to Thomas Moore. Rebekah Pennell, dau. of James, reported for marrying out by a Baptist teacher [minister] to Thomas Walter.
31/3/1766. Esther Hoskins, wife of Joseph, produced a certificate from Middletown, Bucks Co. Benjamin Thomas produced a certificate from Philadelphia.
28/4/1766. Jacob Sharples requested a certificate to Concord for himself, wife Ann and children: John, Nathan, Lydia, Joseph, Jesse, Ann and Jane. Ann Salkeld, dau. of John, now wife of Joseph Larkin, reported for marrying before a priest. James Worrall, son of James of Marple, reported for fornication before marriage. Lydia Beakes produced a certificate from Middletown. Lydia Beakes produced a certificate from Middletown. Ann Howell, wife of Jacob, requested a certificate to Concord. Sarah Robison, wife of William, requested a certificate to Philadelphia.
26/5/1766. Isaac Gleave requested a certificate to Philadelphia for himself, his wife Mary and children: Rebekah, James and Elizabeth.
30/6/1766. Accounts settled with Elizabeth Taylor for the maintenance of Judith Broom and with Agness Minshall for the maintenance of Rachel Woodward.
28/7/1766. Benjamin Davis, son of Lewis, and Benjamin Maddock, Jr., requested a certificate to Philadelphia.

25/8/1766. William Peast produced a certificate from Darby for himself, wife Ann and son James. Samuel Yarnall, son of Nathan, requested a certificate to Kennett. Isaac Maris offered acknowledgement for himself and his wife Elizabeth for keeping company without consent of her father and marrying by a priest. Lydia Walter, dau. of Isaac Vernon, now wife James Walter, acknowledged fornication and having a bastard child for which she was disowned about 20 years ago, now giving the father's name.

26/9/1766. Jonathan Haycock requested a certificate to Concord to marry Hannah Pile, dau. of Jacob.

27/10/1766. Lydia Walter, wife of James, requested a certificate to Kennett. Robert Taylor, son of Thomas, sometime ago obtained a certificate from this Monthly Meeting which he never delivered and now says it is lost. He is also inclined to join the Church of England.

26/1/1767. Benjamin Worrall, son of John, dec'd, reported for marrying by a priest to one not a member, drinking to excess and neglecting meetings. Ann Massey, wife of Joseph, requested a certificate to Goshen.

23/2/1767. Friends of Darby reported Nathan Bonsall is more careful of late in regard to drinking.

30/3/1767. Elizabeth Worrall, dau. of Benjamin, dec'd, reported for marrying John Walter, not a member, by a priest. Hannah Haycock, wife of Jonathan, produced a certificate from Concord. William West requested a certificate to Philadelphia to marry Hannah Shaw. Nathan Bonsall requested a certificate to Darby.

27/4/1767. Elizabeth Townsend, dau. of Joseph, Jr., dec'd, produced a certificate from Concord. Walter Roberts produced a certificate from Goshen for himself, wife Rebekah and children: Thomas, John and Sarah. [She was Rebekah Williamson from Buckingham.] John Maris, son of George, and Margaret Lewis, dau. of John, reported for marrying by a priest and without consent of their parents. Susanna Edwards, dau. of Nathan, now wife of Andrew Wilson, reported for marrying by a priest to one not of our Society. Rebekah Walter, wife of Thomas, requested a certificate to Concord.

25/5/1767. Deborah Carter, dau. of Nineveh, dec'd, now wife of James Day, Jr., reported marrying by a priest to one not a member. Hannah Hance, dau. of Benjamin, reported for marrying by a priest to George Sing, not a member. Susanna Daugherty, Jr., requested a certificate to Haverford. Elizabeth Howell, wife of Jonathan, requested a certificate to Philadelphia for herself and her children: Sarah, Alice, Thomas, John, Hannah and Mary. Joseph Pennell, son of John, requested a certificate to Philadelphia. David Holton reported for marrying out to one not a member. Elias Vernon reported for marrying by a priest to one not a member and without his father's consent. Samuel Savil reported for absconding from his creditors. Sarah Pile, widow of Samuel, produced a certificate from Concord.

29/6/1767. Samuel Ogden requested a certificate to Burlington.

27/7/1767. Jacob Dunn produced a certificate from Goshen. It appears that John Hampton in 1722 produced a certificate for himself and his wife from Concord but for many years has been removed within the verge of Deer Creek Monthly Meeting without requesting a certificate; a certificate will be prepared. Isaac Salkeld reported for joining the Church of England and being sprinkled or baptized; disowned. Thomas Cummings, an Elder of Chester Meeting, died since the last report to the Quarterly Meeting.

31/8/1767. John James produced a certificate from Wilmington, but being removed, requests a certificate to Goshen. Martha Howell, minor dau. of William Howell, produced a certificate from Philadelphia. Esther Worrall, wife of Edward Worrall and dau. of John Worrall, acknowledged marrying by a priest. Meeting informed that Ann Baker, wife of Jesse, reported for neglecting meetings, for being removed within the verge of Concord for several years and refusing to request a certificate. Samuel Taylor, son of John of Chester, requested and was received into membership.

26/10/1767. Deborah Hance, dau. Benjamin, reported for marrying by a priest to Hiram Hancock. Rebekah Worrall, dau. of James, now wife of Joseph Bell, reported for marrying by a priest to one not a member. Jane Minshall, dau. of John, reported for marrying by a Justice to John Longstreth, he being not in unity with Friends. Elizabeth Townsend, dau. of Joseph, Jr., dec'd, reported for marrying by a priest to Isaac Taylor. David Houlton requested a certificate to Philadelphia.

30/11/1767. Elizabeth Salkeld, dau. of John, reported for marrying by a priest to George Robison. Joshua Lewis reported for neglecting his wife and refusing to cohabit with her, and, as it is reported, for living with another woman.

28/12/1767. Mary Kenny, wife of James, requested a certificate to Bradford. Francis Ruth produced a certificate from Concord. Esther Hoskins is chosen overseer with Elinor Harrison for the women's Chester Meeting in the room of Elizabeth Sharples, dec'd.

29/2/1768. Margaret Cobourn [dau. of Joseph Cobourn] reported for neglecting meetings and keeping bad company. Mary Yarnall, dau. of Philip Yarnall, dec'd, acknowledged her marriage by a priest to Joseph Warner. Isaac Worrall, son of James, reported for removing from these parts leaving a just debt unpaid and by reports has since married his first cousin.

25/3/1768. Thomas West produced a certificate from Concord for himself, wife Sarah and two children, Esther and Thomas. Samuel Yarnall produced a certificate from Concord. Deborah Gregg reported for marrying out to Samuel Dutton.

25/4/1768. Elizabeth Garrison requested a certificate to Concord. Jesse Maris, son of Joseph, dec'd, requested a certificate to Philadelphia. Thomas Taylor, Jr., reported for profane swearing and keeping bad company. Edward Minshall, son of Thomas, requested a certificate to Philadelphia. Edward Bettle produced a certificate from Philadelphia.

30/5/1768. Catharine Davis, dau. of Daniel, dec'd, produced a certificate from Radnor. Grace Howard, dau. of John, reported for marrying out by a Justice to George Good. James Pennell reported for marrying by a Justice.

25/7/1768. John Green requested to be received into membership. Elizabeth Howard, wife of John, reported for neglecting meetings and encouraging her daughter to marry out.

29/8/1768. Sarah Fell, dau. of Edward, dec'd, reported for marrying by a priest to Benjamin Taylor. Caleb Maris requested a certificate to Goshen. Thomas James requested a certificate to Concord.

31/10/1768. Abraham Bunting produced a certificate from Darby. Harvy Lewis reported for marrying by a priest to one not a member and neglecting meetings. Esther Ashton and dau. Esther requested a certificate to Concord.

26/12/1768. John Smith produced a certificate from Darby for himself, wife Martha and son John. John Roberts produced a certificate from Goshen for himself, wife Sarah and daughters, Esther and Rebecca. Isaac Taylor, son of John, reported for neglecting meetings and marrying by a priest to Mary Edwards, dau. of Nathan. Mary Warner, wife of Joseph, requested a certificate to Wilmington.

30/1/1769. Thomas Moore produced a certificate from Chesterfield, NJ, for himself, his wife Elizabeth and children: Amey, James, Thomas, Asa and Elizabeth. Sarah Talbot, wife of John and dau. of John Levis, acknowledged marrying out by a priest. Edith Faris, wife of Ziba, requested a certificate to Wilmington.

27/2/1769. Job Ridgeway requested a certificate to Salem, NJ for himself, wife Mary and 6 children: Elizabeth, Hannah, Daniel, Ann, Lydia and Beulah. Joshua Sharpless requested a certificate for himself and wife Edith to New Garden. Susanna Daugherty requested a certificate to Goshen.

23/3/1769. Benjamin Powell requested a certificate to Haverford to marry Hannah Davis, dau. of William, dec'd. Joseph Sharpless requested a certificate to Goshen to marry Mary Hibberd, dau. of John, dec'd.

24/4/1769. Trustram [Tristram] Smith produced a certificate from Concord. Jane Longstreth, wife of John, and Sarah Starr, wife of James, requested a certificate to Gwynedd. Caleb Squibb requested a certificate to Salem, NJ. Moses Thomson and Veronica Nufer reported for marrying by a Justice. Jonathan Worrall reported for almost wholly neglecting meetings and having let in a prejudice against Friends. Esther Ashton and her dau. having sometime ago received from this meeting a certificate to Concord, now return.

29/5/1769. Jonathan Worrall acknowledged neglecting meetings, but the prejudice let in against Friends still seems to remain. Esther Calvert, dau. of John, reported for marrying by a Justice to Joseph Jobson, not a member. Jonas Preston requested a certificate to Duck Creek for himself, his wife Mary and five children: Mary Pennell, Hannah Lea, Ann Lea, Thomas Lea and Jonas Preston, Jr. Mary Ashbridge, wife of David, requested a certificate to Duck Creek. William Vernon, son of Jonathan, requested a certificate to Concord.

26/6/1769. Prudence Powell, dau. of David, dec'd, reported for marrying by a priest to William Davis. Abraham Bunting requested a certificate to Nottingham.

31/7/1769. Thomas Walter produced a certificate from Concord for himself and wife Rebecca. Mordecai Yarnall produced a certificate from Philadelphia. David Meredith requested a certificate to Gwynedd. David Regester reported for marrying by a priest to one not a member. [Annotation in minutes of 9/22/1769 indicate David Regester married Margaret Black by license of 7 Oct 1768.] Isaac Calvert, son of Thomas, reported for marrying by a priest. Sarah Talbot, wife of John, requested a certificate to Concord.

28/8/1769. Sarah Byers, dau. of Nathan Edward, reported for marrying by a priest to one not a member. Richard Poole produced a certificate from Darby Monthly Meeting. Sarah Gilbert produced a certificate from Abington Monthly Meeting. Jacob Cobourn reported for marrying by a priest to one not a member. Jeremiah Starr reported for drinking to excess.

22/9/1769. Mary Sharples, wife of Joseph, produced a certificate from Goshen. Samuel Yarnall requested a certificate to Kennett.

30/10/1769. Phebe Miller, wife of George, proposed visiting several meetings.

27/11/1769. Hannah Levis, dau. of Samuel, reported for fornication and having a bastard child. Esther Dicks, dau. of Joseph, reported for marrying by a priest.

25/12/1769. Mary Vernon, wife of Jonathan, Jr., produced a certificate from Uwchlan. George Swayne, son of Thomas, requested a certificate to Concord as an apprentice. John Pennell requested a certificate to Philadelphia for himself, wife Martha, and dau. Ann.

29/1/1770. Nathaniel Vernon acknowledged his breach of promise to Robert Squibb in regard to payment of money.

26/2/1770. Hannah Starr, wife of Jeremiah, reported for drinking to excess. Jesse Wilkinson reported for fornication and begetting a bastard child. Benanuel Lownes, son of Benanuel, requested a certificate to Philadelphia as an apprentice. Jacob Dunn reported for neglecting to pay a debt to George Miller.

23/3/1770. Sarah Hampton, dau. of Samuel, dec'd, produced a certificate from Philadelphia. William Cobourn reported for drinking to excess, neglecting meeting and keeping idle company. Jane Yarnall, wife of Nathan, appointed Elder of Middletown Meeting. Nathan Davis requested a certificate to Concord for himself, his wife Hannah and children, Rebecca and Mary.

30/4/1770. Caleb Squibb produced a certificate from Salem. Job Yarnall reported for fornication. Alice Harry, wife of John Harry and dau. of Moses Meredith, reported for marrying by a priest. This meeting has been acquainted by way of complaint that Thomas Low, James and William Cowpland, sons of David Cowpland, Moses Carter, Richard Howard and Peter Dicks, several years ago left these parts without acquainting this Monthly Meeting or seeking to obtain certificates: disowned.

28/5/1770. David Malin reported for neglecting meetings and the nonpayment of debts to Reuben Roberts and Joshua Pennell. Isaac Hoopes, son of Abraham, reported for marrying by a Justice.

25/6/1770. Lazarus Askew produced a certificate from Concord.

30/7/1770. Abigail Lewis requested a certificate to Goshen. Alice Harry requested a certificate to Gwynedd. A certificate signed for Grace Good sometime ago through neglect was not sent to her while there

(Haverford) and was returned to this meeting; she now requests one to Nottingham. Walter Roberts reported for marrying by a Justice to one not a member.

27/8/1770. Samuel Taylor requested a certificate to Philadelphia. William Iddings, Jr., produced a certificate from Exeter. Augustine Pasmore produced a certificate from Newgarden. Mordecai Yarnall, Jr., produced a certificate from Uwchlan. Richard Way produced a certificate from Chesterfield, but as he was reported having returned to Chesterfield, the certificate was endorsed on the back and directed back to that meeting.

21/9/1770. Elizabeth and Esther Yarnall requested a certificate to Wilmington.

29/10/1770. Joseph Garretson, minor, produced a certificate from Concord. Joseph Pilkington requested a certificate to Warrington.

26/11/1700. Priscilla Evans requested a certificate to Goshen. William Swaffer acknowledged that sometime ago as a Justice for the county of Chester he signed as witness to a marriage in which one party was a member of the Society and the other had been disowned.

31/12/1770. Jacob Dunn reported for neglecting to pay a debt to Thomas Swayne and for drinking to excess. John Worrall requested a certificate to Concord to marry Sarah Newlin, dau. of John, dec'd. Sarah Yarnall, dau. of Thomas, dec'd, reported for marrying by a priest to Collin McClyster. [An annotation indicates they m. 25 Sep 1770 at 2nd Presb. Church, Phila.]

28/1/1771. Walter Roberts reported for being frequently in the breach of his promise. Esther Pennell requested a certificate to Concord. Prudence Davis requested a certificate to Haverford. Mary Thompson reported for being among the company of a runaway wedding [Sarah McCleister's] performed at a house of entertainment. Edward Vernon reported for marrying by a priest. John Hoopes reported for drinking to excess and neglecting meetings.

25/2/1771. Nathan Haycock requested a certificate to Haverford to marry Priscilla Thomas, dau. of Michael. Nathaniel Calvert and Mary Worrall, dau. of James Worrall and now wife of Nathaniel Calvert, reported for marrying, they being first cousins. The certificate sent to Philadelphia for Martha Pennell, wife of John, and her dau. Ann has returned.

22/3/1771. Joshua Cowpland reported for being in the practice of administering the oath in the station of the Justice of the Peace. Hannah Starr reported for continuing in the practice of drinking to excess. Benjamin Hoopes and Lydia Worrall, dau. of James, reported for marrying by a magistrate. Certificate received some months ago from Concord Monthly Meeting for Joseph Gibbons, Jr., his wife Margery, and their children. Phebe Horn requested a certificate to Philadelphia. Ann Thompson produced a receipt from Mary Kirk for keeping her mother, Judith Broom, for 65 weeks which amounted to £19.9.0. Isaac Coats, son of Samuel, dec'd, and Rebecca Sharples, dau. of Benjamin, to marry.

29/4/1771. Regarding the charge against Mary Thompson, she claims to have acted under the influence of her husband in some matters, he not being a member. Mary Dicks, dau. of Nathan, reported dec'd. Martha Howell, dau. of William, and Phebe Horn requested a certificate to Philadelphia. Job Vernon reported for marrying by a priest. Joseph Sharples requested a certificate to Kennett for himself, his wife Mary and child. Susannah Ruth produced a certificate from Philadelphia. The marriage of Coats and Sharples is put by on account of the man's indisposition of mind.

27/5/1771. Sarah Worrall, wife of John, produced a certificate from Concord. John Lewis requested a certificate to Haverford for himself, wife Alice and dau. Alice.

20/6/1771. Joshua Cowpland continues in much the same disposition and also neglects meetings. Jesse Maris requested a certificate to Goshen to marry Jane Ashbridge, dau. of George. John Roberts requested a certificate to Goshen for himself, wife Sarah and children: Esther, Rebekah and Lydia. William Pennell, son of James, dec'd, reported for marrying by a priest to his first cousin Elizabeth Pennell, dau. of Samuel, dec'd. [Annotation: m. April 17, 1771 at St. Paul's Church in Phila.]

29/7/1771. Deborah Rogers requested a certificate to Goshen. William Starr, wife --- and children: Hannah, Isaac, Margaret, William and Joshua, requested a certificate to Wilmington. Daniel Sharples, son of Joseph, dec'd, reported by Middletown Meeting for fornication and begetting a bastard child with Rebekah Hains and marrying another woman by a priest. Mary Marshall, wife of William Marshall and dau. of Edward Fell, dec'd, reported for marrying by a priest.

26/8/1771. Jane Longstreth produced a certificate from Gwynedd.

30/9/1771. Jesse Tanyer, son of Joseph, requested a certificate to Goshen. Sarah Pile requested a certificate to Concord. Elizabeth Bartram [wife of Nathan] requested a certificate to Darby. Priscilla Haycock produced a certificate from Haverford. Elizabeth Sharples,

dau. of Nathan Dicks, for marrying by a priest requested a
certificate to Daniel Sharples.

28/10/1771. Hannah Powell, wife of Benjamin, produced a certificate
from Haverford. Isaac Davis produced a certificate from Haverford
for himself, wife Joanna and children, Paschal and Sarah. Isaac
Weaver reported for neglecting to pay debts to Mary Harvy, James
Garrett and Thomas Sharples reported for neglecting meetings.

25/11/1771. David Ogden produced a certificate from Wilmington for
himself, wife Zibiah and children, Ann and Sarah. Robert Cobourn
reported for long neglecting meetings, differing with his wife and
drinking to excess.

30/12/1771. Jane Maris, wife of Jesse, produced a certificate from
Goshen. Joseph Gibbons, Jr., reported for being in the practice of
administering the oath. Meeting informed that Mordecai Yarnall, Jr.,
reported for enlisting in military service and going out of the
province. Joseph Taylor, son of Peter, requested a certificate to
Haverford.

27/1/1772. Nehemiah Davis reported for drinking to excess. John
Haycock, Jr., reported for refusing to comply with Friends' advice in
a matter of controversy with Reuben Roberts.

24/2/1772. John Cobourn reported for drinking to excess and neglecting
meetings. Ann Siddens, wife of William Siddens and dau. of David
Ogden, reported for marrying by a priest to one not a member.
Martha Dotherdy [Daugherty] requested a certificate to Concord.
Dugal Cameron requested a certificate to Uwchlan for himself and
wife Elizabeth. Walter Roberts reported for absconding from his
creditors. Thomas Broom reported for drinking to excess and
neglecting meetings.

30/3/1772. Esther Jobson requested a certificate to Goshen. Joseph
Wilkison reported for drinking to excess and neglecting meetings.
Hugh Lownes, son of Benjamin, dec'd, requested a certificate to
Philadelphia.

27/4/1772. Thomas Thomas requested a certificate to Goshen. Thomas
Swayne requested a certificate to Darby. Evan Taylor and wife
Amay requested a certificate to Nottingham. Hannah Haycock, now
Wolson, dau. of John, reported for marrying by a priest to one not a
member.

25/5/1772. Hannah James produced a certificate from Goshen. Jane
Larkin produced a certificate from Concord. Cornelius Wood
requested a certificate to Goshen for himself, his wife Mary and
children: Isaac, John, Jane, Nathan and Samuel. Daniel Brown
produced a certificate from Uwchlan for himself, wife Susanna, and

children: Joseph, Mary, Margaret, Daniel, John and Joel. James
Wood produced a certificate from Wrightstown for himself, wife
Mary and children: James, John, Aaron, Septimus, Mary, Sarah,
Rachel and Rebekah.

29/6/1772. Catharine Bonsal requested a certificate to Wilmington.

27/7/1772. Nathaniel Squibb reported for attempting to wrong his
neighbor.

31/8/1772. Thomas James produced a certificate from Kennett. Henry
Laurence reported for neglecting or refusing to comply with his
father's will. Abraham Sharples requested a certificate to Concord
for himself and four of his children: Mary, Esther, Abraham and
Rebekah. Thomas Moor requested a certificate to Philadelphia for
himself, his wife Elizabeth and five of their children: James, Thomas,
Asy, Elizabeth and Ann. Lydia Sharples requested a certificate to
Newgarden. Grace Sharples, daus. of Abraham, requested a
certificate to Goshen. Mary Howell [widow of Israel] requested a
certificate to Philadelphia.

25/9/1772. Jacob Hoopes reported for fornication.

26/10/1772. Jonathan Jones produced a certificate from Gwynedd for
himself and his wife Susanna. Elisha Worrall reported for refusing or
neglecting to refer a matter of controversy with Joseph Pratt.
George Davis requested a certificate to Burlington. Hannah Yarnall,
wife of David, reported for drinking to excess and neglecting
meetings. Sarah Harlon [wife of Samuel] produced a certificate from
Kennett. Susannah Brown, wife of Daniel, appointed an elder.

30/11/1772. Joseph West produced a certificate from Kennett for
himself, his wife Susanna and children, Jesse and Rachel. Mary,
Sarah and John Starr, children of Jeremiah and Hannah Starr,
requested a certificate to Exeter. Sarah Massey, wife of Mordecai,
reported for marrying by a priest. Henry Howard reported for
fornication and for marrying by a priest.

28/12/1772. Joseph Haycock reported for refusing to refer a matter in
dispute with Gideon Malin. Joseph Crosly, son of Samuel, requested
a certificate to Uwchlan. Mary Crosly, wife of Samuel, requested a
certificate to Concord for herself [and their son Joseph].

25/1/1773. Isaac McIlvain requested a certificate to Pine Street
Monthly Meeting, Philadelphia. Sarah Howell, dau. of Isaac,
requested a certificate to Darby.

22/2/1773. Agnes Wilkison reported for marrying by a priest to one not
a member. [Wife of Jesse and dau. of David Salkeld, dec'd.] John
Woolley requested a certificate to Goshen to marry Phebe Hoopes,

dau. of Joshua, dec'd. Ambrose Taylor, son of Peter, requested a
certificate to Nottingham to marry Mary Sidwell, dau. of Henry.
Sarah Crozier, dau. of James Crozier, requested to come under the
care of Friends. Susanna Bishop, dau. of Thomas Bishop, requested
to come under the care of Friends. Thomas Pilkington, son of
Thomas, requested a certificate to Bradford. Lydia Worrall, wife of
Thomas, requested a certificate to Concord for herself and three of
their children: Hannah, John and Ann.

26/3/1773. Samuel Carpenter requested to come under the care of
Friends.

26/4/1773. Francis Richardson produced a certificate from Philadelphia
for himself and three of his children: John, Hannah and Deborah.
Samuel Carpenter requested a certificate to Concord to marry
Rachel Dingy [Dingee], dau. of Jacob, and settle there. Aaron
Sharples, son of Benjamin, requested a certificate to Philadelphia.
Certificates being prepared for Sarah Gilbert and Mary James, wife
of Joseph. Joseph Wilkinson continues to drink to excess.

31/5/1773. Martha Worrall, dau. of Jonathan, reported for marrying by
a priest to Jonathan Moore. Thomas Sharples requested a certificate
to Duck Creek for himself, his wife Martha and children: William
Preston, Jonas and Jane. Elijah Worrall reported for beating and
injuring Michal Bready and neglecting meetings; it is thought that he
has occasioned uneasiness between Michal and his wife.

26/7/1773. Phebe Woolley, wife of John, produced a certificate from
Goshen. Martha Levis, dau. of Samuel, now wife of James Hunter,
Jr., reported for marrying by a priest.

30/8/1773. Elijah Worrall reported as still being out of these parts. Jane
Howard, dau. of John, reported for marrying by a priest to Benjamin
Chance. Isaac Maris reported for differing with his brother in a
reproachful manner. William Griffith reported for drinking to excess.

24/9/1773. Mary Chamberlain, wife of John, requested a certificate to
Pipe Creek Monthly Meeting, Frederick Co.

25/10/1773. Frederic Vernon accused by Mary Owen of fornication and
begetting a bastard child. [He denied the charge.]

29/11/1773. Elizabeth Beethom produced a certificate from Lancaster
Monthly Meeting in Old England. Benjamin Powell reported for
refusing or neglecting to refer a matter in controversy with James
Rhoads and for treating him with unbecoming language. Samuel
Levis reported for buying two young Negro slaves.

27/12/1773. Ann Rogers produced a certificate from Gwynedd. Evan
Taylor produced a certificate from Nottingham for himself and wife

Amy. Mary Taylor, wife of Ambrose, produced a certificate from Nottingham. Nathan Haycock reported for marrying by a magistrate to one not a member and too soon after the death of his former wife. Aaron Baker requested to come under the care of Friends. Samuel Lewis, son of John, requested a certificate to Haverford.

31/1/1774. Thomas Wilson produced a certificate from Duck Creek for himself and children: Sarah, Ezekiel, John, James, Mary, Susanna and Thomas. Samuel Levis, Jr., requested a certificate to Darby to marry Elizabeth Garrett, dau. of William. Ann Levis, dau. of John, now wife of John Hunter, reported for marrying by a priest to one not a member. Joseph Meredith, son of Moses, charged with begetting a bastard child by Hannah Worrall, dau. of John.

28/2/1774. Catharine Fairlamb, dau. of John, dec'd, now wife of Peter Hill, reported for marrying by a magistrate to one not a member. Thomas Calvert, Jr., requested a certificate to Kennett.

25/3/1774. Isaac Sharples requested a certificate to Wrightsborough, GA. Ephraim Yarnall acknowledged former misconduct. Ann Cowpland, wife of Joshua, requested a certificate to Salem for herself and four of their children: Caleb, Cadwalader, Sarah and David. Mary Ashbridge, wife of Joshua, requested a certificate to Goshen. Lydia Mendenhall requested a certificate to Concord. Barbara Wilkinson requested a certificate to Fairfax for herself and children, Sarah and Joseph. John Woolley and wife Phebe requested a certificate to Goshen. Aaron Vernon requested a certificate to Warrington for himself, his wife Rachel and children: Margaret, Sarah, Lacy and Rachel. Nathan Yarnall requested a certificate to Philadelphia for son Ellis.

25/4/1774. Rachel Crozer requested that her five daus.: Elizabeth, Rachel, Martha, Esther and Rebeckah [children of James Crozer], be taken in as members. Ambrose Taylor requested a certificate to Newgarden for himself, wife Mary and son Jacob. Deborah Mifflin, wife of Joseph, requested a certificate to Philadelphia.

30/5/1774. Daniel Brown requested a certificate to Hopewell for himself, his wife Susanna and children: Joseph, Mary, Margaret, Daniel, John and Joel. Ann Dutton requested a certificate to Concord. Sarah Salkeld, dau. of John, now wife of Joseph Gill, reported for marrying by a priest to one not a member.

25/7/1774. Isaac Maris reported for drinking to excess. Nathaniel Sharples reported for marrying out of unity [27 Sep 1773, Christ Church, Philadelphia, to Elizabeth Wilkinson] and giving an obligation for a sum of money towards the maintenance of Abigail

Malin's child of which she charged him with being the father.
Women to treat with Abail Malin [dau. of David]. Jacob Talbot
requested a certificate to Concord for himself, his wife Susanna and
children, John and Samuel.

29/8/1774. Samuel Fairlamb and Hannah Richardson, dau. of Francis,
reported for marrying by a priest. Nathaniel Vernon reported for
neglecting to pay debts to Edward Russel and Thomas Swayne and
for neglecting meetings.

23/9/1774. Edward Fell requested a certificate to Richland to marry
Mary Penrose, dau. of Robert, dec'd. Margaret Garret [wife of
Thomas] requested a certificate to Darby. Ann Rogers, dau. of
Robert, reported for fornication and having a bastard child.

31/10/1774. Ann Evans produced a certificate from Philadelphia.
Lyddia, dau. of John Calvert, now wife of David Dunn, reported for
marrying by a priest.

28/11/1774. Ann Hunter requested a certificate to Goshen. Keziah
Harvy requested to become a member.

26/12/1774. John Pennell, son of Thomas, acknowledged outgoing in
marriage. Hannah Wilkinson, wife of William [and dau. of Nathan
Taylor], acknowledged outgoing in marriage. Sarah Robinson
produced a certificate from Philadelphia. Isaac Sumption produced a
certificate from Concord.

30/1/1775. John Pennell requested a certificate to Duck Creek. William
Horn produced a certificate from Philadelphia for himself, his wife
Phebe and their young children, Mary and Elizabeth.

27/2/1775. Mary Fell, wife of Edward, produced a certificate from
Richland. Sarah Gilpin, widow of George, produced a certificate from
Concord. Ephraim Yarnall requested a certificate to Kennett.

24/3/1775. Samuel Yarnall produced a certificate from Kennett.

24/4/1775. Richard Pool requested a certificate to Concord to marry
Agnes Brown. Elisha Worrall reported for not complying with the
advice of Friends to refer a matter in controversy with Isaac Maris.
Jonathan Haycock produced a certificate from Richland. Lydia
Regester, dau. of Robert, dec'd, reported for fornication and having a
bastard child. Gideon Vernon requested a certificate to Goshen to
marry Phebe Farr, dau. of Edward. William Calvert requested a
certificate to Kennett. Elizabeth Scot, wife of John, requested a
certificate to Goshen.

29/5/1775. Isaac Maris continues to drink to excess.

26/6/1775. Raper Hoskins produced a certificate from Burlington.
Benjamin Pyle produced a certificate from Concord. Samuel Carter

acknowledged outgoing in marriage with a recommendation from Friends in North Carolina where he resides; he requested a certificate to Cane Creek. Elinor Harrison is chosen overseer for Chester Women's Meeting along with Sarah Sharples instead of Jane Yarnall, dec'd.

31/7/1775. Abraham Sharples produced a certificate from Concord for himself and children: Abraham, Rebekah, and for his dau's. Mary and Esther.

28/8/1775. Thomas Wilson reported for purchasing a Negro slave for a term of years. Frederic Fairlamb, John Richardson, John Cox and David Cowpland, Jr., reported for being concerned in military preparations. Keziah James [wife of Ezekiel] requested a certificate to Goshen. Thomas Moore produced a certificate from Philadelphia Monthly Meeting for the Southern District for himself, Elizabeth his wife and their children: James, Thomas, Asa, Elizabeth and Ann.

22/9/1775. Patience McClaskey [dau. of Jonathan Worrall of Marple] acknowledged outgoing in marriage. John Flower requested to be taken under the care of Friends [approved]. Daniel Sharples requested a certificate to Goshen to marry Hannah, dau. of Isaac Thomas. Ann Pedrick, widow of John and dau. of John Fairlamb, dec'd, reported for marrying by a magistrate. Esther Kirk, wife of Phillip and widow of Edward Worrall reported for marrying by a priest. Caleb Davis, Thomas Levis, Joseph Lowns, Nathaniel Vernon, Nathaniel Vernon, Jr., Thomas Vernon, Jonathan Vernon, Jr., and Joseph Taylor reported for being concerned in military preparations and combinations respecting government [disowned].

30/10/1775. Phebe Vernon, wife of Gideon, produced a certificate from Goshen. Mary Reece produced a certificate from Goshen for herself and three children: Lydia, Nehemiah and William. Elizabeth Swaffer produced a certificate from Goshen. Hannah Hunter, dau. of Jesse Maris, reported for marrying by a priest [m. 16 Jan 1775 Edward Hunter]. Aaron Ashbridge and Joseph Ashbridge, Jr., reported for being concerned in military preparations. Aaron Ogden reported for marrying by a priest. William Horn reported for neglecting to pay debts to John Nail and William Brown. Elizabeth Scot, widow of John Scot, returned her certificate not having an opportunity to deliver it whilst she lived there.

27/11/1775. Thomas Vernon and John Vernon, sons of Nathaniel Vernon, are in the practice of exercising in the military service agreeable to their father's direction, they being under age. Esther Cobourn, wife of Caleb and dau. of Abraham Ashton, reported for marrying by a priest. Caleb James requested a certificate to Goshen for himself, his wife Mary and children: Aaron, Sarah, Joseph, Mary and Caleb.

29/1/1776. Jonathan Haycock requested a certificate to Darby for himself, wife Hannah and children: Joseph, Isaac, Benjamin, Jacob and Sarah. Benjamin Powell reported for exercising in military discipline.

26/2/1776. Hannah Sharples [wife of Daniel] produced a certificate from Goshen. Jonathan Howell produced an acknowledgment for his past misconduct; also a recommendation from Friends in NC where he now resides. Phebe Travilla [dau. of James Travillo] requested a certificate Goshen.

22/3/1776. Jonathan Morris produced a certificate from Newgarden for himself, wife Alice and children: Cadwalader, Ann, Jonathan, Catharine, Samuel, Evan and Hannah. Jacob Hibberd produced a certificate from Goshen.

28/4/1776. Joseph Sermon produced a certificate from Philadelphia for himself, wife Mary and children: Richard, Isaac, Robert and Jane. Thomas Evans of Edgmont produced manumission for a Negro boy, Samson, otherwise known as Samson Tobias, when he reaches age 21 which will be 6/8/1787.

27/5/1776. Hannah Talbot, dau. of Joseph, now wife of Francis Dutton, reported for marrying by a priest. John Eyre requested a certificate to Concord for himself, his wife Rebecca and children: William, Caleb and Sarah.

24/6/1776. Mary Horn requested a certificate to Goshen. Joseph Talbot requested a certificate to Concord to marry Ann Sharpless.

29/7/1776. Richard Blackham produced a certificate from Philadelphia. Ezra Thomas produced a certificate from Goshen. Abigail Newlin, wife of Cyrus Newlin, and Mary Shipley, wife of Joseph Shipley, requested a certificate to Wilmington. William and John Levis, sons of Samuel, reported for exercising in military discipline and making warlike preparations [disowned]. William Horn reported for falsifying his word and drinking to excess. The certificate granted some time ago for George Davis to Burlington is now returned with an endorsement. Ann Evans produced manumission for a Negro woman named Sarah Tobias, left to her by her dec'd husband Cadwalader Evans, also for Sarah's children, Peter and Charity, and for Sarah's dau. Ruth to secure her freedom at 18.

26/8/1776. Richard Pool, Isaac Sumption and Joshua Weaver reported for exercising in military discipline. Samuel Yarnall requested a

certificate to Concord to marry Hannah Hutton, dau. of John
Hatton, dec'd. Nathan Pennell and wife Susannah requested a
certificate to Concord. Aaron Baker reported for drinking to excess
and neglecting meetings.

30/9/1776. Benjamin Sharples produced manumission for a mulatto boy
under his care. William Edwards, Jr., reported for exercising in
military discipline.

28/10/1776. Thomas Cortney and his wife Ann, formerly Evans,
reported for marrying by a magistrate and further against him for
neglecting to deliver a certificate from this meeting to Goshen. Seth
Worrall and Joshua Levis reported for exercising in the military and
making warlike preparations. John Haycock, Jr., reported for
endeavoring to make it appear in a public place and time that he
was married when he was not, in order to avoid paying a tax.

25/11/1776. Ann Yarnall produced a manumission for a Negro woman.

30/12/1776. Isaac McIlvain produced a certificate from Southern
District, Philadelphia. Augustine Pasmore reported for marrying by a
magistrate. Samuel Worrall reported for removing without a
certificate and exercising in military discipline.

27/1/1777. Jonathan Worrall acknowledged past misconduct and
submitted a recommendation from Friends of Exeter. Hannah
Nuzum acknowledged past misconduct and submitted a
recommendation from Friends of Exeter. Jonathan Worrall
requested certificates to Exeter for himself and his sister Hannah
Nuzum. Samuel Yarnall requested a certificate to Concord.

24/2/1777. Thomas Jacobs produced a certificate from Gwynedd. Elisha
Jones requested a certificate to Wilmington for himself, his wife
Gwen and children: Susannah, Margaret, Jesse, Hannah and
Elizabeth. Thomas James requested a certificate to Newgarden.

31/3/1777. Richard Poole acknowledged fornication before marriage and
drinking to excess. Sarah Wilson requested a certificate to Duck
Creek. Alice Temple, wife of William Temple, requested a certificate
to Kennett. Hannah Hunter, wife of Edward Hunter, requested a
certificate to Goshen. Sarah Becerton requested a certificate to
Philadelphia. Thomas Moore requested a certificate to Uwchlan for
himself, his wife Elizabeth and children: James, Asa, Elizabeth and
Ann. Thomas Pilkington, Jr., produced a certificate from Bradford.
Daniel Regester acknowledged drinking to excess. Samuel and John
Lewis reported for neglecting meetings, joining military service and
going aboard a war vessel.

28/4/1777. Ann Evans produced manumission for a Mulatto girl, Phillis, to be freed at age 21. Isaac Sumption has gone aboard a war vessel in order to be an assistant therein. Frederick Engle and his son John reported for being in the practice of exercising in the military service.

26/5/1777. Thomas Coburn reported for neglecting meetings and drinking to excess. John Edwards reported for neglecting meetings. Nathaniel Holland requested membership for himself, his wife Catherine and children: Mary, Thomas, John, Sarah, Samuel and Nathaniel. Jonathan Jones requested a certificate to Gwynedd for himself, his wife Susannah and children: Isaac, Mary and John. Hannah Dutton requested a certificate to Concord. Sarah Yarnall, dau. of David, requested a certificate to Goshen. Joseph Taylor produced a certificate from Haverford.

30/6/1777. Margaret Malin, wife of David, requested a certificate to Philadelphia for herself and children: Elizabeth, David, John, Elijah, Rachel, Margaret and Enoch; also for their daus. Susannah and Mary Malin to the same meeting. Dinah Russell, widow of Edward, requested a certificate to Southern District, Philadelphia. Sarah Harlon, wife of Samuel, requested a certificate to Warrington. Sarah Doherty [Daugherty] requested a certificate to Concord. Elisha Worrall, son of Jonathan, dec'd, and Ann Dicks, dau. of Joseph, reported for marrying by a magistrate. Gwen Jones, widow of Elisha, requested a certificate to Goshen for herself and children: Susanna, Margeret, Jesse, Hannah and Elizabeth.

28/7/1777. Elisah Worrall and wife did not give a satisfactory account of their marriage. [Annotated remark: Their son Frederick married a dau. of James Hunter of Newtown or Radnor and was father of Prof. J. Hunter Worrall of W. Chester.] Enoch Taylor and Elizabeth Scott, widow of John, reported for marrying out by a magistrate. Jacob Dingee produced a certificate from Concord for himself and wife Hannah. Ambrose Taylor produced a certificate from New Garden for himself, wife Mary and children, Jacob and Mordicai. James Reynolds produced a certificate from Concord. Mary Warner produced a certificate from Philadelphia, Northern District. A deed of manumission was produced from John Reynolds, Hugh Roberts, James Pemberton and Abel James, trustees for Mordicai Yarnall, dec'd, and agreed to by Ann Yarnall, for a Negro named Maria. Robert Pennell reported for drinking to excess, neglecting meetings and encouraging the military service, being a spectator of military

exercises several times. Abraham Williamson requested a certificate
to Goshen to marry Esther James, dau. of Joseph, dec'd.

25/8/1777. Emanuel Walker produced a certificate from Middletown,
Bucks Co., for himself, wife Ann and children: Joseph, Samuel,
Mary, Ann, Beulah, John and Heppzibah. Thomas Moore requested
a certificate to Goshen. John and James West, sons of William West,
reported for engaging in military service and being of loose and
libertine conduct. Joshua Weaver acknowledged the misconduct of
his exercising in military discipline.

28/9/1777. John Edwards reported for purchasing a slave for a number
of years.

27/10/1777. Jonathan Morris reported for having a claim to several
slaves and refusing to manumit them. Thomas Minshall, Jr.,
reported for marrying out.

24/11/1777. Recommendation received from a number of Friends in
North Carolina on behalf of Caleb Harvey informing this meeting
that he was desirous of having his right of membership conveyed to
Cane Creek Monthly Meeting. Thomas Coburn reported for drinking
to excess and neglecting meetings. Mary Hoopes, wife of Isaac,
produced a certificate from Goshen. John Levis and Samuel Levis
reported for holding several slaves in their possession which they
refuse to manumit.

29/12/1777. Jonathan Morris reported for being unwilling to manumit
his slaves. Samuel Levis reported for being unwilling to manumit his
slaves. Joseph Pilkington produced a certificate from Warrington.

26/1/1778. Joseph Sharples produced a certificate from Concord. James
Iddings produced a certificate from Exeter. Thomas Pilkington, Jr.,
reported for marrying by a priest to one not a member. James
Rhoads produced a document of manumission for Negro woman
Patience Jobias. Thomas Pennell reported for marrying by a hireling
priest to one not a member. John Hill requested that he and his
children: [William, Humphry], Hannah, Ann, Rachel, Mary, Lydia
and Tacy, be received into membership. Ann Sharples, dau. of Jacob,
dec'd, produced a certificate from Concord.

23/2/1778. James Iddings requested a certificate to Bradford. Agnes
Wilkinson requested a certificate to Fairfax. Ann Talbot, wife of
Joseph, Sr., produced a certificate from Concord for herself and two
of her children, Martha and Hannah Sharples.

30/3/1778. Nathan Edwards produced a document of manumission to
secure the liberty of a mulatto boy under his care named Richard

Penn. Isaac Davis reported for selling a mulatto woman and two children as slaves. Ezra Thomas requested a certificate to Goshen.

27/4/1778. John Levis produced manumission to secure the liberty of a Negro woman named Flora and her three children: Essex, Frank and Harry. Francis Richardson produced manumission to secure the liberty of a Negro named Present and her three children: Charles, George and Phebe. Seth Worral reported for marrying his first cousin Phebe Worrall, dau. of Benjamin, dec'd, by a hireling priest. Joseph West requested a certificate to Concord for himself, wife Susanna and children: Jesse, Rachel, Mary, Hannah and Joseph. Gideon Vernon has several times appeared with arms and assisted in taking several persons from their dwellings in a violent manner; Friends have waited long in order to get an opportunity with him, he being gone from his habitation. Lydia Worrall, wife of Thomas, produced a certificate from Concord for herself and her three children: Hannah, John and Ann. Lydia Barnard produced a certificate from New Garden. Joseph Thomas produced a certificate from Goshen. Margaret Byrd, formerly Thomson, dau. of John, reported for marrying by a priest to one not a member. Sarah Mattson, formerly Worrall, dau. of Peter, dec'd, reported for marrying by a priest.

25/5/1778. An inquiry was made into the circumstances of several Negro slaves, who it was thought Jonathan Morris had a claim. It was revealed that his brother Samuel Morris, dec'd, by his last will gave the remainder of his estate to him after the debts were paid and appointed him executor. Edward Horn produced a certificate from Newgarden for himself, his wife Mary and son William. Joseph Dingee produced a certificate from Concord. Patience McClaskey produced an acknowledgment and a recommendation from some Friends of Chichester Meeting. Lydia McIlvain requested membership for her children: Judith, John, Lydia, Jeremiah, James, Margaret, Richard and Hugh.

29/6/1778. Evan Taylor reported for neglecting meetings, drinking to excess and engaging as a substitute soldier. Cadwalader Evans produced a certificate from Exeter. Jesse Haines produced a certificate from Goshen.

27/7/1778. Ann Goodwin, Jr., produced a certificate from Goshen.

31/8/1778. Samuel Pennell, son of William, charged with fornication and begetting a bastard child. Patience McClaskey requested a certificate to Concord. Phebe Horn, wife of William, requested a certificate to Darby for herself and her children: Mary, Thomas and Elizabeth.

Eleanor, dau. of John Cox, dec'd, now wife of Slater Lownes, reported for marrying by a priest to one not a member. Mary Mendenhall, wife of Philip, and formerly widow of William Reece, reported for marrying by a priest to one not a member.

25/9/1778. Susanah and Mary Malin were granted certificates to Philadelphia some time ago but were not delivered; copies being produced. Margaret Malin, wife of David, returned the certificate granted to her and several of her children, Elizabeth, David, John, Elijah, Rachel, Margaret and Sarah, some time ago (not having delivered it) and now requested one to Haverford. Jacob Hibberd requested a certificate to Concord to marry Sarah Dutton, dau. of Thomas, dec'd. Rebeckah West, dau. of William, now Haycock, married by a priest to a man in the army and has gone with him. Susanna Neal, wife of John, produced a certificate from Goshen for herself and her children: James, Ann and Lydia. Lysia Yarnall, dau. of David, requested a certificate to Wilmington.

26/10/1778. Mary Jones, dau. of Jesse, produced a certificate from Goshen. Mary McIlvain, dau. of John McIlvain, dec'd, reported for marrying by a hireling teacher to one not of our society, she being removed to Maryland. Deborah Mifflin reported for not delivered her certificate to Philadelphia.

30/11/1778. Margaret Maris, wife of Jesse, produced a certificate from Philadelphia for herself and children: Ann, Richard, Jemima and Elizabeth. Lydia Bernard requested a certificate to Newgarden.

28/12/1778. Thomas Worrall produced a manumission to secure the liberty of a Negro woman named Prudence and her children, Rebekah and Charles, and another to secure the liberty of a man named Abel. Philadelphia Monthly Meeting returned the copy of Sarah Beckerton's certificate with an endorsement signifying she refused to deliver it, had been in the practice of selling liquors to the soldiers and others and is now returned within the verge of this meeting. Robert and William McCoy produced a certificate from Deer Creek and stated that they are about to return. Isaac McIlvain reported for marrying by a priest to one not a member. George Lownes and Mary Lownes, dau. of Benanuel, dec'd, both requested a certificate to Concord. George Hoopes reported for drinking to excess, neglecting meetings and marrying by a hireling priest. Daniel Regester reported for drinking to excess, attending a marriage out of unity and taking the Test [for the military].

25/1/1779. John Edwards, Jr., has taken the Test. John Levis, John Thompson and Edward Horn have taken a Test, the tenor of which

is inconsistent with our religious principles. Edward Horn continues
to keep a public house, entertaining the collectors and others
concerned in the sale of the property taken from Friends for fines
and other demands. Joseph Sermon requested a certificate to
Philadelphia for himself, wife Mary and five children: Richard, Isaac,
Robert, Jane and Hannah. Nathan Edwards reported for neglecting
meetings and refusing to give satisfaction concerning a report of his
taking the Test. Cadwalader Evans and his wife Sarah, dau. of John
Cox, dec'd, reported for marrying by a priest. Jehu Maris requested
a certificate to Haverford to marry Jane Humphrey, dau. of John,
dec'd. Sarah Davis, dau. of Isaac, now wife of Isaac Vanleer,
reported for marrying by a priest to one not a member. Joseph
Yarnall reported for marrying by a priest.

22/2/1779. Sarah Beckerton reportedly was married by a priest since
last meeting to one not a member. Isaac McIlvain reported for
paying part of a fine for not serving in the militia. Joseph Yarnall
told his brother that he was not capable of condemning his conduct
at this time. Lydia Worrall, dau. of John, reported for committing
fornication and begetting a bastard child. Prudence Edwards, dau. of
William, now wife of Seth Thomas, reported for marrying by a priest
to one not a member.

26/3/1779. Mary Penrose produced a certificate from Richland. Thomas
Walter acknowledged purchasing a mare that was taken as a prize.
Joseph Rhoads requested a certificate to Goshen to marry Mary
Ashbridge. Benjamin Powel reported for removing without
requesting a certificate against repeated advise and for paying a fine
in lieu of personal service in the militia. Tacy Roberts, dau. of
Reuben, reported for bearing a child and refusing to satisfy Friends
that she is married. Alice Buckly, formerly Lownes, widow of
Benanuel, reported for marrying by a priest. Rebekah Porter
requested to be taken under the care of Friends. Israel Cox
requested a certificate to Uwchlan.

26/4/1779. William Wood produced a certificate from Wrightstown.
James Malin reported for keeping bad company and taking the Test.
Isaac Levis reported for taking the Test and assisting to lay a tax for
military purposes. Joseph Garretson acknowledged taking the Test
and marrying out of unity. Hannah Calvert, Jr., acknowledged being
at a marriage performed by a priest. Henry Lawrence reported for
taking the Test and assisting to lay a tax for warlike purposes.
Samuel Levis reported for taking the Test and neglecting meetings.
George Davis left these parts, since which it appears he has taken

the Test and Esther Ely, a young woman, has charged him with being the father of her child. Rachel Matson, dau. of Peter Worrall, dec'd, reported for marrying by a priest to one not a member. Abraham Sharples, son of Abram, requested a certificate to Bradford. Phebe Sharples, dau. of Abraham, requested a certificate to Uwchlan.

31/5/1779. Jane Longstreth requested a certificate to Uwchlan. Deborah Calvert reported for fornication and having a bastard child. Mary James produced a certificate from Goshen for herself and four small children: Samuel, Frederick, Abigail and Hannah. Thomas Dell Weaver reported for taking the Test. Ambrose Smedley acknowledged countenancing the fine gatherers taking some receipts which had been given for forage taken by the Army for a fine in lieu of personal service in the militia. Daniel Worrell married by a priest to a young woman who is not a member and has taken some property of his neighbors in a clandestine manner. Frederick Engle reported for engaging in military exercise and also for offering duplicates in order for the collection of taxes, part of which is a fine for not taking the Test.

28/6/1779. Aaron Sharples produced a certificate from Philadelphia, Southern District. Owen Worrall reported for neglecting meetings for some years and for quarreling and fighting of late. Susannah Martin, dau. of Benjamin Worrall, dec'd, reported for marrying out. Agnes Wilkinson reported by Fairfax Monthly Meeting for not delivering her certificate to that meeting and acknowledging adultery before leaving this meeting.

26/7/1779. Jesse Goodwin produced a certificate from Goshen. Jane Maris, wife of Jehu, produced a certificate from Haverford. Phebe Miller returned her minutes to visit families of Goshen Meeting with endorsement from that meeting. Benjamin Sharples, son of Joseph, dec'd, requested a certificate to Concord, being placed as an apprentice to a member there.

30/8/1779. Thomas Sharples produced a certificate from Duck Creek for himself, his wife Martha and children: William, Jonas, Jane, Thomas and Preston. Joseph Newlin produced a certificate from Concord. David Ogden reported for taking the Test, assisting to take a return in order to lay a tax for military purposes and neglecting to attend our religious meetings. John Engle reported again being in the practice of exercising in military discipline, taking the Test and neglecting meetings. Beulah Brumwell requested a certificate to

Philadelphia. Rebekah Baldwin requested a certificate to Goshen. Joseph Dingee requested a certificate to Darby.

24/9/1779. Augustine Pasmore requested a certificate to Concord. Jane Wilson requested that Phebe Pew [Pugh], a child under her care, be received as a member [approved].

25/10/1779. Mary Preston, widow, produced a certificate from Duck Creek for herself and two of her children, Hannah Canby, widow, and Jonas Preston. Mary Rhoads, wife of Joseph, produced a certificate from Goshen. Nathan Milner reported for marrying by a priest to one not a member.

29/11/1779. Mary Cobourn, dau. of John, requested a certificate to Wilmington. Mary Rhoads acknowledged paying a substitute fine for her brother. Mary Yarnall reported in necessitous circumstances. Middletown informed this meeting that Francis Wiseley requested to come under the care of Friends.

31/1/1780. Benjamin Hance, Jr., reported for being in military employ and going to sea in an armed vessel. John Hill requested a certificate to Darby for his son William.

28/2/1780. Seth Pancost [Pancoast], Jr., reported taking the Test. Levi Pilkington requested a certificate to Exeter. John Worrall requested a certificate to Concord to marry Hannah Thatcher, dau. of William. Elizabeth Taylor requested a certificate to Kennett. John Flower by a Friend informed the meeting that his bodily indisposition makes it difficult for him to attend; therefore, he requested a certificate to Philadelphia Monthly Meeting for the Southern District.

24/3/1780. Isabela Cowpland produced two manumissions to free a Negro man named Sip and a Negro woman named Pless. Catherine Hill and Mary Fairlamb (daus. of John Fairlamb, dec'd) requested a certificate to Wilmington. Joseph Newlin requested a certificate to Concord. Mary Brinton, wife of Joseph, produced a certificate from Kennett for herself and her children: Welden, Peggy and Lydia. Rachel James produced a certificate from Goshen.

24/4/1780. Thomas Evans appointed clerk of the [men's] meeting in place of Isaac Sharples, dec'd. Thomas Smedley acknowledged paying part of a fine for not bearing arms and also part of a tax. Hannah West, wife of William, produced a certificate from Philadelphia. Agness Beaven [Bevan] requested a certificate to Philadelphia Monthly Meeting for the Southern District for herself and five children: Ann, David, Isabela, Tacy and Mathew Sollar Beavan [Bevan]. Ann Radcliff, wife of John, formerly Pennell, dau. of John, dec'd, reported for marrying out of unity. Hannah Garetson, wife of

Joseph, formerly Calvert, dau. of John, reported for marrying by a
priest. Baldwin Weaver reported for being in the practice of
exercising in military discipline. James Maris reported for having a
mulatto slave, who he refuses to free, and also for neglecting
meetings. James Haycock reported for paying a fine in lieu of his
personal service in the militia. Jacob Hibberd requested a certificate
to Concord.

29/5/1780. Joseph Davis was charged by a young woman with being the
father of her child, a situation he seems to deny though he
acknowledged having unlawfully accompanied her. Cadwalader
Morris was charged with being the father of a bastard child and
going to sea in an armed vessel. Hannah Malin, dau. of Gideon,
reported for fornication and begetting a bastard child. Susanna
Griffith [dau. of William, dec.] requested a certificate to Concord.
Thomas Walter has countenanced the payment of a demand for the
releasing of his cow that was seized for a substitute fine.

26/6/1780. Sarah Hall [dau. of Samuel] produced a certificate from
Merion. Hugh Lownes produced a certificate from Northern District,
Philadelphia. John Wood and Sarah Dicks, dau. of Nathan, dec'd,
reported for fornication before marriage and for marrying by a
priest. Mary James, widow of Joseph, now wife of Edward
Woodward, reported for marrying by a priest.

31/7/1780. Hannah Worrall, wife of John, produced a certificate from
Concord. Robert Mendenhall, Jr., produced a certificate from
Concord. Abner Rogers requested a certificate to Concord. Memorial
concerning Nathan Yarnall, dec'd, was under consideration.

28/8/1780. Isabela Cowpland produced manumissions to free a Negro
boy named Cudji and two mulatto girls, Rose and Jane. Margery
Squibb, wife of Nathaniel, requested a certificate to Concord for
herself and children: Thomas, Lydia, Robert, Hannah, Enoch and
Elisha. Owen Rhoads acknowledged paying a fine for not serving in
the militia. James Wood, Jr., reported for taking the Test and in
some way joining the militia. Abigail Engle continues to keep a
tavern and entertain people at the sale of goods taken from her
neighbors for fines. William Salkeld had a creature taken from him
for a substitute fine and consented that a certain person redeem it.

22/9/1780. John Evans paid a fine in lieu of personal service. Hannah
Garret, wife of Nathan, Jr., requested a certificate.

30/10/1780. Eleanor Graham, dau. of Henry Hale Graham, requested to
come under the care of Friends. Hannah Powel, wife of Benjamin,
requested a certificate to Concord for herself and children:

Elizabeth, Joshua, Rebeccah, Samuel, Hannah and William.
Rebeckah Porter requested a certificate to Duck Creek. Mary
Worrall, formerly Howard, dau. of John, reported for marrying by a
priest. Mary Haycock, dau. of Joseph, dec'd, reported for marrying
her first cousin, John Haycock, Jr., by a priest. Isaac Hance reported
for marrying out and exercising in military discipline. Lydia Crockson
produced a certificate from Goshen. Jonathan Morris reported for
selling prize rum which his son got by privateering. Peter Dicks, son
of Joseph, reported for meeting with the militia on muster days in
order to save his fines. Hugh Lownes reported for taking the Test
and accepting a duplicate to collect a tax for military purposes.

27/11/1780. Jonathan Morris thought Friends had better disown him as
he did not see quite as Friends did. Alice Edwards, dau. of Joseph,
requested a certificate to Goshen. Nathaniel Newlin produced a
certificate from Nottingham. Joshua Weaver paid all fines demanded
of him.

25/12/1780. Meeting informed by a Friend from Duck Creek that the
Negro which Thomas Wilson had some time in servitude is at liberty.
Jonathan Morris has manumitted all his Negroes. Peter Dicks
admited paying a substitute fine. Thomas Jacobs requested a
certificate to Gwynedd for himself and wife Lydia. James Howard
acknowledged paying a fine for refusing to collect taxes chiefly for
military purposes; also a fine or double tax for not taking the Test of
Abjuration and Allegiance. Margaret Minshal is chosen clerk of
Chester Women's Monthly Meeting in place of Rebekah Sharples,
dec'd.

29/1/1781. Thomas Wilson requested a certificate to Concord for
himself, wife Jane and children: James, Mary, Susannah, Thomas
and George. Hannah Hall, dau. of John, reported for fornication and
begetting a bastard child. Rachel Byrns [wife of William Burns], dau.
of James Worrall, reported for marrying out to one not a member.
Nathan, John and Aaron Worral, sons of Benjamin, dec'd, reported
for neglecting meetings and so far complying with the requisitions
demanded as to attend on muster days, except Nathan, who
attended once. Phebe Worrall reported for neglecting meetings and
countenancing her sons' conduct. Joseph Booth produced a
certificate from Concord. Mordecai and Joseph Lawrence, sons of
Henry, acknowledged taking the Test.

26/2/1781. Jeptha Lightfoot produced a copy of a certificate from
Exeter (the original being lost) for himself and wife Hannah. Richard
Hill Morris produced a certificate from Abington. Ezekiel Wilson

reported for meeting with the militia on muster days and paying a fine in lieu of personal service. Mary Preston requested a certificate to Wilmington for her son Jonas Preston, an apprentice.

23/3/1781. Jacob Dingee reported for marrying Hannah Rogers, dau. of Robert Rogers. Lydia Mendenhall produced a certificate from Darby. Joseph Booth requested a certificate to Hopewell. Ann Radcliff requested a certificate to Northern District, Philadelphia. Sarah West, widow of Thomas, requested a certificate to Concord for herself and children: Esther, Thomas, Rebecca and Joel. Robert Mendenhall, Jr., requested a certificate to Darby to marry Mary Humphrey. Amos Sharples requested a certificate to Kennett.

30/4/1781. Richard Parsons, Jr., produced a certificate from Wrightstown for himself, wife Jemima and their children: Mahlon, Joshua, Naomi, Rebecca, Jemima, Mary and William. William West requested a certificate to Kennett to marry Ann Brinton, dau. of James. Joshua Lawrence reportedly may have taken the Test and complied with other requisitions of like nature. Amy Taylor [wife of Evan Taylor] requested a certificate to Fairfax. Phebe Worrall [now Williams], dau. of John, reported for marrying by a priest to one not a member. Thomas Walter acknowledged paying a substitute fine.

28/5/1781. John Taylor reported for paying a fine in lieu of personal service in the army. Phebe Miller produced a certificate from Exeter. Cornelius Wood produced a certificate from Goshen for himself, wife Mary and their children: John, Jane, Nathan, Samuel, Hannah, Lydia and Mary. George Pennock produced a certificate from Newgarden. Phebe Speakman, formerly Yarnall, produced a certificate from Concord to visit some families of this Monthly Meeting. Benjamin Pyle reported for paying taxes to the immediate purpose of hiring men to go to the army.

25/6/1781. Joseph Sharples requested a certificate to Wilmington. Benjamin Worral reported for paying a substitute fine. Robert Mendenhall requested a certificate to Goshen.

30/7/1781. Mary Hoops, wife of Joseph, requested a certificate to Goshen. Phebe Sharples, dau. of Abraham, produced a certificate from Uwchlan. John Smith and Dorothy Graham to marry. Joseph Ashton reported for removing without a certificate and later marrying by a priest. Richard Maris reported for paying a muster fine and complying with all demands made on him for the purpose of carrying on war.

27/8/1781. Daniel Humphrey, Jr., produced a certificate from Haverford. David Evans produced a certificate from Haverford.

Matthew Wood produced a certificate from Wrightstown for himself, wife Mary and son Jacob. Mary Hoopes requested a certificate to Goshen. Joseph Talbot, Sr., and John Worral, Sr., paid several demands, called taxes, for military purposes, two of which have been for the immediate purpose of hiring and enlisting men to go to the war. Mary Trueman, wife of Morris, requested a certificate to Darby. Martha Martin reported for paying demands made on her husband [Jonathan] for the hiring and enlisting of men to go to war. Abraham Williamson reported for paying a muster fine and taxes for the purpose of hiring men to go to war. David Regester reported for meeting with the militia on muster days. Abraham Pilkinton reported for paying a tax for the purpose of hiring men to go to war. Mary Cox requested a certificate to Concord for son Lawrence Cox.

21/9/1781. Friends appointed to attend the marriage of John Smith and Dorothy Graham report that the marriage is not yet accomplished and not likely to be. Thomas Sharples reported for taking the Test and paying [military] fines and taxes. Joanna Davis, wife of Isaac, requested a certificate to New Garden. Elizabeth Edwards, dau. of Nathan, reported for neglecting meetings, taking liberty in dress and departing from the plain language; she also paid taxes demanded of her father for the immediate purpose of hiring and enlisting men to go to war.

29/10/1781. Esther Jobson, wife of Joseph, produced a certificate from Goshen for herself and their two children: John and Mary. John Lewis produced a certificate from Haverford. Francis Smedley produced a certificate from Goshen. John Vernon reported for meeting with the militia on muster days as one of them and drinking spirituous liquors to excess at times. Richard Blackham requested a certificate to Philadelphia.

26/11/1781. Caleb Harrison, Jr., reported for paying taxes for the immediate purpose of hiring men to go to war. Jonathan Haycock requested a certificate to Richland. Thomas Griffith, son of William, requested a certificate to Goshen, he being placed as an apprentice to a member there. George Smedly requested a certificate to Bradford.

31/12/1781. Priscilla Bishop, wife of Thomas, Jr., produced a certificate from Goshen.

4/1/1782. Margaret Malin returned a certificate granted by this meeting directed to Haverford more than three years ago for her and seven of her children which she neglected to deliver. She also informed this meeting that her dau. Elizabeth has gone out in marriage and her son David met with the militia. John McIlvain requested a certificate to Nottingham, he being placed as an apprentice to a Friend. William Edwards, Sr., has almost wholly neglected meetings and continues to assist in tavern keeping as manager. Abraham Calvert reported for being in the practice of running horse races and laying wagers. Jemima Pilkinton, dau. of Nathan Edwards, reported for marrying by a priest to one not a member and neglecting meetings.

28/1/1782. Nathaniel Newlin produced a certificate from Concord for himself, wife Martha and two children, Esther and William. Susannah Neal, wife of John, requested a certificate to Concord for herself and three of her children: James, Ann and Lydia.

25/2/1782. Eleanor Graham, mother of Dorothy Graham, expressed her dissatisfaction with John Smith [intended future son-in-law] for not being so willing as she desired to receive some goods which she proposed to give to her daughter on such terms as she thought fit and indicated she would not be reconciled to him and would not allow him in her house which seems to have discouraged her daughter from proceeding to her intended marriage. Benjamin Worrall reported for marrying one not a member. Ann Carter, wife of James, requested a certificate to Concord.

22/3/1782. Daniel Pederick produced a certificate from Salem for himself, wife Naomi and 3 children: Kezia, Mary and John. Emanuel Walker requested a certificate to Philadelphia for himself, wife Anne and 5 children: Samuel, Mary, Anne, Bulah and John. Margery Gibbons, wife of Joseph, reported for conduct which, for a considerable time past, has been very inconsistent with our religious profession and has given way to treating her husband with abusive and threatening language.

29/4/1782. David Malin stated he would soon go to sea in an armed vessel. Margaret Haycock, wife of Nathan, requested to come under the care of Friends. John Wilson reported for exercising in military discipline. Mary Brinton, wife of Joseph, requested a certificate to Concord for herself and children: Weldon, Peggy, Lydia and John. Rachel James requested a certificate to Concord. William Wood requested a certificate to Shrewsbury. Thomas Minshall, Jr., charged with fornication and begetting a bastard child.

27/5/1782. James Gibbons produced a certificate from Concord for himself, wife Deborah and children: Samuel, Mary, James, Daniel, Rebeckah and Rachel. John Woolley produced a certificate from Goshen for himself, wife Phebe and children: Samuel, Sarah and John. James Emlen produced a certificate from Newgarden. Jane

Gibbons, dau. of Joseph, now Malcombe, reported for marrying by a priest. Abigail Mercer, wife of Solomon, requested a certificate to Kennett. Raper Hoskins requested a certificate to Philadelphia for himself, wife Eleanor and son Henry. Evan Edwards, apprentice, requested a certificate to Darby. Aaron Sharples requested a certificate to Falls.

24/6/1782. Margaret Malin requested a certificate to Philadelphia for herself and 5 children: John, Elijah, Rachel, Margaret and Enoch. Nathaniel Samms produced a certificate from Abington for himself and wife Sarah. John Morgan produced a certificate from Richland. George Lownes, apprentice, produced a certificate from Concord dated 2/7/1781 and requested a certificate to Kennett.

29/7/1782. Benjamin and Rebeckah Lobb, children of Jacob and Sarah Lobb, produced a certificate from Darby. Joseph Thomas requested a certificate to Goshen. Sarah Reed produced a certificate from Mt. Holly. Sarah Pyle, wife of Benjamin, requested a certificate to Concord with children: Joseph, Hannah, Phebe and Benjamin. Ann Martin, dau. of George, requested a certificate to Uwchlan.

26/8/1782. Ezekiel Wilson requested a certificate to Concord. Lydia Crockson, dau. of Abraham Croxen, requested a certificate to Philadelphia. Isaac Worrall married out to one not a member.

30/9/1782. Caleb, Sarah and David Cowpland, children of Joshua and Ann Cowpland, produced a certificate from Salem. Grace Sharples, dau. of Abraham, produced a certificate from Goshen. Joshua Barnes produced a certificate from Salem. Grace Good produced a certificate from Sadsbury dated 10/22/1777. Joseph Grissel requested to come under the care of Friends. Hannah Yarnall, wife of Peter, requested a certificate to Concord.

28/10/1782. Peter Smedley requested a certificate to Uwchlan for himself and wife Phebe. Hannah Yarnall, wife of Peter, requested a certificate to Concord. George Smedley produced a certificate from Bradford. Caleb Cowpland (apprentice to a Friend) requested a certificate to Philadelphia, Northern District. Ann Carson, dau. of Thomas Worrall, reported for marrying by a priest to one not a member.

25/11/1782. James Barton reported dissenting from our known principles, particularly in believing it necessary to practice water baptism and eating bread and wine in commemoration of Christ's sufferings [disowned]. Paschal Davis reported for removing without requesting a certificate and marriage by a priest. Hannah Pusey [wife of Joshua] requested a certificate to New Garden. Susannah

Martin [wife of Abraham] and Alice Palmer [wife of Asher] requested a certificate to Concord.

29/11/1782. Ezekiel Yarnall requested to come under the care of Friends, [approved].

30/12/1782. Ann Jesop produced a certificate from Falls.

27/1/1783. John Couborn requested a certificate to Concord for himself, his children and his present wife Esther. Joseph Taylor married out of unity to one not a member. Sarah Winder [wife of James] produced a certificate from Falls. Amy Cox [dau. of John, dec'd] requested a certificate to Exeter. Martha Carson requested to come under the care of Friends.

24/2/1783. James Wood requested a certificate to Gwynedd for himself, wife Mary and children: Septimus, Mary, Sarah, Rachel and Rebekah. Aaron Wood requested a certificate to Gwynedd. Joseph Grisell requested a certificate to Concord to marry Priscilla Morrison. James Emlen requested a certificate to Concord to marry Phebe Peirce, dau. of Caleb. Phebe Haycock, dau. of Joseph, dec'd, reported for fornication and begetting a bastard child [she refused to name the father].

31/3/1783. Sarah Bartholomew, formerly Cowpland, dau. of David, dec'd, reported for marrying by a priest to one not a member. Amy Johnson, formerly Rogers, dau. of Robert, reported for marrying by a priest to one not a member. Elizabeth Clerk [wife of Thomas] requested a certificate to Philadelphia. John McIlvain produced a certificate from Nottingham. Tacy Davis, formerly Rhoads, dau. of James Rhoads, dec'd, married by a priest to one not a member. Ann, Richard, Jemima, Elizabeth, William and Margaret Maris, children of Jesse [and Margaret] Maris, Jr., requested a certificate to Philadelphia. Hannah Wilcox, formerly Worrall, dau. of Thomas Worrall, reported for marrying by a priest to one not a member. Nathaniel Newlin, son of Joseph, reported for marrying by a priest to one not a member. John Meredith requested a certificate to Gwynedd for himself, wife Hannah and three children: Eleanor, David and John. John Woolly requested a certificate for himself, wife Phebe and three children: Samuel, Sarah and John.

28/4/1783. Nehemiah Davis requested a certificate to Wilmington for himself, wife Eleanor and 6 children: Mary, Sarah, Elizabeth, William, Dorothy and Susanna and also a certificate to Exeter for his dau. Eleanor. James Gibbons requested a certificate to Darby for himself, wife Deborah and children: Samuel, Mary, James, Daniel, Rebekah and Rachel. Sarah Carter, dau. of Martin Carter, requested to be received into membership. Mary Yarnall, wife of William, requested to be received into membership. Sarah Baker, dau. of Jesse, requested to be received into membership.

2/5/1783. William West, Jr., requested a certificate to Kennett. William Regester requested a certificate for himself, wife Abigail and three children: Jane, Thomas and Robert and also requested a certificate for his eldest dau. Lydia, both certificates to Bradford. Massey Lawrence, dau. of Henry, acknowledged attending a marriage by a priest. Hannah Griffith requested a certificate to Concord for son Enoch (apprentice to a Friend). William Yarnall requested that his three children: William, George and Enoch, be received into membership; Mary his wife also requested to be received.

26/5/1783. Thomas Parry produced a certificate from Abington for himself, wife Elizabeth and three children: Joseph, Sarah and Benjamin. Joseph Taylor acknowledged marrying out. John Hutton produced a certificate from Exeter. Sarah Reed [wife of Robert] requested a certificate to Darby. George Penock requested a certificate to Haverford to marry Mary Leddon, dau. of Abraham. Ambrose Taylor requested a certificate to Wilmington for himself, wife Mary and children: Jacob, Mordicai, Stephen and Abigail.

30/6/1783. John Mendenhall produced a certificate from Concord for himself, wife Tabitha and son Cyrus. John Windor produced a certificate from Falls for himself, wife Margaret and 6 children: James, Abner, Hannah, Sarah, Mary and Ann. Phebe Pasmore, dau. of Augustine, dec'd, produced a certificate from Philadelphia, Southern District. Amelia Vaughn, dau. of Isaac, produced a certificate from Haverford. Phebe Emlen, wife of James, produced a certificate from Concord. Priscilla Grisell, wife of Joseph, produced a certificate from Concord. Sarah West, widow of Thomas, produced a certificate from Concord for herself and 4 children: Esther, Thomas, Rebekah and Joel. Mary Mendenhall, wife of Philip, requested a certificate to Concord for herself and her two children (by a former marriage), Lydia and Nehemiah Reece.

28/7/1783. Jacob Hibberd produced a certificate from Concord for himself, wife Sarah and children: Mary, Hannah and John. Edward Moore produced a certificate from Goshen. Isaac Weaver, Jr., reported for marrying by a priest to one not a member. William Griffith requested a certificate to Concord. Jane Yarnall, wife of James, and Martha Haines, dau. of Isaac, produced a certificate from Goshen.

25/8/1783. Joseph, Mary and Joshua Baker, children of John Baker, dec'd, produced a certificate from Newgarden. Ezra Goodwin requested a certificate to Goshen. Mary Horne, wife of Edward, requested a certificate to Darby for herself and three children: William, Stephen and Davis. Ann Talbot, widow of Joseph, requested a certificate to Darby. Phebe Hatton, wife of Peter, Jr., requested a certificate to Concord.

26/9/1783. Joshua Smedley requested a certificate to Goshen. Eli Yarnall requested a certificate to Haverford to marry Priscilla Walker, dau. of Joseph.

27/10/1783. George Pennock requested a certificate to Philadelphia. Sarah Ashbridge, dau. of Joseph, requested a certificate to Philadelphia. Susannah Couborn, dau. of John, requested a certificate to Concord.

24/11/1783. Rebekah Porter produced a certificate from Duck Creek. Lydia Dicks, dau. of Joseph, reported for fornication and begetting a bastard child. Phebe Tanyear, now Nasmith, dau. of Joseph, dec'd, reported for marrying by a hireling minister to one not a member.

29/12/1783. Levi Lukins produced a certificate from Gwynedd. Ann Larkin [wife of Joseph] requested a certificate to Concord. Joseph Walker reported for removing to Philadelphia about three years ago and neglecting to request a certificate. Springfield Meeting understands that the children of Walter Roberts: Sarah, Thomas, John and Jonathan, live within the limits of Bush River Monthly Meeting, SC, and one of them on behalf of them all, requested a certificate to that meeting, they having removed when very young. James Reynolds requested a certificate to Wilmington. Joshua Yarnall requested a certificate to Philadelphia, Northern District.

26/1/1784. John Nuzum produced a certificate from Exeter.

23/2/1784. Sarah Dougherty produced a certificate from Concord. Mary Porter requested to be received into membership. Alice Cissel, dau. of Reuben Roberts, reported for marrying by a priest to one not a member.

26/3/1784. Amos Sharples produced a certificate from Kennett. Samuel Hall produced a certificate from Goshen. Isaac Weaver acknowledged marrying out. George Pennock requested a certificate to Philadelphia. Priscilla Yarnall, wife of Eli, produced a certificate from Haverford. Ann Rogers [widow of Robert] requested a certificate to Concord for herself and two children, Mary and Lydia, and another certificate to Goshen for their son Abraham. Sarah Taylor [wife of Isaac] requested a certificate to Haverford. William Iddings

requested a certificate to Wilmington for himself, wife Hannah and
children: Jane, Hannah, William, Phebe, Samuel and Thomas. John
Fairlamb requested a certificate to Goshen to marry Susanna
Ashbridge, dau. of George. Joel Sharples requested a certificate to
Bradford to marry Hannah Mendenhall, dau. of Joshua.

26/4/1784. George Lownes produced a certificate from Kennett. Joseph
Walker's case continued, he having gone to sea [disowned].
Nathaniel Holland requested a certificate to Philadelphia, Northern
District, for son John. Nathan Worrall reported for neglecting
meetings and marrying by a priest. Cornelius Wood requested a
certificate to Concord for himself, wife Mary and 6 children: John,
Jane, Nathan, Hannah, Lydia and Mary. Lawrence Cox reported for
removing from this area quite some time ago without requesting a
certificate. Elizabeth Jones, dau. of Isaac Weaver, reported for
marrying by a priest.

31/5/1784. Sarah Pyles, dau. of Isaac, produced a certificate from
Concord. Mary Berry, dau. of David Ogden, reported for marrying by
a priest to one not a member. Abigail Hinkson, dau. of Frederick
Engle, dec'd, reported for marrying out.

28/6/1784. Joseph Hoskins produced a certificate from Burlington.
Joseph Dicks reported for neglecting to pay a just debt to his son
Peter. Martha Worrall, wife of Isaiah, produced a certificate from
Richland. Naomi Pederick, widow of Daniel, requested a certificate
to Salem for herself and four children: Keziah, Mary, John and
Thomas.

26/7/1784. Caleb Martin produced a certificate from Bradford for
himself, wife Hannah and children: Joseph, George, Warrick, Lydia,
Hannah and Ruth; his son Joshua also produced a certificate from
the same meeting. Lawrence Cox returned to reside for some time
within the verge of Middletown Meeting. Esther Pyle, dau. of Isaac,
produced a certificate from Concord. Hannah Sharples, wife of Joel,
produced a certificate from Bradford. Phebe Coppock, dau. of
Abraham Sharples, reported for marrying by a magistrate to one not
a member.

30/8/1784. Isaac Wood produced a certificate from Wilmington. David
Evans and Eleanor Harris, dau. of Caleb, married by a magistrate.
Lydia Regester, dau. of William., produced a certificate from
Bradford. Mary Hance, dau. of Benjamin, reported for fornication
and begetting a bastard child. Ann Jesop, dau. of Samuel, requested
a certificate to Falls Monthly Meeting. Ann Lynn, wife of Joseph,

requested a certificate to Philadelphia. Mahlon Parsons requested a certificate to Gwynedd to marry Mary Wood.

34/9/1784. Joseph West produced a certificate from Concord for himself, wife Susannah and children: Jesse, Rachel, Mary, Hannah, Joseph, William and Susannah. William Regester produced a certificate from Bradford for himself, wife Abigail and three children: Jane, Thomas and Robert. Isaac Weaver, Jr., requested a certificate to Philadelphia. Joseph Pilkington reported for occasioning a Friend to be distressed for a military tax, and also for drinking to excess. Humphrey Hill requested a certificate to Philadelphia. [Annotation: married Alice Howard at Christ Church, Philadelphia, March 3, 1791.] Philip Yarnall, son of David, dec'd, requested a certificate to Wilmington (apprentice).

25/10/1784. Amy Cox, dau. of John, produced a certificate from Exeter.

29/11/1784. Joshua Yarnall produced a certificate from Philadelphia, Northern District. Jonathan Pennell requested a certificate to Darby. Deborah Thatcher, dau. of Richard, dec'd, produced a certificate from Bradford. Hannah Dutton, dau. of Thomas, dec'd, produced a certificate from Concord. Susannah Martin, wife of Thomas, requested a certificate to Haverford. Hannah Chandlee, wife of Goldsmith, requested a certificate to Crooked Run Monthly Meeting. Abigail Yarnall, dau. of Isaac of Edgmont, dec'd, requested membership with Friends.

27/12/1784. Martha Haines, dau. of Isaac, requested a certificate to Newgarden.

31/1/1785. Lydia McIlvain requested a certificate to Concord Monthly Meeting for her son Jeremiah McIlvain. James Haycock reported for neglecting meetings and drinking to excess. Lawrence Cox has for some considerable time removed without a certificate, has much neglected meetings and has taken great liberty in dress [disowned]. George Smedley requested a certificate to Concord to marry Hannah Mercer. Mary Parsons, wife of Mahlon, produced a certificate from Gwynedd. Sarah Kerns, dau. of John Windors, reported for marrying by a magistrate to one not a member.

28/2/1785. William Hill produced a certificate from Bradford. Anna Hill, wife of William, requested a certificate to Darby. John Fairlamb requested a certificate to Wilmington. Thomas Parry requested a certificate to Buckingham for himself, wife Elizabeth and children: Joseph, Sarah, Benjamin and Phebe. Martha Sharples, dau. of Jacob, dec'd, requested a certificate to Concord. Joseph Baker, son of John, dec'd, requested a certificate to Newgarden. Isaac Edwards reported for marrying by a priest.

25/3/1785. Elizabeth Moore, wife of Edward, requested to be received into membership and Edward requested membership for their children: Margaret, Abner, Rachel and Phebe. [On 8/29/1785 they were received into membership including a son Abraham, born after the request.] Mary Marshall, wife of William, requested membership for her 6 children: Massey, William, Hannah, Edward, Rebekah and Joseph. Joseph Talbot requested a certificate to Concord for son James (apprentice to a Friend).

25/4/1785. Naomi Wood, dau. of Richard Parson, reported for marrying out to one not a member. Joseph Grisell requested a certificate to Uwchlan for himself, wife Priscilla and dau. Agnes.

30/5/1785. James Arnold produced a certificate from Goshen. Mary Vernon, wife of Jonathan, Jr., has removed to live away from her husband. George Harris requested a certificate to Philadelphia, Southern District. David Evans requested a certificate to Haverford for himself, wife Eleanor and young dau. Mary. Thomas Walter requested a certificate to Concord for himself, wife Rebekah and 6 children: James, Joseph, Mary, Rachel, Jemima and Phebe. Elizabeth Sharples, widow of Isaac, and Sarah, wife of Joseph Peirce, requested certificates to Concord.

27/6/1785. Jonathan Willis produced a certificate from Philadelphia, Northern District. Susanna Dougherty and her dau. Susannah Dougherty, Jr., produced a certificate from Wilmington. Sarah Carter, dau. of Martin, requested a certificate to Philadelphia. Rachel Taylor requested a certificate to Goshen.

25/7/1785. Andrew Moore produced a certificate from Newgarden. Joseph Thatcher produced a certificate from Concord. John Windors and wife, having been visited on account of their dau. Sarah Kern's marriage, informed the meeting that their daughter's outgoing in marriage was contrary to their minds and that they used some endeavors to prevent it. John Lewis requested membership for four of his minor children: Jane, Franklin, John and Mary [approved]. Frederick and Joseph Dicks, sons of Joseph, attended the militia and answered to their names as such and their father countenanced them by being present; Mahlon and Joshua have met in like manner. John Smith, Jr., dec'd, by his last will bequeathed to the people called Quakers at Chester the sum of £50.

29/8/1785. Joseph Pilkington continues to drink to excess. Jane Clayton, dau. of John, produced a certificate from Bradford. John

Windors, wife Margaret and 6 children: James, Hannah, Mary, Ann, Abner and Mercy. William Evans reported for mustering with militia and for quarreling and fighting. Joseph Engle (apprentice) requested a certificate to Bradford. Jesse Haines requested a certificate to Concord to marry Rachel Otley.

23/9/1785. Asher Palmer produced a certificate from Kennett for himself, wife Alice and son Joseph. John Cobourn produced a certificate from Concord. Mary Cobourn requested a certificate to Wilminton.

31/10/1785. John Hall produced a certificate from Goshen. Lydia Calvert, wife of Abraham, produced a certificate from Goshen Monthly Meeting. William Evans has lately married out of unity. Mathew Wood reported for assembling with the militia and answering to his name as one of them. George Smedley requested a certificate to Uwchlan. Phebe Pugh, dau. of William Pugh, dec'd, requested a certificate to Duck Creek. Asher Palmer and his wife Alice and son Joseph produced a certificate from Kennett Monthly Meeting.

28/11/1785. Lydia, wife of Abraham Calvert, produced a certificate from Goshen. Isaac Eyre requested a certificate to Concord for his son Lewis, he being placed as an apprentice to a Friend. Joseph Talbot and his wife Hannah, requested a certificate to Concord for themselves and children: Hannah, Joseph, Ruth, John and Rachel. Hannah Griffith requested a certificate to Goshen for her son Joseph, he being placed as an apprentice.

26/12/1785. Ann Courtney, wife of Thomas, requested a certificate to Goshen. Priscilla Griffith, dau. of William, dec'd, requested a certificate to Concord. Ann Worrall, wife of James, requested a certificate to Bradford Monthly Meeting. Elias Engle met with the militia several times and answered to his name as one of them.

Benjamin Simcock married Elizabeth, widow of William Boon, as early as 1758. See Administration Book, Philadelphia.

30/1/1786. Richard Hill Morris requested a certificate to Woodbury to marry Mary Mifflin. Francis Smedley requested a certificate to Goshen. Ann Courtney requested a certificate to Goshen. Hannah Robeson, wife of Jonathan, requested a certificate to Haverford. Elizabeth Rhoads, dau. of Joseph, dec'd, now Elizabeth Tyson, reported for marrying by a priest to one not a member. Ann Smedley, widow of Francis, produced a certificate from Goshen. Ann

Otley produced a certificate from Concord. Rachel Haines, wife of Jesse, produced a certificate from Concord.

27/2/1786. Certificate not prepared for Ann Worrall because she left her husband many years ago. [See rough minutes.] James Dilworth produced a certificate from Concord. William Ashbridge, son of George, dec'd, produced a certificate from Goshen. Jonathan Morris requested a certificate to Philadelphia for his son Samuel Morris, apprentice. Phebe Ashbridge, dau. of George, dec'd, produced a certificate from Goshen.

24/3/1786. William Jones produced a certificate from Goshen. George Massey produced a certificate from Goshen. Nathaniel Newlin requested a certificate to Darby for himself, wife Martha and three children: Esther, William and Mary. John Rhoads reported for attending a marriage out of Friends.

24/4/1786. Mary and Grace Sharples, daus. of Abraham, dec'd, requested a certificate to Uwchlan.

29/5/1786. Mary Morris, wife of Richard Hill Morris, produced a certificate from Woodbury. Richard Weaver charged by Margaret Glackin for fornication and begetting a bastard child. Lydia Martin, dau. of Jonathan, reported for fornication and begetting a bastard child. Mary Tucker, wife of Thomas, produced a certificate from Goshen for herself and three children: Benjamin, Ann and Thomas. Hannah Sharples reported dec'd.

26/6/1786. Samuel Hall reported for mustering with the militia. John Nuzum reported for mustering with the militia and charged by Frances Sault with fornication, which he does not deny. Agness Bevan produced a certificate from Philadelphia, Southern District for herself and three children: Isabella, Tacy and Mathew Lawlor. Mary Preston, wife of Davis, widow of Jonas, requested a certificate to Wilmington. Sarah Salkeld, wife of William, requested a certificate to Pipe Creek, with four children: John, Samuel, Mary and Sarah. Hannah Dutton, dau. of Thomas, dec'd, requested a certificate to Concord.

31/7/1786. John Trump produced a certificate from Kennett for himself, wife Hannah and children: Sarah, Daniel and Ann. Reese Nanna produced a certificate from Kennett. John Martin produced a certificate from Uwchlan. Lydia Martin disowned for fornication and begetting a bastard child. Richard Weaver disowned having left these parts. Mary Preston requested a certificate to Wilmington. Sarah Salkeld requested a certificate to Pipe Creek for herself and children. Hannah Dutton requested a certificate to Concord.

Elizabeth Jones, wife of William Jones, formerly disowned, offers acknowledgment of her past behavior and requested reinstatement: (accepted). Mary Harry, dau. of John, produced a certificate from Gwynedd. Isaac Eyre and Abigail Dicks, dau. of Nathan, dec'd, reported for marrying by a magistrate. John Thompson, Jr., Jonathan Maris and Edward Evans acknowledge mustering (with militia). Joshua Parson reported for attending a marriage out. Phebe Pasmore, dau. of Augustine, dec'd, requested a certificate to Nottingham.

28/8/1786. John Rhoads disowned. Samuel Hall disowned. Hannah Cowpland, widow of David, and Edward Vernon reported for marrying by a hireling minister.

22/9/1786. Joshua Parsons acknowledged attending a marriage out. Isaac Wood requested a certificate to Hopewell. Hannah Vernon disowned. Hannah Humphreys, widow of Daniel, produced a certificate from Haverford. Mary Gibbons, dau. of Joseph, and Mathew Ash reported for fornication before marriage. Parry Howard reported for neglecting meetings, mustering with the militia, and charged by Catharine Mullen with fornication.

30/10/1786. Joseph Tucker produced a certificate from Goshen. William Shoemaker produced a certificate from Concord. William Jones requested that his daus., Sarah and Rebecca, be received into membership [approved]. William also requested a certificate to Haverford for himself, his wife Elizabeth and children. David Hall, Jr., acknowledged attending a marriage out. Rachel Taylor, dau. of John, dec'd, produced a certificate from Goshen. Jonathan Thompson reported for mustering with militia. Joseph Pilkington reported still drinking to excess at times.

27/11/1786. Isaac Eyre and wife disowned. Parry Howard disowned. William Jones and family requested a certificate to Haverford. Samuel Maris requested a certificate to Bradford. Joseph Dicks, Jr., reported for mustering with the militia.

25/12/1786. Levi Lukens requested a certificate to Haverford. Jehu Maris reported for cutting timber on his neighbor's property. Philip Dunn reported for keeping bad company, gaming and suspected of forgery. Hannah Squibb, dau. of Nathaniel, produced a certificate from Concord. Thomas Evans reported deceased.

29/1/1787. Humphrey Hill returned his certificate endorsed by Philadelphia Monthly Meeting. George Lownes reported for marrying by a magistrate. Jane Peirce, wife of John, requested a certificate to Concord.

26/2/1787. Esther Pyle, dau. of Isaac, requested a certificate to Darby. Mary Maris, now Lawrance, dau. of Isaac, reported for marrying by a priest to one not a member. John Martin requested a certificate to Uwchlan. Mary Baker, wife of Joseph, requested to be received into membership [approved].

27/3/1787. Priscilla Ashbridge, dau. of Joseph, requested a certificate to Philadelphia. Rebecca Sharples, dau. of Abraham, dec'd, requested a certificate to Sadsbury. Edward Moore and wife Elizabeth requested a certificate to Goshen with children: Margaret, Abner, Rachel, Phebe and Abraham. Joel Sharples requested a certificate to Darby for himself, wife Hannah and son Samuel.

30/4/1787. Mary Ash requested a certificate to Darby.

28/5/1787. Amos Bond produced a certificate from Wilmington. Nathan Milner requested a certificate to Wilmington. Rachel Hayworth, dau. of John, produced a certificate from Goshen. Rachel McCullough reported for drinking to excess and neglecting meetings.

26/6/1787. Joseph Bishop produced a certificate from Concord. Hannah Long, wife of William, requested to become a member. Leah Ashton, wife of Joseph, requested to become a member. Elizabeth Tyson, wife of Levi, requested a certificate to Nottingham.

30/7/1787. Enoch Griffith produced a certificate from Concord. Benjamin Sharples produced a certificate from Concord. Joshua Barns requested a certificate to Salem.

27/8/1787. William Wilson produced a certificate from Sadsbury. Jonathan Willis requested a certificate to Haverford. Mary Tanyer, dau. of Joseph, dec'd, requested a certificate to Haverford. Sarah Carter, dau. of Martain, produced a certificate from Philadelphia.

21/9/1787. Benjamin Yarnall produced a certificate from Wilmington. Elias Engle reported for being married of late in a disreputable manner. James Howard reported for marrying by a magistrate to one not a member. Humphrey Hill, charged by Lydia Swago for fornication and begetting a bastard child. In his will Thomas Evans left £50 to the Monthly Meeting towards a school.

29/10/1787. George Malin, minor, requested a certificate to Philadelphia. Catharine Hill, wife of Peter, produced a certificate from Wilmington. Phebe Iddings, minor dau. of William, produced a certificate from Wilmington. Lydia Shoemaker, dau. of William, produced a certificate from Philadelphia, Southern District. Amy Darlington, wife of Jesse, requested a certificate to Concord.

31/12/1787. Joshua Thomas produced a certificate from Haverford. John Powell, Jr., requested membership. William Wilson reported

for an unsatisfied debt to William Lightfoot. Nathaniel Holland
requested a certificate to Philadelphia for his son Samuel Holland.
Gideon Malin requested a certificate to Philadelphia, Southern
District, for son Gideon. Mary Vernon still neglects meetings. Abigail
Pancost [Pancoast], dau. of Stephen Ogden, dec'd, reported for
marrying out. Lydia Regester, dau. of William, now wife of ---
Yarnall, reported for fornication before marriage.

25/2/1788. Thomas Smedley (representative from Providence Meeting)
was absent on account of the burial of his brother's wife. Joseph
Gibbons, Jr., reported for marrying by a Presbyterian minister.
Margaret Marshall, wife of Humphrey, requested a certificate to
Bradford. John Worrall requested a certificate to Gwynedd to marry
Rebecca Wood, dau. of James.

31/3/1788. William Marshall, a minor, requested a certificate to Goshen.
Samuel Acton, a youth, produced a certificate from Darby. Mary
Marshall requested a certificate to Bush Creek Monthly Meeting,
SC, for herself and children: Hannah, Edward, Rebecca, Joseph and
Sarah. Sarah Winders, wife of James, requested a certificate to Falls
Monthly Meeting. Hannah Fairlamb, dau. of Frederick, reported for
marrying out to --- Engle. Jane Fallows requested to become a
member.

28/4/1788. John Moore produced a certificate from Darby. Deborah
Lightfoot, dau. of Joseph, produced a certificate from Exeter. Amy
Moore, dau. of John, dec'd, produced a certificate from Darby. Isaac
Thompson reported for marrying by a Presbyterian minister to one
not a member and has attended the militia at times. Sarah Weaver,
wife of Isaac, requested a certificate to Westland, or the nearest
meeting where her husband settles, for herself and children:
William, Abraham and Sarah. Sarah Trump, now Brooks, dau. of
John, reported for marrying by a priest to one not a member. Mary
Cobourn, now Young, dau. of John, reported for marrying by a
priest.

26/5/1788. Benjamin Bond and wife produced a certificate from Goshen.
William Wilson reported for fornication with Rebecca Hoskins. John
Trump requested a certificate to Nottingham with wife Hannah
Trump and children, Daniel and Ann. James Weaver requested a
certificate to Westland or elsewhere with his parents. Jane Clayton
requested a certificate to Wilmington. William Hill requested a
certificate to Darby with wife Anna Hill and dau. Mary.

30/6/1788. Nathan Yearsley produced a certificate from Goshen. Martin
Carter produced a certificate from Concord. Jane Wood, dau. of

Cornelius, produced a certificate from Concord. Eleanor Davis produced a certificate from Darby with children: Mary, Sarah, Elizabeth, William, Dorothy and Susanna. John Broomall requested to become a member. Rosanna Bond and husband produced a certificate from Goshen.

28/7/1788. John Davis produced a certificate from Kennett. John Gibbons requested a certificate to Philadelphia, Northern District. Nathaniel Samms and wife requested a certificate to Westland. Jacob Edwards, a minor, requested a certificate to Philadelphia.

25/8/1788. Elizabeth, Hannah and Phebe Morris, daus. of John, dec'd, produced a certificate from Goshen. Rebecca Worrall, wife of John, produced a certificate from Gwynedd.

26/9/1788. Hannah Sharples, dau. of Jacob, dec'd, requested a certificate to Darby. Daniel Sharples requested a certificate to Concord to marry. Jonas Sharples, a minor, requested a certificate to Philadelphia, Southern District. John Hall requested a certificate to Goshen. Cornelius Wood requested a certificate to Darby for son Samuel. Rebecca Parsons, dau. of Richard, reported for fornication and begetting a bastard child.

27/10/1788. John McIlvaine requested a certificate to Newgarden to marry Ann Pennock, dau. of Levis. Joshua Thomas and wife Sarah requested a certificate to Philadelphia. Rebecca Dingee, dau. of Richard Maris, reported for marrying by a priest to one not a member.

24/11/1788. Isaac Dennis produced a certificate from Richland. Susanna Dutton, dau. of Thomas, dec'd, produced a certificate from Wilmington.

29/12/1788. John Hutton and wife Massey requested a certificate to Exeter. John Broomall requested a certificate to Concord. William Williamson requested a certificate to Nottingham to marry [Phebe Passmore]. Cadwalader Evans requested membership for his children: John, William, Thomas and Samuel. Phebe Valentine requested a certificate to Uwchlan.

26/1/1789. Jonathan Sharples requested a certificate to Kennett. Sarah Davis, dau. of Nehemiah, dec., requested a certificate to Concord.

23/2/1789. William Davis, a minor, requested a certificate to Concord. James Paist and Elizabeth Dunn, dau. of Jacob, reported for marrying by a Baptist Teacher. Joshua Parson reported for mustering with militia. Edward Evans reported for mustering with militia. Phebe Howard [now Hammer], dau. of James, reported for fornication before marriage [disowned].

30/3/1789. James Broomall requested to be a member. Peter Taylor, Jr., reported for fornication with Susannah Malin, dau. of Gideon, in an abusive manner and since has married another woman. Mary Graham, dau. of Henry Hale, requested to be a member. Lydia Calvert requested a certificate to Goshen.

27/4/1789. William Ashbridge requested a certificate to Darby. Richard Maris, Jr., reported for mustering with militia. John Rogers reported for marrying by a magistrate to one not a member. Sarah Sharples, wife of Daniel, produced a certificate from Concord. Phebe Williamson, wife of William, produced a certificate from Nottingham. Sarah Pyle, wife of Benjamin, produced a certificate from Concord with children: Joseph, Hannah, Phebe, Benjamin, Sarah, Esther and Mary. Catherine Morris, now Shelcross, dau. of Jonathan, reported for marrying by a magistrate. Esther Garratt requested a certificate to Goshen. Priscilla Yarnall is chosen as clerk for the women's Chester Monthly Meeting in place of Mary Morris, dec.

25/5/1789. Ann Worrall acknowledged marrying out. Sarah Reynolds requested a certificate to Nottingham. Joseph Levis and Sarah Hall, dau. of David, reported for marrying by a magistrate. George Lownes requested a certificate to Kennett.

29/6/1789. Ann McIlvain, wife of John, produced a certificate from Newgarden.

27/7/1789. William Griffith produced a certificate from Concord. Anna Shaw produced a certificate from Philadelphia, Northern District.

31/8/1789. John Buzby produced a certificate from Abington. Elizabeth Atkinson produced a certificate from Philadelphia, Northern District. Ann Griffith produced a certificate from Wilmington. Thomas Calvert reported for fornication with Susanna Worrall, dau. of Peter.

25/9/1789. William Williamson and wife Phebe reported for fornication before marriage [disowned]. Ann Worrall, wife of Elisha, requested a certificate to Haverford.

26/10/1789. Ambrose Smedley requested a certificate to Goshen to marry Elizabeth Yarnall, dau. of Daniel.

30/11/1789. Respecting the marriage of Nathaniel Newlin "the same was orderly solemnized and altho' the company was large yet was in a good degree orderly conducted at the house of entertainment." Mary Newlin requested a certificate to Concord.

28/12/1789. Nathan Wood produced a certificate from Crooked Run, VA. Eleanor Davis, Jr., produced a certificate from Exeter. Enoch Gorman and Martha Thompson, dau. of Moses, reported for marrying by a magistrate [before Thomas Cheyney, Esq., 16 April 1789]. [disowned]

25/1/1790. John Birchall and wife Lydia produced a certificate from Philadelphia. James Birchall, son of John and Lydia, produced a certificate from Philadelphia.

22/2/1790. Joseph Field produced a certificate from Kingwood with wife Achsa and children: Robert, Elizabeth and Susanna. Jeremiah McIlvain produced a certificate from Concord. James Nuzum produced a certificate from Robeson. Nathan Lewis requested a certificate to Concord for himself, wife Sarah and son Job. Benjamin Tucker requested a certificate to Evesham. George Massey requested a certificate to Uwchlan. Benjamin Thomas requested a certificates to Darby for sons Owen and George. Jesse Haines and wife Rachel requested a certificate to Wilmington with their three children: Mary, Jacob and Reuben. Elizabeth Smedley, wife of Ambrose, produced a certificate from Goshen. Susanna Malin, who charged Peter Taylor, Jr. with committing fornication with her in an abusive manner, has since born a child in an unmarried state; advice as to how to deal with the case will be sought at the Quarterly Meeting. Rachel Hayworth, dau. of John, requested a certificate to Haverford.

26/3/1790. George Malin produced a certificate from Philadelphia. Richard Morris requested a certificate to Philadelphia, Southern District. Jesse Maris and wife Jane requested a certificate to Goshen with dau. Rebecca. Cadwalader Evans and wife Sarah requested a certificate to Kingwood with their children: John, William, Thomas and Samuel. Isaac Hoopes requested a certificate to Wilmington for son Abraham. Mary Cox, dau. of John, dec., requested a certificate to Kingwood.

26/4/1790. Edward Churchman produced a certificate from Nottingham with wife Rebecca and children: Caleb, Owen, Phebe and Anne. Asher Lobb produced a certificate from Darby. James Dilworth requested a certificate to Concord. Moses Minshall reported for drinking to excess [disowned]. Lydia Burchall, wife of John, produced a certificate from Philadelphia.

31/5/1790. Joel Sharples produced a certificate from Darby with wife Hannah and son Samuel. James Wood produced a certificate from Gwynedd with wife Mary. It was decided by the Quarterly Meeting Committee that Susanna Malin's conduct was reproachful and she should condemn it or be disowned [disowned]. Sarah Lobb, wife of Jacob, produced a certificate from Darby with children: David and

Elizabeth. Sarah Wood produced a certificate from Gwynedd. Jane Sharples, dau. of Thomas, reported for marrying by a hireling priest to [James] Shaw who is not a member. Phebe Coborn, now Young, dau. of John, reported for marrying by a hireling priest to one not a member.

28/6/1790. Ambrose Taylor produced a certificate from Wilmington with wife Mary and children: Jacob, Mordecai, Stephen, Abijah, Peter and Mary. Richard Nuzum produced a certificate from Robeson with wife Hannah and children: Sarah and Phebe. Mary Preston produced a certificate from Wilmington. Eleoner Davis, dau. of Nehemiah, dec., requested a certificate to Exeter. Hannah Bonsal requested a certificate to Wilmington. Abigail Smedley requested a certificate to Goshen. Rachel Hayworth reported for not delivering her certificate and has since married out; copy of certificate sent to Haverford.

26/7/1790. Beloved Friend Phebe Miller died 21/8/1789. David Garrett produced a certificate from Goshen with wife Esther and son Pennell. William Russell produced a certificate from Goshen with 4 children: Obed, Jesse, John and William. Rachel Hayworth, now Rachel Tool, was refused by Haverford. Samuel West requested a certificate to New Garden. Hannah Russel, dau. of William, produced a certificate from Goshen. Sarah Russell, dau. of William, produced a certificate from Goshen.

24/9/1790. Owen Maris requested a certificate to Goshen.

25/10/1790. Mary Vernon produced a certificate from Concord. Catharine Shelcross requested a certificate to Wilmington. Nathaniel Holland requested a certificate for son Nathaniel to Philadelphia.

28/11/1790. Francis Ruth requested a certificate to Concord. Ann Hibberd, wife of Isaac, requested a certificate to Darby. Susanna Dutton requested a certificate to Concord.

27/12/1790. Jonathan Pennel produced a certificate from Darby. Hannah Edwards, dau. of Nathan, dec., now Hannah Knight, reported for marrying by a magistrate to one not a member. Ann Griffith requested a certificate to Sadsbury. John Wilson acknowledged being concerned in military service.

31/1/1791. John Wilson requested a certificate to Philadelphia, Northern District. Jonas Sharples produced a certificate from Philadelphia, Southern District. George Nuzum produced a certificate from Robeson. Ann Evans requested a certificate for her grandson David Copeland to Philadelphia, Northern District. Hannah Crossley produced a certificate from Concord.

28/2/1791. Jonathan Pennell requested that his children: James and
Henry Hall, minors, be received into membership [approved]. Jacob
Dingee requested a certificate to Kennett for himself and wife
Elizabeth and two children: Elizabeth and Richard. Esther Levis,
dau. of Isaac, reported for marrying by a magistrate to [Edward]
Lewis who is not a member. John Mendenhall appointed treasurer of
fund for relief of the poor in place of Joshua Yarnall, dec. Rachel
Rhoads, dau. of Joseph, dec., reported for marrying by a hireling
priest to [Abel] Worrall who is not a member.

25/3/1791. Seth Evans reported for intended fraudulent dealings with
Philip Kirk who sued him for a bond given by Evans to James
Arnold who assigned it to Kirk, the bond having been given in trade
for land to be patented to Evans which was afterward done.

25/4/1791. William Nuzum produced a certificate from Robeson. Joseph
Webster produced a certificate from Concord with wife Rebecca and
children: William, Ruth and Joseph. Rachel Webster and Mary
Webster, daus. of Joseph, produced a certificate from Concord.
Joshua Harrison and wife Eliza requested a certificate to Sadsbury.
Francis Ruth's certificate returned by Concord Monthly Meeting
with some reasons why they were not willing to receive it. Mary
Thomas requested a certificate to Goshen.

30/5/1791. James Mifflin Gibbons requested a certificate to Sadsbury.
Richard Nuzum appointed overseer in place of Thomas Smedley, dec.
Mary Richards requested a certificate to Philadelphia, Southern
District. Sarah Poole requested a certificate to Wilmington. Thomas
Worrall, Jr., reported for marrying by a hireling teacher to one not a
member. Jesse Pennell requested a certificate to Hopewell. A copy
of the will of James Turner was read in which he left property to
Quakers.

27/6/1791. Ann Downing requested a certificate to Uwchlan. Ann
Pennell produced a certificate from Duck Creek. John Busby
reported for marrying by a magistrate [disowned].

25/7/1791. John Hall and wife Mary produced a certificate from
Concord. Rebecca Hall produced a certificate from Concord. Jephtha
Lightfoot and wife Hannah requested a certificate to Sadsbury with
children: Catharine and Sarah. Jonah Thompson reported for
attending a marriage out. Joshua Thompson reported for attending a
marriage out and mustering with militia [disowned]. Isaac Broomall
requested to be a member. Hannah Gibbons reported for committing
fornication and having a child unmarried [disowned].

29/8/1791. Ann Shaw requested that her children: Jane, William and Sarah, be received into membership.

23/9/1791. Ann Shaw's children: William and Sarah, received into membership, but Friend Shaw advised that daughter Jane, residing in Bucks Co., should make application there. Mary Vernon now lives within the verge of Uwchlan. Thomas West and Elizabeth Maris, dau. of Isaac, reported for marrying by a magistrate. Benjamin West reported for fornication [disowned]. Judith Maris requested a certificate to Gwynedd.

31/10/1791. John Davis requested a certificate to Gunpowder, MD. Hannah Russell, dau. of William, now Hannah Eaches, reported for marrying one not a member [disowned].

28/11/1791. Robert Harrison, a minor, produced a certificate from Philadelphia. William Davis produced a certificate from Concord. Sarah Davis produced a certificate from Concord. Elizabeth Taylor, dau. of Isaac, requested to be a member. Samuel James reported for fornication [disowned]. Isaac Broomall requested a certificate to Concord to marry Lydia Neal.

26/12/1791. Jonas Eyres reported for marrying by a magistrate. Jemima Parsons (now Slaughter), dau. of Richard, reported for marrying by a magistrate to one not a member.

30/1/1792. Henry Lawrence requested a certificate to Philadelphia. Joseph Bishop requested a certificate to Bradford to marry Sarah Pratt. Aaron Pennell requested a certificate to Saratoga, NY. Phebe Griffith requested a certificate to Goshen.

27/2/1792. Gideon Malin produced a certificate from Philadelphia, Southern District. Amy Lawrence produced a certificate from Philadelphia. Sarah Starr, wife of James, produced a certificate from Uwchlan for herself and 5 children: James, Joseph, Rebecca, Mary and John Minchall Starr. Robert Coborn requested to become a member. John Jobson has absconded without settling his affairs [disowned].

23/3/1752. Ann and Sarah Starr produced a certificate from Uwchlan. Esther Larkin produced a certificate from Concord. James Nuzum reported for marrying by a hireling minister to one not a member.

30/4/1792. Edward Fell and Joseph Hoskins appointed to the school committee in place of William Fell, dec., and Christopher Dingee who is aged and infirm. James Nuzum resides in the Forest of Bucks Co., but his father expects him to come down. George Maris requested a certificate to Goshen [disowned]. Esther Lewis requested a certificate to Goshen.

28/5/1792. A letter was produced directed to this meeting from Gideon Vernon, who resides in Nova Scotia, expressive of his desire to make satisfaction to Friends for his deviation from their principles. Mary Baker (dau. of John, dec.), now Massey, reported for marrying by a magistrate to one not a member [disowned]. Benjamin Lobb reported for marrying by a magistrate [disowned]. George Worrall requested a certificate to Goshen.

25/6/1792. Rachel Hill (dau. of John), now Grey, reported for marrying by a magistrate to one not a member [disowned]. Sarah Bishop, wife of Joseph, produced a certificate from Bradford. Lydia Broomal, wife of Isaac, produced a certificate from Concord. Joseph Thomas produced a certificate from Haverford with wife Ann and 4 children: Abishai, Sarah, Mary and John. Virgil Eachus produced a certificate from Bradford. Levi Mattson requested that he and children: Hannah, Caleb and Levi be received as members [his wife unites in this request]. Ann Pennell requested a certificate to Motherkiln [DE].

30/7/1792. Robert Coborn requested a certificate to Concord. Phebe Dick produced a certificate from Philadelphia, Southern District with children: John Jefferies Hart and Hannah Morris Hart. Springfield Preparative Meeting to prepare memorial for William Fell, dec. Eleanor Davis appointed overseer in place of Mary Tucker, dec.

27/8/1792. Levi Mattson and children received into membership. Mary Norris produced a certificate from Philadelphia. Phebe Chandler produced a certificate from Philadelphia. Jeremiah McElvain requested a certificate to Horsham Monthly Meeting to marry Elizabeth Spencer.

21/9/1792. John Kendal produced a certificate from Wilmington with wife Mary and children: Deborah and Jesse. Thomas Tucker, apprentice, requested a certificate to Goshen. Mary Vernon's certificate sent back by Uwchland Monthly Meeting. George Worrall reported for undue liberty in dress and address and manifesting a general deviation from our professed plainness of speech and apparel; he has administered an oath [disowned].

29/10/1792. Thomas Coates produced a certificate from Gwynedd with wife Rachel and dau. Sarah. Joseph Field requested a certificate to Kingwood for himself, wife Achsa and children: Robert, Elizabeth, Susannah and Saramary. Mary West, wife of Samuel, produced a certificate from Londongrove.

26/11/1792. James Thomas reported for marrying by a magistrate [disowned]. John Cobourn requested a certificate to Goshen.

31/12/1792. Sarah Gillingham, wife of James, requested a certificate to Philadelphia, Northern District. Sarah Pyle produced a certificate from Concord. Benjamin Worrall requested a certificate to Robeson. David Yarnall reported for marrying by a magistrate to one not a member [disowned].

28/1/1793. Ambrose Taylor and wife Mary with children: Jacob, Mordecai, Stephen, Abijah, Peter and Mary, granted a certificate to Westland.

25/2/1793. Joel West reported for fornication [disowned]. Maris Worrall requested a certificate to Goshen to marry Rebecca Garrett. Betty Mendenhall produced a certificate from Londongrove directed to Concord and endorsed from thence. Elizabeth McIlvain, wife of Jeremiah, produced a certificate from Horsham.

22/3/1793. Mary Taylor, now residing in Wilmington, reported as in need by Wilmington Friends. John Hall requested a certificate to Uwchlan with wife Mary, and Rebecca Hall, their dau., requested one for herself. Isaac Hoopes requested a certificate to Concord for himself, wife Mary and 6 of their children: Isaac, Jacob, Rachel, Mary, Deborah and Sidney. Eli Hoopes, son of Isaac, requested a certificate to Concord. Esther Dunn (now Sankey), [wife of William Sankey], reported for marrying by a magistrate to one not a member [disowned]. Phebe and Sarah Hoopes, daus. of Isaac and Mary Hoopes, requested certificates to Concord.

7/5/1793. George Thomas produced a certificate from Darby. John Broomall produced a certificate from Concord. Isaac Dennis, accused of fornication, begetting a bastard child and marrying another by a priest. Hannah West (now Pusey), dau. of William, reported for marrying by a magistrate to one not a member.

24/6/1793. Nathan Wood, son of Cornelius, requested a certificate to Hopewell. Hannah Fairlamb, widow of Samuel, requested a certificate to Philadelphia, Southern District. Ellen Lownes acknowledged marrying out by a priest. Rebecca Worrall, wife of Maris, produced a certificate from Goshen.

29/7/1793. Warrick Martin, accused of fornication and begetting a bastard child, has left these parts [disowned]. Nathan Yearsley requested a certificate to Uwchlan.

26/8/1793. Ashur Palmer, wife Alice and children: Joseph, Susannah, Morris and Huldah, requested a certificate to Concord.

30/9/1793. Isaac Dennis reported deceased. Robert Green requested to be a member. Joseph Starr, apprentice, requested a certificate to Goshen (apprentice).

28/10/1793. Thomas Steel produced a certificate from Goshen. Sarah Davis requested to be a member [approved].

25/11/1793. Rebecca Ogden, dau. of Aaron, dec., requested to be a member.

30/12/1793. Andrew produced a certificate from Goshen. Aquilla Starr produced a certificate from Uwchlan. Daniel Broomall and wife Martha requested to become members. Amos Bond reported for marrying by a magistrate [disowned]. Esther West (now Esther Riley) reported for marrying by a magistrate to one not a member. Phebe Taylor, dau. of Isaac, requested to be a member.

27/1/1794. Margaret Sankey requested to be received into membership. Eliza Harrison, wife of Joshua, produced a certificate from Sadsbury with their son Caleb. Elizabeth Branner, wife of George, produced a certificate from Philadelphia, Northern District.

24/2/1794. Jane, Martha and Sarah Davis [sisters] have sued a Friend at law. Hannah Pusey requested a certificate to Newgarden.

30/3/1794. Elizabeth Smith produced a certificate from Kennett. David Hall, Jr., requested a certificate to Concord to marry Hannah Pennell. Joseph and Susanna West requested a certificate to Londongrove with their 5 children: Hannah, Joseph, William, Susanna and Thomas. Evan Morris requested a certificate to Newgarden. Tacy Maris, dau. of Richard, (now Tacy Harrison) reported for marrying by a magistrate [disowned]. Mary West, dau. of Joseph, requested a certificate to Londongrove.

28/4/1794. Benjamin Yarnall, apprentice, son of Benjamin, requested a certificate to Wilmington. Hannah Wood, dau. of Cornelius, reported for fornication, having a bastard child and denying any knowledge thereof [disowned].

26/5/1794. Sarah Lewis produced a certificate from Concord with children: Job, David and Martin. Samuel Acton requested a certificate to Salem. Mary Parsons (dau. of Richard), now Mary Neal, wife of James, reported for fornication [disowned].

30/6/1794. Jonathan Pennell reported for marrying by a magistrate to one not a member [disowned]. William Black produced a certificate from Chesterfield. Hannah Jones, dau. of Norris, dec., produced a certificate from Philadelphia. Hannah Green requested to be a members with her husband Robert and their children: Abel, Joseph, Jane, Lewis, Lydia and Robert. A memorial to be prepared for Phebe Emlen.

28/7/1794. Ann Tucker requested a certificate to Philadelphia, Northern District. Esther Larkin requested a certificate to Concord.

Rachel West, dau. of Joseph, requested a certificate to Londongrove. Nathaniel Worrall requested a certificate to Gwynedd to marry Mary Paul. Joseph Rhoads and wife Mary proposed as Elders. William Gray requested to be a member. Ann Lynn, wife of Joseph, produced a certificate from Philadelphia with children: Mary, Phebe and John. Sarah Dicks, an Elder, died 11/25/1793 in her 82nd year. Phebe Emlen died 10/25/1793, aged about 35 years.

25/8/1794. Thomas Levis, Jr., requested a certificate to Darby to marry Ann Levis. David Howard, who removed several years ago without a certificate, now resides near Redstone Settlement and is married out.

26/9/1794. Hannah Hall, wife of David, produced a certificate from Concord.

27/10/1794. Cornelius Wood and wife Mary requested a certificate to Hopewell. Hannah Vernon reported for fornication and having a child out of wedlock [disowned]. Tamar Lightfoot produced a certificate from Sadsbury.

24/11/1794. Joseph Newlin produced a certificate from Concord. Samuel Black produced a certificate from Mount Holly. Cornelius Wood and wife Mary requested a certificate to Hopewell with their daus.: Jane, Lydia and Mary. Martha Gibbons, wife of John, and son George, produced a certificate from Philadelphia.

29/12/1794. Joseph Engle requested a certificate to Philadelphia, Northern District. Joseph Dicks, Jr., accused of fornication by Sarah Pile [disowned]. William Grey requested a certificate for himself and wife Rachel to Darby. Rebecca West (now Rebecca Edwards), dau. of Thomas, dec., reported for marrying by a magistrate to one not a member.

26/1/1795. Passmore West reported for marrying by a magistrate to one not a member [disowned]. Joseph Tucker and wife Margaret requested a certificate to Philadelphia. Elizabeth Taylor [wife of Enoch] to Bradford.

23/2/1795. Friends of Redstone write that David Howard said he joined the Methodists and had been married by one of their teachers [disowned]. Rachel Bond, wife of Amos, produced a certificate from Wilmington. William Black requested a certificate to Upper Springfield, NJ, to marry Achsa Wright. Joseph Thomas requested a certificate to Exeter with wife Ann and children: Abishai, Sarah, Mary, John and Samuel. John Kendal requested a certificate to Sadsbury with wife Mary and children: Deborah, Jesse and Rebecca. Robert Harrison requested a certificate to Philadelphia.

30/3/1795. Thomas Evans, a minor, produced a certificate from Kennett. Ellen Lownes requested for her children Jane and George to be received as members. Benjamin Sharples requested a certificate to Sadsbury.

27/4/1795. Thomas Clarke produced a certificate from Exeter. Susanna Cloud, wife of William, requested a certificate to Wilmington. Rebecca Hayworth produced a certificate from Haverford. Jonathan Howard acknowledged paying toward hiring substitutes to go out in the militia. Edward Churchman, wife Rebecca and 6 children: Caleb, Owen, Phebe, Anne, Micajah and Hannah, requested a certificate to Concord.

25/5/1795. Aaron Wood produced a certificate from Haverford with wife Elizabeth and children, Moses and Israel. Betty Mendenhall requested a certificate to Darby. Lydia Yarnall requested a certificate to Concord. Sarah Vernon, wife of William, requested a certificate to Concord. Jennett Shaw, a minor, produced a certificate from Middletown. Mary Worrall, wife of Nathaniel, produced a certificate from Gwynedd.

29/6/1795. Ebenezer Cresson produced a certificate from Philadelphia. William Black requested a certificate to Cecil Monthly Meeting, Kent Co., MD. Mary Rhoads chosen clerk for women's Chester Monthly Meeting in place of Priscilla Yarnall, dec.

27/7/1795. John Moore requested a certificate to Darby. Elizabeth Lobb (dau. of Jacob), now Elizabeth Pitt, reported for marrying by a magistrate to one not a member [disowned].

31/8/1795. Israel Yarnall produced a certificate from Goshen. William Davis requested a certificate to Uwchlan. James Maris reported for fornication [disowned]. Leah Ashton requested a certificate to Concord. Deborah Thatcher requested a certificate to Concord. Amy Moore requested a certificate to Darby.

25/9/1795. Edward Hall reported for marrying by a magistrate to one not a member [disowned]. Clement Lawrence requested a certificate to Philadelphia, Northern District. Ann Bowman produced a certificate from Leek Monthly Meeting held at Leek, Staffordshire, England, with an endorsement by Philadelphia Middle Monthly Meeting.

26/10/1795. Isabel Cowpland, minor dau. of David, requested a certificate to Middle Monthly Meeting, Philadelphia.

30/11/1795. Sarah Reese produced a certificate from Goshen.

28/12/1795. George Worrall's acknowledgement accepted, he requested a certificate to Philadelphia, Southern District. Nathan Yearsley produced a certificate from Uwchlan. Ann Lynn, wife of Joseph, and their children: Mary, Phebe, John and Jonathan, requested a certificate to Abington. Elizabeth Smith requested a certificate to Kennett. Joshua Copeland reported for fornication before marriage and marrying by a magistrate. Jonathan Vernon, Jr., meets with the militia as one of them [disowned].

25/1/1796. Joel Malin requested a certificate to Kennett to marry Elizabeth Smith. Jane Cresson requested a certificate to Philadelphia, Northern District. Thomas Coats requested a certificate to Philadelphia, Northern District, for his dau. Sarah, a minor.

29/2/1795. Peggy Levis (dau. of Isaac, dec.), now Peggy Davis, reported for marrying by hireling priest to one not a member [disowned]. Hannah Gibbons produced a certificate from Philadelphia, Northern District. John Evans, Jr. has exercised with the militia [disowned]. Enoch Griffith requested a certificate to Newgarden with wife Rachel and their dau. Ann.

25/3/1796. Caleb Yarnall requested a certificate to Goshen for son Owen, apprentice. Mary Jobson (dau. of Joseph), now Mary Thomson, reported for marrying by a magistrate to one not a member [disowned]. Israel Yarnall requested a certificate to Haverford.

25/4/1796. Joshua Cowpland disowned. Rachel Grey produced a certificate from Darby with children: Martha and William. Susannah Cloud produced a certificate from Wilmington. Sarah Lewis and children: Job, David and Martin requested a certificate to Philadelphia, Southern District. Sarah Nuzum reported for fornication and begetting a child out of wedlock [disowned].

30/5/1796. Elizabeth Branner requested a certificate to Philadelphia, Northern District. Mary Starr requested a certificate to Exeter. Hannah Baker, dau. of Aaron, now Hannah Waddle, reported for committing fornication before marriage [disowned]. Kesse West requested a certificate to Baltimore.

27/6/1796. Nathaniel Hollingsworth produced a certificate from Goshen with wife Abigail and children: Robert, Hannah, Aaron, Thomas and Eli. Betty Crossley produced a certificate from Concord. Elizabeth Malin (formerly Smith), wife of Joel Malin, returned her certificate from Kennett with endorsement. Elizabeth Smith (dau. of John, dec.), now Elizabeth Price, reported for marrying by a hireling minister to one not a member [disowned].

25/7/1796. Tacy Bevan (dau. of David), now Tacy Statia, reported for marrying by a magistrate to one not a member [disowned]. Leah Rhoads (dau. of Joseph, dec.), now Leah Farr, reported for marrying by a magistrate to one not a member; and is removed near to Winchester, VA.

29/8/1796. Sarah Massey [wife of Mordecai] requested a certificate to Warrington.

23/9/1796. Jonas Sharples disowned for marrying by a magistrate to his 1st cousin, Susannah Fairlamb, dau. of Nicholas. Edward Engle disowned for marrying by a magistrate to Mary Eyres, dau. of Isaac. Joseph Worrall disowned for marrying by a magistrate to one not a member. William Shoemaker requested a certificate to Motherkiln [DE] to marry Sarah Bowman. Rebekah Davis, wife of John, requested a certificate to Concord. Rebekah Green produced a certificate from Concord.

31/10/1796. Ashur Lobb requested a certificate to Darby. George Martin left these parts a considerable time ago and since then has been charged by Phebe Evans, Jr., with fornication and begetting a bastard child [disowned]. Mary Crosley, wife of Samuel, produced a certificate from Concord with dau. Mary, a minor. Phebe Evans disowned for fornication and begetting a child out of wedlock.

28/11/1796. Hannah Squibb requested a certificate to Wilmington. Robert Green, wife Hannah and children: Abel, Jane, Lewis, Lydia, Robert and David, requested a certificate to Goshen. Elizabeth Levis, dau. of Samuel, dec., requested a certificate to Philadelphia.

26/12/1796. Mary Ann Corbett, a minor, produced a certificate from Duck Creek, dated 1791, it being misdirected by the death of the Friends who had care of it; she now lives with a Friend of Goshen to whom the certificate is now endorsed. Abigail Pancoast, wife of Seth, requested membership for her children: Hannah, Ann, Esther and Stephen.

30/1/1797. David Bevan, son of Davis, a member of Philadelphia Monthly Meeting, has resided for several years within the verge of this meeting but neglected to request a certificate as they inform this meeting by letter. Ann Cassin, dau. of Thomas Worrall, acknowledged marrying out for which she was formerly disowned. Nathaniel Holland, dec., left £10 by will to this meeting. Jane Regester, dau. of William, requested a certificate to Philadelphia.

27/2/1797. Jesse Darlington produced a certificate from Concord with wife Amy and children: Martha, Rhoda, Samuel and Edward. Thomas Coats and son Moses, a minor, requested a certificate to Gwynedd.

24/3/1797. Joseph Hooton, a minor, produced a certificate from Mount Holly. Thomas Bayliff produced a certificate from Hopewell. Aaron Mendenhall produced a certificate from Bradford. Joseph West produced a certificate from Londongrove. Roger Dicks requested a certificate to Goshen to marry Rebecca Maris. Ann Carson requested a certificate to Philadelphia, Southern District.

24/4/1797. Jesse Reese requested membership. Nathaniel Hollingsworth requested a certificate to Goshen with wife Abigail and children: Robert, Hannah, Aaron, Thomas, Eli and Jesse.

29/5/1797. David Bevan produced a certificate from Philadelphia, Southern District. Mary Sharples produced a certificate from Newgarden with children: Lydia, Phebe, Esther, Rebecca and Joseph. Hannah Bonsall requested a certificate to Philadelphia, Southern District. Cyrus Levis requested a certificate to Philadelphia. Ann Pennell, wife of Jonathan, requested to be a member. William Pennell married one not a member [disowned]. Tamer Lightfoot, now Tamer Worrall, married by a magistrate to one not a member [disowned]. Sarah Coats, dau. of Thomas, having removed to live with her father in Gwynedd, requested a certificate be signed for her - the first to Philadelphia of 2nd month 1796 being mislaid.

26/6/1797. Benjamin Stokes produced a certificate from Radnor with wife Ann and children Susannah and Sarah. Judith Maris and son Jesse produced a certificate from Gwynedd. Rachel Taylor requested a certificate to Gwynedd. Rebecca Garrett requested a certificate to Goshen. William Howard married by a magistrate [disowned]. Elizabeth Gibbons, dau. of Joseph, dec., requested a certificate to Londongrove.

31/7/1797. William Griffith produced a certificate from Philadelphia, Northern District. Isaac Hoops produced a certificate from Concord with wife Mary and 5 of their children: Jacob, Rachel, Mary, Debby and Sidney. Eli Hoops produced a certificate from Concord. Raper Hoskins produced a certificate from Philadelphia with wife Eleanor and children: Abigail, John, Henrietta, Graham and Wyatt. Phebe Walker requested a certificate to Haverford. Mary Lawrance requested a certificate to Philadelphia, Northern District. Rebecca Dicks, wife of Roger, produced a certificate from Goshen. Sarah

Hoopes produced a certificate from Concord. Robert Pennell and
wife Ann requested a certificate to Concord.

28/8/1797. Nicholas Woolis requested for himself and dau. Rachel to be
members [approved]. George Miller, dec., devises land to this
Monthly Meeting.

22/9/1797. Rachel Taylor returned her certificate upon her return from
Gwynedd.

30/10/1797. Sarah Shoemaker, wife of William, produced a certificate
from Motherkiln. John Levis requested a certificate to Darby to
marry Mary Levis. Jesse Reese requested a certificate to Goshen.
George Thomas reported for marrying one not a member
[disowned]. Mary Holland (dau. of Nathaniel, dec.), now Mary Ryon,
reported for marrying by a magistrate to one not a member.

27/11/1797. Mary Sharples, dau. of Joseph, dec., produced a certificate
from Newgarden. Elizabeth Cheyney produced a certificate from
Philadelphia. Aaron Mendenhall requested a certificate to Bradford.
John Broomall requested a certificate to Concord to marry Susanna
Wilson.

25/12/1797. Joseph Regester requested to be a member. John Evans
reported for marrying by a magistrate to one not a member. Hannah
Worrall appointed on committee to have care of the poor in place of
Hannah Sharples, dec. Mary Davis appointed to same committee in
place of Martha Sharples, dec.

29/1/1798. Isaac Malin and 1st cousin Hanna [Hannah Crosley]
disowned for marrying out of unity by a magistrate. Abigail Graham
left £25 in her will for the purpose of education of the poor children
of the Quakers in Delaware County.

26/2/1798. Mary Squibb produced a certificate from Concord. Thomas
Bayliff requested a certificate to Concord. Raper Hoskins and
George Miller appointed to the school committee in place of George
Miller, dec., and Isaac Engle.

23/3/1798. James Starr, Jr. requested a certificate to Catawissey.
Joanna Holland, dau. of Nathaniel, dec., requested a certificate to
Philadelphia, Northern District. Thomas Clark requested a
certificate to Concord.

30/4/1798. Elizabeth Atkinson requested a certificate to Philadelphia,
Northern District. Edward Marshall produced a certificate from
Cane Creek. Acquilla Starr requested a certificate to Catawissey
with wife Abigail and children: Sidney and Engle.

28/5/1798. George Holme produced a certificate from Darby. Amos
Sharples requested a certificate to Darby with wife Lydia and

children: Emily and Omy. Ebenezer Cresson requested a certificate to Woodbury. Rebecca Parsons, wife of Joshua, requested a certificate to Radnor with children: Phebe, Mahlon, John, Neomie and William.

25/6/1798. Esther Lewis, wife of Edward, produced a certificate from Goshen. Susanna Broomall, wife of John, produced a certificate from Concord. Lydia Martin, dau. of Caleb, reported for fornication and begetting a child out of wedlock [disowned]. Nicholas Woollas reported for marrying by a magistrate to one not a member [disowned]. Mary Webster, now Mary Miller, married by a magistrate to one not a member [disowned].

27/8/1798. James Morton produced a certificate from Philadelphia, Southern District. James Broomall requested a certificate to Concord to marry Hannah Dutton. Mordecai Yarnall requested a certificate to Concord. Hannah Sharpless, dau. of Joseph, dec., produced a certificate from Newgarden.

21/9/1798. Bathsheba Eaches [formerly Bathsheba Webb] requested that she and her children: Homer, Joseph, Obed and Hiram be received into membership [with her husband's approval]. Andrew Steel requested a certificate to Concord to marry Susanna Dutton.

29/10/1798. Nathaniel Worrall and wife Mary requested a certificate to Gwynedd with their children: Jonathan, William and Edith.

26/11/1798. Isaac Sharpless produced a certificate from Concord. Thomas Bowman produced a certificate from Motherkiln with children: Rebecca, Thomas and Esther. David Regester received again into membership. Ruth Worrall, wife of Thomas, requested to be a member with her husband and their children: Caleb, Sarah and Peirce. Betty Malin (dau. of Gideon, dec.), now Betty Taylor, reported for marrying by a magistrate to one not a member.

31/12/1798. Preston Eyre reported for associating with the militia to learn the art of war [disowned]. Thomas Worrall reported for drinking to excess. David Regester requested a certificate to Goshen. George Holme requested a certificate to Philadelphia, Southern District.

28/1/1799. Amy Johnson, wife of Joseph, requested a certificate to Concord. Joseph Starr produced a certificate from Goshen. Sarah Wood requested a certificate to Abington for her [minor] dau. Ann. Elizabeth Gibbons (dau. of Joseph, dec.), now Elizabeth Lloyd, reported for not turning in her certificate and marrying by a magistrate to her 1st cousin.

25/2/1799. Ann Maris (dau. of Richard), now Ann Mace, reported for marrying by a magistrate to one not a member. Elizabeth Gibbons, now Elizabeth Lloyd, neglected to deliver her certificate of two years ago and since married her 1st cousin [disowned].

25/3/1799. Joseph Hoskins requested a certificate to Radnor with family. Joseph Maris reported for marrying by a magistrate to one not a member. Mathew Wood requested a certificate to Goshen with his wife Mary and children: Jacob, Elizabeth, Mary, Isaac, Tamer, Abram, Seth and Anne. Thomas Steel requested a certificate to Concord with wife Mary and children, Sidney and Amy (Anna). Isaac Broomall requested a certificate to Concord with wife Lydia and children: John, Daniel and James. Dorothy Davis requested a certificate to Uwchlan. Leah Farr, wife of John, requested a certificate to Hopewell.

29/4/1799. James Wood requested a certificate to Goshen with wife Mary. Mary Lawrence requested membership for her children: John, Isaac, Hannah and Henry, her husband uniting in the request [approved]. Elizabeth Cheyney requested a certificate to Concord. Hannah Broomall, wife of James, produced a certificate from Concord. Susanna Hannum reported for fornication before marriage [disowned].

27/5/1799. Joseph Hoskins requested a certificate to Radnor with wife Mary and children: Amaria and Dorothy Graham. Esther Levis requested a certificate to Darby. Joseph Dickenson removed without requesting a certificate several years ago and has since married out; now he resides in the compass of this meeting [disowned]. Abigail Rhoads (dau. of Joseph, dec.), now Abigail Grim, reported for marrying by a magistrate to one not a member [disowned]. Morris Truman produced a certificate from Darby with wife Mary and children: Joseph, James and Morris.

24/6/1799. Memorials signed for James Emlen and Mary Sharples.

29/7/1799. Sarah Maclister [Macalister] acknowledged marrying out. Robert Newlin produced a certificate from Wilmington. Mary Newlin, wife of Robert, produced a certificate from Falls. Aaron Wood requested a certificate to Goose Creek with wife Elizabeth and children: Moses, Israel, Susannah, Sarah and Catharine. James Yarnall requested membership for himself and 5 minor children: Isaac, Sidney, Rachel, James and Albin. Thomas Dent requested membership. Mary Yarnall, dau. of James, requested membership. Martha Smith, dau. of John, dec., requested a certificate to Concord.

26/8/1799. Sarah Maclister [Macalister] received into membership again. Joseph Griffith produced a certificate from Concord with wife Sarah and son Isaac. Gill Pennington produced a certificate from Radnor with wife Esther and children: William, Benjamin, Sarah, Elizabeth, Joseph and Mary. Andrew Steel requested a certificate to Concord. Jennet Shaw requested a certificate to Goose Creek.

30/9/1799. Aaron Mattson produced a certificate from Goshen. Abraham Hoopes produced a certificate from Wilmington.

28/10/1799. Grace Good requested a certificate to Kennett. Jane Lownes, a minor, requested a certificate to Philadelphia, Northern District. Samuel Black requested a certificate to Duck Creek. Hugh McIlvaine requested a certificate to Philadelphia.

25/11/1799. Ann Worrall, now Ann Garrett, reported for fornication before marriage [disowned].

30/12/1799. Isaac Masey produced a certificate from Goshen.

27/1/1800. Israel Yarnall produced a certificate from Mount Holly. Joseph Pyle requested a certificate to Darby. John Vernon, Jr. and William Nuzum left the neighbourhood some years ago without applying for certificates.

24/2/1800. Luke Cassin produced a certificate from Philadelphia, Southern District, with wife Ann. Anna Martin produced a certificate from Concord. Sarah Pyle requested a certificate to Concord. Catherine Fairlamb, dau. of Nicholas, now Catherine Hinkson, reported for marrying by a magistrate to one not a member.

31/3/1800. Preston Sharpless requested a certificate to Duck Creek. Benjamin Stokes requested a certificate to Philadelphia, Northern District, with wife Ann and children: Susanna, Sarah, Elizabeth and John. Dell Pennell requested a certificate to Darby with wife Hannah and 3 children: Sidney, Hill and Mary Dell. Levi Mattson requested a certificate for son Caleb to Philadelphia, Southern District. Robert Newlin requested a certificate to Wilmington with wife Mary. Bettey Taylor requested a certificate to Concord.

28/4/1800. Thomas Wilson produced a certificate from Bradford with wife Ann and dau. Sarah. George Yarnall reported for marrying by a magistrate to Mary Howard, dau. of James [both disowned]. Mary Morris left £25 by her will to the Monthly Meeting.

26/5/1800. James Starr produced a certificate from Catawissa. Jane Ashbridge, dau. of Joseph, dec., requested a certificate to Philadelphia, Northern District. Rachel Walter requested a certificate to Concord. Hannah James (dau. of Joseph, dec.), now Hannah Lungren, reported for marrying by a magistrate to one not a member. Samuel Sharpless, apprentice, requested a certificate to Wilmington.

30/6/1800. Robert Green produced a certificate from Goshen with wife Hannah and children: Abel, Jane, Lewis, Lydia, Robert, David, Samuel and James. Jesse Reese produced a certificate from Goshen. Jos. Townsend John produced a certificate from Uwchlan. William Davis produced a certificate from Uwchlan. Hannah Lungren's husband would not allow a visit to her but she has sent a few lines requesting she be disowned [disowned]. Joseph Regester and wife Sarah requested a certificate to Wilmington. Phebe Chandler requested a certificate to Burlington. Dorothy Davis produced a certificate from Uwchlan. Abigail Pyle produced a certificate from Darby. Betty Crosley, now Betty Hinkson, reported for marrying by a magistrate to one not a member.

28/7/1800. Nathaniel Worrall produced a certificate from Gwynedd with wife Mary and children: Jonathan, William and Edith. Hannah Massey requested a certificate to Goshen. Esther Sharpless, a minor, dau. of Joseph, dec., requested a certificate to Newgarden. Ann Worrall, a minor, dau. of Rebecca, requested a certificate to Abington.

25/8/1800. Enos Painter produced a certificate from Concord. Rebecca Hayworth produced a certificate from Radnor. William Davis requested a certificate to Gwynedd to marry Rachel Robinson. Richard Nuzum requested a certificate to Redstone with wife Hannah. George Nuzum, their son, requested a certificate to same place. Esther Riley requested membership for her children: Rebecca, Thomas and Sarah. Phebe Nuzum (dau. of Richard Nuzum), now Kirk, reported for marrying her first cousin [disowned]. Hannah Pyle, now Caldwell, reported for marrying by a magistrate to one not a member.

27/10/1800. Thomas Evans requested a certificate to Westland. Luke Cassin requested membership for his son Thomas [approved]. Jesse Reese requested a certificate to Concord to marry Elizabeth Davis. Elizabeth Smedley (dau. of Ambrose), now Elizabeth Kellogg, reported for marrying by a magistrate to one not a member.

24/11/1800. Owen Yarnall produced a certificate from Goshen. Israel Yarnall requested a certificate to Bradford. Sarah Edwards (dau. of William), now Sarah Barton, reported for fornication before marriage.

29/12/1800. William Sharples reported for marrying by a priest. Sarah
   Gibbons, dau. of Joseph, dec., requested a certificate to
   Philadelphia.

ACKNOWLEDGMENTS AND DISOWNMENTS

BAILES, Sarah, formerly of Chester, now distant. Acknowledged marriage by a priest, which was a grief to her parents. 17/2/1733.

BAKER, John, late of Edgmont. Disowned 24/4/1728 for marriage by a priest to one not a member.

BALDWIN, Hannah, dau. of William and Mary Coborn, lately belonging to the meeting ... married one not of the Society ... reported, 28/5/1712.

BALDWIN, John of Chester. Drinking too much liquor. 17/7/1718.

BARBE, Robert and wife Hannah. Acknowledged fornication before marriage. 23/12/1718/9.

BARKLET, Thomas, lately arrived from Talbot Co, Maryland, recorded 26/6/1700.

BECKHAM, Sarah, formerly Norbury. Disowned 29/10/1718 for marrying contrary to discipline.

BENSON, Jean - Taking a husband contrary to the good order, recorded 20/7/1716.

BLEAN, Awbrey. Admitted some time ago. Acknowledged marrying by a priest. 27/5/1730.

BOND, Ann. Acknowledged marrying by a priest to one not a member and without her father's consent. 31/5/1727.

BOOTH, Charles. "I am heartily sorrowfull for all the misteps that I have made wherein I have offended God and his people and I am very sorry that I have been so farr transported into passion as to Quarrill and Strick Huntley." 29/11/1704/5.

BOWER, Mary of the county of Philadelphia - some years past condescended to an entanglement of marriage with a profane person, recorded 19/6/1701.

BRITTAN, Hannah, dau. of Mary Woodward. Acknowledged fornication. 24/7/1733.

BRUMALL, Jane, dau. of John of Nether Providence. Some time past with her father, mother and sister desired to come under the care of the meeting but afterward kept company with a young man not of the Society, contrary to her parents' consent and after her father's death, married him by a priest. Disowned 24/9/1729.

BUNTING, Mary. Went to a priest to be married. 28/7/1724.

CADWALLADER, Elizabeth, dau. of John of Uwchlan, being borne of believing parents. Disowned 26/10/1720 for being overtaken with strong liquor and scandalous behaviour.

CAIN, Rachel. Acknowledged being overtaken with strong liquor some
time before her marriage. 28/4/1725.

CALVERT, Elizabeth, wife of Daniell Calvert of Edgmont, she being
formerly a frequenter of our meetings has taken a husband who is
not of our profession. Disowned. A paper of condemnation given by
Friends of Chester Monthly Meeting on 31/5/1710. Caleb Pusey,
Thomas Minshall, Bartholomew Coppock, John Edgg, Randall
Vernon, Ephraim Jackson, Even Lewis, Nicholas Fairland [Fairlamb],
Jacob Simcock, John Salkeld, Witt Lewis, Margritt Minshall,
Margritt Coppock, Agness Salkeld, Eliner Vernon, Alice Simcock,
Jean Edgg, Lidia Vernon, Mary Lewis, Mary Dell, Mary Asbridge,
Francis [Frances] Worrall, Sarah Minshall.

CALVERT, Elizabeth. Acknowledged marrying out for which she had
been disowned. 30/7/1728.

CALVERT, Judith, Jr. Acknowledged defrauding Peter Dicks of about
three quarters of a pound of butter.

CARTER, Joseph, produced a certificate from Newton Meeting in
Cheshire in old England, recorded 28/9/1698.

CARTER, Joseph. Contrary to the advice of friends "hath actually
married to one who doth not any wayes profess the truth with us."
Disowned. 25/8/1708.

COEBOURN, Elizabeth, dau. of Thomas. Disowned 24/2/1732 for
marriage by a priest to one not a member.

COEBOURN, Joseph of Chester. Kept company with a young woman
under some degree of engagement to another man and that in seven
weeks after the death of his first wife and since married by a priest.
Disowned 25/4/1733.

COEBOURN, Thomas, son of Thomas. Disowned 29/9/1725 for keeping
company with Elizabeth Coebourn, wife of Thomas, dec., who
acknowledged her fear that she was with child by him.

COOKSON, Daniel. Marrying out. 28/7/1719.

COPPOCK, Bartholomew. Drinking over much drink at Darby.
25/12/1709/10.

COPPOCK, Sarah, dau. of Jonathan, dec. Acknowledged marriage by a
priest. 27/8/1729.

CROSBY, John. "Whereas I have unadvisedly broke the good order
established amongst friends in Case of marriage tending to the
breach of unity in the brother hood, and an Example of Looseness to
young people, for which I am heartily sorry and desire the
forgiveness of God and of my Brethren" &C. Dated 20/9/1719. [In
the forgoing statement, Crosby acknowledges his regret for upsetting

friends by marrying out of unity and setting a poor example for the young members.]

CROXSON, Thomas, son of Randall of Providence, "has been under our care by reason of his father and mother being married amongst friends." Disowned 29/9/1731 for drinking and lying.

CROXTON, Randall. ".. drawn into the Excess of Strong Drink at the Buriall of Thomas Powell Jur. which I am sencible not only hurt my own Soule but hath brought Reproach upon the holy Profession of truth ... 28/10/1714.

CROXTON, Randall of Upper Providence. Disowned 24/7/1716 for stealing.

DICK, Martha "... has committed that which is gross and unclean ...", recorded 25/12/1711.

DICKS, Sarah, formerly Sarah Powell, of Providence Township - went to the priest to be married, recorded 29/2/1717.

DOBBS, Richard. Disowned 23/7/1727. Gave way to drunkenness and vile conversation such as cursing, swearing and calling for damnation on himself if he ever married Margaret Woodward which he afterward wished to do.

EDGE, John of Upper Providence. Disowned 30/1/1730 for keeping loose company, drinking to excess and using corrupt language.

EDWARDS, Sarah, dau. of Janne Edwards of Middletown, Chester County, married one not of the Society. Sarah Edwards, now Sarah Pratt, is disowned, recorded 29/5/1717.

ELLBECK, Mary. Admitted some time ago. Disowned 28/12/1731/2 for marrying one not of our profession.

ELLIS, Cadwallader of Goshen. Disowned 30/9/1713.

ELLIS, Mary - "... for want of watchfullness lent mine eare to that seperating rending and deviding spirritt which apeared through George Keith ...", 27/2/1702.

FAWCET, John. "have too much and frequently kept Evill Company which hath tended to the dishonour of truth." 30/6/1708.

FRED, Benjamin. Going down to Chester by his father's order to bring the sheriff to arrest a friend. 8/8/1716.

FRED, John. "Burmingham the 10th of the 7th month 1716. ... I, John Fred, belonging to Concord meeting having arrested a publick friend at the breaking up of a Quarterly meeting held at Concord the last third month contrary to an order established among us..."

FINCHER, John and Martha, acknowledged doing "that we ought not to have done" before marriage. No date. 1700

FINCHER, Mary - having committed a gross evil with him who is not her husband, recorded 24/11/1699.

FISH, Ralph, was formerly from West River in Maryland, recorded 30/6/1703.

FLOWER, Rebecca. Disowned 24/2/1732 for drinking to excess.

GLEAVE, Esther, dau. of John Gleave. In disobedience to her parents married John Croeser, not of the community. Disowned 25/11/1730/1.

GIBSON, Nathan, formerly a member of Chester Monthly Meeting, now of Darby Township. Acknowledged committing fornication with Ann Blunston before marriage. 24/4/1719.

GOODWIN, Thomas, Sr. "Whereas on the 29th Day of the Second months 1724 I went with some of my neighbours to the washing of Sheep and for want of Caer and watchfullness I Drank to much Rum and also Spoak some unsavorry words at the house of the widow Baker in Edgmond all which have been a wounding to my soul and Grief ... grief to my wife and children ..." 27/5/1724.

GOODWIN, Thomas. Acknowledged for drinking too much strong liquor. 30/5/1733. "I who am so near the brink of the Grave."

GORSUCH, William. Acknowledged marrying by a priest. 27/5/1730.

HARDMAN, Edward. "... I have been two Loose in my Life and Conversation ... Since I made profession of Truth ... belying my masters and family as which I have lived with ... also wickedly pretended my self to be sick at Charles Whitakers ... also did greatly wrong my master Samuel Jennings the last night by casting out Disparraging words concerning him at Henry Hollingsworths." 24/4/1706.

HARLIN, Hannah. Acknowledge fornication with her husband before marriage by a priest, bringing trouble on her tender parents. 28/4/1725.

HARRISON, Caleb. Loose and vain way of living and neglecting meetings and drawing out a young woman's affections before the parents' consent is obtained. 15/7/1713.

HARRY, Joseph, son of Joseph. Disowned 26/9/1733 for marriage by a priest to one of another profession.

HASTINGS, John and wife Mary. Married by a Justice. 31/10/1722.

HAYES, Jonathan of Newtown. "Some years ago transported himself into this Province from Europe his native Land where he was brought up and Educated in the way of .. Quakers ..." Disowned 28/9/1720 for marrying out, swearing, drinking to excess and keeping bad company.

HEALD, Kathren - To the Monthly Meeting held at Middletown, "... went too hastily to be married contrary to the good order ...", recorded 25/3/1713.

HOLDSTONE, Sarah, who before marriage was Sarah Phips, married one not of the Society, reported 26/11/1712.

HOLSTON, Sarah. Admitted some time ago at her request. Disowned 30/1/1730 for being "loose and vain in her conversation" and keeping company with a young man at unseasonable times and after an unbecoming manner.

HOSKINS, John of Chester. "have for some considerable time past suffered himself in a large degree to fall into a loose and unchristian conversation, as drinking, gaming and other evils too commonly attending the same but altogether contrary to our Christian Profession." Disowned. 29/9/1708.

HOSKINS, Mary, dau. of Ruth. Disowned for marriage by a priest to one not of the Society. 31/8/1731.

HOWELL, Ann, now REYNOLDS. Acknowledged that for which she had been testified against. 27/6/1733.

HUNTER, Peter. Acknowledged saying at a Monthly Meeting some months ago that John Worrall's servants were stripped at his house and were not abused as was complained of, which was false. Made his mark 2/5/2/1720.

HURFORD, John, produced a certificate dated 22/12/1702/3.

JAMES, Aron [Aaron], lately arrived from Stafford Monthly Meeting in old England for himself and wife, recorded 24/9/1701.

JAMES, Susannah. Acknowledged marrying out and fornication before marriage. 28/7/1730.

JERVIS, Joseph. "Whereas I haveing Some time since Reported that I thought I saw as I was Lying on my Bed Samuell Buckly and that he Put me on Courting his widow and that I should be kind to his Children or the Like and of my Desireing the next Day some Private Discours with his widow which she Prudently Denied but it being but a drea; I do hereby acknowledge that I did not do well in making such use of it and hope for the time to come to be more carefull of my wayes."

JERVIS, Joseph. Selling rum to the Indians.

JERVIS, Joseph of Middletown. Disowned 25/9/1717 for going to Barbadoes without acquainting friends and neglecting to pay his debts.

JONES, David. "Whereas it happened some years past that my servant or servants worked my neighbours horses or mares in my Plantation without my consent or the owners leaves so to do I am sorry for it ... and if any of the horses or mares come to any hurt or damage in my Plantation by my Servants Ile Endeavour to make them payment for the tresspass." 29/3/1704.

JONES, Henry. Acknowledged marrying by a Justice. 28/7/1730(?).

JONES, Mary, wife of David. Recommended from Philadelphia Monthly Meeting. Disowned 24/2/1732 for drinking to excess.

JONES, Sarah. Acknowledged marrying out. Marlborough, 31/4/1722. [Her mark.]

JONES, Thomas. - taking a small quantity of corne from Joseph Jervis in a fraudulent manner. 31/5/1704.

JONES, Thomas. Acknowledged that for which he had been disowned. 31/8/1720.

KENDAL, Thomas, lately arrived from old England from the Monthly Meeting of Settle in Yorkshire, signifying his clearness [to marry], recorded 26/6/1700.

KENDALL, Thomas. "... made offers of marriage to my late servant Rebeckah Swaffer without the consent of her mother and two soone after the death of my wife ... used some indecent & dishonest means to Entangle her affections and secure her to myself." 26/9/1724.

LEA, Isaac. Dancing at John Wades and at other times, having later recollected. Desiring a certificate to Darby 30/8/1721.

LEE, Isaac. Acknowledged fornication with his wife before marriage by a priest. 28/10/1724.

LOWE, Joshua. Frequenting a public house, dated 30/11/1720/1. It appears that he was bound with Joseph Richards, Senr., for his good behaviour in keeping a publick house and when he found that his frequenting the same gave offence to friends he withdrew his obligation which drew on him the revenge of that family.

MACDANIEL, Martha. Produced a certificate from Philadelphia Monthly Meeting, but owing to some reports it was not received since which she has been delivered of a bastard child. Disowned 31/5/1732.

MADDOK, Mordicha, produced a certificate from Newton Meeting in Cheshire in old England dated 7/9/1701, recorded 30/1/1702.

MALIN, Jacob of Providence. Acknowledged being overtaken in drink at a burial. 24/2/1717.

MARIS, George, Lydia WALLY, John BOWETER and his wife, John HOULSTON, John STIDMAN and his wife and family, John HOGKINS and his wife, Walter FAUSET and his wife, John HASTINGS and his wife, Joshua HASTINGS and his wife, Robert

BARBER, Robert PENNEL and his wife and family, produced their certificates to the satisfaction of the meeting, recorded 7/3/1688.

MARIS, George and wife Hannah. Acknowledged fornication before marriage. 28/12/1725/6.

MARIS, Jonathan, son of Richard of Springfield. "hath fallen into an uncommon course of drunkenness." and of late married contrary to discipline. Disowned 30/7/1728.

MARIS, Jonathan. Acknowledged drunkenness and marrying one of another profession - for which he had been disowned. 28/7/1730.

MASSEY, Thomas and wife Sarah. Acknowledged marriage, being first cousins, and fornication before marriage. 27/4/1726.

McCLUER, John, produced a certificate from Radnor Monthly Meeting dated 12/1/-- , recorded 25/3/1702.

MINSHALL, Jacob, Middletown. Disowned 25/2/1715. For endeavoring too much familiarity with the wife of one John Holston of Edmond. Jacob adknowledged the same on 28/2/1715.

MINSHALL, Jacob. Acknowledged that for which he had been disowned. 26/8/1720.

MOORE, Mordecai. Came to our Meeting by certificate from Merion Monthly Meeting. Disowned 28/2/1729 for absconding from his creditors.

MUSGROVE, Mary. Acknowledged marrying by a priest. 30/7/1728.

NEALL, Mary - took her husband John Neal being not a Friend, recorded 4/6/1695.

NORBURY, Rachel. Hath born a bastard child. Disowned 31/5/1732.

OGDEN, David. "about the Later end of Last summer I meeting with my neighbour John Worrall at the Smiths Shopp in Edgmond and having had some Diffence with him a little before about which I having taken some Disgust against him, Do own that I use such Expressions to and conserning him which I ought not to have done Cautioning those there present ... to Deale with him as if they were Dealling with a knave with other unjustifiable expressions both there and some time before at William Gregory's ... And as for those other words .. that he cheated most of his workmen - and that he would bring up his son to be as very a knave as himself &c.; though I do not remember I spoak those words yet if such words were spoaken by me." 21/11/1703/4.

OGDEN, Jonathan of Middletown, yeoman. Acknowledgment of keeping bad company and absconding to escape tha law (but since cleared). 29/2/1717.

234   *EARLY CHURCH RECORDS OF DELAWARE CO., PA*

OWEN, Hannah, wife of John. Disowned 30/1/1730 for leaving her
   husband and children and going away with John Walker, "a man of a
   loose and libertine spirit."
PARSONS, Susannah. Acknowledged marrying by a priest to one not a
   member. 26/4/1732.
PEARSON, John. Disowned 26/10/1726 for drinking to excess and
   fornication with his wife before marriage.
PEARSON, Sarah of Marple. Disowned 24/12/1717/8 for fornication.
PENROSE, Ann. Disowned 31/3/1731 for marriage by a priest to one
   Thomas Willis, not of the Society.
PENROSE, Robert, Jr. Acknowledged drinking "since I left the verge
   of your meeting."
PERKINS, Ann, wife of Caleb. Disowned 25/10/1721. "bearing a child
   less than sixteen weekes after the time of her marriage which lived
   several days."
PHIPPS, Joseph. Quarreling with Christopher Clayton. "I have had a
   great deal of trouble upon my mind for so doing." 1/9/1707.
PHIPPS, Joseph. Allowing his dau. Sarah's marriage to John Holston,
   not a member of the Society. 27/2/1713.
PIERSON, Enoch. Marrying out. Made acknloedgments to his parents
   and his wife's father, William Smith. William Smith so acknowledged
   22/11/1719/20.
POWELL, Mary. Acknowledged marrying out. 22/12/1730/1.
POWELL, Sarah, wife of Thomas Powell, Jr., took her husband
   contrary to advice, recorded 27/2/ .
PRITCHETT, Richard. "I being at the house of old Daniell Williamson
   in harvest time past Did ... Curse and Sweare and [use] other
   unsavorry Expressions ..."24/1/1715/6.
PUGH, Jean - "... have follishly & wickedly defiled my selfe before
   marriage ...", reported 30/4/1712.
PUGH, John. "Whereas John Pughe Taylor now of Chester Township
   Did some agoe request of this meeting that he might marry among
   us upon which he was permitted so to do: But to prevent mistakes
   about him we think it convenient to signifie ... we never owned him
   to be a member ..." Signed by order and in behalf of our Monthly
   Meeting at Middletown the 31/1/1712, (William Lewis, Clerk).
PUSEY, William. "I have suffered myself to have been two much
   overtaken in Drink as also in Letting my mind out after a young
   woman in Relatin to marriage that was not of our communion ..."
   24/5/1707.

RING, Elizabeth, wife of Nathaniel Ring and widow of Thomas
Coebourn. Elizabeth kept company with her deceased husbands first
cousin Thomas Coebourn, son of Thomas, with intentions to marry
too soon after her husband's death and put up a paper to publish
the same, but she has since married Nathaniel Ring although she
feared she was with child by Thomas. Disowned 29/9/1725.

RING, Nathaniel and wife Lydia. Acknowledged fornication before
marriage. 30/7/1728.

ROBINSON, William. "some years past brought a certificate from
Ballycaine Monthly Meeting in the kingdom of Ireland ... But hath
since clendestanly drawn out the affection of a Daughter of Thomas
Parke Contrary to her Parents minds and is married to her by the
Priest. ..." Disowned. 24/4/1728.

ROGERS, Nicholas and Mary. Fornication before marriage. 31/5/1721.

RUSSELL, Dinah. Acknowledged marriage by a priest. 26/8/1730.

SANDERS, Paul, formerly of Philadelphia, recorded 26/3/1701.

SKELTON, Margaret. Admitted some time ago. Disowned 24/2/1732
for marriage by a priest to Patrick Carty.

SIMCOCK, John. Acknowledged his former loose course of life in
frequenting taverns and keeping vain company. Abington,
16/10/1718.

SIMCOCK, Jacob of Ridley. Acknowledged mismanagement of his
property and what his father left him so as to be unable to pay all
his creditors, also occasionally taking a little too much drink.
27/3/1723.

SMITH, John, formerly belonging to the meeting of Pownallfee in
Cheshire in old England, recorded 26/11/1701/2.

SWARFFER, Rebecca. Acknowledged giving Thomas Kendal some
encouragement in courtship too soon after the death of his wife and
without her mother's knowledge and remaining in his service after
he courted her. 26/9/1724. Made her mark.

TANNEER, Martha, wife of Daniel. Disowned 28/7/1724 for marrying
out.

TATE, Katharine, dau. of Randall and Mary Malin of Upper
Providence. Disowned 26/4/1721 for marrying out to one not a
member and against the advice of her parents and Friends.

TAYLOR, Esther. Acknowledged marriage by a priest without her
parents' consent or knowledge. 30/5/1733.

TAYLER, Hannah. Has given occasion whereby the truth hath been
dishonored, 1701.

TAYLOR, John and Elizabeth. Acknowledged fornication before marriage. 29/8/1733.

TAYLOR, Mary, widow - keeping company with John Jones, recorded 29/4/1699.

TAYLOR, Mary. Made her mark. Fornication. 31/10/1722.

TAYLOR, Mary. Acknowledge fornication; disregarded the advice of her mother. 29/3/1723.

TAYLOR, Peter of Caln of Chester Co., allowed his son William to proceed in marriage. 25/6/1716.

TAYLOR, Samuel. Proceeding in marriage against discipline. 28/6/1721.

THOMAS, William. Taking off his hat at a funeral when prayer was made by a separatist (Keithite). 17/8/1707.

THOMPSON, Margery. Acknowledged marrying by a priest. 25/2/1726.

TREGO, James of Edgmont. Disowned 25/12/1716 for quarreling and fighting and marrying a woman not of the Society by a priest.

TREGO, James. Acknowledged that for which he had been disowned. 26/7/1726.

TREGO, William, son of Peter Trego, Sr., of Middletown. Disowned 26/6/1717 for marrying one not a member.

TODHUNTER, Margarett - Disorderly proceeding in marriage, recorded 25/11/1713.

TOMLINSON, Samuell, formerly belonging to Lancaster Meeting in old England, recorded 27/2/1702.

VERNON, Jacob, late of Providence. Acknowledged being overtaken by strong drink. 29/3/1727.

VERNON, John. "at the last Chester fair ... I was drawn into company and was overtaken with strong Drink ..." 24/5/1708.

VERNON, Jacob. "Whereas it happened at Richard Perkers with three more that was with me we Dranke together three pints of Strong Liquor Called by the name of tiff in time I smoaked some tobacco which with the Liquor I not being used to smoaking Did after make me sick and Light headed it being an offence against God." 12 mo. 1702.

VERNON, Thomas, son of Robert, dec. Disowned 27/12/1709/10 for "his vain and Evill Conversation as that of Drinking to Excess, loose Company keeping, cursing, swearing, lying."

VESTAL, Elizabeth. "being led aside to break the pure law of Christ and then being ashamed went to hide my transgression by going inadvisedly to marry in a way not owned by the people among whom I walked." 27/5/1717.

WALN, John. Drinking too much strong liquor. 23/12/1720.

WALN, John of Ridley. Disowned 31/10/1722 for drinking to excess and other disorders.

WELDON, Elizabeth, dau. of John. Disowned 24/2/1727 for marriage by a priest to Thomas South, who was not a member.

WELDON, William. At 22 years of age when he let out his mind to a young woman not of the Society, contrary to the advice of his parents and Friends. Having committed with her he afterwards married her by a Justice of the Peace; now very sorry. 31/6/1719.

WESTON, Mary, formerly Mary Scot. When she became a widow, she gave way to entertain a man into her company of another profession to marriage and did marry him, recorded 9/5/1717.

WHIPPO, Jane, wife of George. Acknowledged fornication before marriage. 27/12/1726/7.

WILLIAMS, Ellis. "in taking a wife I have not observed the method and discipline of friends ..."

WILLIAMS, Lewis and Ann. 29/6/1720. Acknowledged marrying out without parents' consent, whose parents have since forgiven them.

WILLIAMSON, Daniel, Jr. of Newtown. "... as to swear and curse at Chester Spring faire last past." And instead of acknowledgment "he bid us trouble him no more." Disowned 30/11/1715/6.

WILLIAMSON, Hannah - disorderly proceeding in marriage, reported 27/8/1712.

WILLIAMSON, Hannah, formerly Hannah Malin, dau. of Randall Mallin and his wife Mary - married one not of the Society, recorded 27/11/1717/8.

WILLIAMSON, Mary - has given her consent to the marriage of her dau. with one that is not of the Society, recorded 31/1/1712.

WILLIS, Cathrine, dau. of John Maris. Disowned 27/12/1726/7 for fornication with her husband before marriage by a priest.

WILLIS, Katherine. Acknowledged for her outgoings for which she was testified against. 26/9/1733.

WOODWARD, Margaret of Middletown. Acknowledged letting out her affections to Richard Dobbs, one of loose conversation, without her father's consent and afterwards committed fornication with him. 29/2/1728.

WORLEY, Francis. "in my too much hast and passion I did severly and unhansomly correct my late servant Edward Hardman." 28/1/1701.

WORLEY, Susannah, dau. of Francis Worley. Disowned 31/10/1722 for adultery with a married man which she admits.

WORRALL, John of Marple acknowledged "taking to me a wife which was not of the Same Profession." 26/2/1703.

WORRALL, John. 29/6/1720. "Inasmuch as through the wickedness and intollerable behaviour of some of my servant I have been Provoked to Give them such Chastisement as might be thought immoderate (though in my judgment, far short of what their vicious practices required); however, since such correction may seem severe and unbecoming one to Give who makes profession of a more mild and tender Prinsiple and since what I did to those bad servants Gave occasion of offence, I am very sorry for it and Desire you to pass it by hoping for the future with the Lords assistance to be more watchfull over my temper so that no Provocation shall prevail upon me to do what may grieve honest Friends..."

WORRILAW, Ann, dau. of John and Ann of Thornbury. Disowned 25/8/1724 for fornication; refused to name the father.

WORRILAW, Thomas and wife Susanna. Acknowledged fornication before marriage by a priest. 30/8/1727.

WORRILOW, John. Drinking and keeping company with such as drink. 29/1/1714.

WORROLAW, Jean - that Abraham Beaks did lie upon her bed part of one night, she being in bed which has brought great trouble and sorrow upon her, but he was not in bed with her, recorded 2/3/1696.

WORTHINGTON. Samuel and wife Sarah, dau. of Jacob Simcock, both of Springfield. Disowned 26/9/1716 for keeping company without parents' consent and fornication before marriage.

WORTHINGTON, Samuel and wife Sarah of Ridley. 2/10/1716. Acknowledgment.

WORTHINGTON, Samuel. Acknowledged on account of his marriage &c. with Sarah Simcock. 25/9/1717.

WORTHINGTON, Sarah - keeping company without leave of her parents and suffering herself to be shamefully defiled by Samuell Worthington before they were married, recorded 28/8/1717.

ST. PAUL'S PROTESTANT EPISCOPAL CHURCH: CHESTER

MEMBERS ROSTER: 1704-1705

Joseph Abbott, Samuel Adams and wife Elizabeth (Allen), Richard Adams, William Adams and his wife Sarah (Hall), Francis Allen and wife, Nathan Baker and wife Sarah (Collett), Peter Bainton and wife Ann (Keen-Sandelands), Joseph Baldwin and wife Elizabeth (Meales), Thomas Baldwin and wife Mary (Beel), Thomas Barnswell, John Bristow, Charles Brook, Thomas Butterfield and wife Mary, Samuel Byshop and wife, the widow Calvert, Isaac Calvert, Thomas Calvert, John Charles, James Clark and wife, Joseph Cohen, Samuel Colburn and wife, Joseph Collins and wife Mary (Pony), Jeremiah Collett and wife Ann, John Collett, James Cook and wife Catherine, James Cooper and wife Mary (Ludwedge), Gabriel Cox and wife, Robert Crafts and wife Helen (Vannemmon), Philip Davis and wife, James David and wife Martha (Jones), John Davis and wife Mary (Jones), Edward Danger and wife, Swan Derrickson and wife, Evan Edwards and wife, George Evans and wife, David Evans and wife, George Freeman and wife Elinor (Sandelands-Trent), Gabriel Friend and wife, Thomas Gale and wife Elizabeth (Forsithe), Thomas Hall and wife, William Hanby and wife, John Hannum and wife Margery, Tobias Henrichs and wife Jane, Matthias Holman and wife, Alexander Hunter and wife, Benjamin Ingram and wife, Thomas Jenkins and wife, Richard Jenkings and wife, Edward Jennings, Edward Johningsen, Richard Kenterdine, John Langford and wife Joanna (Andree), James Lhwyd and wife Ruth (Host), Peter Longacre and wife Barbara (Friend), James L. Lowry and wife, William Lutton and wife Mary (Jeffreys), David Mandiah, John Marks, Walter Martin and wife Mary (Howell, Sr.), Walter Martin and wife Barbara (Howell), Peter Manesdore and wife, James Maurice and wife Ann (Taylor), John Maxfield, David Meredith and wife Sarah (Rush), James Mills and wife Mary (Cornish), Joseph Mills and wife, Robert Moulder and wife, Rev. Henry Nicols and wife Elizabeth (Gatchell), John Niel and wife, Joseph Noel and wife, Thomas Pedrick and wife Elizabeth (Moulders), Peter Petersen and wife, William Pickels and wife, Henry Pierce and wife, Thomas Powell and wife, John Powell and wife Mary (Howell, Jr.), David Roberts and wife Susanna (Tudor), James Sandelands, Thomas Smith and wife, John Smith and wife, John Somers, John Test, Jr., and wife, Edward Thomas and wife, William Tucker and wife Annie (Brown), John Vannemmon and wife, John Wade and wife, Robert

Walker and wife Lydia, Thomas Waters and wife Margaret (Davis),
Thomas Weston and Wife Rebecca (Sandelands), William Willis and
wife, Thomas Withers and wife Elizabeth, Joseph Worrell and wife,
Jasper Yeates and wife Catherine (Sandelands-Creker).

The following were joined in membership by 1715: John Bright
and wife, Thomas Bright and wife, William Bover and wife Margaret
(Rodes), Thomas Broom and wife Elizabeth (Hannum), Walter Cocks,
James D. Davis and wife, Philip Davis and wife, Thomas Davis and
wife, Thomas Dawson and wife, Graham Durnall, John Durnall,
Thomas Durnall, Eroch Erochson and wife, William Fortescue and wife,
George Hannum, Edward Hughes and wife, Morgan Hughes and wife,
Charles Jones, Robert Jones and wife Margaret (Carel), Hugh Jones
and wife Jane (Pugh), Thomas Linvel and wife Dinah (Richardson),
George Leonard and wife, Richard Mersden and wife Ann (Simons),
Thomas Powell and wife Sarah (Heyse), George Robertson and wife
Sarah (Hall), John Spragg and wife, Magnes Tate and wife Honor
(Williams), John Tyler and wife, Thomas Weston and wife Rebecca
(Bainton), Richard Willatson and wife Catharine (Cook).

BIRTHS, DEATHS AND BAPTISMS

William Abbott, son of Joseph, bapt. 23 Feb 1706.
David Admes, d. 17 Aug 1795, age 33.
Mary Allen, dau. of Francis, bapt. 1707, d. 1707.
Eliza Anderson, 12 Oct 1792, age 2.
Rebecca Ashton, dau. of Richard, babt. 11 Nov 1731.
Rev. Richard Backhouse, rector of St. Paul's from 1728 to 1749, d. 29
    Nov 1749, and his wife Ann. Children: Mary, d. 8 Jul 1731; Mary
    (2nd), bapt. 21 Aug 1732; Isabel, b. 7 Feb 1734, bapt. 15 Feb 1734;
    Richard, b. 16 Sep 1741, bapt. 24 Sep 1741; Allen, d. 6 Aug 1756.
Thomas Baldwin, d. 1731, buried 5 Jul 1731, grave unmarked. Children
    bapt. 6 May 1705: Joseph, Antony, Mary, Martha, Elizabeth.
Jean Barton, dau. of Capt. Barton, bapt. 7 May 1755.
Mary Barton, dau. of Thomas and Sarah, d. 29 Sep 1746.
Sarah Barton, wife of Thomas, d. 3 Oct 1746.
Rebecca Baynton, dau. of Peter and Ann (Sandelands) Baynton, bapt.
    18 Jun 1704.
Ann (Sandelands) Baynton, widow of James Sandelands and wife of
    Peter Baynton, d. 1704, buried 5 Oct 1704, grave unmarked.

Samuel S. Bickerton, son of Jesse and Elizabeth, bapt. 30 Jun 1786.

Benjamin Blackstone, son of Benjamin, Sr., bapt. 30 Aug 1731.

John Bright, son of James, bapt. 14 May 1704.

James Bright, son of Thomas, bapt. 2 Jun 1706.

Charles Brooks. Upon his stone: "Here lyeth the body of Charles Brooks, who died____. And also Frances Brooks, who died 9 Aug 1704, age 56."

Frances Brooks. On a thin slab was scratched the following: "For the memory of Francis Brooks, who died August the 19th, 1704, aged 56." And the following inscription:

> "In barbarian bondage
> and cruel tyranny
> For ten years together
> I served in Slavery.
> After this Mercy brought me
> To my country fair
> And last I drowned was
> In River Delaware."

Thomas Broom. Children: John, bapt. 14 Jun 1713; Mary, bapt. 12 Sep 1714.

Rebekkah Broom, dau. of Samuel and Lydia, bapt. 29 May 1732.

Elizabeth Brown, servant of Jeremiah Collett, buried 1 Nov 1704.

George T. and Matilda Buck. Children: Mabel, bapt. 10 Sep 1704, Isabel, bapt. 10 Sep 1704.

Mary Butterfield, adult, bapt. 14 May 1704.

Samuel B. Byshop. Children: Joseph, bapt. 10 Sep 1704; Rachel, bapt. 10 Sep 1704; Hannah, bapt. 16 Dec 1704; Sarah, bapt. 16 Dec 1704.

John Charles, buried 5 Mar 1708 at St. Paul's.

Thomas Calvert, adult, bapt. 9 Dec 1705.

John Caldwell. Children: John, bapt. 25 Dec 1754; Elizabeth, bapt. 7 Jul 1751.

Elizabeth Campbell, dau. of Peter, bapt. 14 Jun 1713.

Catherine Clark, dau. of James, bapt. 4 Mar 1705.

William Clark, son of James, bapt. 4 Mar 1705.

Mary Cock, dau. of Walter, bapt. 14 Jun 1713.

Lavinia Coeburn, widow, bapt. 14 Jun 1713.

Hannah Colburn, dau. of Samuel, bapt. 28 Dec 1713.

John Cole, dau. of Stephen and Martha, bapt. 3 Nov 1728.

Elizabeth Cole, dau. of Stephen and Martha, bapt. 27 Sep 1730, d. 19 Jun 1731, age 10 months, buried 27 Jun 1731.

Elizabeth Cole, d. 22 Sep 1732, age 70, buried 24 Sep 1732 at St. Paul's.

James Cole, son of Stephen and Martha, bapt. 30 Apr 1732.

Martha Cole, former widow of Stephen Cole, dec., but late the wife of Albert Russell, d. 15 Nov 1761.

Stephen Cole, d. 4 Jan 1744, age 44.

Anne Collett, wife of Jeremiah Collett, d. 15 Oct 1704, buried 11 Jul 1705. *[Some of the graves were removed from Old Saint Paul's grave yard and reburied in other cemeteries as they became available. It is likely that 11 Jul 1705 was the reburial date.]*

Jeremiah Collett, Sr., buried 10 Jul 1706.

John Collett, son of Jeremiah and Anne, buried 5 Jul 1705.

Charles and Margaret Connor. Children: Margaret, b. 19 Feb 1729, bapt. 29 Feb 1729; Catherine, b. 1 Jan 1731, bapt. 17 Mar 1731; Sarah, b. 24 Jan 1733, bapt. 7 Apr 1734; Ann, b. 7 Aug 1735, bapt. 10 Aug 1735; Mary, b. 8 Jun 1738, bapt. 12 Nov 1738, d. 1736, age 6 years 4 months, buried 26 Jun 1736; Margaret (2nd), lived 20 days, buried 25 May 1737; Isabel, b. 4 Feb 1740, bapt. 20 Feb 1740; Charles, b. 13 Mar 1742, bapt. 24 Apr 1743.

Ephraim Cox, son of Gabriel, bapt. 20 Jun 1705.

John Coyle, son of Charles and Martha, bapt. 12 Jan 1732.

Jacob R. Crosby, d. 9 Jul 1798, age 1 year.

Jonas Culin, son of George, bapt. 9 Nov 1732.

Isaac and Rachel Culin. Children: Margaret, b. 5 May 1780; Mary, b. 9 Jun 1783; Daniel, b. 7 Aug 1785; Isaac, b. 30 Jan 1788; Rachel, b. 18 Nov 1790.

Edward Danger. Children: Prudence, bapt. 25 Jan 1705; Mary bapt. 9 May 1708; Margaret, bapt. 16 Apr 1714.

Thomas David, son of Philip, bapt. 11 Sep 1707.

Mary Davis, dau. of James D., bapt. 5 Nov 1704.

James Davis, son of James, bapt. 15 Sep 1706.

Elizabeth Davis, dau. of Thomas, bapt. 15 Mar 1705.

Sarah Davis, dau. of Philip, bapt. 1 May 1706.

Hugh Davis, son of Philip, bapt. 13 Jun 1706.

Christian Davis, son of John, bapt. 3 Jun 1708.

David Dawson, son of Thomas, bapt. 6 Sep 1713.

John C. Dean, son of Henry and Mary, bapt. 24 Jul 1747.

John Derrickson, son of Swan, bapt. 10 Aug 1705, d. 1707, buried 14 Aug 1707.

Mary Derrickson, dau. of Swan, bapt. 8 Sep 1706.

Margaret Dicks, wife of Abraham, d. 24 Nov 1796, age 39.

Richard Entrakin, d. May 1729, age 40. Flat stone about 9 feet northeast of Mather monument.

John Durnald, bapt. 25 Apr 1714.

Thomas Durnald, bapt. 25 Apr 1714.

Graham Durnald, bapt. 25 Apr 1714.

Evan Edwards. Children: Ann, bapt. 6 Jul 1704; James, bapt. 12 May 1706; Prudence, bapt. 12 May 1706.

Mary Ellwell, buried 16 Mar 1708 at St. Paul's.

Elizabeth Engle, wife of John and dau. of John and Phoebe Harper, d. 29 Aug 1784, age 19.

John Erochson, son of Eroch, bapt. 2 Mar 1707.

George Evans, son of George, bapt. 9 Oct 1707.

Elizabeth Evans, dau. of George, bapt. 9 Oct 1707.

David Evans, son of David, bapt. 9 Oct 1707.

John Fergeson, d. 11 Mar 1792, age 61.

Susanna Fortesque, dau. of William, bapt. 10 Apr 1709.

Andrew Frazzar, son of Thomas and Jane, b. 17 Mar 1790, bapt. 11 Apr 1791.

David French, son of Robert, d. Aug 1742.

Robert French, d. 7 Sep 1704. Interred under a three by six foot, syenite slab.

James Friend, son of Gabriel, bapt. 20 Aug 1713.

John Garrett, buried 1707 at St. Matthew's.

Edward Green, son of Thomas G., bapt. 20 Nov 1704.

Henry Green, son of Thomas G., bapt. 14 Nov 1705.

Richard Griffey, bapt. 28 Dec 1713.

John Hanby, son of William, bapt. 5 Aug 1705, d. 16 May 1769.

Sen. James Ham, d. 29 Nov 1809, age 86.

Joyce Ham, wife of Sen. James Ham, d. 29 May 1807, age 70.

John Hannum. Children: Sarah, bapt. 23 Apr 1704; Ann, bapt. 1 Jul 1705; George, buried 15 Feb 1707; George (2nd), bapt. 30 May 1708; John, buried 19 Dec 1707; John (2nd), bapt. 27 Apr 1712.

Tobias Henricks. Children: Henry, bapt. 14 May 1704; Helsha, bapt. 28 Oct 1705; Henry, bapt. 14 Mar 1708.

Yesh Holman, son of Matthias, bapt. 5 Oct 1706.

Mary Howell, adult, bapt. 23 Apr 1704.

Barbara Howell, adult, bapt. 23 Apr 1704.

Morgan Hugh, son of Edward, bapt. 15 Mar 1705.

Elizabeth Hugh, dau. of Morgan, bapt. 27 Sep 1706.

Alexander Hunter. Children: Rachel, bapt. 15 Jun 1704; Elisabeth, bapt. 31 Aug 1706; Sarah, bapt. 25 Apr 1714.

Mary Ingram, dau. of Benjamin J., bapt. 2 Jan 1705.

Paul Jackson, M.D., d. 1767, age 36 years. "Here lieth Paul Jackson, A.M. He was the first who received a Degree in the Colege of Philadelphia. A man of virtue, worth and knowledge."

Sarah Jenking, dau. of Thomas J., bapt. 14 Dec 1704.

Richard Jenkings, son of Richard, bapt. 14 Aug 1707.

Charles John, d. 1707, grave unmarked.

Rebecca Jones, dau. of Charles, bapt. 20 Aug 1704.

Johanna Jones, dau. of Charles, bapt. 1 Mar 1705.

Elizabeth Jones, dau. of Thomas, bapt. 27 Sep 1705.

Robert Jones. Children: Prudence, bapt. 31 Mar 1706; Robert, bapt. 22 Feb 1708; Margaret, 28 Sep 1712.

Mrs. Kindar, d. 1718, grave unmarked.

Thomas Linwall, adult, bapt. 12 May 1766.

Sarah Longacre, wife of Peter Longacre and dau. of James and Mary Barton, d. 19 Jun 1808, age 50. Inscribed upon the stone:

> "Thou are gone before us
> And thy sainted soul has flown
> Where tears are wiped from every eye
> And sorrow is unknown."

George Lownes, d. 26 Oct 1793, age 83.

Elizabeth Lownes, wife of George, d. 10 Mar 1788, age 74.

John Marks, d. 1708, buried 1 May 1708 at St. Paul's, grave unmarked.

Margaret Mather, wife of James, d. 1 Feb 1777, age 68.

James Mather, d. 11 Jan 1780, age 77. Inscribed upon the stone:

> "Though the worm my antient body turns to dust
> Yet I hope my soul in Heaven will live among the
> just."

Betsey McArthur, dau. of Duncan and Peggy, b. Apr 1796, bapt. 6 Mar 1796.

James McMurray, son of John and Mary, b. Apr 1795, bapt. 6 Mar 1796.

Jane Maguire, dau. of Thomas, bapt. 24 Aug 1732.

Peter M. Manesdore, bapt. 27 Dec 1704.

Eleanor Crosby Martin, wife of Dr. William Martin, dau. of John and
Ann Crosby of Ridley, b. 24 Apr 1777, d. 16 Jan 1837.

Walter Martin. Adult children: Walter, bapt. 6 May 1705; John, bapt. 6
May 1705; Mary, bapt. 6 May 1705; Ann, bapt. 6 May 1705;
Elizabeth, bapt. 6 May 1705; Sarah, bapt. 6 May 1705.

William Martin, MD, son of John and Mary Martin, b. 2 Sep 1765 in
Philadelphia, d. 28 Sep 1798 in Chester, buried 28 Sep 1798 at age
33. Died of yellow fever taken while attending the infected crew of a
British vessel lying off Chester.

William Martin, Esq., son of William and Eleanor, b. 17 Sep 1797

James and Margaret Mather. Children: John, b. 29 Aug 1728, bapt. 7
Sep 1728; Margaret, b. 30 July 1731, bapt. 6 Aug 1731; James, b. 4
Dec 1732, bapt. 1 Jan 1733; Rebecca, b. 6 Apr 1737, bapt. 11 Apr
1737; James, b. 5 Apr 1739, bapt. 11 Apr 1739; Rebecca, b. 17 Feb
1740, bapt. 27 Feb 1740; Mary, b. 11 Jun 1742, bapt. 19 Jun 1742.

Ruth Mather, dau. of John, bapt. 21 Apr 1732.

Daniel Meridith, son of Daniel, bapt. 13 Dec 1705.

Mary Mills, wife of James, d. 1704, buried 24 Aug 1704 at St. Paul's,
grave unmarked.

James Mills, son of James, bapt. 24 Aug 1704, d. 1704, buried 2 Sep
1704 at St. Paul's, grave unmarked.

James Mills, d. 1707, buried at St. Paul's, grave unmarked.

Joseph Mills, son of James, buried 20 Apr 1707 at St. Paul's.

Rachell Moore, dau. of James and Rachel, b. Feb 1796, bapt. 6 Mar
1796.

Andrew Moore, dau. of Andrew and Ann, b. 18 Aug 1790, bapt. 9 Apr
1791.

John Morton, b. A.D. 1724, d. April 1777. The monument marking his
grave is a plain shaft of marble nine feet high, its four sides facing
the cardinal points of the compass and without ornament save the
Coat of Arms of the State of Pennsylvania encircled by a wreath of
laurel. Inscribed upon the west side: "Dedicated to the Memory of
John Morton, a member of the First American Congress from the
State of Pennsylvania, assembled in New York in 1765, and of the
next Congress, assembled in Philadelphia in 1774." Upon the south
side: "In 1775 while Speaker of the Assembly of Pennsylvania, John
Morton was elected a member of Congress and in the ever
memorable Session of July, 1776, he attended that august body for
the last time, enshrining his name in the grateful remembrance of
the American People by signing the Declaration of Independence."
Upon the east side: "In voting by States upon the question of the

Independence of the American Colonies, there was a tie until the vote of Pennsylvania was given: two members of which voted in the affirmative and two in the negative. The tie continued until the vote of the last member, John Morton, decided the promulgation of the glorious Diploma of American Freedom." Upon the north side: "John Morton, being censured by some of his friends for his boldness in giving his casting vote for the Declaration of Independence, his prophetic spirit dictated from his death bed the following message to them. 'Tell them they will live to see the hour when they shall acknowledge it to have been the most glorious service I ever rendered to my country'"

Ann Moulder, dau. of Robert, dec'd, and Jane, bapt. 27 Dec 1744.

John Neale, son of Gabriel, bapt. 10 Sept 1732.

Robert Nelson, d. 1797, age 57.

Mary Nichols, dau. of Rev. Henry, bapt. 22 Feb 1708, buried 1 Mar 1708.

Rachel Niel, dau. of John, bapt. 2 Jun 1705.

Mary Noel, dau. of Joseph M., bapt. 19 Nov 1704.

Lydia Nowel, dau. of Joseph M., bapt. 13 Apr 1712.

Lawrence S. Parcum, d. 1705, grave unmarked.

Edward Pavier. Children: Bridget, bapt. 24 Nov 1705; Edward, bapt. 24 Nov 1705; Mary, bapt. 24 Nov 1705; Elizabeth, bapt. 24 Nov 1705.

Thomas Pedrick, adult, bapt. 24 Oct 1704.

Mary Pedrick, dau. of Thomas, bapt. 2 Feb 1706.

Gabriel Peterson, son of Peter, b. 3 Dec 1704.

William Pickels, son of William P., bapt. 3 Dec 1704, d. 1705, buried 24 May 1706 at St. Paul's.

Henry Pierce. Children: Catherine, bapt. 14 Jun 1704; Henry, bapt. 14 Jun 1704; Sarah, bapt. 14 Jun 1704; James, bapt. 7 Mar 1707; Elizabeth, bapt. 27 Nov 1713.

Joseph Powell, son of Joseph, bapt. 9 Sep 1705.

Ann Powell, dau. of Thomas, Jr., bapt. 28 Dec 1713.

Polly Price, wife of William, d. 27 May 1802, age 82 years, 6 months.

Rebecca Price, dau. of James, bapt. 28 Mar 1706.

John Rawtom, son of Charles R., bapt. 27 Dec 1704.

Elizabeth Reed, adult, bapt. 28 Dec 1714.

John Rice, d. 10 Jul 1726, age 33. On a second stone in line with the other about ten feet away: "John Rice, d. 10 Mar 1726, age 33."

Joseph Richards. Children: Ruth, bapt. 22 Apr 1705; Elizabeth, bapt. 22 Sep 1705; Mary, buried 20 Sep 1705; Unnamed, bapt. 9 Jun 1706; Dinah, bapt. 9 Jun 1706; Edward, bapt. 9 Jun 1706.

Edward Richards, Esq., d. 13 Apr 1794, age 56.

Jacob Richards, son of Edward, bapt. 14 Nov 1731.

Susannah Richards, wife of Jacob, d. 10 Aug 1791, age 58.

Catherine Ridgeway, d. 1734, buried at St. Paul's, grave unmarked.

Margaret Rosse, dau. of George, bapt. 7 Oct 1712.

Sarah Rush, adult, bapt. 20 Dec 1704.

Isaac Sandelands, son of John, bapt. 14 Nov 1731.

James Sandelands, merchant, d. 12 April 1692 at age 56, buried under Old St. Paul's.

James Sandelands, Jr., son of James, d. 1707, buried 26 Dec 1707 at St. Paul's, age 29. Believed buried next to his father under an unmarked stone below the church.

Mary Shaw, wife of Samuel, d. 19 Jan 1768, age 40.

Samuel Shaw, b. 1707 in Lincolnshire, England, d. 20 Sep 1783 near Chester.

Unnamed Shields, child of Arthur and Mary, bapt. 29 Aug 1772.

Ann Smith, dau. of John, bapt. 12 Sep 1712.

Anne Smith, d. 1704, buried 13 Jul 1704.

Betsey Smith, dau. of Robert and Jane, b. Mar 1795, bapt. 6 Mar 1796.

John Smith, son of Thomas, bapt. 29 May 1712.

Luke Smith, d. 21 Oct 1789, age 19.

Thomas Smith, son of Thomas, bapt. 29 Mar 1712.

William Smith, d. 30 Mar 1788, age 46.

John Sommers, d. 1708.

Elizabeth Spragg, dau. of John, bapt. 25 Apr 1714.

Sarah Spear, d. 6 Mar 1770, age 69.

Ann Taylor, d. 1731.

John Test, Jr. Children: John, bapt. 10 Nov 1706; Thomas, bapt. 16 Nov 1706; Ann, bapt. 26 Apr 1709.

John Test, son of John Test, Jr., d. 17 May 1727, age 21.

Ann Thomas, dau. of Edward, bapt. 1 Sep 1706.

David Thomas, son of Edward, bapt. 19 Feb 1707.

William Trehearne, d. 3 Oct 1739.

William Tyler, son of John, bapt. 12 Sep 1714.

Deborah Tyler, son of John, bapt. 24 Sep 1714.

Mary E. Upman, dau. of Mary J., b. May 1795, bapt. 6 Mar 1796.

Mary Van Nemmon, dau. of John, bapt. 1705.

Abigail Vernon, dau. of Edward and Mary, d. 15 Dec 1781, age 5 weeks.

Edward Test Vernon, son of Edward and Mary, d. 9 Jul 1785, age 1 day.

James Mather Vernon, son of Edward and Mary, d. 24 Apr 1777, age
about 3 years.
Peter Mather Vernon, son of Edward and Mary, d. 15 Dec 1781, age 2
months.
Rebecca Vernon, dau. of Edward and Mary, d. 15 Dec 1784, age 1 year.
Mary Vernon, wife of Edward Vernon, Esq., d. 16 Oct 1785, age 35.
John Wade. Children: Prudence, bapt. 1 Jul 1705; Robert, bapt. 1 Feb
1708; Rebecca, bapt. 12 Jun 1713.
Joseph Wade, d. 28 Mar 1786, age 34.
Robert Wade, son of Joseph, d. 22 Sep 1781, age 4.
Lydia Walker, dau. of Robert and Lydia, bapt. 12 Jul 1704.
Sarah Waters, dau. of Thomas, bapt. 3 Jun 1708.
Thomas Weaver, d. 20 Aug 1785, age 24.
David Synd Withey, grandson of John, d. 18 Sep 1777, age 11 months.
John Withey, d. 8 Oct 1760, age 58.
Elizabeth Willis, dau. of William, bapt. 14 Dec 1704.
Henry Willis, dau. of William, bapt. 15 Mar 1705.
Elizabeth Withers, wife of Thomas, bapt. 25 Jun 1704, d. 1704, buried
27 Jan 1705 at St. Paul's, unmarked grave.
Thomas and Elizabeth Withers. Children: Jeremiah, bapt. 9 Sep 1705;
Mary, bapt. 9 Sep 1705; Jane, bapt. 9 Sep 1705.
Joseph Worrell, son of Joseph, bapt. 7 May 1704.
John Yeates, son of Jasper and Catherine, bapt. 4 Mar 1705.
Jasper Yeates, son of Jasper and Catherine, bapt. 6 May 1709. Written
in the register beside the record: "Susceptore Carols Gookin,
proefecto"--*Trans.* "Charles Gookin, Lt. Governor, Sponsor."
Jasper Yeates. Negro slaves: Robert and Joseph, bapt. 20 Apr 1712,
Easter.

MARRIAGES

William Adams and Sarah Hall m. 20 Nov 1704.
Samuel Addams and Elizabeth Allen m. 16 May 1704.
Henry Anderson and Sarah Evans m. 24 Mar 1731.
Michael Atkinson and Susannah Weston m. 31 Aug 1729.
Nathan Baker and Sarah Collet m. 15 May 1705.
Joseph Baldwin and Elizabeth Meales m. 6 Feb 1713.
Thomas Baldwin and Mary Beel m. 20 Mar 1714.
Mordecai Bane and Naomi Medley m. 26 Dec 1705.
Thomas Barton and Sarah Mather m. 8 Oct 1730.

Samuel Bear and Catherine Rowland m. 18 May 1729.

John Best and Martha Jones m. 26 Oct 1730.

Benjamin Bourn and Katharine Parker m. 22 Jul 1730.

William Bover and Margaret Rodes m. 7 Nov 1711.

James Bradley and Elizabeth Till m. 15 Jun 1730.

Thomas Broom and Elizabeth Hannum m. 4 Dec 1711.

Soloman Chafferin and Ann Jeffreys m. 29 Sep 1730.

Joseph Collins and Mary Bony m. 7 Dec 1704.

James Cooper and Mary Ludwedge m. 8 Nov 1705.

Andrew Cox and Mary Bishop m. 5 Jan 1730.

Jonathan Cox and Susannah _____ m. 12 Apr 1743.

Robert Crafts and Helsha Vanneman m. 7 Jun 1706.

Evan Davie and Rachel Messer m. 23 Dec 1728.

James Davis and Martha Jones m. 4 Aug 1704.

John Davis and Mary Jones m. 13 Mar 1707.

William Evans and Ann Davis m. 16 Sep 1729.

William Fell and Ann Thompson m. 28 Mar 1731.

Joseph Fetlow and Bridget Long m. 1729.

Thomas Gale and Elizabeth Forsithe m. 24 Sep 1706.

Thomas Garratt and Katherine Lancast m. 21 Apr 1721.

Paul Garren and Mary Hopman m. 20 Apr 1731.

Edward Gofft and Mary Pontou m. 26 Dec 1730.

William Graham and Jennet Morgan m. 22 Nov 1730.

William Hall and Hannah Richardson m. 23 Apr 1731.

George Hart and Elizabeth Lyon m. 17 Feb 1731.

William Hawlow and Mary Davis m. 13 Jun 1731.

Peter Hendrickson and Anna Robinson m. 2 Dec 1729.

Andrew Heydon and Catharine Round m. 21 Dec 1730.

Jacobus Hine and Margaret Morton m. 25 Mar 1731.

Richard Huet and Ann Howell m. 1 Jul 1729.

Richard Iddings and Margaret Phillips m. 18 Apr 1705.

John Ivans and Margaret _____ m. 5 Apr 1743.

Robert Jackson and Margaret Culbertson m. 7 Mar 1730.

Henry Johnson and Dianah Stedham m. 4 May 1731.

Charles Jones and Sarah Peterson m. 24 Apr 1712.

David Jones and Jane Thomas m. 3 Feb 1731.

Hugh Jones and Jane Pugh m. 12 Dec 1706.

Robert Jones and Margaret Carel m. 5 Jun 1705.

George Kowlin [Culin] and Catharine Howman m. 10 Apr 1731.

John Lack and Elizabeth Martin m. 5 May 1730.

James Lhwyd and Ruth Host m. 13 Nov 1706.

Thomas Linvel and Dinah Richards m. 9 Feb 1714.
Thomas Lloyd and Ann Thomas m. 22 Jan 1731.
William Lloyd and Mary _____ m. 1 Dec 1707.
Peter Loaden and Elizabeth Pavery m. 30 May 1731.
Abraham Long and Ann Rumsey m. 27 Mar 1731.
Peter Longacre and Barbara Friend m. 6 Nov 1705.
William Lutton and Mary Jeffrys [Jeffreys] m. 29 May 1705.
John MacDaniel and Mary Robinson m. 10 May 1712.
Richard Mackgee [McGee] and Ann Sandelands m. 13 May 1731.
Patrick MacManes and Hannah Hall m. 5 Jan 1730.
Benjamin Manifold and Annabal [Annabel] Danger m. 10 Nov 1730.
Walter Martin and Mary Howell, Sr., m. 8 Jun 1704.
Walter Martin and Barbara Howell m. 6 Jun 1704.
John Mather and Mary Hoskyns [Hoskins], dau. of Joseph, member of
    Chester Monthly Meeting, Society of Friends, m. 27 Feb 1731.
James Maurice and Ann Taylor m. 2 Jan 1705.
David Meredith and Sarah Rush m. 3 Jan 1705.
Richard Mersden and Ann Simons m. 13 Dec 1713.
Richard Miller and Elizabeth Willson m. 6 Apr 1731.
James Mills and Mary Cornish m. 25 Mar 1704.
Shelsto Mooney and Margaret Cransbury m. 28 Apr 1731.
John Moore and Prudence Brogden m. 17 Jan 1731.
Edward Nicholas and Margaret Miller m. 1 May 1731.
Rev. Henry Nicols and Elizabeth Gatchell m. 17 Apr 1707.
John Norry and Katharine Willson m. 28 May 1731.
William Oliver and Mary Johnson m. 5 Nov 1730.
Christ Ottey and Elizabeth Godfrey m. 5 May 1729.
Philip Ottey and Sarah Baker m. 8 May 1730.
Samuel Owen and Sarah Hues m. 18 Jun 1730.
John Patterson and Margrat Gill m. 3 Apr 1729.
Thomas Pedrick and Elizabeth Moulder m. 6 Dec 1704.
Henry Pierce and Sarah Hunter m. 24 Apr 1729.
Joseph Powell and Mary Powell, Jr., m. 8 Jun 1704.
Thomas Powell and Sarah Heyse m. 3 Feb 1713.
John Rawson and Ann Boon m. 15 Jan 1729.
Richard Richardson and Ann Stocking m. 28 Feb 1731.
William Richardson and Mary Barker m. 25 Sep 1706.
David Roberts and Susanna Tudor m. 3 Nov 1707.
George Robertson and Sarah Hall m. 10 May 1708.
Allen Robinett and Lydia Derrick m. 4 Feb 1729/30.
Joseph Robinet and Barbara Culin m. 9 Mar 1731.

Edward Russell and Dinah Coeburn m. 8 Jun 1730.
John Smith and Margaret Pue m. 25 Mar 1731.
James Summers and Mary Davis m. 24 Nov 1729.
Aaron Thompson and Jane Broomell m. 25 Aug 1729.
Nathaniel Tucker and Annie Brown m. 15 Jan 1706.
Isaac Turniecliff and Ann Neville m. 25 Feb 1731.
John Vanculand and Sarah Houldston m. 24 Aug 1730.
John Wallace and Ellen France m. 30 May 1731.
Thomas Waters and Margaret Davis m. 13 Feb 1707.
James Webb and Martha Fleming m. 5 Apr 1731.
Thomas Weston and Rebecca Bainton m. 25 Nov 1713.
Thomas Wilkinson and Margrat Lloyd m. 17 Nov 1729.
Richard Willatson and Catherine Cook m. 12 Aug 1712.
Thomas Wills and Ann Penrose m. 22 Mar 1731.
John Wood and Margaret Barnett m. 4 Nov 1730.
William Wright and Hannah Ghest m. 15 Mar 1730.
John Wyburn and Mary Price m. 26 Sep 1730.
Edward Young and Esther Thompson m. 25 Aug 1729.
John Young and Mary Barber m. 19 Oct 1730.

"The following are taken from an old scrap found among other church
papers and is in the handwriting of the Rev. Richard Backhouse. The
paper upon which the entries are made was evidently a page torn
from the record book. At the top is written: ` Memorandum. That
I'm to go to Derby to marrie James Meredith & Mary Nicholas & to
take along with me a Lycence or Two in case need require for
anybody else.'"

John Taylor and Mary Barefoot m. 11 Jul 1733.
Robert Skeen and Esther Gregory m. No date.
Titus Dinnius of Lancaster Co. and Margret Cullem [Culin] m. 1 May
1733.
John Smith and Eve Rockafelt m. No date.
Clift Hemmings and Mary Cornwell m. 3 Jun 1733.

On back of page:

John Scott and Mary Hance m. 1 Apr 1733.
Rich. Colse of Lancaster Co. and Jane Burbrom m. No date.
James Meredith and Mary Nicholas m. 2 Feb 1732.
John Aaron and Sarah Heeser m. No date.

Roger Coleburn and Eleanor Higgins m. 22 Feb 1732.
John Fitshue and Mary Jones m. 27 May 1733.

On another scrap in the same handwriting:

Patrick Holly and Rachel Weimas m. 10 Feb 1731.
Nicholas Bozer and Mary Yeates m. No date.
Lewis Lloyd of Philadelphia Co. and Jane Francis of Philadelphia Co.
    m. 14 Feb 1731.
(Name erased) and Margret Brennam m. No date.
Grey Cook and Sarah Barnes m. 20 Feb 1731.
Patrick Carter and Margret Skelton m. 28 Feb 1731.
Jeremiah Garraway of New Castle Co. and Mary Bell m. 25 ___ 1731.
John Ferral and Margret Horton m. 28 May 1732.
Charles Rennells [Reynolds] and Elizabeth Burns m. 11 Jun 1732.
George Coleburn and Eleanor Higgins m. No date.
Patrick Boyd and Rachel Grimson m. 25 Jul 1732.

Memoranda on Register of Burials

"Memor'a - That a child and an apprentice of the widow Cornish were
    buried in the church yard and afterwards Brooks, a waterman, was
    buried in ye same. All of them not being able to be kept for
    Christian Burial in a solemn manner. [signed] Rev. Henry Nichols,
    1704."

"Lawrence Parkum, a Swede who dyed att Eroch Erochson's was
    buried 16 Oct 1705. [signed] Rev. Henry Nichols"

"James, servant of John Marks, was buried the twelfth day of March
    1707/8."

ROBERT FRENCH

Robert French of the Lower Counties (Delaware) married Mary
(Sandelands), widow of William Trent and daughter of James
Sandelands of St. Paul's. According to Mr. Ashmead, French "was a
native of Scotland and a very prominent man in his time filling many
important offices in the colonial government. His son, David, was
Prothonotary of the Courts (chief court clerk) of Delaware in 1728,

Attorney General of the Lower Counties, Speaker of the Assembly and held other offices. He was a fine scholar and a poet of no small ability. He died comparatively young and was buried "by the side of his father," beneath the stone floor of Old St. Paul's Chapel.

Anne, the daughter of Robert French, married for the second time Colonel Nicholas Ridgeley. After Robert French's death, his widow, Mary Sandelands-Trent-French, married for the third time, Robert Gordon, Chief Justice of the Supreme Court of Delaware. Robert French was a member of the Church of England and the founder of Immanuel Church, New Castle, Delaware.

INDEX

251; Nathaniel, 1; Robert, 1,
41, 75, 78, 81, 83, 113, 119,
233; Thomas, 1
BAREFOOT, Mary, 251
BARKER, Mary, 250
BARKLET, Thomas, 227
BARNARD, Sarah, 107, 121;
Thomas, 42, 121
BARNES, Joshua, 195; Sarah, 252
BARNET, Frances, 82; Richard,
77, 78
BARNETT, Margaret, 251
BARNS, Joshua, 205
BARNSWELL, Thomas, 239
BARRAT, James, 96, 99
BARRATT, Mary, 102
BARRET, Benjamin, 85
BARRETT, Benjamin, 82; Giles,
69; Mary, 69
BARRITT, Mary, 96
BARRY, Kathrine, 127; Margaret,
132; Mary, 114, 132; Richard,
114, 121, 130, 132
BARTHOLOMEW, Sarah;   Cowpland,
196
BARTIN, Abraham, 167; Lydia,
167
BARTLET, Thomas, 82
BARTON, Abner, 1; Abraham, 42,
121, 163; Adam, 1; Capt.,
240; Isaac, 42; James, 1,
150, 195, 244; Jean, 240;
Mary, 1, 126, 131, 163, 240,
244; Naomi, 248; Sarah, 1,
96, 105, 240; Sarah Edwards,
225; Thomas, 240, 248
BARTRAM, Ann, 42; Elizabeth, 1,
174; James, 1, 42, 52, 110,
132, 160; John, 42; John Jr,
42; Mary, 1, 52, 107; Nathan,
174; William, 42, 116
BATTEN, James, 42
BATTIN, Hannah, 134; James,
118, 122; Margarett, 94;
Mary, 122; Samuel, 140;
Thomas, 134
BAYLIFF, Thomas, 220, 221
BAYNTON, Ann (Sandelands), 240;
Peter, 240; Rebecca, 240
BAZER, Jane, 73; John, 73
BEAKES, Ann, 62; Lydia, 66,
161, 167; Mary, 66; Steney,
66; Stephen, 66, 105
BEAKS, Abraham, 238
BEALL, John, 75
BEALS, Jacob, 1; John, 1, 113,
119; John Jr, 90; Mary, 1;
Patience, 1; Sarah, 91, 114,
119; William, 1
BEAN, Jean, 94
BEAR, Samuel, 249

BEAVAN, Ann, 158
BEAVEN, Agness, 189
BECERTON, Sarah, 182
BECKAM, Mary, 71; Richard, 71
BECKERTON, Sarah, 186, 187
BECKHAM, Jane, 59; Richard, 59;
Richard Jr, 109; Sarah, 102;
Sarah Norbury, 227; Susannah,
59
BEEL, Mary, 248
BEESON, Alice, 119; Edward, 42;
John, 42
BEETHOM, Elizabeth, 48, 177
BELERBY, Mary, 113
BELL, Abigail, 118; Alice, 122,
131, 147; George, 44; Hannah,
128; Hannah Reyneer, 128;
Isabell, 44, 115; Joseph,
169; Mary, 128, 252; Rachel,
128; Rachel Reyneer, 128;
Rebekah, 169; Samuel, 122,
126, 128
BENNETT, John, 42; Sarah, 103
BENSON, Hannah, 1; James, 1;
Jane, 1; Jean, 98, 227; John,
1; Robert, 1, 103
BERNARD, Lydia, 186
BERRY, Mary Ogden, 199
BESON, Edward, 115; Esther, 115
BEST, John, 249
BETHEL, Joseph, 127, 138;
Katherine, 127, 138;
Kathrine, 127
BETTLE, Edward, 170
BETTY, James, 155
BEVAN, Agness, 189, 203; Ann,
2, 42, 158, 189; Aubery, 115;
Awbrey, 42, 155, 158;
Benjamin, 2; David, 189, 219,
220; Davis, 42, 157, 165,
219; Elizabeth, 2; Isabela,
189; Isabella, 203; Mary, 2,
49, 159; Mather Sollar, 189;
Mordecai, 2; Tacy, 189, 203,
219; Tasey, 153; William, 2,
84
BEVEN, Mary, 84
BEWAN, Tacy, 153
BEZER, Edward, 42; John, 42;
Margarett, 113
BEZOR, Elizabeth, 75
BICKEDIKE, Esther, 166
BICKERDICK, Esther, 124
BICKERDIKE, Esther, 119, 132,
139, 161, 162
BICKERTON, Elizabeth, 241;
Jesse, 241; Samuel S., 241;
Sarah, 152
BICKHAM, Mary, 55, 131;
Richard, 131
BILLERBY, Isaac, 49; Mary, 49,

INDEX 259

Sarah, 144
CAMMS, Henry, 117
CAMPBELL, Elizabeth, 241; Peter, 241
CANBY, Esther, 101; Hannah, 62, 189
CAREL, Margaret, 240, 249
CARPENTER, Samuel, 177
CARSON, Ann, 195, 220; Martha, 196
CARTEE, Patrick, 118
CARTER, Abraham, 128, 163, 165; Ann, 194; Barbara, 151, 152; Deborah, 91, 168; Edward, 43, 75, 77, 143; Hannah, 3, 58, 107, 149, 154; Isabell, 44, 100; James, 44, 194; Jane, 55; Jeremiah, 42, 43, 58, 117, 148; John, 3, 44, 98, 143, 151; Joseph, 77, 82, 83, 86, 228; Lidia, 86; Lydia, 3, 103; Lydia Jr, 44, 101; Margaret, 149; Marlin, 55; Martain, 205; Martin, 196, 201, 206; Mary, 42, 103, 118, 145, 154; Moses, 172; Neneveh, 148; Nineavah, 145; Ninevah, 117, 118, 145; Nineveh, 114, 154, 168; Patrick, 252; Prudence, 3, 62; Robert, 3, 62, 77, 87, 144; Samuel, 151, 179; Sarah, 42, 55, 144, 196, 201, 205; William, 163
CARTLIDGE, Mary, 87
CARTRIGHT, Widow, 89
CARTWRIGHT, Thomas, 76
CARTY, Margaret Skelton, 235; Patrick, 235
CASSIN, Ann, 224; Ann Worrall, 219; Luke, 224, 225; Thomas, 225
CAUDWELL, Mary, 67; Rebeccah, 67
CAVLERT, Joshua, 87
CHAFFERIN, Soloman, 249
CHALER [TAYLOR], Peter, 77
CHAMBERLAIN, John, 121, 177; Letice, 121; Mary, 177; Sarah, 96, 97
CHAMBERLIN, Hannah, 136, 137; John, 166; Joseph, 44, 136; Mary, 44, 166; Robert, 44; Robert Jr, 95; Susannah, 111
CHAMBERS, Katherine, 84
CHANCE, Benjamin, 177; Mary, 157
CHANDLEE, Benjamin, 44; Goldsmith, 44, 200; Hannah, 200; Mary, 44
CHANDLER, Esther, 110; George,

44; Phebe, 213, 225
CHARLES, John, 239, 241
CHEYNEY, Elizabeth, 221, 223; Thomas, 209
CHURCHMAN, Anne, 209, 217; Caleb, 209, 217; Dinah, 3; Edward, 209, 217; George, 3, 75; Hannah, 3, 84, 217; John, 3, 75, 77, 80; Micajah, 217; Owen, 209, 217; Phebe, 209, 217; Rebecca, 209, 217; Susanna, 3; Susannah, 44
CLARK, Catherine, 241; James, 239, 241; Thomas, 221; William, 241
CLARKE, Thomas, 217
CLATON, David, 146; Sarah, 146
CLAYTON, Adam, 156; Christopher, 86, 234; David, 145; Jane, 201, 206; John, 201; Mary, 76, 117, 156; Sarah, 145; William, 75, 117
CLEMMENS, Elizabeth, 81
CLERK, Elizabeth, 196; Thomas, 196
CLIFFORD, Thomas, 107
CLOUD, Ann, 44; Mordecai, 44; Sally Ann, 3; Susanna, 3, 217; Susannah, 218; William, 3, 44, 217
CLOWD, Hannah, 93
COATES, Isaac, 174; Moses, 44; Rachel, 213; Samuel, 174; Sarah, 130, 213; Thomas, 44, 130, 213
COATS, Moses, 220; Sarah, 218, 220; Thomas, 218, 220
COBORN, Dinah, 115; Elizabeth, 107; Hannah, 91, 227; John, 210; Joseph Jr, 101; Mary, 227; Phebe, 210; Rachell, 99; Robert, 212, 213; William, 227
COBORNE, Joseph, 75; William, 75
COBOURN, Caleb, 3, 180; David, 164; Elizabeth, 3, 93; Esther, 180; Jacob, 171; John, 159, 175, 189, 202, 206, 213; Joseph, 3, 170; Joseph Jr, 162; Joshua, 3; Margaret, 170; Martha, 78; Mary, 78, 189, 202, 206; Rachel, 3, 144; Robert, 160, 175; Sarah, 3; Thomas, 3, 78, 162; William, 76, 77, 78, 172
COBURN, Sarah, 123; Thomas, 183, 184
COCK, Mary, 241; Walter, 241
COCKFIELD, Elizabeth, 105
COCKS, Walter, 240

196, 200, 209; Jonathan, 249;
Laurance, 137; Lawrance, 45,
147; Lawrence, 127, 193, 199,
200; Martha, 137; Mary, 45,
47, 141, 147, 153, 193, 209;
Rachel, 137; Sarah, 127, 137,
147
COXE, Amy, 4; Ellen, 4; Israel,
4; Jane, 4; John, 4; John Sr,
4; Lawrence, 4; Mary, 4;
Sarah, 4
COXTON, Randall, 82
COYLE, Charles, 242; John, 242;
Martha, 242
CRAFTS, Helen (Vannemmon), 239;
Robert, 239, 249
CRANSBURY, Margaret, 250
CRESSON, Caleb, 45; Ebenezer,
217, 222; James, 45; Jane,
218; Sarah, 45
CROCKSON, John, 86; Lydia, 191,
195; Randale, 45; Samuel, 45;
Sarah, 88; Sarah Jr, 120
CROKSON, Mary, 148
CROOK, Grace, 84, 86
CROOKHAM, Deborah, 154; James,
154; John, 154; Mary, 154
CROOKSON, Mary, 124
CROSBY, Ann, 245; Elizabeth,
145; Jacob R., 242; John,
102, 228, 245; John Jr, 139;
Katherin, 83; Richard, 141,
145
CROSIER, John, 116; Rachel,
126; Robert, 124
CROSLEY, Alice, 138; Charles,
45, 124; Hannah, 124, 221;
John, 131, 137, 138; Mary,
148, 219; Samuel, 45, 148,
151, 155, 219
CROSLY, Joseph, 176; Mary, 176;
Samuel, 176
CROSSER, Rachel, 126
CROSSLEY, Betty, 218; Charles,
4; Elizabeth, 4; Hannah, 4,
210; John, 4; Samuel, 4
CROXEN, Abraham, 195; John, 4;
Jonathan, 4; Randall, 4;
Samuel, 4; Sarah, 4; Thomas,
4
CROXSON, John, 128; Thomas, 229
CROXTON, Mary, 121; Randale,
135, 144; Randall, 98, 229;
Randle, 95; Samuel, 121, 124;
Thomas, 117
CROZER, Elizabeth, 42, 178;
Esther, 178; James, 42, 59,
178; Martha, 178; Rachel, 42,
178; Rebeckah, 178; Sarah, 59
CROZIER, James, 177; Sarah, 177
CRUKSHANK, Susanna, 164

CULBERTSON, Margaret, 249
CULIN, Barbara, 250; Daniel,
242; George, 242, 249; Isaac,
242; Jonas, 242; Margaret,
242; Margret, 251; Rachel,
242
CULLEN, Margret, 251
CUMMINGS, Ann, 138; Elizabeth,
151; Enoch, 42, 61, 133;
Hannah, 61; Jane, 42, 133;
John, 135; Mary, 61, 138;
Thomas, 45, 114, 169
CUMMINS, Thomas, 156
CUNDALL, William, 102
CUNDILL, William, 102
CURETON, Margret, 78; Richard,
78; William, 78

-D-
DANGER, Annabal, 250; Annabel,
250; Edward, 239, 242;
Margaret, 242; Mary, 242;
Prudence, 242
DARLINGTON, Abraham, 4, 45, 91,
98, 104; Amy, 4, 205, 220;
Benjamin, 4; Deborah, 4;
Edward, 4, 220; Elizabeth, 4,
101, 104; Esther, 143;
Hannah, 45; Jared, 4; Jesse,
4, 45, 205, 220; John, 45,
143; Joshua, 4; Mark, 4;
Martha, 4, 220; Mary, 4;
Rhoda, 4, 220; Samuel, 4,
220; Thomas, 4, 45
DAUGHERTY, Martha, 175; Sarah,
183; Susanna, 171; Susanna
Jr, 168; Susannah, 147
DAUGHTERTY, Sarah, 198
DAVID, Amos, 5; Ann, 85; David,
86, 87; Elis, 77; Ellis, 5,
86, 105; Hannah, 5, 83; Hugh,
97; James, 239; Jane, 5;
John, 85; Jonathan, 5;
Kathren, 95; Lewis, 45, 158;
Martha (Jones), 239; Mary,
127; Meredith, 45; Moses, 45,
127; Philip, 242; Priscilla,
145; Richard, 5; Rowland, 5;
Sarah, 5; Thomas, 242
DAVIE, Evan, 249
DAVIES, Daniel, 45; Elizabeth,
82; Gemina, 101; Mirack, 91;
William, 104, 106
DAVIS, Ann, 55, 149, 249;
Benjamin, 149, 162, 167;
Caleb, 180; Catharine, 170;
Christian, 242; Daniel, 46,
121, 170; David, 94, 98, 138;
Deborah, 45; Dorothy, 196,
207, 223, 225; Edward, 86;
Eleanor, 196, 207, 213;

191, 202, 207, 211, 214;
Julian, 9; Mahlon, 149, 150,
152; Mary, 9, 51, 63, 121,
137, 161, 211, 214; Mathew,
50; Matthew, 50, 149, 150,
167; Rebecca, 141, 149, 211,
214; Richard, 163; Samuel, 9,
50, 73, 190, 198, 203, 204;
Samuell, 50; Sarah, 73, 146,
163, 190, 208, 240, 248, 250;
Susanna, 9; Thomas, 9, 50,
121, 137, 239; Thomas Jr,
161; William, 9, 249
HAM, Joyce, 243; Sen. James,
243
HAMES, Joseph, 165; Sarah, 165
HAMMAN, William, 118
HAMMANS, Ambrose Lewis, 126;
Hannah, 9, 126; Lowery, 126;
Lowry, 119; Margaret, 9, 66;
Martha, 9, 73; Mary, 9, 66;
Sarah, 9, 126, 127; Thomas,
126; William, 9, 66, 73, 126,
127
HAMMER, Phebe Howard, 207
HAMMONS, William, 106
HAMONDS, Margret, 106
HAMPTON, Ann, 107; Elizabeth,
9, 153; John, 107, 169; Mary,
9, 153; Rebecca, 63; Samuel,
9, 50, 64, 141, 151, 153,
172; Sarah, 9, 64, 152, 153,
155, 172; Simon, 50, 63
HAMS, Henry, 77
HAMTON, Rebeccah, 144; Sarah,
144
HANBY, John, 243; William, 239,
243
HANCE, Benjamin, 161, 168, 169,
199; Benjamin Jr, 189;
Deborah, 169; Hannah, 168;
Isaac, 191; Mary, 199; Sarah,
161
HANCOCK, Hiram, 169
HANDBY, John, 108
HANNUM, Ann, 243; Elizabeth,
240, 249; George, 240, 243;
John, 239, 243; Margery, 239;
Sarah, 243; Susanna, 223
HANSON, Mary, 82
HARDIMAN, Edward, 83
HARDMAN, Edward, 85, 230, 237
HARIS, John, 123
HARKER, James, 108
HARLAN, Hannah, 129; Michall,
129
HARLIN, Hannah, 110, 230;
Michael Jr, 110
HARLING, Deborah, 87; George,
87
HARLON, Samuel, 176, 183;

Sarah, 176, 183
HARPER, John, 243; Phoebe, 243
HARRIS, Caleb, 199; Eleanor,
199; Frances, 143; George,
201; Hannah, 147, 148, 160;
Hugh, 41; John, 141, 143,
148; Olive, 41; Roger, 96;
Sarah, 96, 123, 141
HARRISON, Caleb, 9, 10, 43, 50,
58, 74, 93, 94, 135, 154,
215, 230; Caleb Jr, 133, 154,
193; Catharine, 10, 154;
Catherine, 43; Eleanor, 50;
Elener, 133; Elinor, 58, 154,
169, 180; Eliza, 10, 211,
215; Hannah, 9, 50, 58, 154;
John, 9, 135, 136, 138; John
Fairlamb, 10; Joshua, 10, 50,
154, 211, 215; Mary, 74, 136,
138, 154; Richard, 215;
Robert, 212, 216; Samuel
Pancoast, 10; Seth, 10; Tacy
Maris, 215
HARRISS, Sarah, 98
HARRY, Alice, 48, 172; Frances,
139; John, 139, 172, 204;
Jonathan, 48; Joseph, 230;
Mary, 48, 117, 118, 204
HART, Elizabeth, 120; George,
249; Hannah Morris, 213;
John, 120; John Jefferies,
213
HARVEY, Alice, 10, 55; Caleb,
184; Hannah, 127; Job, 115;
Job Jr, 127; Joseph, 10, 55,
86, 115; Joseph Jr, 120;
Keziah, 179; Mary, 10, 55
HARVY, Mary, 175
HASTING, John, 77
HASTINGS, Elizabeth, 10; John,
103, 107, 230, 232; Joshua,
10, 75, 77, 232; Mary, 10,
106, 107, 230
HATTON, Elizabeth, 58, 91;
John, 182; Peter, 50; Peter
Jr, 198; Phebe, 198; Sarah,
50
HAY, Ann, 102
HAYARD, Ann, 162
HAYCOCK, Ann, 50, 101;
Benjamin, 181; Hannah, 63,
144, 168, 175, 181; Isaac,
181; Jacob, 181; James, 190,
200; John, 50, 175; John Jr,
175, 182, 191; Jonathan, 50,
62, 102, 122, 135, 143, 157,
168, 179, 181, 193; Joseph,
63, 143, 144, 176, 181, 191,
196; Margaret, 194; Mary, 62,
191; Nathan, 173, 178, 194;
Phebe, 196; Priscilla, 174;

HOLME, George, 221, 222
HOLSTON, John, 96, 233, 234;
Martha, 76; Sarah, 231
HOLSTONE, Sarah, 92
HOLTON, Elizabeth, 145; John,
145
HOOLSTON, Rebeckah, 76; Sarah,
76
HOOLSTONE, Elizabeth, 76
HOOPES, Abigail, 158; Abraham,
11, 149, 158, 166, 172, 209;
Ann, 11; Benjamin, 174;
Christian, 11; Daniel, 11,
41, 105, 108; Daniell, 60,
71, 73, 77; Deborah, 214;
Eli, 214; Elizabeth, 11, 71,
166; George, 186; Grace, 11,
60, 164; Hannah, 11, 51;
Isaac, 172, 184, 209, 214;
Jacob, 176, 214; Jane, 11,
41, 71, 166; John, 11, 149,
173; Joseph, 51; Joshua, 11,
51, 177; Joshua Jr, 155;
Mary, 11, 73, 184, 193, 214;
Nathan, 11; Phebe, 176, 214;
Rachel, 214; Sarah, 11, 214,
221; Sidney, 214; Stephen,
11, 164; Thomas, 11; Walter,
11
HOOPS, Abraham, 119; Christian,
138; Daniel, 51, 80, 116,
117, 119, 122, 125, 138;
Daniel Jr, 116; Eli, 220;
John, 122; Joseph, 192;
Joshua, 116; Margret, 127;
Mary, 119, 192; Nathan, 51,
127; Sarah, 125; Stephen,
124; Thomas, 82, 122
HOOTON, Joseph, 220
HOPE, Thomas, 80
HOPKINS, John, 74; Mary, 74;
Ruth, 74
HOPMAN, Mary, 249
HORN, Edward, 185, 186, 187;
Elizabeth, 179, 185; Mary,
179, 181, 185; Phebe, 174,
179, 185; Thomas, 185;
William, 179, 180, 181, 185
HORNE, Davis, 198; Edward, 51,
198; Elizabeth, 51; Mary,
198; Stephen, 198; William,
51, 198
HORTON, Margret, 252
HOSKENS, Stephen, 112
HOSKINS, Abigail, 220; Eleanor,
195, 220; Esther, 167, 169;
George, 11; Graham, 220;
Hannah, 80; Henrietta, 220;
Henry, 195; Jane, 128, 129,
145; John, 11, 51, 75, 80,
117, 220, 231; Joseph, 11,

51, 117, 127, 128, 158, 166,
167, 199, 212, 223, 250;
Mary, 11, 51, 81, 117, 223,
231, 250; Raper, 51, 179,
195, 220, 221; Rebecca, 206;
Ruth, 11, 231; Sarah, 116,
133; Stephen, 11, 133; Wyatt,
220
HOSKYNS, Mary, 250
HOST, Ruth, 239, 249
HOUGH, Frances, 76
HOULDSTON, Sarah, 251
HOULSTON, Ann, 11; Elizabeth,
11; John, 11, 232; Sarah, 114
HOULTON, David, 169; John, 161
HOWARD, Alice, 160, 200; David,
216; Elizabeth, 170; Grace,
11, 53, 170; Hannah, 11, 61;
Henry, 11, 52, 53, 58, 61,
100, 121, 153, 159, 176;
James, 11, 159, 160, 191,
205, 207, 224; Jane, 177;
John, 11, 52, 143, 155, 161,
170, 177; Jonathan, 217;
Lawrence, 154, 155; Mary, 11,
58, 224; Parry, 204; Peter,
11, 135; Phebe, 207; Rebecca,
11; Rebekah, 160; Richard,
11, 153, 163, 172; William,
220
HOWARTH, Henry, 51
HOWEL, Esther, 48; Evan, 48,
51, 103; Israel, 51
HOWELL, Abigail, 12, 154;
Abraham, 12, 150; Alice, 168;
Ann, 12, 105, 106, 120, 135,
154, 167, 231, 249; Barbara,
239, 243, 250; Benjamin, 12;
David, 12; Debbe, 154;
Debbie, 12; Deborah, 164;
Eliza, 12; Elizabeth, 12, 42,
84, 140, 142, 145, 146, 168;
Esther, 12, 164, 166; Evan,
12, 52, 99, 121, 150, 164;
Hannah, 12, 168; Hugh, 12,
154; Isaac, 12, 42, 143, 144,
158, 164, 176; isaac, 52;
Israel, 52, 139, 160, 164,
166, 176; Israell, 142;
Jacob, 12, 52, 53, 87, 120,
125, 130, 134, 145, 154, 156,
164, 167; Jacob Jr, 126, 159;
James, 12; John, 12, 52, 78,
120, 168; Jonathan, 12, 140,
144, 146, 161, 163, 168, 181;
Joseph, 12, 130; Joshua, 12;
Martha, 12, 169, 174; Mary,
12, 42, 126, 160, 164, 168,
176, 191, 243; Mary Jr, 239;
Mary Sr, 239, 250; Patience,
138, 141; Rees, 12; Rice, 84;

230
JERMON, Elizabeth, 91
JERSON, Rachall, 134
JERVIS, Joseph, 77, 83, 92, 93,
 98, 99, 100, 231, 232; Phebe,
 142; William, 142
JESOP, Ann, 196, 199; Samuel,
 199
JOANS, Francis, 95; John, 101;
 Margritt, 101; Mary, 111;
 Thomas, 75
JOANS [JONES], Thomas, 79
JOB, Abraham, 13; Andrew, 13,
 75, 77, 84; Archibald, 135,
 139; Benjamin, 13; Caleb, 13;
 Elizabeth, 13, 81, 84; Enoch,
 13; Jacob, 13; Mary, 13;
 Thomas, 13
JOBE [JOB], Andrew, 79
JOBIAS, Patience, 184
JOBSON, Esther, 13, 175, 193;
 John, 193, 212; Joseph, 13,
 171, 193, 218; Mary, 193,
 218; Samuel, 13
JOHN, Ann, 14; Charles, 244;
 Daniel, 14; David, 13; Ellen,
 13; Griffith, 14, 94; Gwen,
 13; Joseph Townsend, 225;
 Margaret, 13; Mary, 13;
 Rachel, 14; Rebecca, 13;
 Samuel, 13; Sarah, 13;
 Susanna, 13; Thomas, 13, 93
JOHNINGSEN, Edward, 239
JOHNSON, Abraham, 162; Amy,
 222; Amy Rogers, 196;
 Benjamin, 53; Henry, 249;
 Humphrey, 79; Joseph, 222;
 Margaret, 53; Mary, 161, 162,
 250; Robert, 53, 196
JOHNSTON, Hannah, 41; Joshua,
 63; Mary, 63
JOLLAND, Henry, 135; Lydia, 135
JONES, Ann, 14, 114, 120;
 Cadwalader, 14; Charles, 53,
 240, 244, 249; David, 14, 17,
 53, 77, 83, 88, 118, 231,
 232, 249; Elinor, 14; Elisha,
 157, 183; Elizabeth, 17, 53,
 82, 107, 183, 204, 244;
 Elizabeth Weaver, 199;
 Francis, 14, 93, 95; Gwen,
 157, 183; Hannah, 6, 14, 86,
 93, 105, 183, 215; Henery,
 116; Henry, 232; Hugh, 240,
 249; Isaac, 183; Jane (Pugh),
 240; Jean [Jane], 86; Jesse,
 183, 186; Johanna, 244; John,
 14, 53, 101, 183, 236;
 Jonathan, 176, 183; Lowry,
 100; Margaret, 60, 244;
 Margaret (Carel), 240;

Margeret, 183; Martha, 14,
 239, 249; Mary, 14, 78, 111,
 118, 122, 183, 186, 232, 239,
 249, 252; Norris, 215; Peter,
 14, 116, 120; Philip, 158;
 Phillip, 153; Prudence, 244;
 Rachel, 14; Rebecca, 14, 129,
 204, 244; Rees, 6, 14, 60,
 86; Richard, 53, 105, 114;
 Robert, 240, 244, 249; Ruth,
 108, 110; Samuel, 14, 93,
 102, 105; Sarah, 14, 92, 204,
 232; Susana, 88, 89; Susanna,
 14, 176, 183; Susannah, 183;
 Thomas, 14, 80, 83, 88, 122,
 232, 244; William, 53, 129,
 146, 203, 204
JONSON, Benjamin, 115; Mary,
 115

 -K-
KEITH, George, 229
KELLEY, William, 99
KELLOGG, Elizabeth; Smedley,
 225
KENDAL, Deborah, 213, 216;
 Jesse, 213, 216; John, 213,
 216; Mary, 213, 216; Rebecca,
 216; Thomas, 232, 235
KENDALE, Benjamin, 53, 122,
 135; Elizabeth, 120; Grace,
 135; Jane, 113, 114; John,
 53, 130; Mary, 50, 53;
 Rebecah, 130; Thomas, 50, 53,
 109, 120
KENDALL, Benjamin, 125; Jean,
 116; Mary, 54, 92; Sarah,
 139; Thomas, 54, 87, 92, 139,
 232
KENDELL, Jane, 72; Thomas, 72
KENERLY, James, 77
KENINSON, Edward, 77
KENNY, Alexander, 54; James,
 54, 169; Mary, 169
KENT, Ann, 84; Jean [Jane], 84,
 86, 87, 85-6; Rees, 86, 87;
 Rice, 84
KENTERDINE, Richard, 239
KERN, Sarah, 201; Sarah
 Windors, 201
KERNS, John, 200; Sarah
 Windors, 200
KEY, Ann, 134; Elizabeth, 116,
 149, 152; Mary, 110; Moses,
 110, 116, 134, 149, 152
KICKS, Deborah, 110
KINDALL, Jane, 14; John, 14;
 Mary, 14; Thomas, 14
KINDAR, Mrs., 244
KINGSMAN, John, 76
KINNESON, Charles, 14; Edward,

14, 83; Hannah, 14; James,
14; Mary, 14; William, 14
KIRK, Esther, 180; Joshua, 159;
Mary, 159, 174; Phebe Nuzum,
225; Philip, 211; Phillip,
180
KIRKBRIDE, Joseph, 98
KNIGHT, Giles, 85; Gyles, 17;
Hannah, 210; Mary, 17, 18, 85
KNOWLES, John, 132
KOWLIN, George, 249

-L-
LACEY, Benjamin, 163
LACK, John, 249
LADD, John, 115, 120;
Katherine, 120; Mary, 115
LANCAST, Katherine, 249
LANCASTER, Thomas, 95
LANDSDELL, Elinor, 101
LANGFORD, Joanna (Andree), 239;
John, 239
LANGHAM, Mary, 44; Robert, 44
LANGLEY, Jane, 76
LANGLY, Jeremiah, 80, 84
LANGWORTHY, John, 76
LARKEN, Elizabeth, 159; John,
159
LARKIN, Ann, 198; Esther, 212,
215; Jane, 72, 150, 175;
John, 54; Joseph, 198;
William, 54, 150
LARKING, Esther, 54; John, 54
LAURENCE, Henry, 176
LAWLOR, Mathew, 203
LAWRANCE, Henry, 54; Henry Jr,
147; Mary, 220; Mary Maris,
205
LAWRENCE, Amy, 212; Clement,
217; Hannah, 14, 54, 223;
Henry, 14, 54, 187, 191, 212,
223; Henry Jr, 167; Isaac,
14, 223; John, 14, 223;
Joseph, 191; Joshua, 14, 192;
Mary, 14, 223; Mordecai, 191
LAXFORD, Ann, 78
LAYCOCK, Hannah, 54; Thomas,
54; William, 54
LEA, Ann, 14, 14, 171;
Elizabeth, 57; George, 141;
Hannah, 14, 43, 100, 119,
141, 171; Isaac, 57, 104,
105, 109, 131, 139, 140, 141,
232; Jacob, 14; James, 131,
132; John, 14, 20, 43, 54,
62, 100, 113, 119, 123, 147,
156; John Jr, 147; Margaret,
132; Margret, 131; Mary, 14,
62, 141; Rachaell, 141;
Rebecca, 140, 141; Rebeccah,
139; Sarah, 57, 131, 141;

Susannah, 150; Thomas, 14,
171
LEASEY, Benjamin, 165
LEDDON, Abraham, 197; Mary, 197
LEE, Isaac, 232; John, 77
LEES, Joseph, 115, 116
LEONARD, George, 240
LESTER, Peter, 76
LEVIES, William, 101
LEVIS, Ann, 178, 216; Cyrus,
220; David, 15; Deborah, 15;
Elizabeth, 54, 101, 219;
Elizabeth Garrett, 15;
Elizabeth Jr, 109; Essex,
185; Esther, 211, 223; Flora,
185; Frank, 185; Hannah, 14,
54, 64, 74, 172; Harry, 185;
Henrietta, 15; Isaac, 54, 58,
187, 211, 218; Jane, 137;
John, 14, 60, 126, 127, 178,
181, 184, 185, 186, 221;
Joseph, 15, 128, 208; Joshua,
182; Kitty Ann, 14; Margaret,
49; Margaretta, 14; Martha,
177; Mary, 14, 15, 49, 54,
58, 60, 65, 132, 221; Peggy,
218; Rebecca, 127; Samuel,
14, 49, 54, 64, 65, 74, 87,
109, 126, 128, 132, 172, 177,
181, 184, 187, 219; Samuel
Jr, 178; Samuell, 56; Sarah,
15, 56; Sarah Ann, 15; Sarah
Pancoast, 15; Thomas, 180;
Thomas Jr, 216; Thomas S.,
15; William, 54, 137, 181
LEWIS, Abigail, 172; Abraham,
55; Agnes, 15; Alice, 122,
139, 150, 158, 160, 174;
Amos, 55; Amy, 158; Ann, 15,
16, 84, 102, 103, 116, 136,
140, 155; David, 15, 55, 116,
215, 218; Deborah, 15;
Edward, 211, 222; Elizabeth,
15, 65, 71; Enos, 15; Esther,
15, 212, 222; Esther Levis,
211; Evan, 15, 55, 84, 85,
91, 102, 132, 134, 160; Evan
Jr, 88; Even, 228; Feby, 93;
Franklin, 15, 201; George,
15; Girzzel, 55; Griffith,
104; Gwen, 15; Hannah, 15,
140, 148, 160; Harvey, 170;
Henry, 79; Jabez, 15; Jane,
15, 201; Jehu, 55, 139, 150,
160; Jeptha, 15; Job, 209,
215, 218; Joel, 160; John,
15, 55, 65, 122, 158, 164,
168, 170, 174, 178, 182, 193,
201; Jonathan, 15; Joseph,
15, 129; Joshua, 15, 143,
146, 147, 151, 169; Josiah,

244; Peggy, 244
MCCALL, Alice, 147; William,
147
MCCAMISH, Ann, 130, 131;
Patrick, 130, 131
MCCHASKEY, James, 161;
Patience, 161
MCCLASKEY, Patience, 180, 185
MCCLEISTER, Sarah, 173
MCCLUER, John, 233
MCCLUNG, Mary, 157, 158, 162;
Robert, 158
MCCLYSTER, Collin, 173
MCCOY, Robert, 186; William,
186
MCCULLOUGH, James, 159; Rachel,
159, 205
MACDANIEL, John, 250; Martha,
232
MCDANIEL, Martha, 118
MCDANIELL, Martha, 107
MACE, Ann Maris, 223
MCELVAIN, Jeremiah, 213
MCGEE, Richard, 250
MCILVAIN, Ann, 16, 208;
Elizabeth, 16, 214; Hugh, 16,
185; Isaac, 158, 176, 182,
186, 187; James, 16, 185;
Jeremiah, 16, 185, 200, 209,
213, 214; John, 16, 48, 158,
159, 162, 185, 186, 194, 196,
208; John Spencer, 16;
Judith, 16, 185; Lydia, 16,
48, 162, 185, 200; Margaret,
16, 48, 185; Mary, 158, 186;
Richard, 16, 185; Spencer, 16
MCILVAINE, Hugh, 224; John, 207
MCILVAN, John, 56; Judith, 56
MACKGEE, Richard, 250
MACLISTER, Sarah, 223, 224
MACMANES, Patrick, 250
MCMICKLE, James, 136
MCMURRAY, James, 244; John,
244; Mary, 244
MACVITTE, Ann, 107
MADDOCK, Benjamin, 120, 122,
144, 166; Benjamin Jr, 167;
Elizabeth, 121, 122, 144,
166; Henry, 78, 125; James,
128; Jane, 78; John, 125;
Mordecai, 75, 120, 121, 122,
123; Mordica, 82; Sarah, 112
MADDOK, Mordicha, 232
MADOCK, Mordecai, 112
MAGUIRE, Jane, 244; Thomas, 244
MAILLEN, Randell, 75
MALCOMBE, Jane Gibbons, 195
MALIN, Aaron, 17; Abail, 179;
Abigail, 179; Abner, 17;
Agnes, 17; Alice, 17, 60;
Ann, 17, 95; Betty, 222;

David, 17, 142, 147, 172,
179, 183, 186, 194; Elijah,
183, 186, 195; Elizabeth, 16,
17, 56, 57, 183, 186, 193;
Elizabeth Smith, 218; Enoch,
183, 195; Esther, 17; George,
17, 56, 205, 209; Gideon, 16,
50, 56, 60, 176, 190, 206,
208, 212, 222; Gideon Sr, 17;
Grace, 17; Hannah, 16, 17,
57, 98, 100, 190, 237; Hannah
Crosley, 221; Harvey, 17;
Isaac, 16, 17, 82, 221;
Jacob, 16, 17, 56, 88, 89,
232; James, 187; Joel, 17,
56, 218; John, 183, 186, 195;
Lydia, 17; Margaret, 17, 147,
183, 186, 193, 195; Mary, 16,
17, 41, 89, 112, 183, 186,
237; Minshall, 17; Orpah, 17;
Phebe, 17, 50, 60; Preston,
17; Pusey, 17; Rachel, 16,
183, 186, 195; Randal, 17;
Randale, 112; Randall, 16,
77, 79, 88, 104, 237; Randle,
20; Rebecca, 17; Samuel, 17;
Sarah, 186; Sarah Ann, 17;
Susanah, 186; Susanna, 16,
17, 89, 209; Susannah, 56,
183, 208; Thomas, 17, 56;
William, 17, 56, 57, 78
MALLIN, Elizabeth, 116; Hannah,
100; Isaac, 116; Jacob, 122;
Kathern, 104; Kathren, 104;
Susannah, 121
MANDIAH, David, 239
MANESDORE, Peter, 239; Peter
M., 244
MANIFOLD, Benjamin, 250
MANLEY, Elizabeth, 166; Thomas,
166
MARIS, Alice, 18, 43, 55, 65;
Ann, 19, 46, 55, 72, 73, 145,
186, 196, 223; Asa, 19;
Caleb, 170; Elizabeth, 18,
19, 42, 46, 57, 64, 168, 186,
196, 212; Ellis, 19; Esther,
18, 119; George, 18, 19, 50,
55, 56, 59, 73, 77, 78, 101,
110, 111, 115, 119, 140, 153,
168, 212, 232, 233; George
Jr, 18; George Sr, 18;
Hannah, 18, 59, 110, 111,
233; Isaac, 168, 177, 178,
179, 205, 212; James, 18, 19,
144, 190, 217; Jane, 18, 19,
153, 175, 188, 209; Jehu,
187, 188, 204; Jemima, 186,
196; Jesse, 18, 56, 140, 146,
170, 174, 175, 180, 186, 196,
209, 220; Jesse J., 18; John,

Hannah, 182, 210, 225; James,
209, 212; John, 203; Phebe,
210, 225; Richard, 210, 211,
225; Sarah, 210, 218;
William, 211, 224

-O-

ODGEN, Jonathan, 99
OGDEN, Aaron, 22, 56, 180, 215;
Abigail, 22, 206; Alice, 148;
Ann, 104, 175; David, 22, 52,
59, 76, 77, 83, 88, 147, 148,
175, 188, 199, 233;
Elizabeth, 22; Eloisa, 22;
Esther, 54, 56, 105, 108,
162; George, 59, 150, 162;
Hannah, 22, 43, 51, 78, 148;
Hugh, 162; James, 22; Jane,
54; John, 22, 59, 105, 106;
Jonathan, 22, 103, 104, 233;
Martha, 22, 41, 81, 88, 139;
Mary, 22, 51, 138, 162, 199;
Nehemiah, 22; Rebecca, 215;
Rebeccah, 56; Samuel, 22, 54,
59, 105, 108, 137, 138, 139,
148, 169; Sarah, 22, 52, 63,
175; Stephan, 59; Stephen,
22, 41, 43, 51, 133, 206;
Zibiah, 175
OLDFIELD, Jonathan, 117, 127;
Mary, 127
OLDHAM, Susana, 87; Thomas, 83
OLDMAN, Thomas, 104
OLIVER, William, 250
OTLEY, Ann, 203; Rachel, 202
OTTEY, Christ, 250; Philip, 250
OUTELOO, Walter, 124
OUTERLOO, Thomas, 124, 126;
Walter, 124
OWEN, Elinor, 70; Elizabeth,
63; Griffith, 20, 21, 85, 86;
Hannah, 115, 234; Jane, 86,
128; John, 51, 56, 59, 63,
91, 115, 156, 234; Kathern,
85; Mary, 177; Rebecca, 56,
85; Robert, 59; Samuel, 250;
Sarah, 21, 85; Susannan, 51;
Thomas, 70

-P-

PAINTER, Enos, 59, 225; James,
59; Jane, 59; Lidia, 85;
Minshall, 140; Samuel, 140;
Susana, 82
PAIRSON, Kathern, 91
PAIST, Alice, 23; Ann, 23, 60;
Charles, 23; Elizabeth, 22,
23; Jacob, 23; James, 23,
207; Jonathan, 23; Mary, 23;
Orpha, 23; Sarah, 22, 23;
Susan, 23; William, 22, 23,

60
PAKER, Susannah, 87
PAKER [PACKER], Robert, 87
PALMER, Abigail, 60; Alice,
196, 202, 214; Asher, 60,
196, 202; Ashur, 214;
Christian, 60; Hannah, 60;
Huldah, 214; John, 60;
Jonathan, 60, 105; Joseph,
202, 214; Morris, 214; Moses,
60; Sarah, 106; Susannah, 214
PANCOAST, Abigail, 219; Abigail
Ogden, 206; Ann, 50, 54, 219;
Eliza, 50; Esther, 54, 130,
139, 219; Hannah, 219;
Hester, 55; John, 23; Mary,
23, 117; Phebe, 54; Rebecca,
23; Samuel, 23, 60; Sarah,
55; Seth, 23, 50, 54, 55, 60,
130, 139, 189, 219; Stephen,
219; William, 23, 60
PARCUM, Lawrence S., 246
PARK, Jonathan, 109; Thomas,
109
PARKE, Jane, 127; Rebecca, 60;
Thomas, 60, 127, 235
PARKER, John, 75, 81; Joseph,
59, 94, 115; Katharine, 249;
Mary, 59, 116; Richard, 79,
80
PARKERS, Joseph, 150
PARKS, Thomas, 111
PARKUM, Lawrence, 252
PARRY, Benjamin, 197, 200;
Elizabeth, 197, 200; Hannah,
142; Joseph, 197, 200; Phebe,
200; Rowland, 141; Sarah,
197, 200; Thomas, 197, 200
PARSON, Joshua, 204, 207;
Richard, 201
PARSONS, George, 24; Hannah,
24; Israel, 24; Jemima, 23,
192, 212; Jemimah, 60; John,
222; Joseph, 23, 118; Joshua,
23, 60, 192, 204, 222;
Mahlon, 23, 24, 192, 200,
222; Mary, 23, 192, 200, 215;
Naomi, 23, 192; Nathaniel,
23; Neomie, 222; Phebe, 23,
222; Rebecca, 23, 192, 207,
222; Richard, 23, 60, 207,
212, 215; Richard Jr, 192;
Samuel, 23; Sarah, 23;
Sidney, 24; Susannah, 234;
William, 23, 60, 192, 222
PARVIN, Francis, 119, 120;
John, 118; Mary, 147; Thomas,
147
PARVIS, Mary, 153; Thomas, 153
PASCALL, Hannah, 125; Thomas,
125

66, 110, 111; Mary, 67;
Richard, 138; Sarah, 97, 100,
138; Thomas, 110
PETELL, Martha, 121
PETERS, John, 133
PETERSEN, Peter, 239
PETERSON, Gabriel, 246; Peter,
246; Sarah, 249
PETHIRICK, Philip, 93
PEW, James, 96; John, 89;
Phebe, 189
PEWSEY, Ann, 100; Elizabeth,
97; Prudence, 94, 95
PHILIPS, Deborah, 115, 146;
Elizabeth, 88, 99; John, 114,
146; Mary, 146
PHILLIPES, William, 90
PHILLIPS, Hannah, 146, 148,
150, 157; John, 146, 148,
150; Margaret, 249; William,
86, 92
PHIPHS, Sarah, 92
PHIPPS, Aaron, 25; George, 25;
John, 25; Joseph, 25, 234;
Mary, 25; Nathan, 25; Samuel,
25; Sarah, 234
PHIPS, Joseph, 79, 80, 86;
Sarah, 79, 231
PICKELS, William, 239, 246;
William P., 246
PICKOW, Phebe, 20
PIERCE, Catherine, 246;
Elizabeth, 246; Henry, 239,
246, 250; James, 246; Sarah,
246
PIERSON, Enoch, 234
PILE, Abigail, 150; Hannah,
168; Jacob, 168; John, 150;
Lidia, 90; Samuel, 169;
Sarah, 82, 169, 174, 216;
Susannah, 130
PILKINGTON, Abraham, 26;
Edward, 54; Joseph, 26, 173,
184, 200, 201, 204; Levi,
189; Rose, 26, 135; Sarah,
54; Thomas, 26, 134, 136,
146, 149, 177; Thomas Jr,
182, 184; Vincent, 162
PILKINTON, Abraham, 193; Jemima
Edwards, 194
PITT, Elizabeth Lobb, 217
PONTOU, Mary, 249
POOL, Richard, 179, 181
POOLAH, Jane, 26
POOLE, Elizabeth, 62; Richard,
171, 182; Sarah, 211;
William, 62
POOLY, Jean, 90
PORTER, Elizabeth, 58, 74;
Mary, 74, 198; Rebeckah, 191;
Rebekah, 58, 187, 198;

William, 58, 74
POTTER, Abraham, 49, 150;
Lydia, 49, 150
POWEL, Benjamin, 187, 190;
Elizabeth, 191; Hannah, 190,
191; Joshua, 191; Rebeccah,
191; Robert, 117; Samuel,
191; William, 191
POWELL, Amelia, 26; Ann, 246;
Benjamin, 152, 171, 175, 177,
181; David, 41, 62, 98, 106,
107, 136, 171; Elizabeth, 26,
118, 119; Esther, 26, 77;
George, 26; Hannah, 43, 146,
175; Isaac, 26; James, 26;
John, 26, 62, 75, 150, 239;
John Jr, 205; Joseph, 26, 43,
77, 246, 250; Joseph Jr, 146;
Margaret, 26, 150; Margret,
148; Mary, 41, 116, 123, 152,
234; Mary (Howell, Jr), 239;
Mary Jr, 250; Prudence, 152,
171; Rebeckah, 87; Robert,
123; Samuel, 152; Sarah, 26,
93, 99, 229, 234; Sarah
(Heyse), 240; Susanna, 26,
152; Susannah, 71, 136;
Thomas, 26, 71, 75, 77, 96,
118, 119, 239, 240, 250;
Thomas Jr, 229, 234, 246
PRAT, Sarah, 99
PRATT, Joseph, 176; Sarah
Edwards, 229; Sarrah, 212
PRESTON, Ann, 47; Davis, 203;
Hannah, 48, 150; James, 26;
Jane, 47, 48, 63, 65; Jonas,
26, 47, 48, 62, 63, 65, 144,
148, 150, 171, 192, 203;
Jonas Jr, 171; Jones, 189;
Martha, 65; Mary, 26, 171,
189, 192, 203, 210; Sarah,
63, 144
PRICE, Elisha, 162, 167;
Elizabeth Smith, 218; Lydia,
167; Mary, 251; Polly, 246;
Rebecca, 246; William, 246
PRICHARD, Edward, 80, 81;
Philip, 84; Richard, 97
PRICHET, Elizabeth, 80, 99
PRICHETT, Elizabeth, 84, 87
PRIOR, Thomas, 153
PRITCHETT, Edward, 81; Richard,
234
PROCTOR, Joshua, 160, 166
PROYER, Thomas, 153
PRYER, Tacy, 155; Thomas, 153,
155
PUE, Margaret, 251
PUGH, James, 96; Jane, 130,
164, 166, 240, 249; Jean,
234; Jesse, 164; John, 90,

91, 130, 234; Katherine, 128;
Phebe, 189, 202; Roger, 127,
129, 137; Sarah, 126, 127,
129, 137; Thomas, 128;
William, 202
PUSEY, Ann, 26, 66, 100; Caleb,
26, 62, 66, 75, 77, 100, 228;
Caleb Jr, 94; Elizabeth, 26,
97; Hannah, 195, 215; Hannah
West, 214; John, 122, 129;
Joshua, 62, 195; Katherine,
122, 129; Kathren, 121;
Lydia, 26; Prudence, 94, 95;
William, 26, 62, 97, 234
PYLE, Abigail, 26; Anderson,
26; Ann, 88; Benjamin, 62,
179, 192, 195, 208; Betty,
225; Daniel, 63, 129; Esther,
199, 205, 208; Gardiner, 26;
Hannah, 195, 208, 225; Isaac,
61, 63, 199, 205; Jacob, 62;
Jane, 62; John, 26, 88, 89;
Joseph, 26, 63, 195, 208,
224; Martha, 26; Mary, 129,
208; Naomi, 26; Phebe, 195,
208; Rebecca, 145; Robert,
63, 88, 145; Sarah, 26, 61,
63, 195, 208, 214, 224;
Susanna, 111, 119; Susannah,
117, 130; William, 26
PYLES, Isaac, 199; Sarah, 199

-R-
RADCLIFF, Ann, 189, 192; John,
189
RALFE, Lydia, 70
RAWSON, John, 250
RAWTOM, Charles R., 246; John,
246
READ, James, 133; Margaret,
159; Thomas, 159
READMAN, Widow, 85
REBESTER, David, 171
REDMELL, John, 97
REDNAP, Joseph, 97
REECE, Lydia, 180, 197; Mary,
180, 197; Nehemiah, 180, 197;
William, 180, 186
REED, Elizabeth, 246; James,
144, 164; Mary, 164; Robert,
197; Sarah, 195, 197
REES, Ann, 55; David, 26, 55;
Edward, 87; Elinor, 26;
Elizabeth, 55; Grace, 26, 87;
Hannah, 26; Henton, 91; Jane,
87, 90; Jean, 89; Lewis, 26,
87; Mary, 26; Rebecca, 26
REESE, Ann, 140; Jesse, 220,
221, 225; Morris, 63; Sarah,
102, 217
REGESTER, Abigail, 197, 200;

Ann, 122; Daniel, 182, 186;
David, 52, 63, 122, 131, 136,
193, 222; Jane, 133, 134,
197, 200, 219; John, 136,
165, 166; Joseph, 63, 221,
225; Lydea, 131; Lydia, 179,
197, 199, 206; Margeret, 63;
Mary, 52; Rebekah, 166;
Robert, 132, 179, 197, 200;
Sarah, 225; Thomas, 197, 200;
William, 158, 197, 199, 200,
206, 219
REGISTER, Rebekah, 41
RENEAR, Joseph, 97
RENNELLS, Charles, 252
REYNEER, Joseph, 126; Mary, 126
REYNERS, Joseph, 63
REYNOLDS, Ann, 120; Ann Howell,
231; Charles, 252; Henry, 26,
63; Jacob, 63; James, 183,
198; John, 183; Margaret, 26;
Prudence, 26, 75; Sarah, 208
RHOADES, Ann, 130; Elizabeth,
49; Hannah, 49; James, 49;
John, 130
RHOADS, Abigail, 26, 223;
achel, 165; Benjamin, 27,
129; Elizabeth, 26, 27, 63,
66, 202; George, 27; Hannah,
27; Isaac, 27, 63; James, 27,
55, 63, 177, 184, 196; Jane,
27, 156; John, 26, 27, 63,
66, 203, 204; Joseph, 26, 27,
63, 165, 187, 189, 202, 211,
216, 219, 223; Katherine,
129; Leah, 219; Mary, 26, 27,
189, 216, 217; Owen, 27, 63,
190; Phebe, 27; Rachel, 211;
Rebecca, 27, 55; Samuel, 27;
Susanna, 27; Tacy, 196;
William, 27
RHODES, Benjamin, 128, 137;
John, 116; Joseph, 117, 128;
Katherine, 137; Mary, 117
RICE, John, 246
RICHARD, Ann, 97
RICHARDS, Abigail, 153; Ann,
76, 97, 153; Deborah, 153;
Dinah, 246, 250; Edward, 246,
247; Elizabeth, 99, 246;
Hannah, 63; Jacob, 247;
Joseph, 76, 77, 246; Joseph
Sr, 232; Joshua, 153; Mary,
153, 211, 246; Moses, 153;
Ruth, 246; Samuel, 63, 152,
153; Sarah, 155; Susanna, 79;
Susannah, 247
RICHARDSON, Charles, 185;
Deborah, 58, 177; Dinah, 240;
Francis, 58, 177, 179, 185;
George, 185; Hannah, 177,

179, 249; John, 177, 180;
Joseph, 63; Joshua, 63;
Kathren, 97; Mary, 63, 112;
Patience, 149, 160; Phebe,
185; Present, 185; Richard,
250; Sarah, 158; William, 250
RICHARS, Samuel, 151
RIDGELEY, Col. Nicholas, 253
RIDGEWAY, Ann, 171; Beulah,
171; Catherine, 247; Daniel,
171; Elizabeth, 171; Hannah,
171; Job, 171; Lydia, 171;
Mary, 171
RIDGWAY, Ann, 161; Beulah, 161;
Daniel, 161; Elizabeth, 161;
Hannah, 161; Job, 160; Lydia,
161; Mary, 160
RILEY, Esther, 27, 225; Esther
West, 215; John, 27; Rebecca,
27, 225; Sarah, 27, 225;
Thomas, 27, 225
RIMINGTON, John, 85, 110;
Sarah, 110
RING, Elizabeth, 235; Lydia,
113, 235; Nathaniel, 63, 110,
113, 128, 129, 142, 235
RINGER, Joseph, 99
RITCHITS, Sarah, 151
ROADES, Joseph, 57; Rebekah, 57
ROADS, Mary, 116
ROBERTS, Abigail, 47; Alice
Cissel, 198; David, 239, 250;
Edward, 88; Elizabeth, 146,
154, 162; Ellis, 64; Elthew,
79; Esther, 170, 174; Grace,
79; Hugh, 183; Jean, 101;
John, 168, 170, 174, 198;
Jonathan, 198; Lydia, 174;
Margaret, 47; Rebecca, 170;
Rebekah, 168, 174; Reuben,
47, 64, 140, 152, 157, 172,
175, 187, 198; Reubin, 135;
Sarah, 168, 170, 174, 198;
Susanna (Tudor), 239; Tacy,
187; Thomas, 168, 198;
Walter, 168, 173, 175, 198;
William, 100
ROBERTSON, George, 240, 250;
Sarah (Hall), 240
ROBESON, Hannah, 202; John, 64;
Jonathan, 64, 202
ROBINET, Joseph, 250; Samuell,
79
ROBINETT, Allen, 250
ROBINSON, Ann, 104; Anna, 249;
George, 88, 104; Katherine,
104; Mary, 67, 88, 145, 146,
149, 151, 250; Rachel, 225;
Sarah, 179; William, 67, 108,
113, 146, 235
ROBISON, George, 169; Sarah,

166, 167; William, 166, 167
ROCKAFELT, Eve, 251
RODES, Margaret, 240, 249
ROGERS, Abner, 190; Abraham,
198; Amy, 196; Ann, 146, 150,
164, 177, 179, 198; Deborah,
174; Hannah, 192; John, 208;
Lydia, 198; Mary, 106, 198,
235; Nicholas, 64, 102, 106,
235; Robert, 146, 156, 159,
161, 179, 192, 198; Robert
Jr, 156
ROMAN, Dorothy, 120
ROODS, Rebekah, 57
ROOKS, Mary, 55
ROOTH, Lawrance, 75
ROSS, Alexander, 84, 93;
Kathern, 94; Kathren, 93;
Mary, 110, 112
ROSSE, George, 247; Margaret,
247
ROUND, Catharine, 249
ROUSE, Patience, 151
ROUTH, Ann, 27, 79; Francis,
27; Francis Jr, 124, 134;
Lawrence, 27; Rachel, 27;
Sarah, 123, 134; Thomas, 27
ROWLAND, Aquilla, 136;
Catherine, 249; Richard, 136;
Samuel, 136; Sarah, 136
RUDMAN, "Widow", 79
RUMFORD, Martha, 128
RUMSEY, Ann, 250
RUSH, Sarah, 239, 247, 250
RUSHTON, Ann, 114; James, 64,
114
RUSSEL, Dinah, 116; Edward,
116, 179; Hannah, 210;
Joseph, 159; Sarah, 210;
William, 210; William Jr, 158
RUSSELL, Albert, 242; Dinah,
115, 183, 235; Edward, 123,
140, 183, 251; Hannah, 212;
James, 165; Jane, 139, 165;
Jesse, 210; John, 210;
Joseph, 164; Mary, 64, 148;
Obed, 210; Sarah, 63;
Susannah, 63; William, 63,
64, 163, 165, 210, 212
RUTH, Barbara, 44; Francis, 44,
57, 158, 169, 210, 211; Jane,
164; Sarah, 123; Susannah,
57, 156, 158, 174
RYON, Mary, 221

-S-
SALKELD, Agnes, 27, 28, 58, 64,
65, 121, 152; Agness, 228;
Ann, 28; David, 28, 64, 132,
135, 176; Davud, 64; Edmond,
28; Elizabeth, 9, 28, 169;

205, 209; Sarah, 29, 30, 31,
72, 180, 208; Susanna, 29,
30; Susannah, 44, 67;
Susannah Fairlamb, 219;
Thomas, 28, 29, 30, 175, 177,
188, 193, 210; William, 29,
30, 65, 125, 188, 226;
William Preston, 177
SHARPLESS, Abigail, 57;
Abraham, 161; Amos, 65; Ann,
161, 163, 181; Benjamin, 48,
62, 65, 154; Benjamin Jr,
154; Daniel, 48, 57, 65, 153;
David, 153; Edith, 48, 171;
Elizabeth, 43; Esther, 161,
225; Geoffrey, 28; George,
65, 152, 159, 161; Grace,
162; Hannah, 61, 67, 222;
Isaac, 222; Jacob, 163, 165;
Jacob Jr, 166; James, 46,
149; Jane, 64, 72; Jesse,
163; John, 43, 52, 65, 67,
152, 163; John Jr, 156, 157;
Joseph, 61, 65, 163, 165,
171, 222, 225; Joshua, 65,
171; Lydia, 64, 152, 161,
163; Margaret, 157; Martha,
62; Mary, 65, 67, 72, 161;
Nathan, 65, 163; Phebe, 52,
161; Preston, 224; Rebekah,
48, 163; Samuel, 64, 72, 225;
Sarah, 46, 48, 62, 65;
Thomas, 65, 163
SHARPLIS, John, 98
SHAW, Ann, 64, 212; Anna, 208;
Anthony, 65, 117, 120;
Hannah, 168; James, 210;
Jane, 212; Jennet, 224;
Jennett, 217; John, 65; Mary,
120, 134, 247; Rebeckah, 65;
Samuel, 247; Sarah, 212;
William, 212
SHELCROSS, Catharine, 210;
Jonathan, 208
SHEPARD, Hannah, 122
SHEPPARD, William, 125
SHEPPERD, William, 122, 131
SHIELDS, Arthur, 247; Mary, 247
SHIPLEY, Ann, 54; Elizabeth,
124, 134; Joseph, 65, 181;
Mary, 65, 133, 181; Thomas,
65, 133, 148; William, 57,
65, 73, 111, 124, 134
SHOEMAKER, Lydia, 205; Sarah,
221; Sarah Bowman, 219;
William, 204, 205, 219, 221
SIDDENS, Ann, 175; William, 175
SIDWELL, Henry, 177; Mary, 177
SIMCOCK, Alice, 31, 52, 84, 86,
228; Benjamin, 31, 92, 124,
164, 202; Elizabeth, 78, 79;

Elizabeth Boon, 202; George,
82; Hannah, 31, 52, 76;
Jacob, 31, 52, 65, 75, 77,
84, 86, 107, 116, 228, 235,
238; Jacob Jr, 90; John, 31,
77, 79, 81, 84, 103, 235;
John Jr, 75, 79; Mary, 31,
77, 86, 100, 103; Samuel,
127; Sarah, 31, 60, 98, 105,
123, 124
SIMCOCKE, John, 75
SIMONS, Ann, 240, 250
SIMPSON, George, 31, 42, 82,
85, 101, 141, 147; Henry, 31;
Lydia, 31, 42; Ruth, 31;
Stephen, 31
SINCLAR, John, 158
SING, George, 168
SINKLER, Margret, 89; Pheby,
104; William, 86, 104
SIRRELL, James, 77
SIVAL, Abraham, 163; Ann, 150,
163; Elizabeth, 163; Enoch,
163; George, 163; John, 163;
Joseph, 163; Mary, 163;
Robert, 163; Samuel, 150
SKEEN, Robert, 251
SKELTON, Margaret, 118, 235;
Margret, 252
SLAIGH, Joseph, 135
SLAUGHTER, Jemima;   Parsons,
212
SLAY, Joseph, 164
SLEA, Joseph, 126
SLEIGH, Joseph, 121
SMEDELY, Sarah, 81
SMEDLEY, Abigail, 210; Ahinoam,
33; Alice, 31, 41; Ambrose,
32, 33, 49, 65, 188, 208,
209, 225; Ann, 132, 202;
Caleb, 32, 163; Deborah, 32;
Elizabeth, 32, 33, 51, 66,
209, 225; Fancis, 193;
Francis, 66, 132, 202;
George, 31, 32, 33, 41, 50,
54, 65, 66, 77, 88, 105, 152,
195, 200, 202; George Jr,
135; Jacob, 32; James, 32;
Jane, 32, 33, 54; Jean, 110;
Joseph, 32; Joshua, 32, 198;
Lydia, 66; Mary, 31, 32, 49,
50, 51, 54, 65, 66; Peter,
32, 66, 195; Phebe, 32, 195;
Samuel, 32, 33; Sarah, 31,
32, 49, 50, 82, 95, 128;
Thomas, 31, 32, 33, 66, 88,
89, 107, 128, 152, 189, 206,
211; William, 32, 33, 51, 66
SMEDLY, Alice, 102; George, 87,
193; Mary, 87; Sarah, 106
SMITH, Ann, 93, 247; Anne, 247;

SWAFFORD, Mary, 100
SWAFOR, Ann, 47; James, 76;
William, 47
SWAFORD, James, 75, 77;
William, 75, 77
SWAGO, Lydia, 205
SWAIN, Elizabeth, 140; Esther,
109; Francis Jr, 135; Mary,
141; Thomas, 141; William,
140
SWAIN ELIZABETH, Mary, 103
SWAINE, Elizabeth, 67, 154;
Francis, 67, 102; George,
154; Jane, 102; Mary, 154;
Phebe, 154; Thomas, 154;
William, 67
SWARFAR, Rebecka, 109
SWARFFER, Rebecca, 235
SWARFORD, William, 103
SWAYNE, Elizabeth, 33, 52, 67;
George, 33, 172; Mary, 33,
51, 139; Phebe, 33, 51;
Samuell, 145; Thomas, 33, 51,
67, 139, 172, 173, 175, 179;
William, 52, 67
SWIFT, Elizabeth, 33; Henry,
33, 111; Mary, 33
SYMCOCK, Jacob, 20

-T-
TAILLER (TAYLOR), Peter, 75
TALBOT, Ann, 184, 198;
Benjamin, 155; Elizabeth, 64,
108, 155, 158, 163; Hannah,
64, 158, 163, 181, 202;
Jacob, 67, 158, 179; James,
201; John, 108, 155, 170,
171, 179, 202; Joseph, 61,
64, 67, 68, 69, 155, 158,
159, 163, 181, 198, 201, 202;
Joseph Sr, 184, 193; Lydia,
159, 163, 166; Mary, 155;
Rachel, 69, 158, 202; Ruth,
202; Samuel, 179; Sarah, 170,
171, 179; Susanna, 61, 163, 179;
Susannah, 158; William, 155
TANNEAR, Not named, 108
TANNEER, Daniel, 235; Martha,
235
TANYEAR, Phebe, 198
TANYER, Jesse, 174; Joseph, 68,
143, 174, 205; Mary, 205
TARBUCK, Lydia, 96
TATE, Honor (Williams), 240;
Katharine Malin, 235;
Kathern, 104; Magnes, 240;
Mary, 235; Randall, 235
TAYLER, Elizabeth, 72, 93;
Hannah, 235; Martha, 89;
Sarah Jr, 101
TAYLOR, Abiah, 116; Abigail,

134, 197; Abijah, 210, 214;
Alice, 116, 167; Amay, 175;
Ambrose, 177, 178, 183, 197,
210, 214; Amy, 178, 192; Ann,
34, 239, 247, 250; Benjamin,
33, 34, 170; Bettey, 224;
Betty Malin, 222; Deborah,
116; Elisha, 163; Elizabeth,
34, 50, 56, 65, 66, 69, 76,
78, 120, 132, 167, 189, 212,
216, 236; Enoch, 34, 183,
216; Esther, 44, 47, 235;
Evan, 34, 68, 175, 177, 185,
192; Frances, 34, 76;
Francis, 68; George, 165;
Hannah, 34, 72, 89, 122;
Isaac, 33, 56, 65, 68, 78,
99, 102, 110, 169, 170, 198,
212, 215; Israel, 157; Jacob,
79, 80, 106, 178, 183, 197,
210, 214; John, 33, 68, 120,
134, 135, 152, 166, 167, 169,
170, 192, 204, 236, 251; John
Jr, 134; John Pughe, 234;
Jonathan, 34, 72, 79, 80, 81,
82, 112; Joseph, 33, 68, 78,
106, 109, 175, 180, 183, 196,
197; Josiah, 34, 55, 68, 77,
78; Margaret, 33, 69; Martha,
34, 79, 80; Mary, 33, 34, 47,
56, 65, 78, 79, 80, 81, 106,
107, 108, 109, 110, 112, 166,
178, 183, 197, 210, 214, 236;
Mordecai, 34, 47, 68, 119,
130, 131, 132, 166, 210, 214;
Mordicai, 183, 197; Nathan,
34, 41, 68, 137, 138, 179;
Peter, 33, 34, 50, 65, 66,
68, 69, 76, 81, 96, 101, 131,
175, 177, 208, 210, 214, 236;
Peter Jr, 91, 209; Phebe, 55,
79, 215; Philip, 68, 84;
Priscilla, 136; Rachel, 34,
55, 201, 204, 220; Rachell,
55, 76; Robert, 68, 75, 77,
78, 79, 139, 140, 141, 157,
168; Ruth, 34, 41, 138;
Samuel, 33, 104, 113, 169,
173, 236; Sarah, 33, 34, 50,
69, 96, 101, 107, 110, 134,
135, 156, 166, 198; Sarah Jr,
101; Stephen, 197, 210, 214;
Susannah, 111; Thomas, 34,
44, 55, 68, 79, 80, 81, 89,
91, 106, 108, 122, 163, 168;
Thomas Jr, 170; William, 33,
79, 96, 162, 236
TEAT, Kathern, 104
TEMPLE, Alice, 182; Thomas, 68;
William, 68, 182
TEST, Ann, 247; John Jr, 239,

247; Thomas, 247
THATCHER, Abigail, 34; Beulah,
34; Deborah, 200, 217; Enos,
34; Hannah, 189; John W., 34;
Joseph, 34, 68, 201; Richard,
200; Sarah, 34, 68; Sidney,
34; Thomas, 34; William, 34,
68, 189
THEACHER, Jane, 77; Richard, 77
THOMAS, Abishai, 34, 213, 216;
Ann, 34, 216, 247, 250;
Benjamin, 68, 167, 209;
David, 247; Edward, 239, 247;
Eliner, 95; Elizabeth, 140;
Ezra, 181, 185; George, 209,
214, 221; Hannah, 180; Isaac,
180; Jacob, 69, 99; James,
88, 89, 103, 213; Jane, 249;
Jean, 89; Jean [Jane], 89;
Jemima, 102; John, 34, 213,
216; John Chew, 34; Joseph,
34, 101, 132, 185, 195, 213,
216; Joshua, 69, 205, 207;
Katherin, 84; Lidia, 88;
Margaret, 131; Margret, 84;
Martha, 34, 114; Mary, 34,
132, 135, 211, 213, 216;
Michael, 173; Owen, 209;
Peter, 69, 76, 77, 84, 88,
99, 131; Peter Jr, 89;
Priscilla, 173; Prudence,
187; Rebecca, 139; Richard,
68, 135, 140; Samuel, 34,
216; Sarah, 34, 69, 88, 207,
213, 216; Seth, 187; Thomas,
69, 175; William, 69, 84, 85,
86, 139, 236
THOMBLINSON, Samuel, 101
THOMKINS, John, 106; Mary, 106
THOMLINSON, Benjamin, 135;
Mary, 101, 135; Samuel, 95
THOMPSON, Aaron, 114, 251; Ann,
174, 249; Edward, 69, 91;
Esther, 251; Henry, 69;
Isaac, 206; John, 186; John
Jr, 204; Jonah, 211;
Jonathan, 204; Joshua, 54,
118, 159, 211; Joshua Jr,
140; Majory, 140; Margaret,
54; Margery, 111, 236;
Margreat, 112; Martha, 140,
162, 208; Mary, 173, 174;
Moses, 208; Peter, 144;
Prudence, 69; Thomas, 142
THOMSON, Daniel, 151; Grace,
165; Hannah, 158, 159, 160;
John, 69, 78, 137, 185;
Joseph, 165; Joshua, 69, 137,
158, 159, 162; Joshua Jr,
139; Margaret, 185; Margery,
140; Martha, 162; Mary, 54;

Mary Jobson, 218; Mordecai,
69, 165; Moses, 164, 165,
171; Nathan, 159, 160;
Robert, 165; Thomas, 78
THORNTON, Deborah, 159, 161;
Robert, 101; Samuel, 161
TIDMARSH, Hannah, 41, 99;
Isaac, 96; Mary, 44, 94;
Rose, 94; Sarah, 94; William,
94, 96, 98, 99
TILL, Elizabeth, 249
TOBIAS, Charity, 181; Peter,
181; Ruth, 181; Samson, 181;
Sarah, 181
TODHUNTER, Abraham, 62;
Margaret, 62; Margarett, 94,
236
TOLBET, Elizabeth, 127
TOLBOT, Benjamin, 127;
Elizabeth, 127
TOMLINSON, Elizabeth, 69, 102;
John, 69, 124; Joseph, 69,
126; Katherine, 126; Mary,
124, 150, 155; Othniel, 150;
Samuell, 83, 236
TOMPKINS, John, 119
TOMSON, Margery, 111
TOOL, Rachel Hayworth, 210
TOWNSEND, Elizabeth, 168, 169;
Francis, 69, 161; Hannah, 34;
John, 34; Joseph, 34, 69,
103, 110, 158; Joseph Jr,
168, 169; Lydia, 158; Martha,
34, 103, 110; Mary, 34, 122;
Rachel, 161; William, 34
TRAVILLA, James, 181; Phebe,
181
TRAVILLER, James, 138, 166;
Katherine, 138; Phebe, 166
TREGO, Ann, 35, 64, 114;
Elizabeth, 120; Hannah, 35;
Jacob, 34, 35, 100; James,
34, 99, 111, 120, 236; John,
35; Judith, 34, 64, 69; Mary,
35, 100, 106, 120; Peter, 34,
64, 69; Rachel, 35; William,
34, 99, 236
TREHARN, Adam, 102
TREHEARNE, William, 247
TREMBLE, James, 123; Lewis,
161; Margaret, 161; Mary, 123
TRENT, Elinor, 239; Mary, 252;
William, 252
TRIGOE, Jacob, 87; Peter, 87
TROTTER, William, 101
TRUEMAN, Mary, 193; Morris, 193
TRUMAN, James, 69, 223; Joseph,
223; Mary, 69, 223; Morris,
69, 223
TRUMP, Ann, 203, 206; Daniel,
203, 206; Hannah, 203, 206;

237; Mary, 84; Nicholas, 70,
84, 90; Richard, 128, 144;
Sarah, 90; Susannah, 128;
William, 70
WALNE, John, 106, 107
WALTER, Edward, 75, 78; James,
168, 201; Jemima, 201; John,
168; Joseph, 201; Lydia, 168;
Mary, 201; Nathaniel, 70;
Phebe, 201; Rachel, 70, 201,
224; Rebecca, 171; Rebekah,
168, 201; Thomas, 167, 168,
171, 187, 190, 192, 201;
William, 70
WARE, Joseph, 78
WARNER, George, 129; Isaac, 47,
70; John, 70, 131; Joseph,
170; Mary, 47, 170, 183;
Sarah, 131; William, 131
WARNOR, Sarah, 112
WARRELOW, John, 73; Thomas, 73
WATERS, Sarah, 248; Thomas,
248, 251
WATSON, Aaron, 134; Margaret,
132; Thomas, 133
WAY, Abel, 167; Elizabeth, 123;
Joshua, 71, 117, 123;
Richard, 173; Robert, 71
WEAMAN, John, 35
WEAVER, Abraham, 36, 206;
Anthony, 76; Baldwin, 36,
190; Elizabeth, 36, 71, 119,
125, 149, 199; Isaac, 35, 36,
71, 138, 149, 175, 198, 199,
206; Isaac Jr, 197, 200;
James, 36, 206; Joshua, 35,
181, 184, 191; Jude, 150;
Mary, 125, 138; Richard, 36,
71, 119, 125, 149, 203;
Sarah, 35, 36, 206; Thomas,
248; Thomas Dell, 35, 188;
Valentine, 150, 156; William,
36, 206
WEBB, Bathsheba, 74, 222;
Elizabeth, 119; James, 251;
Rebeckah, 71; William Jr, 71,
119; William Sr, 71
WEBSTER, Joseph, 49, 71, 211;
Mary, 211, 222; Rachel, 49,
211; Rebecca, 71, 211;
Rebeccah, 49; Ruth, 211;
Sarah, 104; William, 71, 211
WEIMAS, Rachel, 252
WELDEN, Elizabeth, 111; Hannah,
114
WELDIN, Ann, 100
WELDING, John, 98
WELDON, Benjamin, 113, 121;
Elizabeth, 237; John, 71,
120; William, 132, 133, 237
WEST, Anne, 36; Benjamin, 166,

212; Caleb D., 36; Eliza, 36;
Elizabeth, 36; Esther, 170,
192, 197, 215; Hannah, 36,
185, 189, 200, 214, 215;
James, 166, 184; Jane, 128,
129; Jesse, 176, 185, 200;
Joel, 192, 197, 214; John,
166, 184; Joseph, 129, 176,
185, 200, 215, 216, 220;
Joshua P., 36; Kesse, 218;
Mary, 36, 185, 200, 213, 215;
Passmore, 216; Pusey, 36;
Rachel, 176, 185, 200, 216;
Rebecca, 192, 216; Rebeckah,
186; Rebekah, 166, 197;
Samuel, 36, 210, 213; Sarah,
36, 164, 170, 192, 197; Sarah
Ann, 36; Susanna, 176, 185,
215; Susannah, 200; Thomas,
36, 71, 164, 170, 192, 197,
212, 215, 216; Thomas H., 36;
William, 36, 71, 101, 166,
168, 184, 186, 189, 192, 200,
214, 215; William Jr, 197
WESTON, Mary Scot, 237; Rebecca
(Bainton), 240; Susannah,
248; Thomas, 240, 251
WETHERBY, David, 143
WHARTON, John, 71; Rachel, 71;
Robert, 85, 86; Thomas, 71
WHIPPE, Jane, 128
WHIPPO, George, 131, 237; Jane,
111, 131, 237
WHITACER, Charles, 76, 80
WHITACRE, Charles, 96, 117;
Samuel, 116; Susannah, 117
WHITAKER, Charles, 230
WHITEACER, James, 78
WHITEACRE, Charles, 111; Sarah,
111
WHITEAKER, Ann, 69; Charles,
69, 116, 117; Hannah, 69;
Samuel, 116; Sarah, 112;
Susannah, 117
WHITTACREE, James, 75
WICKERSHAM, Ann, 123; James,
71, 123
WILCOX, Hannah Worrall, 196;
Samuel, 157, 159, 161
WILEY, Martha, 159; Mary, 159;
Rebeccah, 144; Rebekah, 158;
Thomas, 144; Vincent, 159
WILKINS, Mary, 109; William,
71, 109
WILKINSON, Agnes, 184, 188;
Barbara, 160, 178; Elizabeth,
120, 178; Hannah, 179; Jesse,
160, 172; Joseph, 160, 177,
178; Sarah, 160, 178; Thomas,
251; William, 179
WILKISON, Agnes, 176; Jesse,

WOODIER [WOODYAR], George, 81
WOODMANSEE, William, 75
WOODMANSON, William, 76, 77
WOODWARD, Abigail, 37, 70, 150,
151, 162; Alice, 120; Edward,
37, 45, 46, 52, 70, 72, 99,
105, 112, 120, 133, 157, 162,
190; Edward Jr, 137;
Elizabeth, 93, 133; Hannah,
37, 46, 52, 227; James, 153;
Jane, 37, 126, 154; Jean
[Jane], 89; Jesse, 72, 145,
151, 154; Joseph, 37, 92, 99,
126; Lydia, 157; Margaret,
37, 70, 112, 113, 229, 237;
Mary, 37, 45, 121, 124, 227;
Mary James, 190; Prudence,
151, 154; Rachel, 148, 160,
167; Rachell, 83, 107, 122;
Richard, 37, 72, 83, 100,
124; Richard Sr, 37; Sarah,
49, 95, 154; Susannah, 37,
124; Thomas, 72, 77, 83, 107,
122, 148, 151; William, 37
WOODWARTH, Prudence, 145
WOODWORS, Martha, 79
WOODWORTH, Abigail, 151, 156;
Alice, 106; Ann, 80;
Elizabeth, 132; Richard, 100;
Susana, 92; Thomas, 151
WOOLEY, Sarah, 135; Thomas, 135
WOOLIS, Nicholas, 221; Rachel,
221
WOOLLAS, Nicholas, 222
WOOLLEY, Ann, 60; John, 164,
176, 177, 178, 194; Phebe,
177, 178, 194; Robert, 163;
Samuel, 194; Sarah, 194;
Thomas, 60
WOOLLY, John, 196; Phebe, 196;
Samuel, 196; Sarah, 196
WOOLY, Ann, 163; Robert, 163;
Sarah, 163; Thomas, 115, 116
WORALL, John, 75
WORLEY, Francis, 79, 102, 106,
237; Henry, 77, 81, 106;
Mary, 81, 118; Rebeckah, 50;
Susannah, 106, 109, 237
WORLY, Francis, 75; Henry, 75,
105; Mary, 105; Susana, 106;
Susannah, 107
WOROLOW, Susannah, 111
WORRAL, Aaron, 191; Benjamin,
191, 192; John, 72, 191; John
Sr, 193; Jonathan, 112, 167;
Mary, 167; Nathan, 191;
Peter, 112; Seth, 185
WORRALL, Abel, 186, 211;
Abigail, 37, 38, 63, 67, 68,
151; Ann, 38, 46, 166, 177,
202, 203, 208, 224, 225;

Benjamin, 72, 168, 185, 188,
194, 214; Caleb, 222; Caleb
Peirce, 38; Charles, 186;
Edith, 38, 222, 225; Edward,
169; Elijah, 177; Elisah,
183; Elisha, 72, 176, 179,
183, 208; Elizabeth, 37, 38,
64, 159, 166, 168; Esther,
169; Frances, 37, 82, 88,
228; Francis, 228; Frederick,
183; George, 145, 150, 213,
217; Hannah, 38, 73, 132,
159, 177, 178, 190, 196, 221;
Isaac, 170, 195; Isaiah, 199;
Jacob, 161, 162; James, 72,
154, 159, 167, 169, 170, 173,
174, 191, 202; John, 37, 38,
72, 73, 75, 76, 77, 78, 82,
83, 88, 92, 97, 101, 103,
104, 122, 126, 132, 135, 139,
140, 145, 149, 150, 162, 163,
165, 166, 168, 169, 173, 174,
177, 178, 187, 189, 190, 191,
206, 207, 231, 233, 237, 238;
Jonathan, 139, 166, 171, 177,
180, 182, 183, 222, 225;
Jonathan Paul, 38; Joseph,
72, 141, 149, 166, 219;
Joshua, 73, 163; Lydia, 174,
177, 185, 187; Margaret, 72;
Maris, 214; Martha, 177, 199;
Mary, 37, 38, 59, 63, 84,
114, 140, 141, 153, 157, 165,
173, 217, 222, 225; Mary
Howell, 191; Mary Peirce, 38;
Nathan, 199; Nathaniel, 38,
216, 217, 222, 225; Owen,
188; Peirce, 222; Peter, 37,
38, 63, 68, 72, 126, 149,
150, 151, 153, 154, 155, 163,
185, 188, 208; Phebe, 38, 46,
59, 156, 185, 191, 192;
Priscilla, 150; Prof. J.
Hunter, 183; Prudence, 186;
Rachel, 37, 38; Rachel
Rhoads, 211; Rebecca, 207,
214, 225; Rebekah, 169, 186;
Richard Thatcher, 38; Ruth,
38, 222; Samuel, 150, 151,
182; Sarah, 37, 38, 134, 153,
174, 185, 222; Seth, 182;
Susanna, 208; Tamer
Lightfoot, 220; Thomas, 37,
38, 73, 74, 140, 153, 157,
162, 166, 177, 186, 195, 196,
219, 222; Thomas Jr, 211;
William, 38, 46, 59, 154,
222, 225
WORRALLOW, John, 85, 87; Mary,
87
WORRALOW, Ann Jr, 108

Other Heritage Books by John Pitts Launey:

Early Church Records of Delaware County, Pennsylvania, Volumes 1 and 2
First Families of Chester County, Pennsylvania: Volumes 1 and 2

Other Heritage Books by F. Edward Wright:

Abstracts of Bucks County, Pennsylvania Wills, 1685-1785
Abstracts of Cumberland County, Pennsylvania Wills, 1750-1785
Abstracts of Cumberland County, Pennsylvania Wills, 1785-1825
Abstracts of Philadelphia County Wills, 1726-1747
Abstracts of Philadelphia County Wills, 1748-1763
Abstracts of Philadelphia County Wills, 1763-1784
Abstracts of Philadelphia County Wills, 1777-1790
Abstracts of Philadelphia County Wills, 1790-1802
Abstracts of Philadelphia County Wills, 1802-1809
Abstracts of Philadelphia County Wills, 1810-1815
Abstracts of Philadelphia County Wills, 1815-1819
Abstracts of Philadelphia County Wills, 1820-1825
Abstracts of Philadelphia County, Pennsylvania Wills, 1682-1726
Abstracts of South Central Pennsylvania Newspapers, Volume 1, 1785-1790
Abstracts of South Central Pennsylvania Newspapers, Volume 3, 1796-1800
Abstracts of the Newspapers of Georgetown and the Federal City, 1789-99
Abstracts of York County, Pennsylvania Wills, 1749-1819

Bucks County, Pennsylvania Church Records of the 17th and 18th Centuries
Volume 2: Quaker Records: Falls and Middletown Monthly Meetings
Anna Miller Watring and F. Edward Wright

Caroline County, Maryland Marriages, Births and Deaths, 1850-1880

Citizens of the Eastern Shore of Maryland, 1659-1750

Cumberland County, Pennsylvania Church Records of the 18th Century

Delaware Newspaper Abstracts, Volume 1: 1786-1795

Early Charles County, Maryland Settlers, 1658-1745
Marlene Strawser Bates and F. Edward Wright

Early Church Records of Alexandria City and Fairfax County, Virginia
F. Edward Wright and Wesley E. Pippenger

Early Church Records of New Castle County, Delaware, Volume 1, 1701-1800

Frederick County Militia in the War of 1812
Sallie A. Mallick and F. Edward Wright

Inhabitants of Baltimore County, 1692-1763

Land Records of Sussex County, Delaware, 1769-1782

Land Records of Sussex County, Delaware, 1782-1789
Elaine Hastings Mason and F. Edward Wright

Marriage Licenses of Washington, District of Columbia, 1811-1830

Marriages and Deaths from the Newspapers of Allegany and
Washington Counties, Maryland, 1820-1830

Marriages and Deaths from The York Recorder, 1821-1830

Marriages and Deaths in the Newspapers of Frederick and
Montgomery Counties, Maryland, 1820-1830

Marriages and Deaths in the Newspapers of Lancaster County, Pennsylvania, 1821-1830

Marriages and Deaths in the Newspapers of Lancaster County, Pennsylvania, 1831-1840

Marriages and Deaths of Cumberland County, [Pennsylvania], 1821-1830

Maryland Calendar of Wills Volume 9: 1744-1749

Maryland Calendar of Wills Volume 10: 1748-1753

Maryland Calendar of Wills Volume 11: 1753-1760

Maryland Calendar of Wills Volume 12: 1759-1764

Maryland Calendar of Wills Volume 13: 1764-1767

Maryland Calendar of Wills Volume 14: 1767-1772

Maryland Calendar of Wills Volume 15: 1772-1774

Maryland Calendar of Wills Volume 16: 1774-1777

Maryland Eastern Shore Newspaper Abstracts, Volume 1: 1790-1805

Maryland Eastern Shore Newspaper Abstracts, Volume 2: 1806-1812

Maryland Eastern Shore Newspaper Abstracts, Volume 3: 1813-1818

Maryland Eastern Shore Newspaper Abstracts, Volume 4: 1819-1824

Maryland Eastern Shore Newspaper Abstracts, Volume 5: Northern Counties, 1825-1829
F. Edward Wright and Irma Harper

Maryland Eastern Shore Newspaper Abstracts, Volume 6: Southern Counties, 1825-1829

Maryland Eastern Shore Newspaper Abstracts, Volume 7: Northern Counties, 1830-1834
Irma Harper and F. Edward Wright

Maryland Eastern Shore Newspaper Abstracts, Volume 8: Southern Counties, 1830-1834

Maryland Militia in the Revolutionary War
S. Eugene Clements and F. Edward Wright

Newspaper Abstracts of Allegany and Washington Counties, 1811-1815

Newspaper Abstracts of Cecil and Harford Counties, [Maryland], 1822-1830

Newspaper Abstracts of Frederick County, [Maryland], 1816-1819

Newspaper Abstracts of Frederick County, 1811-1815

Sketches of Maryland Eastern Shoremen

Tax List of Chester County, Pennsylvania 1768

Tax List of York County, Pennsylvania 1779

Washington County Church Records of the 18th Century, 1768-1800

Western Maryland Newspaper Abstracts, Volume 1: 1786-1798

Western Maryland Newspaper Abstracts, Volume 2: 1799-1805

Western Maryland Newspaper Abstracts, Volume 3: 1806-1810

Wills of Chester County, Pennsylvania, 1766-1778

Breinigsville, PA USA
14 June 2010
239886BV00005B/44/P